The Checkbook IRA
Why You Want It, Why You Need It

The Checkbook IRA
Why You Want It, Why You Need It

_____

A private conversation with a top retirement tax attorney

Adam Bergman, Esq.

ISBN: 1515284816
ISBN 13: 9781515284819
Library of Congress Control Number: 2015912468
CreateSpace Independent Publishing Platform
North Charleston, South Carolina

Contents

Introduction

How to Invest in What You Know and Understand

"Know what you own, and know why you own it."
—Peter Lynch, former manager, The Magellan Fund

What's the best way to build your wealth for retirement?

Go to the personal finance section of any bookstore and you will see that there are as many theories about how to get rich as there are books on the shelves.

As someone who has participated in and carefully watched the retirement investment industry for many years, I can tell you that not all those theories and approaches have your best interests in mind. All experts and institutions have angles, interests, and points of view about your money that benefit them. So in the interest of full disclosure, I want to tell you about my point of view before we get started.

I believe:

1) Anyone can become wealthy by retirement if he or she invests in retirement savings vehicles.
2) The earlier you start to set aside income and invest it for retirement the better.
3) It's never too late to start.

4) The investment industry wants you to invest in their products because they make more money as a result.

5) Your wealth generally grows faster and is more secure when you invest in what you know and understand.

Accordingly, the company I've built, IRA Financial Group & IRA Financial Trust Company, is designed to help you invest money for retirement through retirement savings vehicles that you can establish, manage, and control.

This book is about one of the best approaches available to independent-minded people who want to take charge of building their wealth for retirement: the self-directed IRA.

The Peter Principle vs. the Herd Instinct

Peter Lynch, the former manager of the Magellan Fund, was one of the wisest and most successful investors in history. One of his principles of investing was "Know what you own and why you own it."

I agree with that premise. But therein lies a problem.

Because of the way the retirement investment industry is constructed, most of us are encouraged to invest in mutual funds or a variety of financial products we've never heard of and barely understand.

So where does this leave us?

Think of a mutual fund you've invested in or heard mentioned in the news. You might understand and appreciate the basic principle of its investment strategy. Maybe it's an aggressive growth fund or an emerging market fund or a value fund. But what companies is it invested in? What is the mix of those companies? What do you know about any of them? Peter Lynch would advise you to know those companies very well. Is that even possible? You're probably not a full-time investor like Peter. You probably don't have access to the conference calls, meetings, and parties that Peter gets access to in order to assess the character and intelligence of the CEO. No one is letting you know that things are looking up or down in a particular sector. When it comes to comparing your knowledge of what you own with the knowledge of Wall Street insiders, you simply don't have a chance.

Now, there's nothing wrong with owning stocks and investing in mutual funds or other mainstream financial products. The majority of retirement investors invest their hard-earned retirement funds in financial products that involve stocks and financial instruments they know nothing about—and yet most earn healthy returns on their retirement investments. For example, according to historical records, the average annual return for the S&P 500 since its inception in 1928 through 2014 is approximately 10 percent. Investing in mainstream financial products may mean following the herd, but sometimes following the herd can feel safe, secure, and easy.

There are times, however, when being in the herd is the last thing you want. The financial crisis of 2008 was one such time. If you were close to retirement age when that devastating economic crash occurred, you probably saw your dreams of retirement shatter. Many retirement accounts were down by more than 45 percent within just a few months. And chances are, five or six years later, your retirement wealth still hasn't recovered. Indeed, many retirement investors liquidated their retirement accounts and turned to money market accounts with little return as a result.

While you may feel distraught and frustrated by that devastation, you probably didn't even know you had a choice in the matter. After all, your financial adviser steered you into those mysterious financial products because they were the best available to you.

Or so you were told.

Freedom and Flexibility

Most people believe that their IRA or 401(k) is limited to investments in stocks, mutual funds, and financial instruments offered by the big financial institutions. Very few people know that they can invest their IRA or former employer 401(k) plan assets into alternative investments such as:

- Real estate
- Precious metals

- Gold
- Private equity funds
- Private businesses
- Peer-to-peer lending
- Mutual funds
- Tax liens
- And more…

Why don't they know this? It's not because they are uneducated, indifferent, or not curious—they simply have not been told. There are two reasons.

First, the majority of retirement investment advisers don't know either. I was a tax attorney at several of the largest law firms in the country for close to ten years and I worked with some of the most highly respected senior tax attorneys in practice today. But whenever I mentioned to such people that IRA funds may be invested in real estate, they did not believe me. Indeed, when I showed that I had worked with a client to use retirement funds to buy a commercial real estate property, and that the transaction was perfectly legal from an IRS standpoint, they were shocked. In one case, one of the senior partners took out his smartphone and visited the IRS website to see if such a transaction was allowed. It was, and is. My point is not to embarrass my law firm or its respected tax attorneys but to demonstrate that even the most sophisticated of investors and tax attorneys are unaware of the possibility of making alternative asset investments using retirement funds.

Second, it's not in the financial interests of the traditional institutional investment companies—such as Bank of America, Charles Schwab, or E-Trade—to encourage you to make alternative investments using retirement funds. They make money when you invest in their financial products and keep your money there for a long time, whether through highly profitable trading commissions or by leveraging the power of your savings. They make no money when you use your money to invest in alternative or nontraditional investments such as a plot of land or a private business. They get no commissions as a result. They lose access to your money too. Why would they inform you, then, that such a strategy was permissible and possibly even preferable depending on the circumstances?

Yet, such nontraditional or alternative retirement asset investments are perfectly legal. The IRS has permitted them since 1974. It says so right on the IRS website.

And the best way to make those investments is through the self-directed IRA.

Getting in on a Good Thing

In the investment world, there's always been a myth that you can get in early on a good thing and make a killing.

Well, in the case of the self-directed IRA, there's definitely some truth to that myth.

Today, out of the roughly 47 million Individual Retirement Accounts in the United States, estimates suggest that only 2 percent to 4 percent of them are self-directed. Basically, this means that almost 95 percent of Americans with Individual Retirement Accounts only invest their retirement funds in traditional equity-type investments such as stocks and mutual funds.

Before you opened this book, you might have believed that such traditional investments were the only and best way to go.

The nontraditional and self-directed retirement market was relatively small and unknown prior to 2008. A small segment of the investment retirement community were early adopters—they had heard about the nontraditional asset option and took advantage of buying real estate, precious metals, and so on. Following 2008 that approach began to become more mainstream. The reason was simple—the blow to retirement savings in the stock market collapse demonstrated the importance of diversifying your portfolio and understanding what you invest in.

In the past few years, the movement toward nontraditional investments has picked up steam. I can't tell you how many times a week I get a call asking me whether such investments are permissible and how to make them happen. Those calls come from a cross section of investors, too: old, young, rich, middle-class, as well as from those new to investing and others who are professional investors.

Nor are my experiences skewed by my own limited perspective. According to a McKinsey & Company report, "The Mainstreaming of Alternative Investments," global alternatives reached record levels of $6.5 trillion by the end of 2011, having grown at a five-year rate of over seven times that of traditional asset classes. And a variety of respected researchers, including from the Federal Reserve Board, the IRS, and the National Association of Government Defined Contribution Administrators, even institutional investors expect to have 28 percent of their portfolios allocated to alternative investments by 2013, up 26 percent from 2010.

That means more and more people are putting more and more of their retirement assets into nontraditional investments.

Is This Book for You?

I've written this book for people who want to take charge of their retirement by building their wealth with a balance of nontraditional and traditional investments into assets they know and understand.

Specifically, I have written it for people who:

1) Are between 25 and 70 years of age and have already accumulated a sizable amount of money in their former employers' 401(k) plans or through an IRA, and now have the freedom to invest that money as they see fit
2) Have knowledge, experience, or insight into alternative investment opportunities, such as real estate, that they would like to leverage
3) Are excited about being more active, thoughtful, and deliberate in building their retirement wealth.

On its own, this book will not make you rich. But it will give you the tools you need to take charge of managing your retirement investments and invest in what you know. It is up to you to do your homework and leverage your knowledge, experience, and insight to make the best decisions in line with your investment ideas.

The self-directed IRA is a golden ticket to retirement investment independence. It offers a kind of investment diversification and security not available with traditional retirement investments.

There are a variety of ways to self-direct your own retirement fund investments—via a custodian or through a special purpose limited liability company (LLC). This book will tell you everything you need to know about taking charge of your retirement fund investments through a self-directed IRA so you can benefit from the investment, security, and tax advantages available. I will describe the extensive opportunities permissible under IRS rules for IRAs, and show you how to determine which options serve you best. I will clarify the IRS rules that govern transactions not prohibited for IRA funds so that you can make any investment with peace of mind. You will also develop the clarity needed to identify and avoid potential fraud, which has recently become more pronounced in the retirement investment community.

Most of all, this book will show you that investing retirement funds does not have to be scary—and it is never dull. In fact, it is exhilarating and empowering to invest in something you know well and understand deeply. The ability to unlock a new world of investment opportunities is at your fingertips. This book will show you how easy it is to do so and how rewarding taking those steps can be.

I

How Rich Got Started with a Self-Directed IRA

The commercials make saving for retirement look so easy, don't they?

Picture a husband and wife in their midforties sitting down with a financial adviser in one scene, laughing and playing with their children at a lake or along a hiking trail in the next, and holding hands in the last scene while standing before a beautiful sunset.

Whatever the story, the people that are depicted in retirement commercials always appear to have a sense of control over their lives. They're good-looking and healthy. Even if they're going through a major career or life change, all their options feel rich with possibility. Their lives are basically secure. Their marriage is solid. Their kids are headed for great things. They already live in a beautiful home—that lakeside ranch house nestled in the woods, or that condominium downtown near the riverside park. The sunset or the view is always amazing. Even the music is serene but hopeful and optimistic.

I bet that when it comes to finances in general and retirement savings in particular, your life feels a little different. A lot more hurried and rushed. More of a nagging sense that there are things you should have taken care of years ago but never had time to do. A lot of uncertainty about your financial stability in the face of pressing needs. A lot of confusion about the best path forward.

Don't worry. You're not alone. Most of my clients—from the very wealthy and outwardly successful to those struggling every month to make ends meet—are dealing with the same pressure, stress, and confusion. It's just life. And life is not a commercial. Fortunately, we can, with a little instruction and guidance, gain mastery over certain key areas of our lives that truly matter in the long run.

One of the most important of those priorities is taking steps today to ensure we will have enough money to live comfortably when we retire. The path to that future is neither complicated nor difficult. And yet the first step is a doozy because it requires learning something new and taking action to make things better in the long term rather than solving the more immediate problems of today.

I've written this book to make that first step and the journey that follows a lot simpler for you. I'm going to tell you how retirement saving works in general, first by describing the various types of Individual Retirement Accounts (IRAs) that you may already have heard of and even be using. And then I'm going to tell you a lot more about a type of IRA you probably haven't encountered before—the self-directed IRA. I'll explain the difference between the more commonly used approaches and the approach I'm advocating in this book—the self-directed IRA, which allows you to leverage your own background, knowledge, and passion to grow your retirement savings directly. And in my experience, that hands-on capability and heightened personal interest makes all the difference in the world. People who have special knowledge or insight in an investment area are more attentive about their money and more motivated to grow it. They take action and stick to a plan because it's fun and it feels good to have all the power in their hands.

But first, let me tell you about someone who wouldn't appear in one of those commercials I described but who may seem familiar nevertheless. I consider this person to be very typical of the clients I work with when setting up a self-directed IRA. I call him Rich.

The Story of Rich

Today, Rich is a consultant and real estate investor. He's forty-seven years old, and he lives in Houston, Texas, with his wife and three children. He plays a decent game of golf, enjoys off-road ATV riding, and loves to travel to old Western towns across the Southwest and in Wyoming, South Dakota, and Montana. His wife, Donna, has been an account manager for a PR firm for the past ten years, but she's thinking more and more about starting her own consulting business. Rich and Donna's older two children are athletes, and the third likes books and school but has some health problems that require a lot of care and monitoring. Other than that, generally speaking, everything is going pretty well.

That wasn't the case four years ago when Rich was laid off. The Great Recession in 2008 hit Rich's Fortune 100 oil and gas company, where he worked as a midlevel executive in the finance department, hard. He avoided the first round of layoffs with relief, but then his group was sold to a European company and everyone at Rich's level in his department was let go.

Though Rich had a college degree and fourteen years of experience climbing the ladder with one company in a growing industry, he found it next to impossible to secure a new job in 2009 and 2010. It was a really hard time for him and his family. His severance package and unemployment insurance ran out, and they began to eat away at Rich's personal savings. His youngest daughter's health needs meant they were always worried about health insurance. And without any steady income except the odd contract with his old company or any promising possibilities of full-time employment on the horizon, Rich started thinking a lot more creatively about what he could do with his life to provide for his family.

Before he'd earned his degree in engineering and gone into corporate America, Rich had been happiest when he was thinking about buying and developing real estate properties. His father had gotten into that line when he retired, snapping up pieces of commercial real estate or rental properties, then making some improvements to position the property for a better sale. Rich had used all his savings to join his dad on the purchase of a small apartment building during his second year of college, then they'd bought a piece of undeveloped land on the highway near a new overpass. For a while those business prospects had kindled Rich's interest like nothing else. Then his father got sick, sold all his investment properties, and moved to Florida. Lacking his dad's initiative and guidance, Rich returned his focus to his engineering studies. Still, he often found himself thinking of a building or piece of land that would be a good deal, and what could be made of it.

One day, during his long stretch of unemployment, Rich realized it just wasn't going to happen for him. Every year the colleges were churning out hundreds of cheap alternatives to his middle management role. No one was going to pick him up from the trash heap. It was a low moment. But that same afternoon an old college friend named John, a tax attorney, mentioned a real estate investment class he was taking and thought Rich would be interested in.

"We're three classes in already, but the information is great," John said. "Why don't you sign up and we can start talking about real estate investment opportunities after class."

Rich jumped at the invitation.

Even after his first class, Rich started to feel good about things again. John was a great sounding board for ideas, and his enthusiasm was infectious. The market had been depressed for the past few years. It was ready to start ramping up. Rich felt like real estate would give him a chance to take charge of his own future.

After he developed some solid ideas and built a business plan around them, Rich was ready to start investing. The only problem was that he needed capital. He still had about $45,000 in savings but he knew that wasn't going to be enough to get a real estate business under way. So he approached a number of local banks about securing financing for some terrific projects but got turned down every time. This was particularly frustrating because Rich was capable of putting down over 25 percent equity for each deal— far more than the banks had been willing to take when their questionable lending practices had caused the country's financial problems in the first place. All that Rich really had left, as ammunition, was the $215,000 he had put aside in his previous employer's 401(k) plan. That was for retirement, and he hated the idea of paying taxes on it and taking away his and Donna's retirement security.

As luck or chance would have it, the very next day Rich had an opportunity fall into his lap. Another friend, Simon, who worked at a consulting firm in the energy industry told him about an opening that would be a perfect fit for Rich. Rich said he would send him a résumé that evening. A week later, Rich was interviewed, and a week after that, he was offered the position. The job did not pay as well as Rich's previous one, but the company was solid. The only thing holding Rich back was the excitement he'd been feeling about getting into real estate investment more seriously.

That night after class, Rich told John about his dilemma.

"I've been looking for a job for so long, it's crazy that I have misgivings now that I suddenly have an opportunity again. But I really wanted to give this real estate investment idea a shot."

John was able to set Rich straight.

"Are you kidding me?" John asked. "This is perfect. The hardest thing about investing in real estate is having a secure foundation to work from. You can earn a full-time salary at your new position now and still buy properties. That way you can let your investments mature and make smart decisions about when to turn them over."

"That's true," Rich agreed, "but actually, I think the hardest thing about investing in real estate is having the capital to get started."

"You already have the capital," John said.

"I told you, all I've got is $45,000 in savings. That's not enough to do any of the deals I have in mind."

"You also said you have two hundred grand in your former employer's 401(k)."

"It's $215,000 to be exact, but I don't want to pay taxes on that and use my retirement savings."

"You don't have to pay taxes on it. You can actually use retirement funds to invest in property and other alternative asset investments."

"How can I do that?"

"By converting your 401(k) to a self-directed IRA."

"A *self-directed* IRA? What's that?"

"It's an IRA that allows you to make a broader range of investments than a normal IRA, including real estate, tax liens, precious metals, and private businesses."

"Oh," Rich said. "I didn't know you could do that. That's kind of mind-boggling."

"Not many people do know that. Even a lot of financial experts don't understand the full potential of a self-directed IRA."

"I wish I knew more."

"Well, I happen to be a tax attorney who knows quite a bit. I can fill you in."

"Would you?"

"As long as you buy the coffee and promise to leverage your retirement savings to grow your wealth, I'm happy to."

"That's a deal. How do we start?"

"Where everything starts. At the beginning."

Two Lattes, One Muffin, and a Self-Directed IRA

Introduction

At the coffee shop, Rich bought two lattes and a muffin and brought them over to the table. John pulled out a pad of paper and a pen.

"Okay," John said, "before we get into the details and the background. Let me give you an overview."

John took a sip of his latte and began.

"Individual Retirement Arrangements (IRAs), as defined by the Internal Revenue Service (IRS), exist in many forms. You've probably heard of the most common type—the Individual Retirement Account or IRA…"

"They have the same acronym?" Rich asked.

"Yes. But don't let that confuse you. There are around 47 million IRAs in existence today. Believe it or not, most of those 47 million IRAs could be considered self-directed IRAs."

"Wait," Rich said. "Are you saying that most IRA holders are using their IRAs to invest in real estate, precious metals, tax liens, or private businesses?"

"Unfortunately not," John answered. "Even if it's allowed under IRS rules, they're not doing that. But what I am saying is that the majority of all IRA investments are technically self-directed since the IRA holder is typically the one who determines what type of investments will be made with his or her IRA."

"You mean, the way my wife selects the mutual funds or even stocks that her IRA purchases?"

"Exactly. When your wife, or any IRA holder, decides which investments to make using his or her IRA, that individual is technically self-directing his or her IRA investment. I wish that more people knew, however, that the IRS allows them to do more than simply select mutual funds or stocks to buy when making IRA investments."

"But I'm getting the feeling that not all IRAs, even those that are technically self-directed, would allow me to make real estate investments."

"That's correct. Whether or not an IRA is a self-directed IRA depends on two factors—control and investment opportunities."

"My wife's IRA is through Fidelity, so I bet she doesn't have that much control."

"Correct again. The 'traditional financial institution' self-directed IRA is by far the most popular type of self-directed IRA. Like your wife, the majority of all IRAs are held at traditional financial institutions, such as Fidelity, Vanguard, Charles Schwab, Bank of America, Merrill Lynch, and so on. Many traditional financial institutions advertise themselves as offering a self-directed IRA, but what that really means is that you will be limited to purchasing stocks, mutual funds, bonds, and other traditional types of investments that earn the institution commission. In other words, you need the consent of your IRA custodian before making an investment."

"What's an IRA custodian?"

"A custodian is your IRA trustee. Basically, that's the institution that holds your IRA account. By law, every retirement account must be held at a custodian or trustee. A trustee may be a bank, trust company, credit union, or a large brokerage firm that is licensed by the IRS. IRS regulations require that either a qualified trustee or custodian hold the IRA assets on behalf of the IRA owner."

"Are there some financial custodians that will allow you to invest in areas you want to invest in?"

"Yes. A true self-directed IRA custodian is known as a passive custodian—and a passive custodian allows the IRA holder to engage in nontraditional investments like real estate. What it generally doesn't do is offer investment advice."

"Can you trust them?" Rich asked.

"Good question. As long as the institution is authorized to establish IRAs and holds the retirement funds at a Federal Deposit Insurance Corporation (FDIC), you have no worries about your money being safe."

"So, to get this straight," Rich said, "when you have a self-directed IRA at a traditional financial institution, you're technically able to self-direct your IRA investments. But you're probably limited to investing in the financial products offered by the financial institution."

"That's right," John answered. "For example, a financial institution such as Vanguard or Fidelity will allow you to select the type of investments for your own IRA, but your choices are generally limited to the financial products they offer. In other words, stocks, mutual funds, and bonds. They won't permit you to make alternative asset investments such as real estate, precious metals, private business investments, foreign currency, options, and so on."

"Why won't they allow me to purchase real estate with my IRA if it's permitted by the IRS?"

"It's just business. Financial institutions are in business to earn profit and generate strong earnings for shareholders. Like any business, they're motivated to enhance the bottom line. So they require IRA holders to invest in financial products they market and sell. That way they can earn a fee or commission and probably gain use of the funds. In fact, they make money by using the funds they have on deposit for their own investment purposes or to hold as financial reserves."

"In other words, they don't make any money by allowing you to purchase real estate or other alternative asset investments, so it doesn't make any sense to let you do that."

"Exactly. If they could make money when you bought real estate with your IRA funds, they'd probably allow you to do that. But when an IRA holder buys real estate, the parties that benefit from the investment are the seller of the property, the real estate agent, the title insurance company, and the closing attorney. On the other hand, if an IRA holder uses IRA assets to purchase mutual funds or stocks, the financial institution selling you those stocks benefits directly from the investment."

"So if they let you shift your IRA assets away from financial products that generate their fees and commissions to nontraditional investments such as real estate, that's going to negatively affect the financial institution's bottom line."

"Right. It'll reduce the financial institutions profits for sure, and probably put a strain on their financial reserves. So, most traditional financial institutions just don't allow it."

"So tell me about the financial institutions that allow me to make nontraditional investments with my IRA funds."

"Okay," John said. "There are two kinds of those, too. Ready?"

Custodian-Controlled Self-Directed IRAs without Checkbook Control

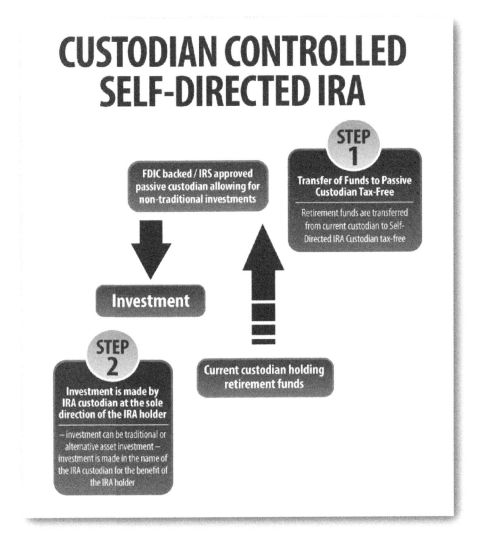

John took another sip of his latte and drew a line on the yellow pad.

"Unlike the traditional financial institutions such as Fidelity, Vanguard, Charles Schwab, or Bank of America, there are a number of financial institutions or IRA custodians that do allow IRA holders to make nontraditional investments with their IRA funds."

"Have I heard of them?"

"Maybe. They include Equity Trust, Pensco Trust, and IRA Financial Trust, for example."

"Sounds sort of familiar. How are they different from the Vanguards?"

"They have a slightly different business model. Unlike a traditional financial institution, which makes the majority of its IRA-related earnings on commissions and fees associated with stocks, mutual funds, bonds, and other equity of debt–type investments, these custodians typically generate their profits through annual account valuation fees and transaction fees."

"Okay, so they charge you an annual fee or a fee whenever you do something with your money, or both?"

"Exactly. They generally permit you to make alternative asset investments such as real estate."

"I still don't like that word *permit*." Rich laughed. "It's my money, right?"

"It is," John said, "but even in this type of financial institution you still don't have 'checkbook control.' In other words, you need custodian consent to enter into and execute any transaction."

"Sounds like a pain."

"Well, it can be. In fact, like any bureaucratic matter, it can be very inefficient. There are typically long delays between asking for consent and getting approval, and on top of that there can be high custodian fees associated with the transaction. So, before engaging in an IRA investment, they require you to get the consent of the custodian. You'll need to provide the custodian with the transaction documents for review as part of their transaction review process. And even upon approval, your IRA investment would be made in the name of the custodian for the benefit of ("FBO") the IRA holder's IRA. So, for example, ABC Trust Company FBO Rich Smith IRA. This doesn't give the IRA owner any privacy or limited liability protection."

"Sounding less appealing by the minute."

"And the minutes can count, right, when you're trying to pounce on an opportunity."

"And the fees, too. I don't like the sound of that."

"You shouldn't. It's common for a moderately active investor with $1 million in assets with a self-directed IRA custodian without checkbook control to end up paying from $500 to $1,500 in aggregate annual fees (including account value fee, transaction fees, and approval letters)."

"And they can still say no to your investment idea?"

"They sure can. There's no guarantee that the custodian will approve your investment even though the investment would not violate IRS rules. Overall, with a custodian-controlled self-directed IRA, even though you will generally be permitted to make most alternative-asset IRA investments, time delays and high custodian fees are a major downside. For example, if Jim, the guy who sits in the front row of class, wants to use his retirement funds to invest in real estate, let's say he elects to use a custodian-controlled self-directed IRA to make the investment. He selects ABC Trust Company as the IRA custodian. Before making the real estate investment, Jim would be required to provide all real estate transaction documents, including the purchase agreement and all ancillary purchase documents to ABC Trust Company for review and signature. Then ABC Trust Company must approve the transaction. If the transaction is approved, Jim needs to wait for ABC Trust Company to sign all documents before proceeding with the real estate purchase. In other words, even before Jim makes an offer on a piece of real estate, he's required to seek ABC Trust Company's consent as well as receive all required signatures before the offer can be submitted. Then, the funds required to make the purchase would be transferred directly from ABC Trust Company, and Jim would be required to pay an annual account fee based on the annual value of his IRA as well as fees for each IRA transaction."

"So, for Jim to pull that real estate deal off, he's got to hope no one else snaps it up before him, ABC Trust Company has to make the purchase for him, and he's got to pay them fees on top of all the fees and costs of the transaction."

"That's correct."

"I'm assuming there's a better way."

"You're right, there is."

The Self-Directed IRA LLC with "Checkbook Control"

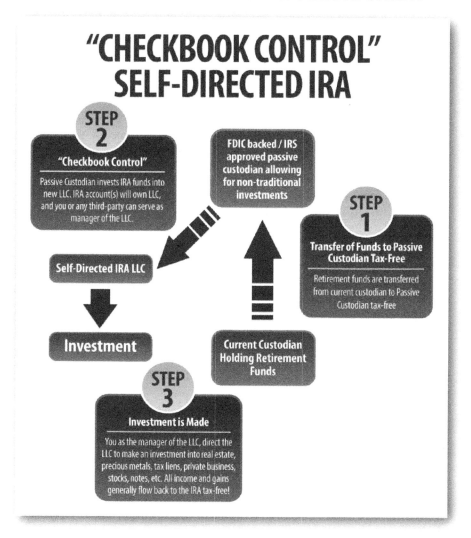

The lattes were finished, and Rich sat back as John told him a very interesting story.

Beginning in the mid-1990s, a new type of self-directed IRA structure started taking shape allowing the IRA holder to make IRA investments directly without seeking the consent of a custodian. Unlike a custodian-controlled self-directed IRA, which requires the IRA holder to seek the consent of the custodian before making investments, with a self-directed IRA LLC with "Checkbook Control," a limited liability company (LLC) is established that is owned by the IRA account and managed by the IRA account holder. A Passive Custodian then transfers the IRA holder's IRA funds to the LLC's bank account providing the IRA holder, as manager of the LLC, with checkbook control over his or her IRA funds.

"So," John said, "with a 'truly' self-directed IRA, the IRA holder has total control over his or her IRA funds."

"No need to get custodian consent?"

"Right. You no longer have to get each investment approved by the custodian of the account. Instead, all your investment decisions are made by you, as the manager of the LLC, or by any third-party manager you assign."

John continued. Like the financial institutions and custodians that offer custodian-controlled self-directed IRA, there are a number of trust companies that serve as passive custodians allowing for true self-directed IRA LLC with checkbook control investments, such as IRA Financial Trust. The popularity of self-directed IRA LLC with checkbook control is increasing each year. More and more custodians are getting more comfortable with their clients using these types of investment structures for their IRA funds.

"What do you think?" John asked.

"I think it sounds great, and I'd love to learn more. Can you teach me what I need to know?"

John said that he could, without much problem. In fact, he'd come prepared to get that ball rolling.

"I have a pamphlet here on IRAs in general. Why don't you read this, or read as much as you'd like, and then we can talk about getting started after class on Thursday."

"That sounds great," Rich said. And he took the pamphlet from John titled, "What Is an IRA?"

What Makes This Book Different

There are lots of books about retirement savings, and plenty that deal with different retirement investment vehicles like IRAs. This book's aim is to be the first that examines the checkbook control self-directed IRA LLC solution in depth. In it, I will show you and Rich and others like you why the self-directed IRA LLC solution is quickly becoming the most popular self-directed retirement solution for alternative asset investments. Other books have featured the self-directed IRA, but this book will mainly focus on the checkbook control self-directed IRA LLC structure and its inner workings.

So, if you, like Rich, want to study up on IRAs first, I suggest you turn to the next chapter and read as much or as little as you'd like. Then, let's move on to Chapter 3, and we can continue our conversation about the self-directed IRA with a difference.

II

What's an IRA?

Rich's head was spinning in a good way when he got home that night. He felt like the weight of the world had been lifted from his shoulders and that there were great possibilities before him. Not only could he accept the job at the energy consulting company, but he could continue to pursue his dream of becoming a real estate investor—and he could leverage his retirement funds (while continuing to grow them) to do so. He explained the gist of all that to Donna, knowing that there was a lot more he needed to learn still before he got started. Even so, Donna and he enjoyed one of their most relaxed and pleasant nights in a while, drinking some wine on the porch while they talked about the future with a sense of hope rather than dread.

On his own the next day, Rich opened up the pamphlet John had given him on the basics of IRAs. He'd heard the term *IRA* a million times in his life, but he really wanted to make sure he understood the fundamentals before he got deeper into the nuances of the self-directed IRA with checkbook control.

The Basics

IRAs exist in many forms. The most common type is the traditional IRA, also known as the regular or original IRA, to which any person with earnings from employment may contribute. These types of IRA plans are referred to as contributory IRAs. IRAs that are used to receive assets distributed from other retirement plans are called rollover IRAs. Roth IRAs combine the features of a regular IRA and a savings plan to produce a hybrid that adheres to its own set of rules. SEPs and SIMPLE IRAs are technically IRAs even though their rules are quite similar to those of qualified plans.

An IRA, like the trust under an employer's qualified 401(k) plan, is exempt from tax pursuant to Internal Revenue Code (IRC) Section 408(e)(i), and an individual maintaining an IRA usually is not taxed on principal or earnings of the account or annuity until they are distributed by the trustee, custodian, or insurance company. A deductible contribution to an IRA thus offers the same tax advantage as an employer's contribution to a qualified plan: deferral of taxation of the contributed funds and investment returns thereon until the funds are withdrawn at retirement.

IRAs can be invested in securities, real estate, or virtually any other asset except life insurance, artworks, precious metals, and other collectibles. An IRA is subject to some of the prohibited transaction rules of IRC Section 4975, which impose excise taxes on self-dealing transactions, and may be subject to the unrelated business income tax (UBIT) if it invests in a trade or business via a pass-through entity (i.e., LLC) or uses margins or a non-recourse loan.

The History of the IRA

In 1974, The Employee Retirement Income Security Act of 1974 (ERISA) was enacted, giving us IRAs. IRAs were created by Congress to encourage savings by employees not covered by qualified plans of their employers.

In doing so, Congress was trying to solve a simple but major problem. For many millions of employees, provision is made for their retirement out of tax-free dollars by their participation in qualified retirement plans. However, many more employees do not have the opportunity to participate in qualified plans. Often, plans are not available because an employer is not willing to incur the costs of contributing to a retirement plan since, in general, the employer is required to contribute funds that are in addition to the compensation otherwise paid to employees. Employees who are not covered under a qualified plan are disadvantaged by the fact that earnings on their retirement savings are subject to tax and grow more slowly than the tax-sheltered earnings on contributions to a qualified plan[1].

Unlike a 401(k) and related salary reduction plans, IRAs are not run by employers. The enactment of IRAs extended to workers without pensions the same kind of tax advantages already granted to pension funds and the self-employed.

Starting in 1975, individuals were allowed to set up separate accounts at financial institutions and deduct the value of their contributions from their current taxable income. Only employees without employer pension plans were eligible to contribute, and their annual contributions were limited to 15 percent of pay or a maximum of $1,500. The investment returns of these accounts were also excluded from taxable income in the year earned, but withdrawals were to be included in taxable income in the year they occurred. To encourage use of the accounts for retirement saving, ERISA set a penalty of 10 percent additional tax on withdrawals by taxpayers before age 59½.

The Economic Recovery Tax Act of 1981 expanded IRA eligibility and increased maximum contributions. Starting in 1982, all persons with earnings could contribute to IRAs, whether or not they were in a pension plan, and the maximum contribution was increased to 100 percent of earnings or $2,000. In response, tax returns with IRA contributions jumped from 4 percent of all returns with wage and salary income in 1981 to 14 percent in 1982 and 18 percent in 1986. The Tax Reform Act of 1986 restricted deductible IRA contributions. Starting in 1987, the act allowed deductible contributions only by an individual who was not covered by an employer pension plan (and whose spouse was not covered), and who had adjusted gross income between $25,000 and $35,000 (or, for joint returns, $40,000 to $50,000). Those not qualifying for deductible contributions could still make nondeductible

---

1   HR Rep. No. 779, 93d Cong., 2d Sess., reprinted in 1974-3 CB 244, 367–368. See HR Rep. No. 220, 105th Cong., 1st Sess. 775 (1997).

IRA contributions, thereby benefiting from the exclusion of investment returns from taxable income. The restriction caused tax returns with deductible IRA contributions to drop to 8 percent of all returns in 1987 and to decline slowly from there, reaching 4 percent in 1997.

The Taxpayer Relief Act of 1997 substantially raised the income limits applying to taxpayers covered by an employer plan. Eventually, those limits would be $50,000 to $60,000 for single taxpayers (2005 and after) and $80,000 to $100,000 for married taxpayers (2007 and after). Even higher limits ($150,000 to $160,000) were enacted for married taxpayers previously disqualified from making deductible contributions solely by virtue of a spouse being covered by an employer plan. The act also allows individuals to elect back-loaded IRAs, called "Roth" IRAs, in which contributions are not deductible, but withdrawals, assuming certain age and holding requirements are satisfied, are not taxed—a treatment similar to that of a tax-exempt bond. These IRAs are phased out between $116,000 and $131,000 of income for singles, and $183,000 to $193,000 for joint returns. All but the highest-income taxpayers will thus be eligible for some type of fully tax-favored IRA. Regulations imposing penalties on premature withdrawals were also relaxed so that the accounts may be used to save for higher education expenses or the first purchase of a home.

The Economic Growth and Tax Relief Reconciliation Act of 2001 (EGTRRA) increased the maximum allowable contribution to both deductible IRAs and Roth IRAs. For taxpayers under age 50, the limit would reach $5,000 in 2008 and then would be indexed for inflation. Taxpayers age 50 and above are allowed to make additional contributions up to a limit that would reach $1,000 in 2006. In 2015, an individual could make a maximum pretax or after-tax (Roth) IRA contribution of up to $5,500 or $6,500 if over the age of 50.

While the primary point of the IRA rules is to assist with the gathering of retirement savings, a set of rollover rules is also included, which allow funds to be transferred tax-free from one IRA to another and allow employees to avoid tax on some distributions from qualified plans by contributing the distributed money or property to an IRA.

The Popularity of the IRA

According to the Employee Benefits Research Institute, as of 2012, Individual Retirement Accounts (IRAs) are a vital component of US retirement savings, holding more than 25 percent of all retirement assets in the nation. A substantial portion of these IRA assets originated in other tax-qualified retirement plans, such as defined benefit plans (pensions) and 401(k) plans, and were moved to IRAs through rollovers from those plans. Thus, a sizable percentage of current IRA accounts are a repository for assets built up in the employment-based retirement system, as individuals hold money in them before or during retirement.

According to the ICI Research Perspective publication of November 2013, there were $5.7 trillion in IRA assets at the end of the second quarter of 2013. IRAs represented more than one-quarter of US total retirement market assets, compared with 17 percent two decades ago. IRAs also have risen in importance on household balance sheets. In June 2013, IRA assets were 9 percent of all household financial assets, up from 4 percent of assets two decades ago. In May 2013, 46.1 million or 38 percent of US households reported they owned IRAs.

Traditional IRAs were the most common type of IRA owned, followed by Roth IRAs and employer-sponsored IRAs, such as SEP IRAs.

What Is an IRA?

An individual retirement account (IRA) is a trust or custodial account set up in the United States for the exclusive benefit of you or your beneficiaries. The account is created by a written document. The document must show that the account meets all of the following requirements:

- The trustee or custodian must be a bank, a federally insured credit union, trust company, a savings and loan association, or an entity approved by the IRS to act as trustee or custodian.
- The trustee or custodian generally cannot accept contributions of more than the deductible amount for the year. However, rollover

contributions and employer contributions to a simplified employee pension (SEP) can be more than this amount.

- Contributions, except for rollover contributions, must be in cash. (See Rollovers.)
- You must have a nonforfeitable right to the amount at all times.
- Money in your account cannot be used to buy a life insurance policy.
- Assets in your account cannot be combined with other property, except in a common trust fund or common investment fund.
- You must start receiving distributions by April 1 of the year following the year in which you reach age 70½ (required minimum distributions).

There are two kinds of IRAs: individual retirement accounts (trusts and custodial) and annuities (contracts).

How Do I Set Up an IRA?

An individual may establish an IRA with a bank, savings and loan association, credit union, trust company, brokerage firm, or other organization that can demonstrate to the IRS the ability to lawfully administer the IRA account. The trustee or custodian must be a bank, a federally insured credit union, a savings and loan association, or an entity approved by the IRS to act as trustee or custodian. An individual retirement annuity is generally established through an insurance company.

To establish an IRA, the IRA holder and the financial organization offering the IRA must agree upon certain terms and conditions in writing. An IRA is established when the individual and the financial institution sign and receive the IRA opening documents. You can set up an IRA at any time. When the IRA is opened, it is essentially a trust with no investments. The IRA is funded when the IRA owner makes contributions or funds are transferred or rolled over from another retirement account.

Who Tends to Set Up IRAs?

IRA owners tend to be savers. According to the same ICI Research Perspective publication from November 2013, the median financial assets of IRA-owning households were eight times greater than the median financial assets of households that did not own IRAs. Also, IRA owners are more likely to be married, employed, and have college or postgraduate degrees than households that do not own IRAs.

How Many IRAs Can I Have?

An IRA holder may have an unlimited number of IRAs with one or more financial organizations. For example, you can set up an IRA with Bank X in Year One and make a contribution and then set up another IRA with Bank Y in Year One. Although you can establish more than one IRA, the IRA annual contribution limits applies to all IRAs together. So, if you are under fifty years old and have three different IRAs, as of 2015 you cannot make IRA contributions in an amount that will exceed $5,500 including all your IRA accounts ($6,500 if you are over the age of 50). The contribution can be allocated to one IRA or divided among all or some of the other IRA accounts.

Can I Have an IRA if I Also Contribute to Another Retirement Account?

If both you and your spouse have compensation and are under age 70½, each of you can set up an IRA. You can have a traditional IRA whether or not you are covered by any other retirement plan. However, you may not be able to deduct all of your contributions if you or your spouse is covered by an employer retirement plan.

If you and your spouse file a joint return, only one of you needs to have compensation. You and your spouse cannot both participate in the same IRA.

The Traditional IRA

A traditional IRA primarily is a tax-deferred retirement savings vehicle. Tax is generally deferred on traditional IRA contributions and earnings until the year the IRA owner takes a distribution. A traditional IRA is essentially any IRA that is not a Roth IRA or a SIMPLE IRA. In general, if you have income from working for yourself or someone else, you may establish and contribute to an IRA. The IRA can be a special account that you can set up with a bank, brokerage firm, or other institutional custodian. Alternatively, it can be an individual retirement annuity that you can purchase from an insurance company.

Who Can Set Up a Traditional IRA?

You can set up and make contributions to a traditional IRA if:

- You (or, if you file a joint return, your spouse) received taxable compensation during the year, and
- You were not age 70½ by the end of the year.

You can generally set up a traditional IRA if you have income from working for yourself or someone else. If your only income is social security or passive income, such as interest, dividends, rental income, or capital gains, that income would not be considered earned income and would not be considered income available for purposes of making an IRA contribution.

Tax-Deductible Contributions

With traditional IRA contributions, you have the ability to take tax deductions. This was designed to encourage savings for retirement.

When you take advantage of tax deferral by investing in your employer-sponsored retirement plan, you not only put off paying income taxes on the money you contribute, you may also save money on the taxes you eventually will pay.

The money you contribute to a traditional IRA is pretax, which means that the contribution is deducted from your gross income and goes directly into your retirement savings plan, so you're left with a smaller dollar amount in your paycheck that can be taxed by the IRS. As a result, you'll pay less in your current income taxes for the year, because according to the IRS, you've earned less money. This can help you reduce your income tax liability.

The benefit of tax-deductible contributions is simple. For example, if you are in a 30 percent income tax bracket and you contribute $5,000 to a traditional IRA in a year, that's $5,000 of your salary on which you're not paying taxes this year, so you will be able to reduce your annual income tax bill by approximately $1,500 ($5,000 x 30 percent). In other words, you will receive an income tax deduction for the $5,000 contribution, which will save you approximately $1,500 in tax payments. By making tax-deductible contributions, you are essentially paying yourself to save for your retirement.

All earnings generated from traditional IRA contributions are tax-deferred until distributed.

What Is Tax Deferral?

Tax deferral literally means that you are putting off paying tax. The most common types of tax-deferred investments include those in IRAs or Qualified Retirement Plans [i.e., 401(k)s]. Tax deferral means that all income, gains, and earnings, such as interest, dividends, rental income, royalties, or capital gains will accumulate tax-free until the investor or IRA owner withdraws the funds and takes possession of them. As long as the funds remain in the retirement account, the funds will grow tax-free. This allows your retirement funds to grow at a much faster pace than if the funds were held personally, allowing you to build for your retirement more quickly. And when you withdraw your IRA funds in the form of a distribution after you retire, you will likely be in a lower tax bracket and be able to keep more of what you accumulated. So, using a traditional IRA as a retirement savings vehicle, not only are you not paying taxes on the money you invested, you could be paying them at a lower rate when you finally do "take home" your money.

As long as the funds remain in the account, they grow without taxes eroding their value. This enables assets to accumulate at a faster rate, giving you an edge when saving for the long term.

What Are the Advantages of Tax Deferral?

By using an IRA to make investments, the IRA owner is able to defer taxes on any investment returns, thus, allowing the IRA owner to benefit in three ways. The first benefit is tax-free growth: Instead of paying tax on the returns of an investment, tax is paid only at a later date, leaving the investment to grow tax-free without interruption. The second benefit of tax deferral is that IRA investments are usually made when the IRA owner is in his or her highest income earning years and is thus subject to tax at a higher tax rate. The third benefit is the ability to defer taxes on investments in the face of increased federal income tax rates. With tax rates at a historic low (the highest income tax bracket in 1986 was 50 percent and in 2000 was 39.6 percent), the likelihood of higher federal income tax rates in the near future are significant, especially with the financial strain the baby-boomer generation is expected to have on the federal budget. Thus, the ability to defer tax on investments until the IRA owner is 70½ and likely in a low income tax bracket makes an IRA a highly attractive investment vehicle.

Tax Deferral by the Numbers

The following examples illustrate the powerful advantage of tax-deferred contributions and compounding through a traditional IRA versus making contributions to a taxable account.

Example #1:
Joe is forty years old and makes a $5,000 contribution to an IRA. Assume Joe is in a 30 percent federal income tax bracket. Joe invests his IRA funds and receives a 6 percent average annual return. When Joe retires at age 70, his $5,000 contribution would be worth $21,609.71. If Joe invested the $5,000 personally, the account would only be worth $14,033.97.

Example #2:
Jane is thirty-five years old and makes a $5,000 contribution to an IRA. Jane makes a $5,000 contribution to her IRA each year until she reaches the age of 70. Assume Jane is in a 30 percent federal income tax bracket. Further assume that Jane was able to generate a 7 percent average annual return on her investment. When Jane retires at the age of 70, her IRA account would be worth $792,950.21. If Jane made these $5,000 contributions though a taxable account, the account would only be worth $490,707.49.

Contributions
IRC Section 219(a) permits a deduction for contributions to IRAs, which is allowable only if the contribution is in cash, the contributor is under the age of 70½ at the end of the taxable year, and the contribution is not a rollover. Also, a deductible contribution may not be made to an IRA that was started by another person and acquired by the taxpayer as beneficiary on that person's death unless the taxpayer is the surviving spouse.

How Much Can Be Contributed?
Traditional IRAs may receive several types of contributions: regular, spousal, rollover, transfer, recharacterization, and catchup contributions.

Regular Contributions:
To be eligible to make regular contributions to a traditional IRA, an individual must satisfy the age requirements for that year and have earned income.

Age
There is a maximum age restriction on when traditional IRA contributions can be made under the law. IRA owners cannot make IRA contributions beginning in the year in which they attain age 70½ Therefore, IRA owners who reach their 70th birthday before July 1 of a given year cannot make an IRA contribution for that year they will be 70½ before the end of the year.

There is no minimum age for making IRA contributions; however, financial institutions may have rules restricting minors from signing contracts.

Qualified Compensation
Individuals must have qualified compensation in order to be eligible to contribute to an IRA. In general, individuals must earn income from personal services rendered. The personal services rendered must be performed in the year the compensation is received. For most individuals, the income is shown on IRS Form W-2, Wage and Tax Statement, or IRS Form 1099-MISC.

What Is Compensation?
Generally, compensation is what you earn from working.

Wages, Salaries, Etc.
Wages, salaries, tips, professional fees, bonuses, and other amounts you receive for providing personal services are compensation.

Commissions

An amount you receive that is a percentage of profits or sales price is compensation.

Self-Employment Income

If you are self-employed (a sole proprietor or a partner), compensation is the net earnings from your trade or business (provided your personal services are a material income-producing factor) reduced by the total of:

- The deduction for contributions made on your behalf to retirement plans, and
- The deduction allowed for one-half of your self-employment taxes.

Alimony and Separate Maintenance

For IRA purposes, compensation includes any taxable alimony and separate maintenance payments you receive under a decree of divorce or separate maintenance.

Military Differential Pay

For IRA purposes, compensation includes military differential pay you receive.

Nontaxable Combat Pay

If you were a member of the US Armed Forces, compensation includes any nontaxable combat pay you received.

What Is Not Compensation?

Compensation does not include any of the following items:

- Earnings and profits from property, such as rental income, interest income, and dividend income.
- Pension or annuity income.

- Deferred compensation received (compensation payments postponed from a past year).
- Income from a partnership for which you do not provide services that are a material income-producing factor.
- Any amounts (other than combat pay) you exclude from income, such as foreign earned income and housing costs.
- Income from social security and worker's compensation.

What IS and is NOT Compensation for Purposes of an IRA

Compensation includes...

Wage / Salaries

Commissions

Self-employment income

Alimony and separate maintenance

Military differential pay

Nontaxable combat pay

Compensation does NOT include...

Earnings and profits from real estate investments

Interest and dividend income

Pension or annuity income

Deferred compensation

- Income from certain partnerships that does not involve [?]
  - Any amounts you exclude from income
- Income from social security and worker's compensation

What if Both Spouses Have Compensation?

If both you and your spouse have compensation and are under age 70½, each of you can set up an IRA. You cannot both participate in the same IRA. If you file a joint return, only one of you needs to have compensation for each spouse to open his or her own IRA.

Contribution Limits

Under the IRA rules, a contribution is deemed to have been made during a taxable year if it is made not later than the due date of that year's return (not including extensions) and is "made on account of such taxable year." For a taxpayer whose taxable year is the calendar year, a contribution for any year can thus be made as late as April 15 of the following year. For example, for 2015, you will be permitted to make IRA contributions up until April 15, 2016.

Regular Contributions

A regular traditional IRA contribution is limited to the lessor of the annual contribution limit or 100 percent of the individual's eligible compensation.

Example 1:

If Jim earned $25,000 in W-2 compensation in a year and is under 50 years of age, Jim would be permitted to make a $5,500 IRA contribution in 2015.

Example 2:

If Jim earned only $4,000 in W-2 compensation in a year and is under 50 years of age, Jim would only be permitted to make an IRA contribution of $4,000.

For the year 2015, you may contribute a maximum of $5,500 each year, or $6,500 if you will reach the age of 50 by the end of the year. If you are not covered by an employer's retirement plan, you may take a deduction on your tax return for your contribution. However, if you are covered by an employer's plan, your IRA may be fully or partially deductible or not deductible at all depending on how much gross income you have.

Catchup Contributions

Individuals who reach age 50 or older before the end of the taxable year may be eligible to contribute an additional amount to a traditional IRA as a catchup contribution. The maximum annual amount that individuals may contribute to a traditional IRA as a catchup contribution is $1,000.

Spousal Contributions

If an individual has no qualified compensation income but his or her spouse does, that individual may generally make a contribution to his or her IRA based on his or her spouse's compensation. This is generally referred to as "spousal contributions."

To be eligible for spousal contributions to a traditional IRA, the spouse without compensation income must not have reached the age of 70½ in the calendar year in which the contribution is being made. Also, to be eligible, the spouse must have eligible compensation and the couple must file a joint federal income tax return.

The traditional IRA contribution limits are applied to each spouse as a separate IRA holder. Thus, if both a husband and wife are eligible to make IRA contributions, the IRA contribution limit for the couple in 2015 is the lessor of $11,000 (plus catchup contributions, if eligible) or 100 percent of the combined eligible compensation. However, no more than the individual IRA individual contribution limit ($5,500, plus catchup contributions, if eligible) may be contributed to either spouse's IRA.

If a spousal contribution is made, the spouse without compensation must establish a separate IRA. However, the compensated spouse is not required to have an IRA in order for the noncompensated spouse to make an IRA contribution.

Example 1:

Jim and Jane are married and both earn $25,000 in W-2 compensation annually. Jim and Jane are both under 50 years of age. Jim and Jane would each be permitted to make a $5,500 yearly IRA contribution for 2015.

Example 2:

Jim and Jane are married. Jim and Jane are both under 50 years of age. Jim did not earn any yearly compensation, but Jane earned $50,000 in W-2 annual compensation. Jim would still be able to make a spousal contribution of $5,000 based on Jane's eligible compensation for 2015.

Can I Contribute Less than the Maximum Allowed Contributions?

You are not required to make maximum contributions to your IRA each year. In fact, you are not required to make any contributions to your IRA in any year. However, if contributions to your traditional IRA for a year were less than the limit, you cannot contribute more after the due date of your return for that year to make up the difference.

Example:

Jim, who is 47, earned $47,000 in year 2014. Although he can contribute up to $5,500 for that year, Jim only made a contribution of $3,700. After April 15, 2015, Jim cannot make up the difference between his actual contributions for 2014 ($3,700) and his 2014 limit ($5,500). He cannot contribute $1,800 more than the limit for any later year.

What Happens if I Contribute More than the Maximum Contributions?

If contributions to your IRA for a year were more than the maximum IRA contribution limit, for that year, you can generally apply the excess contribution in one year to a later year if the contributions for that later year are less than the maximum allowed for that year. However, a penalty or additional tax may apply.

In general, if the excess contributions for a year are not withdrawn by the date your return for the year is due (including extensions), you are subject to a 6 percent tax. You must pay the 6 percent tax each year on excess amounts that remain in your traditional IRA at the end of your tax year. The tax cannot be more than 6 percent of the combined value of all your IRAs as of the end of your tax year. (The additional tax is figured on Form 5329.)

Example:

Jane is thirty-nine years old and single, her compensation is $25,000, and she contributed $6,000 to her traditional IRA for 2015. Jane has made an excess contribution to her IRA of $500 ($6,000 minus the $5,500 limit). The contribution earned $10 interest in 2014 and $5 interest in 2015 before the due date of the return, including extensions. Jane does not withdraw the $500 and the interest it earned by the due date of this return, including extensions. Jane would be liable for tax on the excess contribution made.

What Happens if I Withdraw an Excess Contribution Made by the Due Date of Filing My Tax Return?

You will not have to pay the 6 percent tax on an excess IRA contribution if you withdraw an excess contribution made during a tax year and you also withdraw any interest or other income earned on the excess contribution. You must complete your withdrawal by the date your tax return for that year is due, including extensions.

What Happens to the Excess Contributions That Were Withdrawn?

If you made an excess IRA contribution for the taxable year and withdrew the excess contribution prior to the filing of your tax return, you would not include the excess contribution in your gross income if both of the following conditions are met:

- No deduction was taken for the excess contribution.
- You withdraw the interest or other income earned on the excess contribution.

You can take into account any loss on the contribution while it was in the IRA when calculating the amount that must be withdrawn. For example, if you made an excess IRA contribution and the funds were used to make an investment that has since lost value (there is a loss) the net income you must withdraw may be a negative amount.

What Happens to the Income or Interest Earned on the Excess Contribution?

You must include in your gross income the interest or other income that was earned on the excess contribution. Report it on your return for the year in which the excess contribution was made. Your withdrawal of interest or other income may be subject to an additional 10 percent tax on early distributions, which I'll discuss later.

Are All Contributions to a Traditional IRA Deductible?

Before 1987, IRA owners were allowed to deduct all eligible traditional IRA contributions on their federal income tax returns. The Tax Reform Act of 1986 put restrictions on who may claim income tax deductions for traditional IRA contributions, but it allowed IRA owners to make nondeductible contributions.

If I Have a 401(k) Can I Still Contribute to an IRA?

In the past, an active participant in an employer-sponsored retirement plan could not have an IRA. This restriction was removed in 1981, but it reappeared in modified form in 1986. Since 1986, the normal ceiling on deductible IRA contributions has been reduced if the taxpayer is an "active participant" of a qualified retirement plan and his or her adjusted gross income exceeds a threshold amount. In other words, rather than disqualifying all employees participating in employer-sponsored plans, the IRA deduction is phased out for taxpayers whose incomes exceed specified thresholds.

What IRA Contributions Are Deductible?

In general, an IRA owner is able to deduct a traditional IRA contribution, or a portion of an IRA contribution, depending on the IRA owner's active participation in an employer-sponsored retirement plan, such as a 401(k) plan; marital status; and modified adjusted gross income (MAGI).

Active Participation in an Employer-Sponsored Retirement Plan

An IRA owner is an active participant in an employer-sponsored retirement plan if he or she is participating in or receiving contributions from an employer-sponsored retirement plan, such as a 401(k) plan. In other words, an individual is an active participant for any taxable year during which benefits accrue to him or her under a qualified plan, such as a 401(k) plan maintained by his or her employer. If an individual is an active participant in an employer-sponsored retirement plan, the deductibility of an IRA contribution depends on the IRA owner's MAGI.

If I'm Married and Only One Spouse Is an Active Participant in a Plan, How Do We Determine MAGI?

If you file a joint income tax return with your spouse, and only one spouse is considered an active participant, the deductibility of the traditional IRA contribution made by the spouse who is not an active participant in an employer-sponsored retirement plan is dependent on the couple's MAGI.

What Type of Plans Are Considered "Retirement Plans" for Deductibility Purposes?

An IRA owner is treated as an active participant in an employer-sponsored retirement plan if the IRA owner is an active participant in any of the following retirement plans:

- A qualified plan described in IRC Section 401(a), including a 401(k) plan
- An annuity plan described in IRC Section 403(a)
- An annuity contract or custodial account described in IRC Section 403(b)
- A SEP Plan described in IRC Section 408(p)
- A trust described in IRC Section 501(c)(18)
- A plan for federal, state, or local government employees or for an agency or instrumentality thereof [other than an IRC Section 457(b) Plan].

What Is the Modified Adjusted Gross Income (MAGI) Threshold?

In general, for purposes of determining the deductibility of traditional IRA contributions, an individual's MAGI is calculated to be the individual's adjusted gross income without taking into consideration the tax deduction for traditional IRA contributions. An individual's MAGI can be found on the individual's federal income tax return (i.e., IRS Form 1040, US Individual Income Tax Return).

For an individual who is an active participant in an employer-sponsored retirement plan or is married to an active participant, the deductibility of a traditional IRA contribution depends on such individual's MAGI as illustrated on the IRS Form 1040.

If the IRA owner's MAGI is equal to or below the annual minimum threshold, the IRA owner is eligible to take a deduction for the full amount of the IRA contribution up to the statutory limit (i.e., $5,500 if the individual is under the age of 50). However, if the individual's MAGI exceeds the minimum threshold, the IRA owner will only be able to deduct a portion of the traditional IRA contribution until the maximum qualifying income level is reached.

What Is the Traditional IRA Deductibility Threshold for 2015?

In 2015, if you are single and covered by an employer's plan, your contribution is fully deductible if your adjusted gross income (AGI) is less than $61,000 and not deductible at all when your AGI reaches $70,000. Between $61,000 and $71,000 the deduction is gradually phased out. For married individuals, the phase-out range is from $98,000 to $118,000, if the IRA participant is covered by an employer plan. For an IRA participant who is not covered by a plan but whose spouse is covered, the phase-out range is $183,000 to $193,000.

Why Is the Traditional IRA Deduction Threshold So Low?

It is believed that the relatively low ceiling on IRA deductions is intended to keep IRAs from becoming a significant alternative to qualified plans for highly compensated employees.

Traditional IRA Nondeductible Contributions

An individual who is unable to deduct all or part of a traditional IRA contribution is still permitted to make a nondeductible traditional IRA contribution of up to the lessor of the applicable annual limit (i.e., $5,500 if the individual is under the age of 50 for 2015) or 100 percent of earned income.

An IRA owner who makes a nondeductible traditional IRA contribution must report the nondeductible amount to the IRS on Form 8606, which should be filed with the IRA owner's individual federal income tax return (Form 1040).

Who Is Responsible for Determining the Deductibility of a Traditional IRA Contribution?

The IRA owner and not the IRA custodian is responsible for determining the deductibility of a traditional IRA contribution.

How Do the Contributions Limits Apply to Husband and Wives?

Generally, the husband and wife are treated separately under the IRA rules. If both spouses are employed, each can deduct contributions up to the lesser of the dollar ceiling or 100 percent of that spouse's compensation.

Can I Still Make IRA Contributions Even if I Earn More Money than the Phase-Out Limit?

A taxpayer phased out of making tax-deductible contributions is still allowed to make nondeductible contributions in the amount of $5,500 or $6,500, as applicable for 2015.

Distributions

The IRS's approach to helping people invest and save their retirement funds is a lot like a football game. If the quarterback takes too much time calling an offensive play, the team will face a penalty. Similarly, if a traditional IRA owner withdraws his or her funds too early from an IRA, the IRA owner will face an early distribution tax. On the other hand, if the quarterback calls an offensive play too quickly before his teammates are ready, the team will be in violation of the rules, just as you will face a penalty for taking an early distribution from your traditional IRA.

The required distribution rules are believed to have been designed by Congress to ensure that IRAs are mainly used as retirement savings vehicles, not as a medium to build wealth for transfer to heirs.

In general, the distribution rules deal separately for distributions to IRA owners and distributions to beneficiaries after the death of an IRA owner.

When Can Distributions Be Taken from an IRA?

An IRA owner may take distributions from his or her IRA at any time. The determination of whether the distribution is taxed depends on the type of IRA (i.e., traditional or Roth); the age of the IRA owner; and in the case of a Roth IRA, the duration of time the account has been established.

Are Traditional IRA Distributions Subject to Tax?

Yes—the IRA owner is required to include traditional IRA distributions in his or her taxable gross income. The IRA owner who receives a distribution will report the distribution on his or her individual federal income tax return (Form 1040) and pay tax on the distribution based on the individual's federal income tax rate.

What Type of Transactions Are Exempted from the Traditional IRA Distribution Rules?

In general, the following IRA-related transactions are not treated as distributions subject to tax:

- Rollovers
- Transfers
- Recharacterizations
- Revoked IRA within seven-day period
- The portion of a distribution relating to nondeductible traditional IRA contributions

Early Distributions

In general, traditional IRAs are designed to encourage retirement saving and at the same time discourage people from taking money away from their retirement savings before reaching the age of 59½ The age 59½ was selected by Congress because it was believed to be the age when one began transitioning from active employment to retirement.

Are Early Distributions Subject to an Additional Tax?

Yes. In general, the IRS assesses a 10 percent penalty on the taxable portion of early distributions. However, the 10 percent early distribution penalty does not apply in the following situations:

1. **Death of the IRA Owner:**
   An IRA distribution to beneficiaries is not subject to the 10 percent early distribution penalty. In other words, upon the death of the IRA owner, the distribution of the owner's IRA to his or her beneficiaries is not subject to the 10 percent penalty.

2. **Disability:**
   Distributions received by a disabled IRA owner are not subject to the 10 percent early distribution penalty. Prior to making the disability distribution, the financial organization may require written evidence from the disabled IRA owner to verify disability. The IRA owner can demonstrate this by using IRS Form 1040, Schedule R, Credit for the Elderly or Disabled.

3. **Rollovers and Conversions:**
   Amounts rolled over to an IRA or properly converted to an IRA are not subject to the 10 percent early distribution penalty.

4. **First-Time Homebuyer Expenses:**
   Distributions taken for qualified first-time homebuyer expenses are not subject to the 10 percent early distribution penalty. There is a $10,000 lifetime limit with this exemption.

5. **Return of Nondeductible Contributions:**
   The 10 percent early distribution penalty would not apply to the portion of a distribution that represents a return of nondeductible contributions or after-tax assets received through a rollover.

6. **Substantially Equal Periodic Payment:**

   The 10 percent early distribution penalty shall not apply to distributions that are part of a series of substantially equal periodic payments made at least annually over the IRA owner's life expectancy or joint life expectancy of the IRA owner and his or her beneficiary. The IRA holder must make a specific election under IRC Section 72 with the IRA custodian to take advantage of this election. The rules that apply to this option are quite complex, so it is best to consult with a tax attorney or CPA.

7. **Health Insurance:**

   An IRA owner who received federal or state unemployment compensation for twelve consecutive weeks may take IRA distributions to pay for health insurance. These distributions are not subject to the 10 percent early distribution penalty. The IRA owner must take a distribution in the year he received his unemployment or in the year that follows. This exemption does not apply to distributions taken more than 60 days after the IRA owner regains employment.

8. **Medical Expenses:**

   Distributions used for reimbursed medical expenses that exceed 7.5 percent of the IRA owner's adjusted gross income are not subject to the 10 percent early distribution penalty.

9. **Higher Education Expenses:**

   IRA distributions used for qualified education expenses of the IRA owner, his or her spouse, or the spouse's child or grandchild are not subject to the 10 percent early distribution penalty.

10. **IRS Levy:**

    Distributions taken because of IRS tax levies imposed on the IRA owner are not subject to the 10 percent early distribution penalty.

11. **Qualified Reservist Distributions:**
Qualified reservists (including National Guard personnel) called to active duty after September 11, 2001, for a period of at least 180 days or an indefinite amount of time, are permitted to take penalty-free distributions from their IRA. This applies to distributions taken between the date of the order or call to duty and the end of the active-duty period. **Note:** The distribution taken will still be subject to federal income tax.

Required Distributions to IRA Owners

The required minimum distribution rules (RMD) were created in order to guarantee the flow of IRA funds into the federal income tax system as well as to encourage IRA owners to use their retirement funds during their retirement.

You don't have to be concerned about taking distributions from a retirement plan until the year in which you turn 70½ To avoid penalty, an IRA owner must comply with what are called the required distribution rules, also known as the minimum distribution rules. The required distribution rules require that an IRA owner take a minimum distribution amount from his or her retirement account each year, generally beginning in the year the IRA owner turns 70½. April 1 of the year following the calendar year during which the owner reaches age 70½ is the "required beginning date." The minimum distribution amount for a "distribution calendar year" is the owner's "account" for the year, divided by an "applicable distribution period." An owner's distribution calendar years are the years during which he or she reaches age 70½ and each subsequent year during his or her life. The "applicable distribution period" changes annually and is usually taken from a Uniform Lifetime Table found in the IRC. It is, for example, 27.4 for the distribution calendar year during which an owner reaches age 70, 18.7 for the year of his or her 80th birthday, and 11.4 for the year during which an owner turns 90. The minimum distribution for the first distribution calendar year must be made by April 1 of the following year (the required beginning date), and distributions for the distribution calendar year containing the required beginning date and all other years must be made by the end of the year. (Please see Exhibit A to view a copy of the Uniform Lifetime Table.)

If your spouse is your beneficiary and is more than ten years younger than you, you will be required to use a different and more favorable table called the Joint Life and Last Survivor Table. (Please see Exhibit B to view a copy of the Joint Life and Last Survivor Table.)

What Is the Required Beginning Date?

The IRA owner must begin taking RMDs in the year he or she turns 70½ The IRA owner may delay taking the first year's RMD until April 1 following the year in which they reach age 70½. This April 1 date is called the required beginning date (RBD). In all subsequent years, RMDs must be taken by December 31.

For example: Joe turned age 70 on June 23, 2013, and therefore will be age 70½ in 2013. Joe must take his 2013 RMD by April 1, 2014. Joe would also need to take his second RMD—the 2014 RMD—by December 31, 2014.

How Do You Calculate the RMD?

To determine an RMD for an IRA, the IRA owner will need to divide the December 31 prior year-end IRA balance by the applicable distribution period.

IRA Balance

_____ = RMD

Distribution Period

A. IRA BALANCE
    THE IRA owner's IRA balance on December 31 of the prior year is used to calculate an RMD. Any outstanding rollovers, transfers, and recharacterizations must be added to the prior year-end balance.

B. Distribution Period
    The distribution period applicable to an IRA owner is a number that represents the average life expectancy tables.

In general, during an IRA owner's lifetime, the IRS final regulations provide for a uniform distribution period equal to the joint life expectancy of the IRA owner and a hypothetical beneficiary exactly ten years younger. The life expectancy is determined using a Uniform Lifetime Table issued by the IRS each year. In order to obtain the applicable distribution period, simply use the age of the IRA owner in the year for which the distribution is being taken and refer to the Uniform Lifetime Table issued by the IRS.

Exception to Using the Uniform Lifetime Table

An exception to using the Uniform Lifetime Table arises if an IRA owner's spouse who is more than ten years younger than the IRA owner is named as the sole beneficiary of the IRA. In this case, the IRA owner may use a longer distribution period as determined by the actual joint life expectancy found in the IRS's Joint and Last Survivor Table. Note that the new IRA owner may take a distribution in excess of the RMD amount.

Who Is Responsible for Making the RMD Calculations?

The IRA custodian (the financial institutions) is required to submit reports to the IRS and to the IRA owner regarding RMDs. If an RMD is required to be taken from an IRA for a calendar year and the IRA owner is alive at the beginning of the year, the IRA custodian that held the IRA as of December 31 of the prior year must provide a statement to the IRA owner to report the due date of the RMD and, in most cases, the amount that is due. The IRA custodian is required to send this report to the IRA owner by January 31 of the year for which the RMD is required.

What if the RMD Is Not Made?

If an IRA owner's distribution from his or her IRA is less than the year's RMD amount, the difference is an excess accumulation, and the IRA owner is subject to a 50 percent penalty tax, which must be paid to the IRS. The IRA custodian does not assess or collect the penalty as the penalty is paid to the IRS with the filing of Form 5329, Additional Taxes on Qualified Plans and Other Tax-Favored Accounts. For example, if the IRA owner was required to take an RMD of $1,000 but only took a $500 distribution, the IRA owner would be subject to a penalty tax of $250 (amount of distribution shortfall less $500 multiplied by 50 percent penalty).

Beneficiary Distributions

When an IRA owner dies, the financial institution holding the IRA account must follow certain procedures when making distributions to the beneficiaries of a deceased IRA owner. It is important to remember that if the IRA beneficiary does not take a required distribution, he or she will be subject to a 50 percent excess accumulation penalty. For example, if an IRA beneficiary was required to take a distribution of $1,000 but only took a distribution of $500, the IRA beneficiary would be subject to a penalty tax of $250 (amount of distribution shortfall less $500 multiplied by 50 percent penalty).

Beneficiary Distribution Options

There are a number of distribution options available to a designated IRA beneficiary, generally dependent on whether the deceased IRA owner's sole primary beneficiary is a spouse and whether the deceased IRA owner has reached 70½, the age for RMDs. Remember, a living IRA owner is not required to take an RMD until the IRA owner reaches the age of 70½.

Distribution Option if the IRA Beneficiary Is a Spouse and the IRA Owner Was under the Age of 70½ When He or She Died

If an IRA owner dies before he or she reaches the age of 70½ and designates a spouse as the primary and sole beneficiary, the spouse IRA beneficiary has the following options:

1. **Transfer:** A surviving spouse who is sole beneficiary of a deceased spouse's IRA and has an "unlimited right to withdraw" from it may, at any time after the owner's death, elect to treat the IRA as though he or she were its owner rather than its beneficiary. The election may only be made if the spouse is the only beneficiary of the IRA. In other words, the deceased IRA owner's IRA may be transferred to the surviving spouse's IRA. Essentially, the surviving spouse may roll over the deceased IRA owner's IRA into his or her own.

2. **Life Expectancy Rule:** Minimum distributions to an electing surviving spouse are determined under the rules for the deceased IRA owner, not the rules for beneficiaries, except that the election may not cause there to be a minimum distribution for the year of the owner's death if the owner died before his or her required beginning date. For example, if a surviving spouse is seventy-five years old when a sixty-four-year-old IRA owner dies, no distribution is required for the year of death, even if the spouse makes the election, even though the spouse's required beginning date occurred before that year. An electing spouse is treated as IRA owner "for all purposes under the IRC," including the premature withdrawal penalty. In other words, a surviving spouse can wait until the year the deceased spouse would have turned 70½ to begin receiving required distributions. This deferral option is only available to a surviving spouse IRA beneficiary. The surviving spouse can choose the option even if she is over the age of 70½ as long as the account remains in the deceased IRA owner's name.

If a surviving spouse elects to use the Life Expectancy Payment methods to take IRA distributions, the surviving spouse would have to do the following:

a. Ascertain the IRA Value: The surviving spouse must determine the IRA value of the deceased IRA owner's balance as of December 31 of the year before the IRA owner would have turned 70½ to calculate the first required distribution.

b. Calculate the Applicable Distribution Period: Using the surviving spouse's age in the year the deceased IRA owner would have turned 70½, the surviving spouse must look up the appropriate life expectancy factor as provided by the IRS—also called the Applicable Distribution Period.

c. Calculate the Required Distribution: The surviving spouse would need to calculate the first required distribution, which is calculated by dividing the account balance by the Applicable Distribution Period. That amount must be distributed by December 31 of the year in which the deceased IRA owner would have turned 70½.

Example 1:

Joe was born June 10, 1939, and died on July 1, 2007, at age 68—before reaching his RBD. His wife, Jane, is the sole beneficiary of his IRA. Jane will elect to use the life expectancy rule to determine required distributions. Jane will be able to defer distributions until the year 2010, the year Joe would have turned 70½. To compute the required distribution, Jane would have to use the account balance as of December 31, 2009, the year before Joe would have turned 70½.

Example 2:

If Jim was the sole primary beneficiary of his wife's IRA when she died during 2007 at age 68, distributions to him must begin by the end of the calendar year during which his wife would have reached age 70½. If that year is 2009 and Jim is sixty-five years old on his birthday during 2009, the applicable distribution period for the year is 21, which is his life expectancy as of that birthday, and the minimum distribution for the year is the account balance as of the end of 2008, divided by 21.

3. **Five-Year Rule:** If the surviving spouse elects to use the five-year method, all of the deceased IRA holder's IRA assets must be distributed within five years of the IRA holder's death. In actuality, the surviving spouse has a little more than five years to withdraw the IRA assets.

This is because the official distribution deadline is December 31 of the year continuing the fifth anniversary of the IRA holder's death. For example if the IRA holder dies on April 12, 2009, the deceased IRA holder's IRA assets would not need to be completely distributed until December 31, 2014—five years and almost nine months.

A. How much must be distributed over the five-year period?
    The five-year rule option only requires that all assets be distributed from the IRA account by December 31 of the year of the fifth anniversary of the IRA holder's death, but is places no limitations on the amount of each annual payment. What this means is that the IRA beneficiary can receive the entire amount as a lump sum immediately after the IRA holder's death, in equal monthly installments or even nothing at all until December 31 of the fifth and final year.

When Is Using the Five-Year Rule Mandatory for an IRA Beneficiary?

The five-year rule option is mandatory for an IRA beneficiary when both of the following occur:

1. The IRA holders dies before the age of 70½
2. The deceased IRA holder's IRA did not designate a beneficiary as of September 30 of the year of his or her death.

What Distribution Is Required When the Surviving Spouse Beneficiary Dies?

If a surviving spouse beneficiary inherits an IRA and begins taking required distributions on December 31 of the year after the deceased IRA holder's death but dies before all assets of the retirement account are distributed, the surviving spouse's beneficiary must take distributions in the following form:

• In the year of the surviving spouse's death, the spouse's beneficiary will divide the account balance as of December 31 of the year before the surviving spouse's death by the Applicable

Distribution Period (ADP) for the surviving spouse in the year of the spouse's death.

- For the second year and beyond, the surviving spouse's beneficiary will reduce the ADP determined in the above paragraph by one and divide it into the account balance as of the previous December 31. This computation continues using this method until the entire IRA account has a zero balance.

Distribution Option if the IRA Beneficiary Is a Nonspouse and the IRA Owner was under the Age of 70½ When He or She Died

If an IRA holders dies and designates a nonspouse a beneficiary as the primary beneficiary of his or her IRA, the nonspouse beneficiary will typically have only one option for taking IRA distributions—the life expectancy rules.

The Life Expectancy Rules

The IRS allows a nonspouse beneficiary to use the life expectancy rules to calculate the IRA required distributions after the deceased IRA holder's death. The IRA distributions must begin to be taken no later than December 31 of the year after the death of the deceased IRA holder's death. There are no additional opportunities for delaying IRA distributions for nonspouse beneficiaries.

If distributions are made under the life expectancy rule to a designated nonspouse beneficiary, the ADP for the calendar year immediately after the year of the IRA owner's death is the beneficiary's remaining life expectancy as of his or her birthday during that year, and the applicable period is reduced by one for each subsequent distribution calendar year. Unlike in the case of a spouse beneficiary, which is required to use the life expectancy of the deceased IRA owner for purposes of calculating the annual required distribution amount, a nonspouse beneficiary is required to use his or her life expectancy when calculating the annual required distribution amounts. For example, if Mary is designated as sole beneficiary of an IRA of her mother, who dies during 2007, her first distribution calendar year is 2008. If she becomes sixty years old during that year, the applicable distribution period would be based on the life expectancy of a 60-year-old.

Five-Year Rule

The five-year rule applies to a nonspouse beneficiary if allowed by the IRA's terms, or at the election of the deceased IRA owner or beneficiary.

Can a Nonspouse IRA Beneficiary Do a Roth IRA Conversion?

No. If a nonspouse IRA beneficiary inherits an IRA, the nonspouse IRA beneficiary does not have the option to convert the traditional inherited IRA to a Roth IRA.

Distribution Option if the IRA Beneficiary Is a Nonindividual (i.e., a Qualified Trust) and the IRA Owner Was under the Age of 70½ When He or She Died

In general, if a nonindividual, such as a trust, is designated as the beneficiary of an IRA and the IRA owner was under the age of 70½ when he or she died, the "qualified" trust would have the option to distribute the funds over a five-year period or based on the life expectancy of the oldest beneficiary of the "qualified" trust.

What Is the Advantage of Designating a Trust as IRA Beneficiary?

There are a number of advantages to naming a trust as beneficiary of an IRA. The most common purpose is for estate tax purposes. The use of a trust for estate-planning purposes is a common method used to minimize estate taxes and maximize the amount that can be transferred to family members tax-free.

The trust and estate tax rules are quite complex and beyond the scope of this book, but below is a brief overview of how the estate tax rules work.

Maximizing Your Estate Tax "Exclusion Amount"

Upon death, federal law allows each individual to transfer a certain amount, known as the "exclusion amount" of his or her assets tax-free. The "exclusion amount" for 2015 is $5.43 million or $10.86 million per couple. What this means is that an individual can transfer $5.43 million to his or her heirs over a lifetime without the transfer being subject to estate tax. In addition, an individual may transfer an unlimited amount upon his or death to a surviving spouse tax-free. Without proper estate planning, an individual may squander some or all of the "exclusion amount."

For example, a husband and wife have a combined net worth of less than $11 million. If the husband dies in 2015 and leaves all his assets to his wife, never using his $5 million exclusion amount, the wife would receive all the funds tax-free since all funds transferred to a surviving spouse are tax-free; however, when the surviving spouse dies, she would only be able to use her exclusion amount to pass her assets to her children, which would likely be insufficient to protect all assets from estate tax. In other words, if the husband had given his $5 million to the children when he died instead of to his spouse, his entire estate could have been transferred tax-free, and the surviving spouse could have used his or her exclusion amount to shelter the assets from tax that would pass to the children upon her subsequent death. Now, some might say, "Wait a minute. Do I really want to leave so much money to my children without any restrictions?" This is where the idea of using a trust has so much value. By designating a trust as the IRA beneficiary, when the husband dies, he can direct his $5 million exclusion amount to the trust, which can designate his wife as the trust beneficiary and then the children upon her death. Because the assets of the trust do not belong to the wife technically, upon her death the trust's assets can be passed to the children tax-free, allowing the wife to give additional amounts. Thus, by using the trust, the husband was able to use his exclusion to pass his assets to his spouse and upon her death to his children tax-free as well as freeing up his wife's exclusion to transfer additional funds to her children in satisfaction of her "exclusion amount."

Maintaining Control after Death

In certain situations, the IRA holder may wish to maintain some control and impose some oversight about how distributable IRA funds may be spent by a beneficiary of a "qualified trust." For example, if the IRA holder has a special needs child who relies on government benefits, (ii) the beneficiary is a minor, or (iii) the beneficiary has financial difficulties or has substance abuse problems. Using a trust can provide the IRA holder with the assurance that an appointed trustee will have control in terms of the amount of trust funds that are being distributed.

What Happens to the RMDs if an IRA Owner Does Not Have a Designated Beneficiary?

If an IRA owner does not have a designated beneficiary for his or her IRA, then the distribution options are limited. In essence, if the beneficiary of the deceased IRA owner's IRA is not designated, and if the IRA owner dies before his or her required beginning distribution date, the five-year distribution rule would apply and the entire IRA account must be distributed by December 31 of the year containing the fifth anniversary of the IRA owner's death.

If there is no designated IRA beneficiary, the life expectancy rule is not an option and the IRA beneficiary as per the deceased IRA holder's will or pursuant to probate must use the five-year rule.

What Happens to the RMD if an IRA Owner Dies and Has Multiple IRAs with Different Beneficiaries?

If an IRA owner dies and has multiple IRAs with different beneficiaries, then each IRA is treated separately for purposes of the required distribution rules. In other words, the determination of which distribution rules would apply would be applied separately for each IRA.

What Happens if an IRA Owner Dies and Has Multiple Beneficiaries for One IRA?

There are specific distribution rules that would apply in determining the required IRA distributions in the case of an IRA owner who dies with an IRA, which has multiple beneficiaries.

The date for determining the beneficiaries of an IRA is September 30 of the year following the IRA holder's death. If, on that date, all the beneficiaries of the deceased IRA owner's IRA are designated beneficiaries, then the beneficiaries have until December 31 to divide the account so that each beneficiary gets his or her separate share. If the IRA is split in a timely manner, then the required distribution rules would apply separately to each share of the split IRA.

In a case in which you have multiple beneficiaries for a deceased IRA owner's IRA, all beneficiaries are treated as nonspouse beneficiaries even if one of them is your spouse. As a result, the most limiting rules—those that will generally produce the most accelerated distribution payment schedule—will apply to all beneficiaries. For example, if a deceased IRA owner names her spouse and children, the beneficiaries must choose from the options available to the surviving spouse's children because children have more restricted distribution options than spouses.

The Life Expectancy Rules

The life expectancy distribution rule generally applies when there are multiple IRA beneficiaries on a single IRA. However, the least favorable distribution period is the one the IRA beneficiaries are required to use. The IRA must be distributed over the single life expectancy of the oldest beneficiary. This will ultimately create the largest possible annual distribution and as a result will reduce the size of the IRA the quickest (exactly what the government wants). The oldest beneficiary's life expectancy is determined based on his or her age in the first distribution year. Once the distribution amount is determined, it is allocated among the IRA beneficiaries pro rata based on their IRA interests.

For example, Joe who is forty-five years old dies in 2014 and names his mother and his two children as equal beneficiaries of his IRA. The beneficiaries will use the life expectancy method for determining the distribution amounts. Since Joe's mother is the oldest beneficiary, Joe's IRA must be distributed over her life expectancy.

Five-Year Rule

If, by the IRA's terms, or at the election of the deceased IRA owner or beneficiary, the five-year distribution option were selected, the five-year distribution option would apply to all beneficiaries. Even if the life expectancy option would be available to the spouse, the spouse would nevertheless be prohibited from using the life expectancy option if the spouse is one of the multiple beneficiaries since the five-year option would be the least favorable distribution period.

How Is the IRA Transferred to the Beneficiaries?

When transferring the deceased IRA owner's account to the beneficiaries, the IRA assets must be transferred directly from the current custodian of the IRA to the beneficiary's new IRA custodian. The beneficiary must not have control of any of the IRA funds at any time.

In the case of a nonspouse beneficiary, the account must remain in the name of the deceased IRA holder. Thus, in the case of a nonspouse beneficiary, the IRA must remain in the name of the deceased IRA owner. However, if the spouse is one of the beneficiaries, the spouse would be able to roll his or her share into an existing or new IRA in the spouse's name.

Whose Name Should Go on the Account?

In the case of a nonspouse beneficiary, the IRS requires that the new account be in the name of the deceased IRA holder's name. (If a spouse is named as the beneficiary, then the spouse may roll over the deceased spouse's IRA into an IRA in the name of the spouse.) Typically, many custodians will modify the name of the account by including the name of the deceased IRA owner and the beneficiary. For example, Dave Smith died, leaving his IRA to his two children, John and Steve. The children elect to split the IRA into two separate IRAs so that each can manage his own account. The IRA custodian set up the two new IRA accounts in Dave's name and transferred half of Dave's original IRA into each one. The title on John's account would be something like: Dave Smith, Deceased, for the benefit of (or FBO) John

Smith. The other account is titled Dave Smith, Deceased, for the benefit of (or FBO) Steve Smith.

How Is This Reported to the IRS?

IRA custodians are required to comply with a number of reporting requirements after an IRA holder dies. Generally the IRA custodian must file Form 5498 for each beneficiary. The IRS would use this information to determine the source of the IRA funds and determine the liability for required distributions, if any. The form must be filed by the IRA custodian each year until the account has a zero balance.

Distribution Option if the IRA Beneficiary Is a Spouse and the IRA Owner Was over the Age of 70½ When He or She Died

If an IRA owner dies after he or she reaches the age of 70½ and designates a spouse as the primary and sole beneficiary, the spouse IRA beneficiary has the following options:

Life Expectancy Rule

Minimum distributions to an elected surviving spouse are determined under the rules for the deceased IRA owner, not the rules for beneficiaries, except that the election may not cause there to be a minimum distribution for the year of the owner's death if the owner died before his or her required beginning date. The minimum required distributions for the year of the deceased spouse's death will be calculated in the same way as what would have applied had the deceased spouse been alive. The surviving spouse will use the Uniform Lifetime Table issued by the IRS each year and find the ADP for the deceased spouse based on his or her age in the year of his or her death. Then the surviving spouse would divide the deceased spouse's IRA balance as of December 31 of the previous year by the ADP.

Note: If the surviving spouse is more than ten years younger than the deceased spouse and if the deceased spouse was using the Joint and Last

Survivor Table for purposes of determining the annual required IRA distributions, the surviving spouse would use the same table to find the ADP in the year of the deceased spouse's death.

I Thought a Surviving Spouse Can Treat the Deceased Spouse's IRA as His or Her Own?

Correct. A surviving spouse beneficiary has the option of treating a deceased spouse's IRA as his or her own. However, if the deceased spouse died after the age of 70½, the surviving spouse must take the required distribution for the year of the surviving spouse's death before the surviving spouse can make the account his or her own. It is important to remember that once the deceased spouse's IRA has been transferred into the surviving spouse's name, all the required distribution rules apply as though the surviving spouse were the original owner.

What Happens for Required Distributions in Year Two if the Surviving Spouse Is Younger than the Deceased Spouse?

If the surviving spouse is younger than the deceased spouse, beginning in the second year, he or she is required to take minimum required distributions (assuming the spouse does not roll over the IRA into his or her name); the surviving spouse will use his or her own age to determine the ADP each year.

What Happens for Required Distributions in Year Two if the Surviving Spouse Is Older than the Deceased Spouse?

If the surviving spouse is older than the deceased spouse, the surviving spouse will calculate the required distribution amount using the greater of:

- The deceased spouse's life expectancy at the time of his or her death, reduced by one each subsequent year, or
- The surviving spouse's life expectancy, redetermined each year using his or her age, looking up the ADP in the Single Life Table

Since the surviving spouse is permitted to elect to use the largest ADP (the most favorable to the surviving spouse), typically the surviving spouse will start out using the deceased spouse's life expectancy and then switch to his or her own once the ADP surpasses the deceased spouse's life expectancy.

Rollover

A surviving spouse has the option of rolling over a deceased spouse's IRA into his or her own IRA or can leave the IRA in the name of the deceased spouse. In general, a surviving spouse has several ways of making a deceased spouse's IRA his or her own:

- Rolling over the IRA into a new or existing IRA in the name of the surviving spouse
- Failing to take post-death required minimum distributions in a timely manner
- Contributing an additional amount to the deceased spouse's IRA

What Do Most Surviving Spouses Do?

Most surviving spouses elect to roll over a deceased spouse's IRA into his or her own. At the time the rollover is complete, the deceased spouse's IRA will belong to the surviving spouse in every respect. This means that the surviving spouse can name a new IRA beneficiary and that the surviving spouse's age—not the deceased IRA owner's—will determine whether required minimum distributions must be taken.

Example 1:

Jane, a surviving spouse, was sixty-five years old when her husband Steve, who was 74, died. Jane elects to roll Steve's IRA into her own. Since Jane was under 70½ at the time of Steve's death, Steve's required minimum distributions may be stopped until Jane reaches the age of 70½ Then Jane must begin taking required distributions using the Uniform Lifetime Table to determine her ADP.

Example 2:
Tina, a surviving spouse, was 75 when her husband Dave, who was 77, died. After Dave's death, Tina rolled Dave's IRA over into her own. Since Tina was over the age of 70½ when Dave died, Tina is required to take a distribution in the year of Dave's death and then she must take a distribution on her own behalf since Dave's IRA is now in her name.

Remember, if the deceased spouse was over the age of 70½ at the date of his or death, the surviving spouse is required to take the required minimum distribution for the deceased spouse for the year of the deceased spouse's death before the surviving spouse can complete the IRA rollover to his or her name.

Is There a Deadline for Doing the Rollover?
The IRC imposes no deadline for a surviving spouse to convert a deceased spouse's IRA into his or her own account. The election can generally be made anytime, months or years after the deceased spouse's death, as long as the surviving spouse continues to take the required minimum distributions.

If the surviving spouse is over the age of 59½, then waiting to do the rollover has no benefit since the spouse can technically take distributions from his or her own IRA without penalty. However, if the surviving spouse is under the age of 59½, by rolling over the IRA of a deceased spouse who was over the age 70½ at the time of his or her death, into his or her own IRA may not be advantageous if the surviving spouse wishes to access those funds without penalty. Remember, if the surviving spouse is under the age of 59½, once the IRA is rolled over from the deceased spouse's to the surviving spouse's account, it becomes the spouse's IRA in every respect.

Can a Surviving Spouse Convert a Deceased Spouse's IRA into a Roth IRA?
If the deceased spouse had a traditional IRA, in order to convert the traditional IRA to a Roth IRA, the surviving spouse would first have to roll over the deceased spouse's IRA to a traditional IRA in the surviving spouse's

name. Once the assets are in the surviving spouse's IRA, the surviving spouse may convert the account to a Roth IRA.

Distribution Option if the IRA Beneficiary Is a Nonspouse and the IRA Owner Was over the Age of 70½ When He or She Died

The IRS allows a nonspouse beneficiary to use the life expectancy rules to calculate the IRA required distributions after the deceased IRA holder's death. The IRA distributions must begin to be taken no later than December 31 of the year after the death of the deceased IRA holder's death. There are no additional opportunities for delaying IRA distributions for nonspouse beneficiaries.

In the Year of Death

In the year of the death of the deceased IRA owner, if the deceased IRA owner had not yet taken the required minimum distributions for the year, the nonspouse IRA beneficiary is required to take the minimum distribution before the end of the year. The IRA beneficiary will use the Uniform Lifetime Table based on the age of the deceased IRA owner. If the deceased IRA owner had already taken the required minimum distribution for that year, then the nonspouse beneficiary is not required to take another distribution that year.

Second Year and After

Starting in the year after the IRA owner's death, minimum required distributions are determined based on whether the nonspouse beneficiary is older or younger than the deceased IRA owner.

Younger Nonspouse Beneficiary

In the case in which the nonspouse beneficiary is younger than the deceased IRA owner, the nonspouse beneficiary would calculate the required distributions for the second year and beyond using the beneficiary's single life expectancy as provided by the IRS (see Exhibit C) in the year after the deceased IRA owner's death. In subsequent years, the nonspouse beneficiary will reduce the ADP by one each year.

Older Nonspouse Beneficiary

In the case in which the nonspouse beneficiary is older than the deceased IRA owner, the nonspouse beneficiary would calculate the required distributions using the deceased IRA owner's single life expectancy in the year of the deceased IRA owner's death, reduced by one. In subsequent years, the nonspouse beneficiary will reduce the ADP by one each year.

For example, Jim turned 70½ in 2004 and began taking required distributions from his IRA at that time. Jim's designated beneficiary was his sister Tracy, who turned 72 in 2004. Jim had been using the Uniform Lifetime Table, as provided by the IRS, for purposes of determining the required minimum distributions. Jim died in 2007 after taking his required minimum distributions for the year. In 2008, the year after his death, Tracy is required to take a distribution based on Jim's single life expectancy. Tracy would have to determine her life expectancy in 2007, the year of Jim's death, and reduce it by one.

Can a Nonspouse Beneficiary Do a Rollover?

No. A nonspouse beneficiary is not permitted to roll over a deceased IRA owner's IRA into the nonspouse beneficiary's own IRA. Any attempted rollover would be treated as a taxable distribution.

Can a Nonspouse Beneficiary Convert the Deceased IRA Owner's Traditional IRA to a Roth IRA?

No. If a nonspouse beneficiary inherits an IRA, the nonspouse beneficiary is not permitted to convert the traditional inherited IRA into a Roth IRA.

What Happens if the Deceased IRA Owner Designates Multiple Nonspouse Beneficiaries?

If the deceased IRA owner designates more than one nonspouse beneficiary for a single IRA, then the required minimum distributions will be calculated as though the nonspouse beneficiary with the shortest life expectancy (oldest beneficiary) was the sole beneficiary. The one exception to this rule is that if the nonspouse beneficiary with the shortest life expectancy (the oldest beneficiary) is older than the deceased IRA owner at the date of his or her death, the designated nonspouse beneficiaries will be required to use the deceased IRA owner's single life expectancy to calculate the required minimum distributions after his or her death.

Distribution Option if the IRA Beneficiary Is a Nonindividual (i.e., a Qualified Trust) and the IRA Owner Was under the Age of 70½ When He or She Died

In general, if you name a trust as a beneficiary of your IRA, and if the trust is treated as a "qualified trust" by meeting certain requirements, you would look through the trust to determine the beneficiary. The trust beneficiary would be treated as a designated beneficiary for the purposes of computing required minimum distributions.

What Happens if the Trust Has Multiple Beneficiaries?

If a trust has multiple beneficiaries, the multiple beneficiaries would be required to take minimum required distributions based on a single life expectancy using the life expectancy of the oldest beneficiary.

Selecting a trust as beneficiary of an IRA may provide certain estate-planning benefits; however, it may also cause certain beneficiaries of the trust to take greater required minimum distributions than they would have been required to take if a trust was not used and, instead, the IRA holder designated such person(s) as beneficiaries of the IRA.

The following is a chart that summarizes the most common Required Minimum Distributions

Options if the IRA Owner dies BEFORE the age of 70 ½

Spouse is the Sole Designated Beneficiary	• Five-year rule
	• Life expectancy payments
	
	  ° Payments must begin by the later of December 31 of the year following the year of the account holder's death or December 31 of the year the account holder would have attained 70 ½.
	
	  ° The life expectancy for the first distribution year and for subsequent years' payment is determined using the spouse beneficiary's
	
	  NOTE: Beginning in the year following the spouse beneficiary's death, payments are calculated using the spouse beneficiary's age on December 31 of the year of the spouse's death, nonrecalcuated.
	
	• Spouse beneficiary may roll over decedent's plan account to own IRA, to an eligible plan, or to an inherited IRA

Nonspouse Beneficiary	• Five-year rule
	• Life expectancy payments
	
	  ° Payments must begin by the later of December 31 of the year following the year of the account holder's death.
	
	  ° The life expectancy used in the first distribution year is the single life expectancy of the oldest designated beneficiary (unless separate accounting applies) in the year following the year of IRA holder's death.
	
	  ° Subsequent years' payments are determined using nonrecalculation.
	
	• Nonspouse beneficiary may directly roll over plan account to an inherited IRA.

Options if the IRA Owner Dies After the Age of 70½

The following is a chart that summarizes the Required Minimum Distributions

Spouse is the Sole Designated Beneficiary	• Life expectancy payments
	◦ Payments must begin by December 31 of the year following the year of the account holder's death.
	◦ The life expectancy used for the first distribution year is the longer of the single life expectancy of the spouse beneficiary in the year following the accounts holder's death or the account holder's single life expectancy in the year of death, reduced by one.
	◦ Subsequent years' payments are determined using recalculation if using the spouse beneficiary's life expectancy (if surviving spouse is younger than deceased spouse) and nonrecalculation if using the accounts holder's life expectancy (if surviving spouse is older than deceased spouse)
	NOTE: If the spouse's life expectancy is used, beginning in the year following the spouse beneficiary's death, payments are determined using the spouse beneficiary's age on December 31 of the year of death, nonrecalculated.
	• Spouse beneficiary may roll over decedent's plan account to own IRA, to eligible plan, or to an inherited IRA and may be subject to RMD rules depending on age of surviving spouse
Nonspouse Beneficiary	• Life expectancy payments
	◦ Payments must begin by December 31 of the year following the year of the account holder's death.
	◦ The life expectancy used for the first distribution year is the longer of the single life expectancy of the oldest designated beneficiary (unless separate accounting applies) in the year following the accounts holder's death or the account holder's single life expectancy in the year of death, reduced by one.
	◦ Subsequent years' payments are determined using nonrecalculation.
	• Nonspouse beneficiary may directly roll over decedent's plan account to an inherited IRA and would be subject to the RMD rules

The Roth IRA

In 1997, Congress, under the Taxpayer Relief Act, introduced the Roth IRA to be like a traditional IRA but with a few attractive modifications. The big advantage of a Roth IRA is that if you qualify to make contributions, all distributions from the Roth IRA are tax-free—even the investment returns—as long as the distributions meet certain requirements. In addition, unlike traditional IRAs, you may contribute to a Roth IRA for as long as you continue to have earned income (in the case of a traditional IRA, you can't make contributions after you reach age 70½). The rules for the Roth IRA are found in the IRC under Section 408A.

What Is a Roth IRA?

A Roth IRA is an IRA that the owner designates as a Roth IRA. A Roth IRA is generally subject to the rules for traditional IRAs. For example, traditional and Roth IRAs and their owners are identically affected by the rules treating an IRA as distributing its assets if the IRA engages in a prohibited transaction or the owner borrows against it. The reporting requirements for IRAs also apply to Roth IRAs. However, several rules, described below, apply uniquely to Roth IRAs.

The most attractive feature of the Roth IRA is that even though contributions are not deductible, all distributions, including the earnings and appreciation on all Roth contributions, are tax-free if certain conditions are met.

Roth IRA Characteristics

The following is an overview of the tax characteristics of the Roth IRA:

- **Contributions Are Not Tax-Deductible:**
  Unlike with a traditional IRA, an individual is not permitted to take an income tax deduction for their Roth IRA contributions. All Roth IRA contributions are made with after-tax dollars. This means that the amount of the contribution is treated as basis in the IRA.

- **Earnings Are Tax-Deferred:**
  Earnings and gains from a Roth IRA are tax-deferred and may be tax-exempt if certain conditions are met (a "qualified distribution"). This means that all income and gains generated by a Roth IRA investment are not subject to income tax.

- **Tax-Free Earnings:**
  The attraction of the Roth IRA is based on the fact that qualified distributions of Roth earnings are tax-free. As long as certain conditions are met and the distribution is a

qualified distribution, the Roth IRA owner will never pay tax on any Roth distributions received.

Roth IRA Contributions

An individual may make several types of contributions, including regular, spousal, conversion, and catchup contributions.

Regular Contributions

In the case of a Roth IRA, there are no maximum age restrictions for making Roth IRA contributions; however, there are income restrictions that must be met.

No Maximum or Minimum Age Restriction

Unlike with traditional IRAs, there is no maximum age restriction for making Roth IRA contributions. As long as the individual satisfies the required income guidelines, he or she may make Roth IRA contributions even after the age of 70½. In addition, federal law does not impose minimum age restrictions for making Roth IRA contributions. However, typically, most financial institutions will verify the appropriate state laws relating to minors signing contracts.

What Is the Eligible Compensation Requirement?

Earned Income: As with a traditional IRA, an individual must generally have earned income from personal services rendered in order to be eligible to make Roth IRA contributions.

What Is Compensation?

Compensation includes wages, salaries, tips, professional fees, bonuses, and other amounts received for providing personal services. It also includes commissions, self-employment income, nontaxable combat pay, military differential pay, and taxable alimony and separate maintenance payments.

What Are the Income Limits for Making Roth IRA Contributions?

Unlike in traditional IRAs, to be eligible to contribute to a Roth IRA, an individual or married couple must have a Modified Adjusted Gross Income (MAGI) below a certain income limit as prescribed by the IRS. If the individual or married couple has MAGI equal to or greater than the applicable income threshold limit, the individual is not eligible to make Roth IRA contributions. If an individual has income less than the applicable income threshold but more than the specified minimum threshold, the amount of Roth IRA contributions the individual is eligible to make is phased out.

For the tax year 2015, the applicable Roth IRA contribution income threshold levels are as follows:

For a *single filer*, the Roth IRA contribution MAGI limit is $116,000 to $131,000.

For a *married couple filing a joint Federal Income Tax Return*, the Roth IRA contribution MAGI limit is $183,000 to $193,000.

For married individuals living together but filing separate Federal Income Tax Returns, the contribution phase-out range is $0 to $10,000.

How Do You Calculate the MAGI?

An individual is not permitted to make a Roth IRA contribution if the individual's MAGI exceeds a certain income threshold as provided by the IRS each year. When calculating an individual's MAGI, the following adjustments must be made to the individual's Adjusted Gross Income (AGI) as shown on the Federal Income Tax Return. The AGI is a number used to determine your federal income tax. AGI is your gross income minus deductions. Deductions include retirement account contributions, health insurance contributions (for self-employed persons), trade or business expenses, depreciation on rental property, losses from sales of property, alimony payments, medical savings account contributions, moving expenses, and charitable cash contributions. The AGI does not include standard or itemized deductions or personal exemptions.

- Subtract any converted Roth IRA amount
- Subtract any Roth IRA rollovers from a qualified plan
- Subtract any minimum required distributions from an IRA
- Add traditional IRA deductions
- Add student loan interest deductions
- Add tuition and fees deduction
- Add domestic production activities deduction
- Add foreign earned income exclusion
- Add foreign housing exclusion or deduction
- Add exclusion of qualified bond interest shown on Form 8815
- Add exclusion of employer-provided adoption benefits shown on Form 8839

What Happens if an Individual's MAGI Is Above the Roth IRA Income Threshold?

If an individual's MAGI is above the Roth IRA contribution MAGI limit, the individual's Roth IRA contribution limit is gradually reduced.

Roth IRA Contributions

A regular contribution to a Roth IRA is generally limited to the lesser of the annual contribution limit or 100 percent of the individual's compensation. The Roth IRA contribution limit is the same as the traditional IRA limit. For the year 2015, the annual Roth IRA contribution limit for an individual under the age of 50 is $5,500, and $6,500 for an individual over the age of 50. An individual making Roth IRA contributions must reduce those contributions by the amount of any contributions made to a traditional IRA. In other words, the annual IRA contribution limit for 2015 ($5,500 or $6,500) applies to all IRAs and cannot be applied separately to one or more traditional IRAs or Roth IRAs. For example, if Jim had a traditional and Roth IRA and was under the age of 50, Jim could *not* make a $5,500 contribution to both his traditional IRA and Roth IRA. Jim would be limited to making a $5,500 contribution to his traditional IRA, Roth IRA, or some sort of combination contribution made to both his traditional and Roth IRA as long as the combined contribution does not exceed $5,500 for 2015.

How Do I Calculate the Roth IRA Contribution Reduction?

If the amount you can contribute must be reduced, figure your reduced contribution limit as follows:

1. Start with your modified AGI.
2. Subtract from the amount in (1):
   a. $183,000 if filing a joint return or qualifying widow(er),
   b. $-0- if married filing a separate return, and you lived with your spouse at any time during the year, or
   c. $116,000 for all other individuals.
3. Divide the result in (2) by $15,000 ($10,000 if filing a joint return, qualifying widow(er), or married filing a separate return and you lived with your spouse at any time during the year).
4. Multiply the maximum contribution limit (before reduction by this adjustment and before reduction for any contributions to traditional IRAs) by the result in (3).
5. Subtract the result in (4) from the maximum contribution limit before this reduction. The result is your reduced contribution limit.

How Do the Catchup Contribution Rules Work for Roth IRAs?

Like with a traditional IRA, an individual who turns 50 before the end of the taxable year may be eligible to make Roth IRA catchup contributions. The maximum amount that an individual over the age of 50 may contribute annually as a catchup contribution is $1,000 for 2015. An individual must reduce a Roth IRA contribution by any catchup contribution made to a traditional IRA.

Can I Make Roth IRA Contributions if I Have No Eligible Compensation but My Spouse Does?

As with a traditional IRA contribution, an individual with no eligible compensation but who is married may generally make a Roth IRA contribution based on his or her spouse's compensation. This is often referred to as a "spousal contribution."

What Are the Rules for Making a Roth IRA Spousal Contribution?

A. **No Age Requirement:** There is no maximum age restriction for making a spousal Roth IRA contribution. In other words, spousal Roth IRA contributions may be made even after the spouse with no compensation reaches the age of 70½.

B. **Eligible Compensation:** Like with a regular IRA contribution, a spouse must have earned income from personal services.

C. **Joint Tax Return:** In order to be eligible for a spousal contribution, the married couple must file a joint federal income tax return.

D. **Spousal Contribution Limit:** The maximum combined spousal contribution limit is the lesser of the annual contribution limit (including catchup contributions if applicable) per married couple, or 100 percent of the married couple's combined compensation (reduced by any traditional IRA contributions). For example, if both spouses are under the age of 50, the maximum combined spousal contribution limit is $5,500 per spouse or a combined $11,000 annual contribution limit for 2015. As I discussed earlier, the maximum annual contribution amount is decreased for married couples with MAGI in the phase-out range of $183,000 to $193,000 for the year 2015.

When Are Roth IRA Contributions Due?

An individual must make regular or spousal Roth IRA contributions to either a traditional or Roth IRA by the individual's due date of his or her federal income tax return (not including extensions) for the tax year. April 15 is the due date for IRA contributions for most individuals who file a federal income tax return.

Can I Make IRA Contributions After January 1 for the Previous Year?

As long as the IRA contributions for the previous year are made between January 1 and April 15.

Note: If April 15 falls on a Saturday, Sunday, or legal holiday, the individual will generally have until the next business day to make the IRA contribution. If April 15 falls on a weekend or legal holiday, the IRS will typically announce the Federal Income Tax Return and IRA contribution due date at the beginning of the year. These types of contributions are generally referred to as carryback contributions. The IRA owner must generally make a written irrevocable election designating an IRA contribution as a carryback IRA contribution.

What if I Mail the Contribution Check on April 15? When Is It Treated as Received by the Custodian?

If an IRA contribution is mailed to the financial institution (IRA custodian), it is treated as timely contributed if it is postmarked by the due date for making IRA contributions (i.e., April 15).

What if I Contribute Too Much?

A 6 percent excise tax applies to any excess contribution to a Roth IRA.

What Happens if I Correct this Mistake Prior to Filing My Tax Return?

Any excess Roth IRA contribution that is withdrawn on or before the due date (including extensions) for filing your tax return for the year is treated as an amount not contributed. This rule only applies if any earnings (i.e., income or gains) from the contributions are also withdrawn.

Can I Apply the Excess Contributions to the Following Year?

If an individual makes Roth IRA contributions in excess of the annual limit (for 2015, $5,500 if the individual is under the age of 50 and $6,500 if the individual is over the age of 50), he or she can apply the excess Roth IRA contribution made to a subsequent year as long as the contribution made in the subsequent year is less than the annual contribution limit for that year.

Roth IRA Distributions

The difference between a traditional IRA and a Roth IRA is most evident in the treatment of distributions.

As a brief reminder, in the case of a traditional IRA, an IRA distribution is taxed as ordinary income unless it is rolled over into another retirement plan. If the individual is under the age of 59½ when the distribution is made, a 10 percent excise tax would apply to the distribution in addition to the ordinary income tax due on the value of the distribution. If the individual is over the age of 70½ at the time the distribution is taken, then no excise tax applies; however, the individual is required to pay ordinary income tax on the amount of the traditional IRA distribution. Remember also that an individual over the age of 70½ is required to take minimum annual distributions based on a percentage of the individual's total IRA value at the end of the year. Each year the IRS releases a table that determines the amount of the required minimum distribution.

Determining the Tax Status of Roth IRA Distributions: The Ordering Rules

In order to determine which contributions, rollovers, or earnings are distributed from a Roth IRA, the IRS has established a set of ordering rules. Under the ordering rules, the first Roth IRA assets distributed are considered to be a return of the amounts contributed to the Roth IRA. Once the total Roth IRA contributions that have been made have been completely distributed, the ordering rules require that the next assets to be distributed are any rollover or conversion amounts (excluding designed Roth IRA account rollovers), if any. Once all those types of assets have been distributed, any further Roth IRA distributions would come from any earnings accumulated by the Roth IRA investments.

Aren't All Roth IRA Distributions Tax-Free? Should I Care About the Ordering Rules?

Yes and no. If an individual is over the age of 59½ and the Roth IRA account has been established for at least five years, then any distributions from a Roth IRA would be tax-free (qualified distributions). However, in the case of a nonqualified distribution (discussed below in more detail), the ordering of the distributions is significant because of the different tax and penalty consequences that could apply based on the type of asset distributed (i.e., Roth IRA contribution, which is always nontaxable vs. Roth IRA earnings, which may be taxable).

What Is a Qualified Roth IRA Distribution?

A qualified distribution from a Roth IRA is not subject to tax or penalty when made. To have a qualified distribution, the Roth IRA owner must have satisfied a *five-year waiting period* (starting with the first taxable year in which the Roth IRA owner made a contribution to any Roth IRA) and must meet any one of the following requirements:

- Reached the age of 59½
- Qualify as disabled
- Qualify as a first-time homebuyer ($10,000 limitation)
- Death

How Is the Five-Year Waiting Period Calculated?

In order for a Roth IRA distribution to be a qualified distribution, one of the requirements is that the Roth IRA owner must have satisfied a five-year waiting period (starting with the first taxable year in which the Roth IRA owner made a contribution to any Roth IRA). For purposes of calculating the five-year rule, all Roth IRA accounts are treated as one account. Therefore, as long as an individual has made a contribution to a Roth IRA, the five-year waiting period would begin running at that point.

For example, Joe established a Roth IRA in 2007 at age 55 and made a contribution of $1,000. In 2013, at age 61, Joe decided to establish another Roth IRA. Because Joe established a Roth IRA account more than five years ago, Joe has already satisfied the five-year rule and would thus be able to take distributions of after-tax contributions and investment income and gains from either Roth IRA tax-free, even the recent Roth IRA that was opened less than five years ago.

Helpful Tip

Even if you do not currently have any interest in opening a Roth IRA, you may at some point, so if you are under 59½, you may want to establish a Roth IRA with just a minimal amount, even $1, just to start the five-year waiting period. This way, if you ever want to make Roth IRA contributions in the future, you would have already likely satisfied the five-year waiting period, and as long as you are over 59½, you would be able to take distributions of after-tax contributions and investment income and gains from your Roth IRA(s) tax-free. Note: There are separate five-year waiting periods in the case of Roth IRA conversions.

Distribution of After-Tax Contributions

In the case of a Roth IRA, the amount you contribute is never subject to tax when it comes out. Even if you take it a day after you contribute it and are under 59½, the amount you contributed to your Roth IRA is never subject to tax. The reason for this is simple—you already paid tax on that amount, so the IRS isn't going to tax it again. Remember, in the case of a traditional IRA, the amount you contribute is pretax—meaning you have not paid tax on that amount and, in fact, you have likely received a tax-deduction for the contribution amount, which is why the contribution amount will be subject to tax upon withdrawal.

Because all Roth contributions are never subject to tax upon withdrawal, any distribution taken from a Roth IRA is considered to be a return of your Roth IRA contributions until all Roth IRA contributions you have made over the years have been withdrawn. This rule applies to all Roth IRA contributions you made—even if you have more than one Roth IRA. This means that all Roth IRA contributions are withdrawn tax-free before Roth IRA earnings are recovered. Therefore, once you make a Roth IRA contribution, you will always be able to withdraw that money tax-free. For this reason, some people use the Roth IRA as an emergency fund. If they ever get into a financial jam and need money, they will always have the ability to withdraw the Roth IRA contributions tax-free and without penalty, which would not be the case if a traditional IRA contribution was made.

For example, Joe began making Roth IRA contributions of $5,000 each year beginning in 2006. By the beginning of 2011, Joe's Roth IRA had grown to $35,000. Of that amount, $25,000 was from Joe's annual contributions and $10,000 was from investment gains. In March 2011, Joe was in a difficult financial position and needed additional funds to help pay some personal bills. Joe decided to withdraw $25,000 from his Roth IRA. The $25,000 is not subject to tax because Joe's distribution is deemed to be a return of his contributions. However, if Joe decided to withdraw $30,000, the first $25,000 would be tax-free because it is a return of his contributions. The excess $5,000 would be subject to income tax and a 10 percent excise tax if Joe was under the age of 59½ and the Roth IRA had been open for less than five years.

What Happens if You Die Before the Five-Year Waiting Period Is Up?

If a Roth IRA owner dies before satisfying the five-year waiting period, the Roth IRA owner's beneficiary is required to wait until the Roth IRA owner would have satisfied it for the distribution to be qualified.

What Is a Nonqualified Distribution?

Any distribution from a Roth IRA that is not treated as a "qualified" distribution is by default treated as a "nonqualified" distribution. In other words, if the five-year waiting period has not been satisfied or if one of the qualifying events has *not* occurred:

- Reach the age 59½
- Qualify as disabled
- Qualify as a first-time home buyer (up to a lifetime $10,000 limitation)
- Death

How Are Nonqualified Distributions Treated?

A nonqualified distribution is treated much like a traditional IRA distribution. The Roth IRA contributions you made will always come out tax-free, but the earnings generated by your Roth IRA will be subject to income tax.

Roth IRA Distribution Ordering Rules

In order to determine which Roth IRA distributions are taxable, it is important to determine which part of the distribution is attributable to Roth IRA contributions and which part is attributable to Roth IRA earnings. It would be nice if you could pick and choose which amount can come out of your Roth IRA first, but unfortunately the IRS has established ordering rules for how to take Roth IRA distributions.

1. Roth IRA Contributions

As discussed earlier, the contributions you made to your Roth IRA are distributed first. The amount you contributed to your Roth IRA (contributory basis) is always withdrawn tax-free and penalty free, irrespective of whether the distribution is treated as a qualified or nonqualified distribution.

2. Conversion and Retirement Plan Rollover Assets

Once all Roth IRA contributions have been distributed, then any conversion and retirement plan rollover assets are distributed first by year with the taxable accounts that were subject to tax upon conversion (i.e., traditional IRA), and then the nontaxable accounts (i.e., nondeductible traditional IRA) for that year distributed second. For example, if a Roth IRA owner did a conversion and rollover in 2013 and 2014, her 2013 conversion rollover assets are distributed before her 2014 Roth IRA conversion/rollover assets. As long as the Roth rollover amount is treated as a qualified distribution, it will not be subject to tax upon withdrawal. In addition, a nonqualified distribution of nontaxable conversion or rollover assets (nondeductible traditional IRA) is not taxable, nor is it subject to a 10 percent early distribution penalty. However, a nonqualified distribution of taxable conversion of retirement rollover assets (i.e., traditional IRA) being distributed within five years of being converted to a Roth IRA is not subject to tax but would be subject to a 10 percent early distribution tax. The reason for this is that since you have already paid tax on the conversion, the IRS felt it would not be fair to double tax that amount but still wanted to impose a penalty for the early withdrawal.

3. Roth IRA Earnings

If a Roth IRA owner takes a nonqualified distribution, any portion of the distribution that represents earnings or appreciation of the Roth IRA contributions for the year is subject to ordinary income tax and a 10 percent early distribution penalty, unless she qualifies for a penalty exception (i.e., reached the age of 59½, death, disability, etc.). For example, Ben, who is 52 years old, began making Roth IRA contributions of $4,000 each year beginning in 2011. By the beginning of 2014, Ben's Roth IRA had grown to $26,000. Of that amount, $16,000 was from Ben's annual contributions and $10,000 was from earnings or investment gains. In February 2015, Ben was in a difficult financial position and needed additional funds to help pay some personal bills. Ben decided to withdraw his entire Roth IRA amount: $26,000. The $16,000 would not be subject to tax because Ben's distribution is deemed to be a return of his contributions. However, the $10,000 of earnings, or investment appreciation, would be subject to income tax and a 10 percent early distribution penalty since Ben was under the age of 59½ and the Roth IRA had been open for less than five years. In contrast, if at the time of the distribution, the Roth IRA had been established for longer than five years and Ben was over the age of 59, then the entire $25,000 distribution, even the investment earnings, could be withdrawn tax-free.

As you can see, the timing for taking a Roth IRA distribution can have significant tax implications. For example, if you take a Roth IRA distribution after you turn 59½ and the Roth IRA account has been established for longer than five years, then the entire distribution is tax-free. In contrast, if you took a Roth IRA distribution prior to turning 59½ or before the account had been open for more than five years, you would be subject to ordinary income tax and even an early distribution tax on any earnings or appreciation.

Helpful Tip

Remember, in order to satisfy the Roth IRA qualified distribution rules, the Roth IRA holder must be over the age of 59½ *and* the Roth IRA account must have been open for at least five years.

Alternatively, if you converted a traditional IRA to a Roth IRA and then took a distribution before the Roth IRA have been open for five years, a 10 percent early distribution penalty would be triggered. Hence, the origin and timing of a Roth asset has a dramatic impact on the potential tax treatment of a Roth IRA distribution. That being said, if you can hold off taking Roth IRA distributions for at least five years from the establishment of the Roth IRA and after you have reached the age of 59½, you will not have to pay tax on any Roth distribution, regardless of whether it is a contribution, conversion/rollover, or investment earnings.

The following is a summary of the Roth IRA ordering rules and the tax and penalty that may apply:

Order of Roth IRA Assets for Distribution	"Qualified" Distribution	"Nonqualified" Distribution
Amount contributed to Roth IRA	Not subject to tax or penalty	Not subject to tax or penalty
Amounts converted to a Roth IRA that were subject to tax	Not subject to tax or penalty	Not subject to tax but subject to a 10% early distribution penalty
Amounts converted to a Roth IRA that were not subject to tax	Not subject to tax or penalty	Not subject to tax or penalty
Roth IRA earnings and investments gains	Not subject to tax or penalty	Subject to tax and 10% early distribution penalty

No Required Minimum Distributions

Unlike with a traditional IRA, a Roth IRA owner is never required to take a Roth IRA distribution. In other words, the required minimum distribution rules do not apply to Roth IRA owners. This is one of the main differences between a traditional IRA and a Roth IRA. With a traditional IRA, the IRA owner is required to begin taking required minimum distributions when she reaches the age of 70½, whereas, in the case of a Roth IRA, the owner is never required to take a distribution—allowing the Roth IRA owner to accumulate retirement funds tax-free and then pass those funds on to another generation. The reason is likely due to the IRS's belief that since the Roth IRA was structured to provide for tax-free distributions there was no real need to require distributions since the account was growing tax-free anyway and there was no opportunity for the IRS to collect any tax revenue.

Does My Roth IRA Beneficiary Need to Take Distributions After I Die?

As with a traditional IRA, the answer depends on whether a spouse has been designated as a beneficiary of your Roth IRA. The options available to a designated beneficiary of a Roth IRA generally follow the options available to a beneficiary of a traditional IRA when the traditional IRA owner dies before the age of 70½. Unlike with a traditional IRA, however, a Roth IRA owner is not required to take Roth IRA distributions, but certain Roth IRA beneficiaries may be required to take distributions.

What Happens if the Roth IRA Beneficiary Is a Spouse?

In the case of a spouse who is designated as the beneficiary of his or her spouse's Roth IRA, the spouse beneficiary has several options when it comes to Roth IRA distributions. The options include the:

- Five-year rule
- Life expectancy payments
- Transfer to own spouse's Roth IRA
- Distribute and roll over

Under all these options, the spouse would be able to take Roth IRA distributions tax-free as long as the distribution would be treated as "qualified" under the Roth IRA rules. The spouse would not be required to take RMDs for the Roth IRA.

What Happens if the Roth IRA Beneficiary Is a Nonspouse?

A nonspouse beneficiary of the Roth IRA holder is subject to the RMD rules. Like with a traditional IRA, a nonspouse beneficiary of a Roth IRA may apply the five-year rule or life expectancy rule for determining when Roth IRA distributions must be taken. As long as the Roth distributions are "qualified," there will be no tax due on the distribution when taken by the nonspouse beneficiary.

How Are Roth IRA Distributions Reported to the IRS?

The IRS is able to monitor whether a Roth IRA distribution is subject to tax or penalty by requiring IRA Custodians (financial organizations) and Roth IRA owners to report when Roth IRA assets are withdrawn. The IRS achieves this by generally comparing Form 1099-R with what the Roth IRA owner reports on his or her federal income tax return.

Differences Between a Traditional IRA and a Roth IRA

As a reminder, the following chart outlines the different characteristics and tax distinctions between a traditional IRA and Roth IRA.

Traditional IRA	Roth IRA
Tax-deductible contributions	Contributions are not tax deductible. Contributions made to a Roth IRA are from after-tax dollars.
Distributions may be taken by age 59½ and are mandatory by 70½.	No mandatory distribution age. With a Roth IRA you are not required to take distributions ever.

Taxes are paid on amount of distributions (10 percent excise tax may apply if withdrawn prior to age 59½)	No taxes on distributions if rules and regulations are followed.
Available to everyone; no income restrictions with earned income	• For 2015, subject to adjustments each year, Single filers, Head of Household, or Married Filing Separately (and you did not live with your spouse during the year) with modified adjusted gross income up to $131,000 can make a full contribution. Contributions are phased out starting at $116,000 and you cannot make a contribution if your adjusted gross income is in excess of $131,000. • Joint filers with modified adjusted gross income up to $193,000 can make a full contribution. Once again, this contribution is phased out starting at $183,000 and you cannot make a contribution if your adjusted gross income is in excess of $193,000.
Funds can be used to purchase a variety of investments (stocks, real estate, precious metals, notes, etc.)	Funds can be used to purchase a variety of investments (stocks, real estate, precious metals, notes, etc.)
IRA investments grow tax-free until distribution (tax deferral)	All earnings and principal are 100 percent tax-free if rules and regulations are followed. No tax on distributions so maximum tax-deferral.

Income/gains from IRA investments are tax-free.	Income/gains from IRA investments are tax-free.
Purchasing a real estate property, then taking possession of the property after 59½ would be subject to tax.	Purchasing a domestic or foreign real estate property, then taking possession after 59½ would be tax-free.

Financial Institution Reporting Requirements for Roth IRA Distributions

The Roth IRA custodian (financial institution) is required to report Roth IRA distributions using Form 1099-R. The gross distribution amount is reported in Box 1. This should include any federal income tax withheld. Box 2A, taxable amount, is left blank. For Box 2B, "Taxable amount not determined" must be checked. Box 7 is where it would be indicated whether the distribution was qualified or nonqualified. Code Q would be included if the distribution is qualified and code J would be used if the distribution was nonqualified.

Roth IRA Owner's Reporting Requirements

The Roth IRA owner is required to compute the taxable amount of a Roth IRA distribution. Form 1099-R instructions direct the Roth IRA owner to the instructions to Form 1040 and to Form 8606 for additional information on calculating the taxable amount of a Roth distribution.

In any year that the Roth IRA owner takes a nonqualified distribution from a Roth IRA, the Roth IRA owner must file Form 8606 with the IRS to report the distribution.

In any year that the Roth IRA owner takes a qualified distribution, the Roth IRA owner is not required to file Form 8606 with the IRS. Instead, a Roth IRA owner who takes a qualified distribution will report the distribution directly on IRS Form 1040.

What Is a SEP IRA?

A Simplified Employee Pension (SEP) plan provides business owners with a simplified method to contribute toward their employees' retirement as well as their own retirement savings. A SEP is essentially an employer-sponsored profit-sharing plan. Contributions are made to an individual retirement account or annuity (IRA) set up for each plan participant (a SEP IRA). The main difference between a SEP IRA and a traditional IRA and Roth IRA is that a SEP IRA must be established by a business whereas a traditional IRA and Roth IRA are established by individuals. In other words, an individual who is not an owner of a business cannot establish a SEP IRA.

A SEP-IRA account is a traditional IRA and follows the same investment, distribution, and rollover rules as traditional IRAs.

Employees must be included in the SEP plan if they have:

- Reached age 21
- Received at least $550 in compensation from your business for the year
- Worked for your business in at least three of the last five years.

The three-of-five eligibility rule means you must include any employee in your plan who has worked for you in any three of the last five years (as long as the employee has satisfied the other plan eligibility requirements). This is the most restrictive eligibility requirement allowable. You can choose to use less restrictive participation rules in your plan, such as allowing employees to participate immediately after they start work or after a shorter period of employment. If you use the three-of-five rule, you must count any work, no matter how little, in each of the previous five years. Use plan years (often the calendar year), not years based on the date the employee started working for you.

Back in the coffee shop, John said, "Using the three-five rule is a nifty way for business owners to make SEP IRA contributions for themselves without having to make contributions for their employees. "However, once the three-five rule is met, the employer is required to provide all eligible employees with equal-percentage profit-sharing contributions."

"So the three-five rule could help the business owner out for a couple of years, but after that, the employer is required to provide all eligible employees with a SEP IRA contribution using the same percentage it used for the business owner?" asked Rich.

"That is correct," John said.

"How do the contributions work?" Rich asked.

"The contributions you make to each employee's SEP IRA each year cannot exceed the lesser of:

- 25 percent of compensation (20 percent in the case of a sole proprietorship of single member LLC), or
- $53,000 for 2015.

"There are *no* catchup contributions for a SEP IRA as there are for a 401(k) plan."

These limits apply to contributions you make for your employees to all defined contribution plans, which includes SEPs. Compensation up to $265,000 in 2015 of an employee's compensation may be considered. Also, contributions must be made in cash and you cannot contribute property.

What Is a SIMPLE IRA?

A SIMPLE (Savings Incentive Match Plan for Employees) IRA plan allows employees and employers to contribute to traditional IRAs set up for employees. Like a SEP IRA, a SIMPLE IRA can only be established by a business. Employees may choose to make salary reduction contributions and the employer is required to make either matching or nonelective contributions. Contributions are made to an individual retirement account or annuity (IRA) set up for each employee (a SIMPLE IRA).

A SIMPLE IRA plan account is an IRA and follows the same investment, distribution, and rollover rules as a traditional IRA.

Any employer (including self-employed individuals, tax-exempt organizations, and governmental entities) that had no more than a hundred employees with $5,000 or more in compensation during the preceding calendar year (the "hundred-employee limitation") can establish a SIMPLE IRA plan. You can set up a SIMPLE IRA plan effective on any date between January 1 and October 1 provided you (or any predecessor employer) didn't previously maintain a SIMPLE IRA plan. If you're a new employer that came into existence after October 1 of the year, you can establish the SIMPLE IRA plan as soon as administratively feasible after your business came into existence.

All employees who received at least $5,000 in compensation from you during any two preceding calendar years (whether or not consecutive) and who are reasonably expected to receive at least $5,000 in compensation during the calendar year are eligible to participate in the SIMPLE IRA plan for the calendar year.

Each eligible employee may make a salary reduction contribution and the employer must make either a matching contribution or nonelective contribution.

An employee may defer up to $12,500 in 2015 (subject to cost-of-living adjustments for later years).

Employees age 50 or over can make a catchup contribution of up to $3,000 in 2015 (subject to cost-of-living adjustments for later years).

With respect to employer contributions, the employer is generally required to either:

- Match each employee's salary reduction contribution on a dollar-for-dollar basis up to 3 percent of the employee's compensation (not limited by the annual compensation limit), or;
- Make nonelective contributions of 2 percent of the employee's compensation up to the annual limit of $265,000 for 2015, subject to cost-of-living adjustments in later years).

If you choose to make nonelective contributions, you must make them for all eligible employees whether or not they make salary reduction contributions.

With respect to the 3 percent match, you may elect to reduce the 3 percent matching contributions for a calendar year, but only if:

- The limit isn't reduced below 1 percent;
- The limit isn't reduced for more than two years out of the five-year period that ends with (and includes) the year for which the election is effective; and
- You notify employees of the reduced limit within a reasonable time before the sixty-day election period during which employees can enter into salary reduction agreements.

Generally, the same tax results apply to distributions from a SIMPLE IRA as to distributions from a regular IRA with one notable exception. During the two-year period, you may transfer an amount in a SIMPLE IRA to another SIMPLE IRA in a tax-free trustee-to-trustee transfer. If, during this two-year period, an amount is paid from a SIMPLE IRA directly to another IRA that is not a SIMPLE IRA, then the payment is treated as a distribution from the SIMPLE IRA and a contribution to the other IRA that doesn't qualify as a rollover contribution. After the expiration of the two-year period, you may transfer an amount in a SIMPLE IRA to any IRA or 401(k) plan without tax. In addition, a SIMPLE IRA has an exclusive plan rule, which does not allow a business to adopt both a SIMPLE IRA and a solo 401(k) Plan in the same taxable year. Whereas, a business can adopt both a SEP IRA and a 401(k) plan.

Tax Advantages of Using an IRA

There are always great tax advantages to saving for retirement, but this is especially easy to do with an IRA. Not only are you reducing your immediate tax burden by making tax-deferred contributions to the plan, but also all the income and gains generated by your IRA are generally directed back to your plan tax-deferred or tax-free in the case of an after-tax (Roth) account.

All of this means that you can build more wealth at a faster rate. The advantages of saving money for retirement are not as well understood as they should be. In particular, tax deferrals are wildly underappreciated.

The concept of tax deferral is premised on the notion that all income and gains generated by a pretax retirement account investment flow back into the retirement account tax-free. So, instead of paying tax on the returns of a self-directed IRA investment such as real estate, tax is paid only at a later date, leaving the investment to grow unhindered. For example, if an IRA invested $100,000 in 2013 and the account earned $15,000 in 2013, the investor would not owe tax on that $15,000 in 2013. Instead, the IRA holder would be required to pay the taxes when he or she withdraws the money from the IRA, which could be many years later. Assuming the IRA holder mentioned above is in a 30 percent federal income tax bracket, she avoided paying $5,000 in federal income taxes on the $15,000 earned on the IRA investment in 2013. That would have left $10,000 in the account, which would only produce an $800 return assuming an 8 percent rate of return. Whereas, at an 8 percent annual return, the IRA earnings actually go on to produce $1,200 in total if we go back to the original account balance of $15,000. The beauty of tax deferral is that the deferral compounds each year.

Even more eye-popping, take the example of Ben. Ben is thirty years old when he decides to start an IRA. He has a current retirement account balance of zero at that time. Assuming Ben decides to make annual IRA contributions of just $3,500 each year until he reaches the retirement age of 70, and that he is able to generate an average annualized rate of return of 9 percent with a prevailing tax rate of 25 percent, then, at age 70, Ben will have $1,289,022 of tax-deferred income in his IRA. In contrast, if that money had been invested outside of a retirement account as personal funds, the same assumptions produce just $699,475.

In other words, using an IRA allows Ben to accumulate an additional $589,547 of wealth. While Ben is not rich, he is able to put about $67 a week away for his retirement account every year. This small amount of money will turn into more than a million dollars for Ben by the time he retires.

Tax Advantages of Using a Roth IRA

It always comes down to the taxes. With a Roth IRA, as long as you have some patience and can wait until you are over 59½ and have had the Roth IRA open at least five years, all Roth IRA contributions, income, and appreciation will be tax-free. That means no federal or state income tax, ever, upon withdrawal, and not simply tax-deferred growth but tax-free growth. As a tax attorney, I have to say, things don't get much better than that

In order to get a better handle on the potential advantages of making after-tax Roth contributions, it is helpful to run several possible scenarios:

Starting balance: $0
Annual contribution: $1,500
Current age: 35
Age of retirement: 70
Expected rate of return: 8 percent
Marginal tax rate: 25 percent
Total amount of contributions: $52,000

At age 70, with a Roth IRA, the individual would have $279,153 tax-free, a tax savings of $177,181.

Starting balance: $0
Annual contribution: $5,500
Current age: 30
Age of retirement: 65
Expected rate of return: 9.77 percent
Marginal tax rate: 25 percent
Total amount of contributions: $192,000

At age 65 with a Roth IRA, the individual would have $1,552,705.118 tax-free, a tax savings of $876,642.

Now, assuming the individual wanted to retire at age 70:

Starting balance: $0
Annual contribution: $5,500
Current age: 30
Age of retirement: 70
Expected rate of return: 9.77 percent
Marginal tax rate: 25 percent
Total amount of contributions: $200,000

At age 70 with a Roth IRA, the individual would have $2,510,367 tax-free, a tax savings of $1,282,637.

Starting Balance: $0
Annual contribution: $3,500
Current Age: 38
Age of retirement: 70
Expected rate of return: 8 percent
Marginal tax rate: 25 percent
Total amount of contributions: $112,000

At age 70 with a Roth IRA, the individual would have $507,327 tax-free, a tax savings of $337,201.

The examples above show the enormous retirement benefits of making after-tax (Roth) contributions starting at a young age and on a consistent basis. That being said, there is certainly nothing wrong with having a million dollars or so in a pretax retirement account; although, if your federal and state income tax rate was at 50 percent when you retired, that million-dollar-plus retirement account would still be nice, but definitely not as nice as being able to live off the money tax-free without ever having to pay tax on the money again. Taking this a step further, one can argue, that with a 50 percent tax rate, having $1 million in a Roth IRA plan is like having $1.5 million in a pretax account. Numbers never lie—the hard part is turning down an accountant who is pushing for you to make the pretax contribution so it reduces your current income tax and makes him or her look better in your eyes. You need to think long term by focusing on the advantages of tapping a tax-free account when you retire, especially if taxes will be higher than they are now.

Should I Make Roth or Pretax Contributions?

Often tax professionals and financial advisers are asked whether it makes sense to make a Roth after-tax contribution or a pretax contribution. The upside with Roth contributions is that your Roth withdrawals in retirement (including any earnings and gains on your Roth contributions) are completely federal income tax-free if you meet certain requirements.

When deciding whether you should make Roth contributions, before-tax contributions, or a combination of the two, here are some important considerations:

If you feel your tax rate in retirement will be higher than it is today, Roth contributions may make sense for you. If you expect your tax rate to be lower in retirement than during your working years, you may benefit more from making before-tax contributions and paying taxes when you withdraw your money. It is hard to imagine now, but we are currently in a historically low tax-rate environment. For most of the century, including some boom times, top-bracket income tax rates were much higher than they are today. In fact, during the 1950s and early 1960s, the top bracket income tax rate was over 90 percent. In light of our growing deficit, social security shortfall, and heavy government spending, it is not far off to suggest that income tax rates will be higher when you retire than they are now. Of course, no one knows what will happen tomorrow when it comes to Congress and taxes, and especially not in twenty or thirty years, so an educated guess is all one can make.

How confident are you in your expected returns? If you are very confident that your investments and/or cash flow from your investments are relatively secure and will grow over time, a Roth account would make sense. Bear in mind that many people felt that Enron, Lehman Brothers, and Bear Stearns were safe investments and suitable for Roth funds and we all know how those companies turned out. In general, Roth IRA investments seem to work well with real-estate-income-producing investments as well as dividend-growth investments in which the cash flows are generally perceived as stable.

The further away your retirement the greater opportunity for tax-free growth and the more potential you have for tax-free gains. Basically, if you will not be retiring in the near future, Roth contributions may make a good deal of sense, since your account has more time potentially to grow in value. This may make the tax advantages of Roth contributions even more important to you—although Roth dollars can benefit retirement savers of all ages.

Important considerations in determining whether to make pretax IRA or after-tax (Roth) IRA contributions

	Pre-tax Contribution	After-Tax (Roth) contribution
Your age	Getting older potentially reduces the attractiveness of a Roth	The younger you are Roth offers greater advantages
Need for current income tax deduction	The greater the need the greater benefit for a pre-tax contribution	The less the need the more attractive the Roth contribution becomes
Future tax rates	The belief that tax rates will be lower when you retire increase the attractiveness of the pre-tax contribution	The belief that future tax rates will be higher increase attractiveness of Roth
Investment confidence	The less confident you are in the stock market or your 401(k) plan investment options the more attractive the pre-tax account will be because at least you will benefit from a current tax deduction	The more confident you are in your investment returns and their growth over the years, the more attractive the Roth account becomes because all future appreciation will be tax-free

III

The Self-Directed IRA Checkbook
Control Solution

Rich felt both full of knowledge and full of questions by the time the next real estate class took place. He listened intently to the lecturer and took good notes, but he was also very eager to meet with John after class and learn more about the self-directed IRA.

When class ended, he saw that John was packing his stuff up fairly quickly and was dressed a little more formally than usual. Still, John's greeting was enthusiastic as ever.

"Hey, great class, wasn't it?" John said.

"Yeah. I learned a lot more than I even thought I would," Rich said. "Speaking of which, I read through the material you gave me on the IRA, and I'm ready to learn more about the 'checkbook control' self-directed IRA now, if you have the time."

"The real self-directed IRA," John corrected, "not the one the banks and financial institutions tell you about."

"Exactly."

"I thought you'd be excited. Unfortunately, I have some plans tonight, but I brought you another pamphlet figuring you'd be ready for more."

John handed Rich a pamphlet.

"What's this one on?"

"It's the story behind the story of the self-directed IRA LLC with 'checkbook control.' Basically, it's about the history of how it came to be, and the case law that determined the legality of what an IRA holder can and can't do when it comes to directing their own IRA funds."

"Sounds perfect."

"Yeah, the background is a little dry, but it's important to know so that you really understand what's permitted by the IRS and how you can take advantage of the best opportunities."

"Great. I'll read it. Thanks," Rich said.

"No problem," John answered. "I have no plans next week, so if you're free after Tuesday's class we can really get into the brass tacks of how it all works."

"I like the sound of that," Rich said. "With everything I'm learning about real estate development, I'm eager to get rolling."

"Okay. Read up. Have a great weekend. And I'll see you Tuesday."

The Background of the Self-Directed IRA with "Checkbook Control"

The ability to invest retirement funds in a newly established special purpose entity owned 100 percent by an IRA and managed by the IRA holder has been deemed legal by the Tax Court since 1996. However, not until recently did the Tax Court confirm specifically that the use of a newly established LLC wholly owned by an IRA and managed by the IRA holder would not trigger a prohibited transaction.

The legality of using IRA funds to invest in a special purpose entity wholly owned by the IRA and managed by the IRA holder first came into question in the 1990s.

The following information will provide a detailed overview of the case law and legal foundation surrounding the checkbook control self-directed IRA solution. The structure discussed in this book goes by many names, including "checkbook IRA," "checkbook control IRA," "self-directed IRA LLC," and "IRA LLC." All of these names refer to the same concept: a special purpose entity wholly owned by one or more IRAs to make investments. We will be using these terms interchangeably. Some may find the information somewhat dense and heavily legal, but the fact is that the validity of the structure is founded on the merits of a Tax Court case and an IRS ruling. In order to offer an accurate and comprehensive summary of the legal process that led to the IRS formally accepting the checkbook control IRA solution as a legal investment structure, a detailed description of a number of tax rulings is important.

How Did the Checkbook Control Self-Directed IRA Start?

Beginning in the early 1990s, individuals began using special purpose entities wholly owned by their IRA to make investments. Investors wanted the ability to have more control over their IRA investments, and with the emergence of new forms of pass-through entities developing, tax professionals started exploring the use of these entities to make retirement account investments.

The Checkbook Control Self-Directed IRA Is Tested

The idea of using an entity owned by an IRA to make investments was first reviewed by the Tax Court in *Swanson v. Commissioner* 106 T.C. 76 (1996).

Underlying Dispute

The underlying facts involved James Swanson's (the taxpayer's) combined use of two entities owned exclusively by his IRAs to defer income recognition.

James Swanson was the sole shareholder of H & S Swansons' Tool Company, an S corporation that builds and paints component parts for domestic and foreign equipment manufacturers. Following the advice of tax counsel, Swanson arranged in 1985 for the establishment of Swansons' Worldwide, Inc. ("Worldwide"), a Domestic International Sales Company

("DISC"). A DISC is a domestic corporation, usually a subsidiary, that is typically used to defer tax on income generated by the entity.

Although, Mr. Swanson did not use an LLC, the Swanson case was really the first case that addressed the ability to use any entity wholly owned by an IRA and managed by the IRA holder to make tax-deferred investments.

Mr. Swanson appointed as trustee and custodian of IRA No. 1 Florida National Bank, who retained the power to direct its investments. Mr. Swanson then directed Florida National to execute a subscription agreement to purchase 2,500 shares of Worldwide original issue stock. The shares were issued and IRA No. 1 became the sole shareholder of Worldwide. Mr. Swanson then engineered a similar transaction with a second IRA at another bank.

The IRS Attack

The IRS issued a notice of deficiency to Mr. Swanson in June 1992. The IRS stated that prohibited transactions had occurred causing IRAs No. 1 and No. 2 to be terminated. The IRC does not describe what a self-directed IRA can invest in, only what it *cannot* invest in. IRC Sections 408 & 4975 prohibit disqualified persons from engaging in certain types of transactions. The purpose of these rules is to encourage the use of IRAs for accumulation of retirement savings and to prohibit those in control of IRAs from taking advantage of the tax benefits for their personal account.

The IRS made the following arguments:

- Mr. Swanson is a disqualified person within the meaning of IRC Section 4975(e)(2)(A) of the Code as a fiduciary because he has the express authority to control the investments of IRA No. 1.
- Mr. Swanson is also an officer and director of Swansons' Worldwide. Therefore, direct or indirect transactions described by IRC Section 4975(c)

  (1) between Swansons' Worldwide and IRA No. 1 constitute prohibited transactions.
- Mr. Swanson, as an officer and director of Worldwide, directed the payment of dividends from Worldwide to IRA No. 1.

- At the time of the purchase of the Swanson Worldwide stock, Mr. Swanson was a fiduciary of his IRA and the sole director of Swansons' Worldwide.

The sale of stock by Swansons' Worldwide to Mr. Swanson's IRA constituted a prohibited transaction within the meaning of IRC Section 4975(c)(1)(A) of the code.

Mr. Swanson's Position in Response to the IRS

Mr. Swanson took the position in his Tax Court petition that no prohibited transaction had occurred. His position was that since the Worldwide shares issued to IRA No. 1 were original issue, no sale or exchange occurred. Also, he stated that as the director and president of Worldwide, Swanson engaged in no activities on behalf of Worldwide that benefited him other than as beneficiary of IRA No. 1. Mr. Swanson made similar points with respect to IRA No. 2.

The IRS Concedes the Prohibited Transaction Issue

The IRS conceded the prohibited transaction issue in the Swanson case on July 12, 1993, when it filed a notice of no objection to an earlier motion by Swanson for partial summary judgment on that issue. In other words, the IRS concluded that it would no longer pursue its position that Swansons' use of a newly established entity (wholly owned by an IRA and managed by the IRA holder to make investments) was a prohibited transaction. In light of this, Mr. Swanson sought litigation costs against the IRS on the prohibited transaction issue.

The Tax Court Rebuffs IRS Arguments on IRA Prohibited Transaction Issue and Imposes Litigation Costs

The IRS argued that its litigation position with respect to the IRA prohibited transaction issue was substantially justified. The Tax Court disagreed with the IRS's position, finding that it was unreasonable for the IRS to claim that a prohibited transaction occurred when Worldwide's stock was acquired by IRA No. 1 for the following reasons:

- The stock acquired by the IRA was newly issued. Before that time, Worldwide had no shares or shareholders. A corporation without shares doesn't fit within the definition of a disqualified person under the prohibited transaction rules pursuant to IRC 4975. As a result, the corporation, Worldwide, only became a disqualified person with respect to IRA No. 1 investment into Worldwide only after the Worldwide stock was issued to IRA No. 1.
- It was only after Worldwide issued its stock to IRA No. 1 that Mr. Swanson held a beneficial interest in Worldwide's stock. Mr. Swanson was not a disqualified person as president and director of Worldwide until after the stock was issued to IRA No. 1.
- The payment of dividends by Worldwide to IRA No. 1 was not a self-dealing prohibited transaction under IRC section 4975(c)(1)(E). The only benefit Mr. Swanson realized from the payments of dividends by Worldwide related solely to his status as beneficiary of IRA No. 1, which is not a prohibited transaction.
- It was only after Worldwide issued its stock to IRA NO. 1 that Mr. Swanson held a beneficial interest in Worldwide's stock. Therefore, the issuance of stock to IRA No. 1 did not constitute a prohibited transaction.
  - It was only after Worldwide issued its stock to IRA NO. 1 that Mr.
  - Swanson held a beneficial interest in Worldwide's stock. Mr. Swanson's only benefit would be as beneficiary of the IRA, which is not a prohibited transaction.
  - The Tax Court reached similar conclusions with respect to IRA No. 2.

The Checkbook Control Self-Directed IRA Solution Is Born

In deciding the Swanson case, the Tax Court agreed with Mr. Swanson's position that the IRS pursuance of the prohibited transaction claim with respect to the two IRA investments was not justified and should be sanctioned.

"We must apportion the award of fees sought by petitioners (Swanson) between the DISC (IRA) issue, for which respondent (IRS) was not substantially justified."
—Tax Court in *Swanson v. Commissioner* 106 T.C. 76 (1996).

What Did We Learn from the Swanson Tax Court case?

An IRA can own an Interest in a new entity managed by the IRA holder. The Swanson case helped establish that an IRA holder is permitted to establish a new entity wholly owned by his or her IRA in order to make IRA investments. The Swanson case makes it clear that only after the IRA has acquired the stock of the newly established entity does the entity become a disqualified person. The significance of the Swanson case is that it was the first case that firmly established that an IRA could invest in a wholly owned entity to make investments without tax or penalty.

An IRA Holder Can Manage the Newly Formed Entity Owned by the IRA

The Swanson case makes it clear that an IRA holder may serve as manager, director, or officer of the newly established entity owned by his or her IRA. The Tax Court held that Mr. Swanson was not a disqualified person as president and director of Worldwide until after the stock was issued to IRA NO. 1. The Tax Court went on to say that as long as the IRA holder serving as manager is not directly or indirectly *personally benefiting* from any IRA LLC investment, there would be no prohibited transaction even though the manager is a fiduciary and a disqualified person pursuant to IRC Section 4975. In other words, by having the IRA invested in an entity such as an LLC of which the IRA owner is the manager, the Swanson case suggests that the IRA holder can serve as manager of the LLC and have checkbook control over his or her IRA funds without triggering the prohibited transaction rules as long as no direct or indirect personal benefit was derived by the manager from the IRA LLC investment.

It's the IRA Investment, Not the Investment Vehicle Being
Used to Make the IRA Investment, that Counts

The Tax Court in *Swanson* made it clear that it was only after Worldwide issued its stock to IRA No. 1 that Mr. Swanson held a beneficial interest in Worldwide's stock. Therefore, the Tax Court is holding that only once the IRA funds have been invested into the newly established entity does the analysis begin of whether an IRA transaction is prohibited. Said another way, the Tax Court is contending that the use of an entity owned wholly by an IRA is not material as to whether a prohibited transaction occurred. The use of a wholly owned entity to make an investment is essentially no different if the IRA made the investment itself with respect to the prohibited transaction rules. The Swanson case helps show that what is really important in determining whether a prohibited transaction occurred is not whether the IRA made the investment directly or via a wholly owned newly established special purpose entity, but what investment was ultimately made using IRA funds.

First the US Tax Court, Now the IRS Confirms the Legality of the Checkbook IRA Structure

In general, after 1993 when the IRS conceded the IRA prohibited transaction issue in Swanson, a number of attorneys began exploring the impact of the Swanson decision. At about that time, the "LLC" entity began emerging as the entity of choice for investment transactions and was becoming recognized by all fifty states as an entity that provided limited liability protection and pass-through tax treatment.

During this time, a number of attorneys began experimenting with the use of the LLC as an investment vehicle. Attorneys began establishing special purpose LLCs wholly owned by an IRA as a vehicle for making real estate and other investments. Since an LLC is a pass-through entity, it does not pay federal income tax—its owner does. But since the IRA is the sole owner of the LLC and an IRA is tax-exempt pursuant to IRC Section 408, no tax is generally due on the IRA LLC investment. This, coupled with the ability to make investments quickly and with limited custodian intervention, was gaining popularity quickly with the American public.

What Is an LLC?

An LLC is a separate legal entity that is formed under the authority of a state statute. All fifty states and the District of Columbia have enacted limited liability company statutes. Generally, the statutes contain similar basic procedures and elements that are required to establish the LLC. From a corporate standpoint, the LLC is respected as a separate entity and offers its members, in the case of a self-directed IRA LLC, the IRA, limited liability protection. In other words, owners and members of the LLC are not liable for the debts, obligations, and liabilities of the LLC. Whereas, from a tax perspective, an LLC is not taxed on any income it earns or generates. Instead, all taxable revenues and expenses are passed through to the owners of the entity who would then be responsible for the payment of tax on those revenues or expenses. Because of the flow-through tax treatment of the LLC and the limited liability protection it offers, the LLC has quickly become the most popular entity for new businesses as well as for IRA investments.

The corporate and tax principles of the LLC will be discussed in detail in the next chapter.

The increasing popularity of the checkbook control IRA caught the IRS's attention. In light of their defeat in *Swanson* and their new position that a checkbook IRA is not prohibited, the IRS felt it was important that it provide clear rules and audit guidance to the IRS audit agents on the checkbook IRA structure.

The IRS Offers Guidance to Its Audit Agents on the Legality of the Checkbook Control IRA

IRS Field Service Advice (FSA) Memorandum 200128011 was the first IRS drafted opinion that confirmed the ruling of Swanson that held that the funding of a new entity by an IRA for self-directing assets was not a prohibited transaction pursuant to IRC Section 4975. An FSA is issued by the IRS to IRS field agents to guide them in conduct of tax audits. The facts presented in the FSA closely mirrored those in the Swanson case.

The Facts

USCorp is a domestic subchapter S corporation. The father owns a majority of the shares of USCorp. The father's three minor children own the remaining shares of USCorp equally. USCorp is in the business of selling Product A, and some of its sales are made for export.

Father and each child own separate IRAs. Each of the four IRAs acquired a 25 percent interest in FSC A, a foreign sales corporation ("FSC"). USCorp entered into service and commission agreements with FSC A. During Taxable Year 1, FSC made a cash distribution to its IRA shareholders, out of earnings and profits derived from foreign trade income relating to USCorp exports. The IRAs owning FSC each received an equal amount of funds.

The IRS Opinion and Confirmation of the Legality of the Checkbook IRA

The IRS advised that, based on *Swanson*, neither issuance of stock in the newly established entity (FSC) to the IRA's owners nor the payment of dividends by the FSC to the IRAs constituted direct prohibited transaction.

As stated by the IRS in the FSA, "in light of Swanson, we conclude that a prohibited transaction did not occur under IRC Section 4975(c)(1)(A) in the original issuance of the stock of FSC to the IRAs in this case… We further conclude, considering Swanson, that we should not maintain that the ownership of FSC stock by the IRAs, together with the payment of dividends by FSC to the IRAs, constitutes a prohibited transaction under IRC Section 4975(c)(1)(E)." The IRS further stated, "this case should not be pursued as one involving prohibited transactions."

Tax Court Confirms Legality of Checkbook IRA LLC Structure

Even though the Tax Court and IRS clearly approved the use of retirement funds to own an entity for investments and be managed by the IRA holder, neither the IRS nor the Tax Court specifically addressed the actual use of an LLC as the special purpose vehicle for making IRA investments.

On October 29, 2013, the Tax Court offered direct confirmation that the use of a newly established special purpose LLC wholly owned by an IRA and managed by the IRA holder would not trigger an IRS prohibited transaction.

In T.L. Ellis, TC Memo. 2013-245, Mr. Terry Ellis retired with about $300,000 in his 401(k) retirement plan, which he subsequently rolled over into a newly created self-directed IRA.

The taxpayer then created an LLC called CST Investments, LLC ("CST LLC"), taxed as a corporation and had his IRA invest the $300,000 into CST LLC in return for 100 percent interest in the entity. CST LLC was formed to engage in the business of used-car sales. The taxpayer managed the used-car business through CST LLC and received a modest salary.

The facts of Ellis clearly show that a prohibited transaction occurred. As you will learn later on in the book, you cannot use IRA funds in any manner that personally benefits you directly or indirectly. Hence, using IRA funds to invest in a business that the IRA holder will earn a salary from is clearly a prohibited transaction. The IRS could have just made this argument and would have been successful in the case. What is interesting about the Ellis case is that in light of the Swanson case and FSA 200128011, the IRS still pursued the concept that establishing a special purpose entity, in this case an LLC, wholly owned by the IRA and managed by the IRA holder, would trigger a prohibited transaction.

The IRS argued that the formation of CST LLC was a prohibited transaction under IRC Section 4975, which prohibits self-dealing. The Tax Court disagreed and, citing the Swanson case, ruled that even though the taxpayer acted as a fiduciary to the IRA (and was therefore a disqualified person under IRC Section 4975), the LLC itself was not a disqualified person at the time of the IRA investment into the LLC. It was only AFTER the investment that the LLC would be considered a disqualified person because it was owned by Mr. Ellis's IRA, a disqualified person.

The Tax Court concluded that the petitioners did not engage in a prohibited transaction when they caused Mr. Ellis's IRA to invest in CST LLC. Additionally, the IRS also claimed that the taxpayer had engaged in a prohibited transaction by receiving a salary from the LLC. The court agreed with the IRS on this point. Although the LLC (and not the IRA) was officially paying the taxpayer's salary, the Tax Court concluded that since the IRA was the sole owner of the LLC, and that the LLC was the IRA's only investment, the taxpayer (a disqualified person) was essentially being paid by his IRA.

The impact of the Tax Court's ruling in TC Memo 2013-245 is significant because it directly confirms the legality of the self-directed IRA LLC solution by validating that a retirement account can fund a newly established LLC without triggering a prohibited transaction.

As confirmed in Swanson and later by the IRS in FSA Memorandum 200128011 and TC Memo 2013-245, using retirement funds to invest in a newly established LLC wholly owned by an IRA and managed by the IRA holder is not a prohibited transaction. In light of *Swanson* and TC Memo 2013-245, it is evident that the Tax Court believes firmly that using IRA funds to invest in a newly established LLC will not trigger a prohibited transaction and is 100 percent legal.

Helpful Tip

When identifying whether a prohibited transaction occurred in connection with an IRA investment, the Tax Court is holding that the actual investment made by the IRA-owned LLC is what is relevant and not whether an LLC or other type of newly established special purpose investment vehicle was used.

Why Do Some IRA Custodians Continue to Claim that the Checkbook Control Structure Is Risky?

In light of the Ellis case, some IRA custodians are still telling clients that using a checkbook control self-directed IRA could be risky and even trigger an IRS audit. The reason for their concern is obvious—they would like more of your money and higher account fees.

As we already learned, there are two ways to hold self-directed IRA alternative asset investments—either custodian-controlled or "checkbook control." With the custodian-controlled self-directed IRA the IRA custodian is more directly involved in the IRA investment and is actually the party signing the transaction documents and issuing payments. The work this requires on the custodian's part earns them higher annual IRA account fees and, in most cases, per-transaction fees as well. You can't blame them—they are arranging to sign the necessary transaction documents for your IRA investment while corresponding with you and the other transaction party on various aspects of the transaction. All this takes time and effort, which is reflected in their annual fees.

In the case of a checkbook control self-directed IRA LLC, the IRA holder, as manager of the IRA LLC, is the party responsible for signing all IRA transaction documents as well as for funding the investment. This takes most of the work away from the custodian and, accordingly, requires a much more passive type of custodian. Of course, the more passive the IRA custodian is, the less they can charge you, as the IRA holder, in fees.

Full-service IRA custodians are aware of the checkbook IRA and its ability to provide the IRA holder with greater control and freedom with their retirement funds. Greater control and investment freedom translates into lower custodian fees and makes it much harder for these IRA custodians to compete with the IRA passive custodian that is servicing checkbook control IRAs. We shouldn't be surprised, then, that some IRA custodians have been more vocal in expressing their belief that a checkbook control self-directed IRA could be risky or even lead to an IRS audit.

Well, Is It True? Is Checkbook Control an IRS Audit Risk?

No one really knows what triggers an IRS audit. The IRS does not publicly reveal how it determines who gets audited—and this is especially true in the case of retirement funds. It is not inconceivable to argue that an individual or business would likely be more susceptible to an IRS audit than a retirement account that is not subject to tax. However, no one outside of the IRS knows for sure what specifically triggers an IRS audit. When it comes to IRA funds and IRS reporting, we do know several things for sure.

To report a self-directed IRA to the IRS, every IRA administrator or custodian is required to complete and file an IRS Form 5498. One of the main purposes of IRS Form 5498 is to give the IRS access to the annual valuation of IRA funds on a year-to-year basis. IRA valuations are also needed for in-kind distributions and, in addition, required-minimum-distribution calculations are based on year-end IRA values.

IRS Form 5498 also reports your total annual contributions to an IRA account and identifies the type of retirement account you have, such as a traditional IRA, Roth IRA, SEP IRA, or SIMPLE IRA. Form 5498 also lets the IRS know the amounts that you roll over or transfer from other types of retirement accounts into this IRA. The "custodian" of your IRA, typically the bank or other institution that manages your account, will mail a copy of this form to both you and the IRS. Form 5498 requests information pertaining to the IRA account, including the name and address of the IRA custodian, the amount of any IRA contributions or distributions taken during the year, and, most specifically, the value of the IRA account as of December 31 of the previous year.

However, in order to address IRA valuation abuses, in 2013, the IRS proposed additional reporting requirements for hard-to-value IRA assets, on both Form 5498 (for contributions) and on Form 1099-R (for distributions). This reporting will begin in 2015.

According to the IRS, "New information-reporting requirements are proposed to apply to certain IRA investments with no readily available fair market value." Reportable investments may include:

- Non–publicly traded stock
- Partnership or [limited-liability] interests
- Real estate, options
- Other hard-to-value investments

When the requirements take effect, IRA custodians will have to code IRS Form 5498 as well IRS Form 1099-R to indicate transactions involving assets without a clear value. The IRS has stated that the main purpose of this change is to get a better handle on valuations that are being used for distribution purposes for hard-to-value IRA assets, such as real estate, but it certainly will provide the IRS more insight than they have right now in terms of the type of assets that are being purchased with retirement funds.

With approximately 47 million IRAs in the United States and over 90 percent of IRAs invested in traditional assets, such as stocks and mutual funds, coupled with the fact that IRAs do not pay tax, it is not expected that the IRS will begin targeting retirement accounts. According to reports, because the IRS was short on personnel and funding, the agency audited only 0.86 percent of all individual tax returns in 2014. And the 2015 audit rate will definitely fall even lower as the agency's resources continue to shrink. The audit rates for IRAs is believed to be significantly lower largely because almost all IRAs are invested in traditional assets, such as stocks, which are easy to value and are not prohibited transaction candidates, two of the main reasons the IRS would audit an IRA. As you have read above, using a special purpose entity wholly owned by an IRA will not trigger a prohibited transaction, regardless of how any IRS Form 5498 will be coded.

Throughout this book, you'll learn that when it comes to making IRA investments, the type of self-directed IRA structure you use is not as important as the ultimate investment that will be made. This is relevant from a financial standpoint as well as from an IRS prohibited transaction standpoint. The main theme of the Tax Court cases discussed above is that the IRS is more concerned with what your IRA will be investing in rather than the vehicle used to make the investment. Whether you use a DISC, LLC, partnership, or corporation to make your investment is not as relevant as to what the IRA-owned entity will invest in when it comes to the IRS determining whether your IRA engaged in a prohibited transaction. Thanks to the Ellis case, we now know for sure that an IRA can wholly own an LLC and be managed by the IRA holder and make investments without triggering the IRS prohibited transaction rules. The next chapter will show you—and Rich—how that checkbook control solution works.

IV

The Self-Directed IRA LLC: How It Works

The next week, Rich felt ready for a detailed discussion with John on the self-directed IRA. Unfortunately, an email from their real estate professor came in late that afternoon canceling class due to a family emergency. Rich was disappointed to not see John for another week. He was elated, however, when John texted twenty minutes later and suggested they get together at the school anyway.

"We can grab a big table and use the time to do a deep dive into how the self-directed IRA LLC works," John suggested.

"Sounds great!" Rich replied.

The Overview

Rich and John set up at a table, and John laid out some folders and pamphlets.

"Okay," John said, "Now that you've learned that you can use your retirement funds to make alternative asset investments, such as real estate, precious metals, hard money loans, or purchase a business, let's discuss in detail exactly how you can establish the self-directed IRA structure of your choice."

"I still can't believe I didn't know about this before," Rich said.

"You'd think with over 47 million IRAs out there," John said, "more people would know about it. But there's no incentive for the banks or major financial institutions to publicize this. If you have $250,000 in an IRA account at a major financial institution and own a number of mutual funds, the financial institution will typically earn fees from facilitating these investments. If, however, you took your $250,000 and bought precious metals or real estate, the financial institution will no longer have use of those funds or the ability to generate any more fees on the funds."

"No wonder I never see any commercials or ads about this."

"Yes, they don't want to lose your business," John agreed. "But if the 2008 financial crisis taught us anything, it is that Americans need a more diversified and well-balanced retirement portfolio, and they can't always trust the establishment to tell them what's in their best interests."

"That's for sure," Rich said. "So, besides real estate and precious metals, what can I invest in using my self-directed IRA?"

"The IRC doesn't describe what a self-directed IRA can invest in, only what it *cannot* invest in," Rich said.

"That's interesting," John said.

"Absolutely. IRC Sections 408 & 4975 prohibit 'disqualified persons' from engaging in certain type of transactions because the IRS wants to encourage the use of IRAs for accumulation of retirement savings and to prohibit those in control of IRAs from taking advantage of the tax benefits for their personal account."

"I guess that makes sense. The government wants me to have money when I retire."

"It does. Prohibited transaction rules are based on the premise that investments involving IRAs and related parties should be handled in a way that benefits the retirement account and not the IRA owner. The outline for these rules can be found in IRC Section 4975, and we'll discuss them in greater detail another time, but, in general, as long as you are not purchasing life insurance, certain collectibles (like antiques, rugs, stamps, and so on), or investing in a transaction that directly or indirectly personally benefits a disqualified person, the transaction can be made via a self-directed IRA without triggering an IRS prohibited transaction."

"And what's a disqualified person again?"

"Generally, a 'disqualified person' is the IRA holder, any ancestors or lineal descendants of the IRA holder, and entities in which the IRA holder holds a controlling equity or management interest."

"Okay," Rich said, "that's fine because I have funds from a former employer's 401(k) plan. So assuming I want to establish a self-directed IRA, can I use my existing 401(k) plan funds from my former employer?"

"Yes," John answered. "A self-directed IRA may be funded by a transfer from another IRA account or through a rollover from an eligible defined contribution plan. Those include qualified 401(k) retirement plans under IRC Section 401(a), 403(a), 403(b), and governmental 457(b) plans. When the funds are coming from an IRA and going directly to the self-directed IRA, that process is considered an IRA transfer. If you are moving over retirement funds other than an IRA, such as your former employer's 401(k) plan funds, the process of moving the funds is called a rollover. In both instances—an IRA transfer or a rollover—the movement of funds to the new self-directed IRA is tax- and penalty-free."

"If I start contributing to my new employer's 401(k) plan," Rich asked, "can I immediately roll those funds over to my new self-directed IRA account?"

"There are only a few established ways to take money out of a 401(k) plan," John replied. "The most common method is via a distribution. A distribution is essentially a term for taking funds from a retirement account and turning tax-exempt funds into personal funds that are no longer exempt from tax."

"And you can't just do that whenever you want, right?" Rich asked.

"Generally," John said, "you may not take a distribution from a 401(k) plan until a certain event occurs, often called a triggering event. The actions that trigger a distribution under a 401(k) plan will change depending on the type of plan documents your plan has adopted.

Typically, distributions of elective deferrals cannot be made until one of the following occurs—"

John put a sheet of paper on the table, and Rich read the list:

- You reach age 59½
- The plan terminates and you do not establish or maintain a successor-defined contribution plan
- You have a severance of employment
- You become disabled
- You die
- You incur a financial hardship

"In other words," John said, "because you are under 59½, you will not be able to gain access to your current employer 401(k) plan funds until you either turn 59½, leave your job, or the company terminates the plan."

"Okay," Rich said, "so help me understand my situation. I will have approximately $215,000 of former employer 401(k) plan funds to use for real estate investing and assume I do not need a triggering event to move the funds to an IRA. "That is correct," replied John.

"Do I need to roll over all the retirement funds at once?"

"Not really, no. You can roll over as little or as much of your former 401(k) plan funds to a new self-directed IRA as you like. Just make sure you'll continue to have access to those funds from your former employer."

"Okay. That's what I thought. So my plan is to start with $125,000, which will allow me to buy two homes to get my real estate development investments going."

"Sounds good," John said. "Once you've got that decision out of the way, you need to think about how to structure the self-directed IRA."

"Right. I've read about the custodian-controlled self-directed IRA and the checkbook control self-directed IRA LLC. Is that what you mean?"

"Yes," John said.

"Well, which structure do you think will work best for me?" Rich asked.

"As you know," John said, "a self-directed IRA is a type of IRA structure that allows the IRA holder (meaning you) to have more control over your retirement funds. A self-directed IRA is not a new type of IRA. It is simply the vehicle that allows you to make traditional as well as alternative asset investments with your IRA funds."

"Right," Rich said. "But there are different kinds."

"Yes," John said. "There are essentially three types of self-directed IRAs. There is no right answer as to which type of self-directed IRA you should establish. However, there are certain important factors that you should evaluate before determining which type of self-directed IRA will work best for you."

John pulled out another sheet of paper, and Rich peered at it closely.

- Type of investments you will be making with the self-directed IRA:
    - Traditional investments
    - Alternative asset investments
    - Mixture of both
- Would like capacity to make alternative investments
- Frequency of investments
    - Only have enough funds for one investment
    - Multiple investments
- Level of concern about transaction fees
- Value of IRA account:
    - Small IRA account
    - Large IRA account
- Concerned about annual account fees
- Holding period of IRA investment
    - Long term: very little account activity
    - Frequent transactions: i.e., house flipping
- Level of concern about transaction fees
- Speed of investments
    - Need to make investments quickly: i.e., tax lien auction
    - Time is not a factor

- How important is it to have "checkbook control"?
- Ongoing activities of investment
  - Very little: i.e., hedge fund investment
  - Considerable: i.e., payment for ongoing property improvements

"Let's review the three types of self-directed IRA structures so that you can take each of the factors on this list and determine which IRA structure will best suit your investment and financial goals," John said.

"Okay," Rich said.

"Remember," John said, "there's no right answer. Everything is based on the particular facts and circumstances surrounding the way you intend to use your self-directed IRA."

1. Financial Institution–Offered Self-Directed IRA

"The most popular self-directed IRA account offered is the financial institution self-directed IRA," John said.

"Let me guess why it's popular," Rich said. "The banks are pushing it."

"Correct," Rich smiled. "It's typically offered by the major financial institutions such as Bank of America, Wells Fargo, Fidelity, Vanguard, and so on. With this type of self-directed IRA, the IRA holder is usually only able to make IRA investments offered by the financial institution, such as stocks, mutual funds, and ETFs (exchange-traded funds). Even though these types of IRA accounts are called 'self-directed IRA' accounts they are very limited in their investment scope and don't allow IRA investors to make any nontraditional investments, such as real estate."

"How do the financial institutions get away with limiting the investment options available?" Rich asked.

"A financial institution that offers IRA accounts is not required to offer its IRA investors the opportunity to make all allowable types of IRA investments. For example, even though real estate is an IRS-approved investment, an IRA custodian is not required or obligated to offer that investment option. That's why most financial institutions offering IRA accounts will restrict the IRA investment option to financial products they already offer. They don't earn anything when they allow their clients to pull money out of the IRA account to buy real estate from a third party."

"Got it," Rich said.

2. Custodian-Controlled Self-Directed IRA

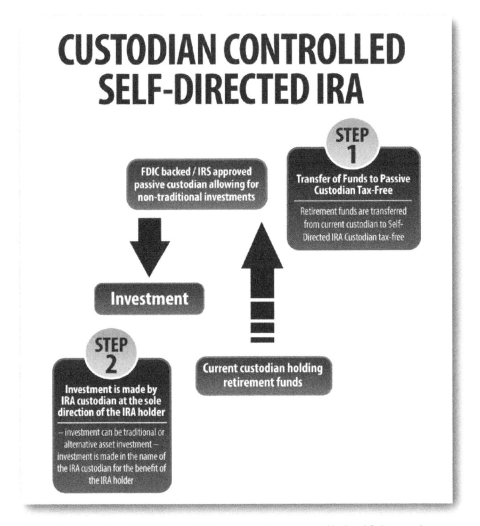

"On the other hand," John said, "a custodian-controlled self-directed IRA offers an IRA investor more investment options than a financial institution self-directed IRA."

"Hold on a second, John," Rich said. "Can you explain this concept of IRA custodian in greater detail?"

"Sure," John said. "With a custodian-controlled self-directed IRA, a special nonbank trust company will serve as the custodian of the IRA. In most cases, these special nonbank custodians are established in South Dakota because of the more lenient capital requirements there."

"In South Dakota? Sounds like the Wild West."

"Not at all. It's very controlled and regulated. In fact, these IRA custodians are governed by the South Dakota Trust laws and are permitted to establish IRA accounts as per the IRC. Since the majority of IRA custodians are nonbank custodians, the IRA account funds are deposited in an omnibus custodial account at an FDIC-insured bank or financial institution that the trust company administers."

"You mean the funds are not held by the custodian directly?"

"That's right. The majority of IRA trust companies do not actually touch the IRA funds; they simply provide all required IRA administration. The IRA funds are deposited in an FDIC-insured bank or financial institution that the IRA custodian controls and will then invest at the client's sole direction."

"Do they do anything else for you other than administration?"

"Unlike a traditional financial institution," John said, "like Vanguard or Schwab, the majority of custodians that offer self-directed IRAs for alternative asset investments don't provide investment advice or sell or market financial products. They make their money by opening and administering self-directed IRA accounts. Usually, they charge annual and transaction account fees. In some cases, fees are based on your account value as well."

"Here's my worry. I've never heard of the majority of these custodians. How can I be sure that they won't just steal my IRA funds?"

"Great question," John said. "The whole idea around the self-directed IRA is that the custodian will only make investments at the direction of the IRA holder. The IRA custodian is not considered a fiduciary to the self-directed IRA since it does not offer any investment advice or have control over the investment decisions you make for the account. The IRA custodian can only move the IRA assets at the behest of the IRA holder. And remember, IRA funds deposited in an FDIC-insured account are protected and guaranteed by the government up to $250,000 until you withdraw them. On top of everything else, almost all IRA custodians carry two types of insurance policies to cover any theft or fraud: an 'Errors and Omission Insurance Policy,' and a 'Crime Insurance Policy.'

"The errors and omission insurance policy is kept in the event of errors that may occur with processing any given transaction where funds are lost and are not able to be recovered. This policy does not cover fraud or crimes committed by our employees. The errors and omission policy provides coverage of up to $1 million. Whereas, the crime insurance policy is kept in the event of a malicious or deliberate removal of funds from our investor's account(s). This policy also provides coverage of up to $1 million."

"Okay," Rich said, "I feel much better about using a special IRS custodian to make self-directed IRA investments when I know my money is so protected. The big question I have then is do I want to use a custodian-controlled self-directed IRA or a checkbook control self-directed IRA LLC?"

John nodded.

"That's a very important decision that really depends on several factors."

He took out his pen and drew a few lines on the notepad.

"The first question you need to answer," John continued, "is what type of investment will you be making? You might make a different decision about the type of self-directed IRA structure you should develop depending on whether you invest in real estate or do a one-off private equity investment. Also, the amount of retirement funds you'll be using matters since IRA custodian fees are an important consideration. And there's also the frequency and number of investments you'll be doing with your self-directed IRA account."

"Well, in my case," Rich said, "I plan on using about $150,000 of my $215,000 retirement fund to buy real estate and possibly make some hard money loans. So, maybe I'll buy one home and do one to two hard money loans. I'd like the loans to be short term—under 18 months—and I'd like to continue making more loans as each comes due. For the real estate, I envision holding the home for about a year while renting it out, then selling it and looking to buy one or two more homes with that money. I really hope to buy the home straight out in cash, without any leverage."

"Great," John said. "So you'll be doing multiple transactions from your self-directed IRA. Let me ask you a question, though. How important is limited liability protection to you?"

Rich sat back. "You know, I heard about limited liability protection in one of our classes, so I think it's probably important, but how critical is it for the majority of my retirement assets to be invested in an LLC?"

"That's another great question. Let's talk about LLCs for a bit so you really understand."

3. The Self-Directed IRA LLC

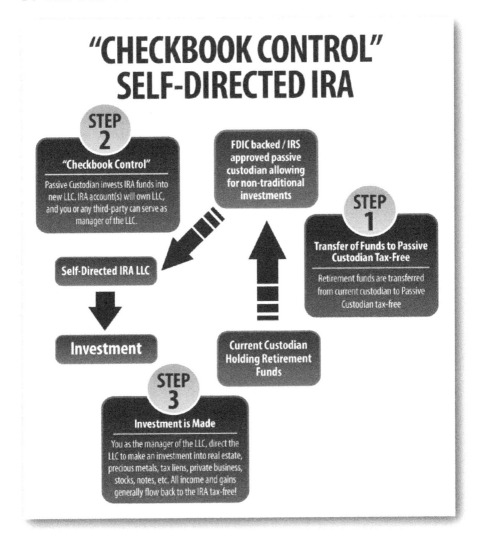

"The LLC was invented in 1977," John began, "when Wyoming became the first state to enact an LLC statute. In 1982 Florida enacted the second LLC act to attract new business to the state. Today, all fifty states and the

District of Columbia have enacted statutes that provide for the creation and governance of LLCs. Generally, the statutes contain similar basic procedures and elements that are required to establish the LLC. As a result, most businesses can be organized as an LLC in any of those jurisdictions, but laws governing LLCs can vary by location.

"In other words," John continued, "an LLC is formed under, exists, and is governed by a state statute that determines how an LLC in that state is formed, registered, and terminated. The statutes also generally provide that either the LLC adopt an Article of Organization, an Operating Agreement, or use the default provisions of the statute to determine other matters that affect the operation of the LLC."

"Are they as common as they seem?" Rich asked.

"They're very common," John answered. "According to some reports, there are close to 4 million LLCs in the United States. And probably a significant majority of all new entities formed in the United States are LLCs. They've really taken over from the C Corporation and S Corporation to become the most widely established entity in the United States, and everything I've read suggests the trend will accelerate as more and more people get comfortable with the LLC."

"So what are the advantages?" Rich asked.

"Initially, there was a question as to whether LLCs would be classified as partnerships, and receive favorable pass-through tax treatment, or be classified and taxed as a corporation for federal income tax purposes."

"How did it turn out?" Rich asked.

"The best of both worlds," John answered. "The Treasury Department and the IRS enacted Treasury Regulations Section 301.7701, which entitled the LLC to elect to be treated for federal income tax purposes either as a partnership or a corporation. The regulation also contained certain default provisions for a situation in which no election was made. Generally, an LLC with two or more members that does not make an election will be treated as a partnership and receive pass-through tax treatment, and an

LLC with only one member will be disregarded as a separate entity from its owner, meaning it is treated as a sole proprietorship and not taxed as a corporation."

"Sounds flexible."

"Yes, very," John agreed. "And an LLC has broad possibilities for its structure, operation, and management. But each state has certain mandatory and default provisions. Mandatory provisions are those rules that must be complied with, and default provisions are rules that take effect if the LLC's Certificate of Formation or Operating Agreement do not address them. In general, LLC statutes are interpreted liberally in order to give maximum effect to the freedom of contract and to the enforceability of operating agreements."

"So does that limited liability aspect affect retirement funds?" Rich asked.

"That's the whole point," John said. "An LLC offers its members (who are usually its owners) limited liability for the LLC investments. In other words, owners and members of the LLC are not liable for the debts, obligations, and liabilities of the LLC. Since, in most cases, your retirement account may be your most valuable asset, protecting that from attack from creditors is extremely important. By using an LLC, you can shield your IRA assets held outside the LLC from creditor attack."

"I get it," Rich said. "If I'm using my IRA funds to invest in real estate or make hard loans, I really want to shield those funds from attacks by creditors if anything goes wrong."

"Exactly," John said. "You want to invest, but you also want to protect. So structuring your self-directed IRA as an LLC can be really effective. That's why people use LLCs for a broad range of business and investment purposes."

John passed Rich a pamphlet.

"Here's a good overview," John said, "that explains why an LLC is so popular for business and investment purposes and a few case studies for how it works in practice."

Rich took a look.

The Popularity of the LLC

Why is the LLC so popular?

Because it:

- Is easy and inexpensive to form
- Is recognized by all states
- Provides limited liability for all members
- Has one level of tax for federal income tax and state income tax purposes (in most cases)
- Provides pass-through of business losses to the member or members
- Can utilize a corporate management structure
- Can have one member or multiple members
- Offers flexibility in distributing cash to the members
- Offers flexibility in allocating profits/losses to the members
- Offers flexibility in conducting business affairs
- Can exist indefinitely

Of this list of great features, the most popular are (1) the limited liability protection and (2) the pass-through tax treatment.

1. Limited Liability Protection

In general, limited liability is where a person's financial liability or exposure is limited to a fixed sum, most commonly the value of a person's investment in a company or partnership. If a company with limited liability is sued, then the plaintiffs are suing the company, not its owners or investors. A shareholder or owner in an entity with limited liability protection, such as an LLC, is not personally liable for any of the debts of the company, other than for the value of their investment in that company.

The following is an example that highlights the advantages of limited liability protection in the case of a self-directed IRA.

Alan has $500,000 in a retirement account and wants to purchase real estate. Alan establishes a new LLC that will be owned 100 percent by his IRA—a self-directed IRA LLC. Alan directs his IRA passive custodian to invest $200,000 into the new LLC, and the LLC purchases the property. Each year the property generates $20,000 of rental income tax-free. After year five, Alan has accumulated $80,000 of income in his self-directed IRA LLC account. In year six, an accident occurs on the property owned by the LLC, and the LLC is sued. Unfortunately, Alan's insurance policy will not cover the entire claim. Because Alan has used an LLC to make the investment and not made the investment directly through a custodian-controlled self-directed IRA, the $300,000 of IRA assets held outside of the LLC will be shielded from creditor attack due to the limited liability feature of the LLC. If Alan had made the real estate investment directly using a custodian-controlled self-directed IRA, and not using an LLC, his entire IRA ($500,000) could have been subject to attack by creditors.

2. Pass-Through Tax Treatment

LLCs are not taxed on any income they earn or generate. Instead, all taxable income and expenses are passed through to the owners of the entity who would then be responsible for the payment of tax. In other words, there is no federal income tax imposed on any income or gains generated by the LLC, only the owners would be subject to tax. Some states do impose a franchise tax or annual fee on the LLC, which we will examine later in this chapter.

LLC Owned by One Owner

If there is only one member in the company, the LLC is treated as a "disregarded entity" for tax purposes, and an individual owner would report the LLC's income or loss on Schedule C of his or her individual tax return. Thus, income from the LLC is taxed at the individual tax rates. In the case of a self-directed IRA LLC, we will see that there will be no individual level-tax because an IRA is exempt from tax under IRC Sections 408 and 408A for a Roth IRA.

LLC Owned by Two or More Owners

In the case of an LLC owned by two or more owners, the LLC is treated as a partnership for federal income tax purposes. A partnership does not pay tax.

Its owners do (or do not, in the case of an IRA). But a partnership is still required to file a partnership tax return—IRS Form 1065. Under partnership tax treatment, each member of the LLC, as is the case for all partners of a partnership, annually receives a Form K-1 reporting the member's distributive share of the LLC's income or loss that is then reported on the member's individual income tax return.

LLC Questions

"That's very helpful," Rich said. "And it brings to mind a few questions."

"Fire away," John said.

"I'll only be using one IRA, but I have multiple traditional IRAs at different financial institutions. For tax purposes, will they be treated as multiple owners or one owner?"

"That's a good question," John said. "You can roll over any type of retirement account into a self-directed IRA structure. Generally, all pretax IRAs can be merged into one traditional IRA account. So, if you have multiple pretax IRA accounts you can use one IRA account to invest in the LLC, which would make the LLC a single member LLC. However, if you had a pretax account and an after-tax account (Roth) and wanted to have funds from both accounts to invest in the new LLC, then you would need to open two IRA accounts: one traditional IRA and one Roth IRA account and then the two accounts would invest in the new LLC. The LLC would then have two owners and the LLC would be considered a partnership for income tax purposes. There would be no partnership level-tax that would be due, but a partnership return would be required to be filed."

"I get it," Rich said. "Is there an advantage to having a single member LLC vs. a partnership?"

"Generally, it's to your advantage to have an LLC that is treated as a disregarded entity for tax purposes because a disregarded entity is not required to file a federal income tax return. For many people this is important because not having to file a partnership tax return is certainly easier and less costly than having to hire a CPA and a tax preparer, or use an online filing service to file the partnership tax return. Also, some people believe that the less paperwork that is filed with the IRS the better. In both cases, there would be no tax imposed at the LLC level and no tax should be imposed at the member level if the member(s) is a retirement account. Using retirement funds to invest in a newly established LLC is Tax Court–approved and perfectly legal. As long as you will not be engaged in a prohibited transaction, there is nothing to be worried about when it comes to filing a return. And not having to file a return is certainly much easier and requires no cost."

"What about my wife? She has an IRA with approximately $100,000 that has been invested in stocks for over five years, and her results have been mixed. Would she be able to invest her IRA funds along with my IRA funds in one LLC?"

"Yeah, a lot of people ask me that. Neither the Tax Court nor the IRS has spoken about whether two or more IRAs can be owners of an entity, such as an LLC, to make investments. However, almost all IRA custodians that work with the checkbook control self-directed IRA LLC allow for multiple IRAs to fund an LLC. The reasoning behind this can be found in the Tax Court's ruling in the Swanson case. The Swanson case helped establish that an IRA holder is permitted to establish a new entity wholly owned by his or her IRA in order to make IRA investments. The Swanson case makes it clear that only after the IRA has acquired the stock of the newly established entity does the entity become a disqualified person. So, as long as both IRA funds are contributed to the newly established LLC at the same time, the Swanson case holds that the entity is not disqualified at that point and two or more IRA funds can become owners of the LLC. This is the position held by most of the IRA custodians who work with checkbook control self-directed IRA LLCs."

"I'm wondering about my Roth," Rich said. "I have a small Roth IRA that I may want to use in the structure. Can I use it and would that cause the LLC to be treated as a partnership for tax purposes?"

"There is no formal IRS guidance on the ability to use pretax and Roth IRA funds in one LLC," John answered. "However, as in the case of having a newly established entity funded by multiple IRAs at the same time, the Swanson Tax Court case does provide some clarification on this question. Under the Swanson case, the stock that Mr. Swanson's IRA acquired was newly issued. Before that time, Worldwide (the entity that would be owned by the IRA) had no shares or shareholders. A corporation without shares doesn't fit within the definition of a disqualified person under the prohibited transaction rules. As a result, Mr. Swanson only became a disqualified person with respect to the IRA investment into Worldwide after the Worldwide stock was issued to the IRA. In other words, if we establish a new LLC funded by a pretax IRA and an after-tax (Roth) IRA at the same time, then the entity will only become disqualified after the IRA investment. For those reasons, it seems that the LLC could be owned by multiple IRA accounts, including your spouse."

John took a breath.

"Then come the details," he continued. "When using a pretax IRA and Roth IRA in one LLC, the ownership of the LLC will be based on the amount contributed by each IRA account. For example, if the traditional IRA contributed $80,000 and the Roth IRA contributed $20,000, the traditional IRA would own 80 percent of the LLC and the Roth IRA would own 20 percent of the LLC. So, all profits and losses as well as LLC distributions would go pro rata to the IRA members based on their percentage interests. Since the LLC has more than one owner, it is treated as a partnership for tax purposes and an IRS Form 1065 is required to be filed. Also, each IRA will need to open a separate IRA account with the IRA custodian."

Rich furrowed his brow, and thought it through.

"Couldn't I set up a separate LLC for each IRA account so as to avoid having to file a partnership return?" he asked.

John nodded. "Yup, that could work. By using separate IRA-owned LLCs, one for your pretax IRA and one for your Roth IRA, you would be able to avoid the requirement of filing a tax return. Another interesting advantage of keeping your pretax and Roth IRA funds separate is that you can make specific investments for your pretax IRA and for your Roth IRA, whereas, if you used an LLC that was owned proportionally by each IRA account, all LLC profits and losses would be allocated to each IRA. This means that you would not be able to have a specific investment for your pretax IRA and a specific investment for your Roth IRA. Do you follow?"

"I think so," Rich said. "Can you give me an example, though?"

"Sure. Let's say the IRA LLC was going to buy two real estate properties. You could not have property A owned by the traditional IRA and property B owned by the Roth IRA since the assets would be owned by the LLC and then proportionally be owned by each of the owners based on their ownership of the LLC. It's the same concept as if you bought stock in a public company. If you owned 1 percent of Apple Inc., then you own 1 percent of everything Apple Inc. owns. Apple can't tell you that you only own 1 percent of the iPod division, and nothing in the iTunes business. Owning specific assets in a Roth IRA might be attractive to some people because the Roth investment could generate significant tax-free income. But if that asset were in a pretax IRA it would be subject to tax upon distribution. The same could be said about an asset, such as currency, that has very high gain potential and the individual retirement account holder wants those gains to go 100 percent to the Roth IRA. The only way to do this is to have the Roth IRA asset own the asset exclusively through the LLC. Of course, if you did not use an LLC and opted for the custodian option, you can buy the asset directly via the self-directed IRA custodian account."

"I get it," Rich said. "But what about if I decided to establish an LLC today and wanted to add additional retirement funds to the self-directed IRA LLC structure? Can I do that?"

"I get this question a lot," John nodded. "When it comes to determining what type of an investment is permitted by the IRS-prohibited transaction rules, the IRS does not describe what a self-directed IRA can invest in, only what it *cannot* invest in. IRC Sections 408 & 4975 prohibit disqualified persons from engaging in certain types of transactions. The IRS is essentially concerned that someone will personally benefit from using his or her retirement funds without paying a tax or penalty if under the age of 59½. In a situation where only retirement funds are being used for an investment and no personal funds are being used, it would be quite hard for the IRS to argue that any prohibited transaction under IRC 4975 would be triggered since there is no risk of self-dealing and the only benefit that would be real-ized by the IRA holder would be as the beneficiary of the IRA. IRC 4975(d) (9) states that a prohibited transaction would not occur if the only benefit one would recognize were as the beneficiary (owner) of the IRA. So, if you have an LLC wholly owned by an IRA and additional IRA funds are being contributed to the LLC, the only benefit being derived would be as benefi-ciary of the IRA, which is not a prohibited transaction as per IRC 4975(d) (9). IRC Section 4975(d)(9) states that the prohibited transaction rules un-der IRC Section 4975(c) shall not apply to: receipt by a disqualified person of any benefit to which he may be entitled as a participant or beneficiary in the plan, as long as the benefit is computed and paid on a basis that is consistent with the terms of the plan as applied to all other participants and beneficiaries. Just like if you used your IRA to buy Apple stock and Apple went up in value, the only benefit you would derive is as the beneficiary of your IRA. You would not receive any personal benefit until you took the stock or cash from the sale of the stock as a distribution. The Swanson case offers some insight into this question as well. In *Swanson*, the IRS tried to argue that dividend payments from the IRA-owned entity to the IRA were a prohibited transaction. The Tax Court held that the IRS was not substan-tially justified in maintaining that the payments of dividends to IRA No. 1 constituted prohibited transactions. Taking this analysis a step further, it is safe to say the Tax Court is saying that as long as the only benefit being generated from the activity is not a personal benefit and is solely a benefit that your IRA is entitled to, it would not rise to the level of a prohibited transaction. So let's take the case of an IRA holder whose IRA owned 100 percent of an LLC and wanted to add funds to the LLC. The IRA owned 100 percent of the LLC before the funds were contributed and would own 100 percent of the LLC after the funds were contributed. All LLC income and gains would still be allocated to the IRA. The only benefit the IRA holder is receiving is that the LLC is now technically worth more because of the contribution of funds, which under IRC Section 4975(d)(9) would be exempt from the prohibited transaction rules. In fact, most of the IRA custodians allow for IRAs from spouses or third parties to be invested in one LLC. The position these IRA custodians take along with most tax professionals is that there would no self-dealing or personal benefit that could trigger a prohibited transaction from the situation described above since no personal funds are involved."

"Okay," Rich said, "so using an LLC to make an IRA investment seems like an interesting concept. Why would I want to use an LLC versus another type of entity, such as a corporation?"

The Advantages of an LLC over a C Corporation

A C corporation is a standard business corporation. It is called a C corporation because it is taxed under subsection C of the IRC.

John explained that an LLC enjoys many of the same advantages as a C corporation, and retains many of the characteristics of unincorporated entities such as partnerships and sole proprietorships. Like a C corporation, the LLC offers its members limited liability (a member is generally only liable up to the amount contributed to the LLC), and like a partnership, the LLC's earnings are not subject to an entity level of tax (only one level of tax imposes directly to the member). However, a C corporation imposes a double level of tax (entity level and shareholder level) on distributable income.

For example, let's say an LLC generates $100 of profits and let's further assume that the individual and corporate tax rate is 20 percent. In the case of an LLC, the LLC would not pay tax and only the owner would be subject to tax on the net profits allocated. In this case, the individual would receive $100, would pay 20 percent tax and would have a net of $80. On the other hand, if that individual used a corporation to make an investment that generated $100 of profits, the corporation would pay tax on $100, which would be $20 (20 percent of $100). Then if the corporation wanted to distribute the $80 of earnings to the individual shareholder, the individual shareholder would then be required to pay tax on the $80 received, which would be another $16 of tax paid, leaving the individual shareholder with just $64. So, with an LLC, the individual would be left with $80, and with a C corporation that same person would be left with just $64.

Like the shareholders of a C corporation, the owners/members of an LLC are generally not liable for the debts of the business beyond the extent of their investment. The owners can operate the business with the security of knowing that their personal assets are protected from the entity's creditors. There are exceptions, such as an instance when an individual member personally guarantees the debts or liabilities incurred by the LLC.

Unlike a C corporation, an LLC is treated as a partnership for federal income tax purposes. This can provide a number of important benefits to the owners. Partnership earnings are not subject to an entity-level federal income tax; instead, they "flow-through" to the owners, in proportion to the owners' respective interests in profits, and are reported on the owners' individual tax returns (one level of tax). Thus, earnings of an LLC are taxed only once. An LLC that is taxable as a partnership can also provide special allocations of tax benefits to specific members.

The Advantages of an LLC over an S corporation

Next, John explained the advantages of an LLC over an S corporation. LLCs and S corporations are similar in many ways. From a tax perspective, both are treated as pass-through entities (no double taxation). Both entities provide limited liability to the owners of the business.

The LLC, however, offers far more flexibility than an S corporation. In order to be considered an S corporation, a company must meet the following requirements:

- The entity must not have more than 100 shareholders
- Shareholders must be US citizens or residents, and must be natural persons, so corporate shareholders, partnerships, and multi-member LLCs are excluded
- The entity must have only one class of stock
- Profits and losses must be allocated to shareholders proportionately to each one's interest in the company
- Corporate formalities must be followed

Since an IRA is a trust and not a natural person, an IRA would not be an eligible shareholder for purposes of establishing an S corporation. Therefore, the only real option for establishing an investment vehicle for an IRA is the LLC or C corporation.

However, from a non-IRA perspective, the one nice feature of using an S corporation is that if you are self-employed you can generally reduce your social security income tax. As a self-employed person, you usually have to pay higher social security and Medicare taxes, collectively known as self-employment taxes, than if you were an employee of a company. But if you organize your business as an S corporation, you can classify some of your income as salary and some as a distribution. You'll still be liable for self-employment taxes on the salary portion of your income, but you'll just pay ordinary income tax on the distribution portion. Depending on how you divide your income, you could save a substantial amount of self-employment taxes just by converting to an S corporation. (Note: The amount of salary you take is something the IRS will look closely at.)

LLCs Are Under No Such Restrictions

To sum it up, many tax professionals believe it is better to use an LLC over an S corporation because an LLC:

- Has no restrictions on the type and number of classes of ownership interests
- Can own stock of another entity or corporation
- Is more flexible in structure and organization
- Is more flexible with respect to distributions of available cash and the allocation of net profits and net losses
- Is more flexible with respect to termination
- Is more flexible with respect to transfer of interests in the LLC

Rich nodded when John had finished talking.

"I really like all the features of an LLC," Rich said, "and I can see why so many new businesses and IRA investors use it as an investment vehicle.

What are the costs associated with establishing a self-directed IRA LLC vs. a custodian-controlled self-directed IRA?"

"I love the way you think," John said. "These need to be really practical decisions."

John started by talking about the custodian-controlled self-directed IRA. The majority of full-service IRA trust companies will generally charge a fee to open and administer the self-directed IRA account, either have a flat annual fee or an annual fee based on the value of the self-directed IRA account. In addition, some of these self-directed IRA trust companies will also include a fee per self-directed IRA transaction. Remember, with a custodian-controlled self-directed IRA account the custodian is actively involved in the papering and execution of the transaction, which is time-consuming and does take a degree of effort on the side of the custodian. It is for this reason that full-service custodian fees tend to be higher than when you use a checkbook control structure.

"How high does it get?" Rich asked.

"For example," John explained, "if you will be investing between $100,000 and $199,000 of IRA funds initially, the average full-service IRA custodian fee will be between $400 and $699 depending on the custodian. These fees might be higher if you are doing multiple investments. If your self-directed IRA account gained in value and went above $200,000, then the average full-service self-directed IRA custodian fee would be between $500 and $850 a year. Again, these fees would probably increase depending on the custodian you choose and whether you do multiple investments. All fees are taken from your IRA account."

"Why am I paying so much if the account is self-directed?" Rich asked. "After all, I'm the one directing the custodian to make the investment, and the custodian doesn't provide any investment advice or even serve as fiduciary of my IRA account."

"Right," John said. "But the fees your IRA pays allow the IRA custodian to properly establish your IRA account, maintain it, direct your IRA investments, and administer the IRA account. For example, if you directed the IRA custodian to make a real estate investment on behalf of your IRA, the IRA custodian needs to review and sign all real estate transaction documents.

The custodian will then need to process your investment direction and send the funds to the appropriate place to purchase the real estate. On an annual basis, the IRA custodian will then be required to complete and file IRS Form 5498—IRA Contribution Information—which provides the IRS with updated valuation information on your IRA. In addition, the IRA custodian will be required to report to the IRS all IRA contributions and distributions as well as any Roth IRA conversions made during the year. That's why, even if you will be the one selecting your investment and directing the custodian to make the investment, the IRA custodian will be somewhat involved in the establishment of the self-directed IRA account, the self-directed IRA transaction process, as well as in the annual administration of the account. So in reality, if you have $200,000 in your self-directed IRA and elected to use the custodian to make the self-directed IRA investment, you would be paying approximately 0.5 percent of your account value each year in fees. That may or may not seem fair to you, but that is generally what the cost will be to make self-directed IRA investments through a custodian."

"Okay. What about the checkbook control self-directed IRA LLC structure?" Rich asked.

"Right," John said. "As you may recall, with a checkbook control self-directed IRA LLC structure, the IRA investment activity is happening at the LLC level and not at the IRA custodian level. For example, once your IRA funds have been transferred to the IRA custodian, that IRA custodian would then invest the funds into an LLC in return for a 100 percent interest in the LLC. Procedurally the funds are then sent from the custodian to the LLC bank account where the manager of the IRA LLC has control over the LLC assets. From the local LLC bank account, the IRA manager, typically the IRA holder, can make the investment by check or wire transfer. Because all the investment activity is happening at the LLC level and not the IRA custodian level, overall the fees for using an IRA custodian for a checkbook control self-directed IRA LLC is typically less expensive than a custodian-controlled self-directed IRA. The reason is quite simple—the checkbook control IRA custodian does less work. Once the IRA funds have been invested in the LLC in return for ownership in the LLC, all investment activity happens at the LLC level. In other words, the IRA holder does not need to go through the IRA custodian to complete the IRA LLC investment. As manager of the LLC, the IRA holder can simply make the investment by check or wire straight from the IRA LLC bank account. The IRA custodian is not required to approve the investment and is not involved in any facet of the transaction, including the preparation and execution of any of the investment documentation, as well as the funding of the transaction. The majority of the IRA custodians in the market that work with checkbook control self-directed IRA LLC accounts charge a flat fee that is not based on account value of transactions. The average IRA custodian fee for the first year fee for establishing a checkbook control self-directed IRA LLC is generally around $199 to $250, and after year one the fee typically drops to an average of between $135 and $199. The initial fee is typically a little higher because of the need to establish the self-directed IRA account, which is a onetime event."

"That sound a lot more self-directed" Rich said.

"Yes," John agreed. "I can go through the costs for establishing an LLC for your self-directed IRA and some ancillary costs for the structure, but what do you think? Is using an LLC for your self-directed IRA investment something you want to pursue?"

"I think so," Rich said. "Because I plan on making multiple real estate investments and making some hard money loans and possible even some tax liens, the fees are not as important to me as the fact that I will be able to make investments more quickly and have a bit more control over my IRA funds. I'm not saying that the savings in fees aren't important— saving $300 to $400 a year is really nice considering it adds up to over $3,000 if I keep the account for ten years. But the ability to make investments quickly from the comfort of a local bank by check or wire wins the day for me."

"That makes sense," John said. "Now let's talk about where you want to form you LLC. What state do you expect to buy real estate in at the outset?"

"I know I'll start off in Texas," Rich said. "But I can see myself moving to other states and doing hard money loans and possible tax liens wherever opportunities are best. Why is the state so important?"

"Well, if you're buying real estate," John said, "I definitely recommend you form the LLC in the state where the real estate will be located to save on having to pay multiple filing fees. A state actually deems the LLC to be engaged in a trade or business if it owns property in that state. For example, if you own property in New York via an LLC, that state will deem you to be engaged in a trade or business and you would have to register the LLC with the state. If you formed the LLC in New York, that would not be an issue, but if you formed the LLC in another state such as Delaware, then you would have to register your Delaware LLC as a foreign LLC in New York and pay New York fees. Then you could avail your LLC of the limited liability protection afforded by using an LLC. Taking this a step further, if you, for example, bought real estate in New York with a foreign LLC—let's say the LLC was formed in New Jersey—and there was a claim against the LLC, the plaintiff can try to argue that no limited liability protection existed because the LLC was not registered in New York and thus not able to avail itself of the New York limited liability laws."

"So, the decision of where to form the LLC can have a financial impact on my IRA," Rich said.

"Exactly," John said. "For example, California imposes an $800 minimum franchise fee on every LLC doing business in the state. So, if you will not be buying real estate in California, then I would form the LLC in another state, such as Wyoming or Nevada. The residence of the IRA owner is not necessarily relevant to where the LLC should be formed because the LLC will be owned by the IRA and not the individual IRA holder. So, in your case, Rich, since you will be purchasing real estate with your IRA LLC in Texas, I would form your LLC in Texas. That way you won't incur any additional LLC formation or annual fees."

"I have read a lot about people forming LLCs in Delaware, Nevada, and Wyoming," Rich said. "Should I think about this for my IRA?"

"In general," John began, "states such as Delaware, Nevada, or Wyoming are really popular for LLC formation purposes for a number of reasons. In the case of Delaware, the best reason for forming an LLC is that LLC laws are considered well-established. Experts think Delaware is very pro company management. It also has a separate court system, the Court of Chancery, which is a court of equity and not a court of law. As a court of equity, there are no juries, and all cases are heard by judges, called chancellors. Delaware has many years of case law, and this provides a lot of certainty to company management and their counsel when making business decisions. Delaware also does not have any state tax and is considered to have very strong confidentiality protection for its members. For example, the Delaware Articles of Formation generally do not ask for the members and managers of the LLC and only ask for the name and address of the registered agent, which can be any person or entity with an address in the state. These confidentiality rules are expected to change because the federal government has started putting pressure on Delaware and some other states over concerns of terrorism funding and the ability to identify the owners of certain entities."

"Amazing," Rich said, "that a state can have such a different tradition."

"Yes," John said. "Like Delaware, Nevada and Wyoming do not have state taxes and also share similar confidentiality characteristics. Now, if you were forming an entity that you would own personally or were looking to establish a fund that would attract foreign investors, then I would suggest considering Delaware. That's because the LLC will be owned by your IRA and not you personally. IRAs, as I will explain, are protected from personal bankruptcy and, in most states, protected from creditor attack, so confidentiality is not as important. Also, IRAs don't pay income tax so state tax exemption is also not as important as you might initially think."

"Okay," Rich said, "that makes sense. So if I am buying real estate in Texas, forming the LLC in Texas is the most cost-effective approach. What about if I was buying precious metals or just making hard money loans?"

"In general, you should form the LLC in the state where the LLC will be conducting business or, in the case of an IRA, making the investment," John said. "Like real estate, if the business is being conducted in State A and you will be using an LLC then the LLC should generally be registered to do business in State A. But if you form the LLC in State B, then the LLC must register as a foreign LLC in State A in order for it to avail itself of the limited liability protection in the state. So the question then becomes, what happens if the activity in the state does not rise to the level of a trade or business, such as buying stocks, holding precious metals, or making a loan? Well, if you were doing this activity personally and not using IRA funds, then you could technically form the LLC in any state and then operate your investment activity as you see fit since the state where you are operating will likely not deem that activity to be a trade or business."

"So you pay taxes where you do business regardless?" Rich asked.

"Exactly," John said. "From a state tax perspective, where you form your LLC for personal business purposes is not as relevant because the state where you perform the activity will tax you on the income generated in the state. For example, if you operate an online business in New York, even if you have established a Delaware LLC for your business, because the income is being generated or sourced in New York, the state of New York will tax you on that income. Of course, you have to pay federal income tax on the income no matter where it is earned."

"Can I form the LLC myself since I have formed LLCs before?" Rich asked.

"This is a good question that I get a lot from clients," John replied. "Technically you can form your own LLC and you do not have to be an attorney to form an LLC in the majority of states. However, when it comes to an LLC owned by a retirement account, there are several important requirements that must be satisfied in order for the LLC to be established correctly. In addition, the majority of self-directed IRA custodians require that an attorney or tax professional sign off on the establishment of the LLC and the drafting of the self-directed IRA LLC operating agreement. Furthermore, as a disqualified person, forming your own LLC could be considered a prohibited transaction under the IRS rules, as we will discuss in greater detail later on. All in all, I don't think it's a great idea for a nontax professional to form their own self-directed IRA LLC. With the establishment fees so insignificant I just don't feel it's worth the risk of establishing the LLC incorrectly by, for example, identifying the LLC as member-managed instead of manager-managed. Don't worry; I will touch on the whole LLC establishment process in more detail shortly."

"So how does that all work for a self-directed IRA?" Rich asked.

"Since an IRA does not pay income tax," John said, "choosing the right state of formation depends on the type of activity being performed. As I said, real estate is treated as a business activity by most states, so even though an IRA would not be subject to tax on income or gains generated by the real estate from a federal tax perspective, gaining limited liability protection for the asset would require you to form the LLC in the state where the real estate is located or to file an LLC that was formed in a different state as a foreign LLC in that state. Some people suggest always forming the LLC in a state such as Delaware or Nevada, and we talked about the reasons for this, but that would require you to incur dual-state filing fees—the state filing fees from Delaware, for example, as well as the fees associated with establishing the LLC in the state where the real estate is located. Also, forming the LLC in a state such as Wyoming that has no state income tax or a state such as Missouri that has no LLC annual fees, will not allow you to circumvent any annual LLC franchise or state fees associated with the LLC where the real estate is located. So, if you established a self-directed IRA LLC in Missouri but bought property in California, you would be required to register the Missouri LLC to do business in California and would become subject to the California annual franchise fee. Again, because owning real estate by an LLC will deem that the LLC be treated as engaged in a trade or business in the state, even if your IRA will own the real estate and you consider it a passive asset, the states do not and will be required to register a foreign LLC to do business in that state if you want to avail yourself of the limited liability protection."

"What happens if I don't care about limited liability protection?" Rich asked. "Do I still have to register a foreign LLC in the state when I buy real estate?"

"Yes," John said. "Most likely the title insurance company or attorney handling your real estate transaction will want to see paperwork showing that you are authorized to transact business in the state. So even if you don't want to form the LLC in the state where you will be buying the real estate or register an LLC formed in another state as a foreign LLC in the state, you will likely be required to do so in any event in order to close on your real estate transaction."

"So explain to me how things change if I don't buy real estate and will only do hard money loans or purchase precious metals?" Rich asked.

Where to Form Your IRA LLC

"Right. Let's get back on track. As I said, the determination of whether you will need to open your LLC in the state where the investment will be made is based on the actual investment. Owning real estate in an LLC will require you to form the LLC in the state where the real estate will be located or file the LLC to register as a foreign LLC in that state. Some of the other popular investments typically made with a self-directed IRA include these."

John showed Rich a list:

- Mortgages
- Mortgage pools
- Deeds
- Private loans
- Tax liens
- Private businesses
- Limited Liability Companies
- Limited Liability Partnerships
- Private placements
- Precious metals and certain coins
- Stocks, bonds, mutual funds
- Foreign currencies

"As you can see," John continued, "these are all passive types of investment activities that would take a significant amount of activity to turn the investment into a business. For example, it would take a significant amount of activity for the IRS to make the claim that you weren't a stock investor but a stock trader. The same goes for buying and selling precious metals or making loans. Most self-directed IRA investors will make a couple of loans a year, which is clearly not a business. In order for your hard money loan investments to turn into a lending business it would require a lot more than a couple of loans a year. The IRS doesn't offer a clear number as it is generally based on the facts and circumstances involved. However, the IRS does offer some guidance as it pertains to stock investments versus stock trading as a business, which is helpful when examining whether a self-directed IRA investment would be considered a business."

John explained that, to be engaged in business as a trader in securities, you must meet all of the following conditions:

- You must seek to profit from daily market movements in the prices of securities and not from dividends, interest, or capital appreciation
- Your activity must be substantial
- You must carry on the activity with continuity and regularity.

And he told Rich to consider the following facts and circumstances in determining if an activity is a securities trading business:

- Typical holding periods for securities bought and sold
- The frequency and dollar amount of your trades during the year
- The extent to which you pursue the activity to produce income for a livelihood
- The amount of time you devote to the activity.

"So, if the nature of your trading activities does not qualify as a business," Rich said, "you are considered an investor, and not a trader. Right?"

John nodded. "I've worked with thousands of self-directed IRA clients and I have yet to come across a self-directed IRA client whose investment activities could be deemed to rise to the level of a trade or business. This applies to stock, currencies, options, hard money loans, and so on."

"So," Rich said, "since a self-directed IRA does not pay tax on any income or gains, why would we care if the activity is treated as an investment or business?"

"That's actually an important distinction for two reasons," John said. "The first is where you form your LLC. If the investment would not rise to the level of a trade or business, then you can technically form your LLC in any state. This means that even if you live in California and are buying stocks or making hard money loans with your retirement funds, you can form the IRA LLC in any other state. You'll see why that matters when we talk about state filing fees and annual fee requirements. But, for example, California imposes an $800 minimum franchise fee on all LLCs doing business in the state. So, if you bought real estate in California, you would be required to form the LLC in California. But if you were just buying stocks or investing in a hedge fund, then you would not be required to form the LLC in California, potentially saving you at least $800 a year, which really adds up."

"So, does it matter where I live when figuring out where to form my self-directed IRA LLC?" Rich asked.

"Well, remember," John said, "when it comes to a self-directed IRA LLC, the LLC is actually owned by your IRA and not you personally. So, your personal residence is not very relevant when it comes to determining the state of formation for your IRA LLC. What's more relevant is the type of investments that will be done in your self-directed IRA LLC. For example, real estate investments would merit you forming the LLC in the state where the real estate will be located, but if you were investing in options or a private business, then forming the LLC in any state of your choosing would be an option."

"You mentioned a private business," Rich said, "I know you'll be explaining the IRS-prohibited transaction rules in greater detail later on, but assuming I am not personally involved in the business and nor is any disqualified person, do I have to form the self-directed IRA LLC in the state where the business will be located?"

"When you're just a passive investor in the underlying private business your IRA LLC will be investing in, the private business investment will be treated as any other passive investment, such as stocks or precious metals, which will allow you to form the self-directed IRA LLC in any state—not necessarily the state where the underlying private business is located. That means that if you will be investing in a company that does business in New York, your self-directed IRA LLC can generally be formed in any state and will not be required to register to do business in New York. As a passive investor of a New York company, your LLC will not be considered to be engaged in a trade or business in New York."

"I think I understand," Rich said. "If I will be buying real estate with my IRA I should form the LLC in the state where the LLC will be located. On the other hand, if I'll be investing more in passive assets, such as precious metals, private businesses, or hard money loans, then I could technically form the LLC in any state, although I should be wary of states like California, which have high annual fees."

"Exactly. You've got it."

"So what are the fees like for establishing an LLC?" Rich asked.

John handed Rich a report that he had prepared, that as of January 1, 2015, provided all the state LLC filing fees and annual report or franchise fees (see Exhibit D). "I think this will give you a good foundation for understanding the costs involved in establishing an LLC."

"Wow, thanks, John, that's really helpful," Rich said. "It looks like there are quite a few states that do not have any annual fees. What happens if I don't have an address in a state I want to establish an LLC in? How can I get the LLC formed?"

"In order to form the LLC in a state, the LLC needs to have a registered agent in that state," John said. "Any person can serve as the registered agent. All you need is an address. In fact, there's a whole industry of registered agent companies that will sell you an address in the state. The registered agent receives service of process at a legal address within the jurisdiction where legal documents may be served during business hours. It is the registered agent's duty to then forward that service of process to the entity's designated contact, usually the company's legal team."

"I had no idea that sort of thing existed," Rich said.

"I know, right? The registered agent also receives official government documents including franchise tax notices and annual report forms. Registered agents may also notify business entities whether or not they are in 'good standing' or not."

"So, all I need to do is hire a registered agent company that will provide me with an address in the state where I want to form the LLC," Rich said.

"Yup," John said. "The registered agent fee is typically between $100 and $200 for the year. I put together a few cost scenarios using general market pricing so you can calculate whether the checkbook control self-directed IRA LLC solution makes sense for you. I will cover this again later, but all self-directed IRA fees should be paid with IRA funds and no personal funds should be used."

"Great," Rich said.

Together, they looked at some examples.

Self-Directed IRA Establishment Fees

Example 1:

Jim, who resides in Missouri, wants to use his retirement funds to invest in real estate and is debating between using a checkbook control self-directed IRA LLC and a self-directed IRA without checkbook control. Jim has $150,000 in his IRA that he wishes to use for real estate.

If Jim selects Custodian X as the custodian—a full service self-directed IRA custodian who does not work with checkbook control—Jim will be paying approximately $575 each year for a custodian plus will he require custodian approval to purchase or sell a real estate investment. Over a four-year period, Jim would pay approximately $2,300 to Custodian X for custodian services.

On the other hand, if Jim elects to use a self-directed IRA LLC checkbook control structure, he would pay approximately $1,000 in year one, including the LLC setup. However, for every year thereafter Jim would only be required to pay approximately $150 per year for maintenance of the checkbook control structure. Thus, over a four-year period, Jim would be required to pay approximately $1,600, a saving of at least $700, plus Jim would get the ability to have more control over his retirement funds.

Example 2:

Beth, who resides in Michigan, wants to use her retirement funds to invest in precious metals and is debating between using a checkbook control self-directed IRA LLC and a self-directed IRA without checkbook control. Beth has approximately $280,000 in retirement funds that she wants to use for precious metals and other alternative assets.

If Beth selects Custodian Y as the custodian—a full-service self-directed IRA custodian who does not work with checkbook control—she would pay approximately $675 each year for a custodian plus she would require custodian approval to purchase or sell precious metals. Over a six-year period, Beth would pay approximately $4,050 to Custodian Y for custodian services.

Alternatively, if Beth elects to use a self-directed IRA LLC checkbook control structure, she would pay approximately $1,000 in year one. However, for every year thereafter she would only be required to pay approximately $150 per year for maintenance of the checkbook control structure. Thus, over a six-year period, Beth would be required to pay approximately $1,900, saving approximately $2,150.

Example 3:

Dan, who resides in Kentucky, wants to use his retirement funds to invest in real estate and is debating between using a checkbook control self-directed IRA LLC and a self-directed IRA without checkbook control. Dan has $200,000 in retirement funds that he wants to use to buy real estate.

If Dan selects Custodian Z as the self-directed IRA custodian without checkbook control, Dan will be paying approximately $600 each year for a custodian, plus he will require custodian approval to purchase or sell a real estate investment. Over a five-year period, Dan would pay approximately $3,000 to Custodian Z for custodian services.

Alternatively, if Dan elects to establish a self-directed IRA LLC checkbook control structure, he would pay approximately $1,000 in year one. However, for every year thereafter, Dan would only be required to pay approximately $150 per year for maintenance of the checkbook control structure. Thus, over a five-year period, Jim would be required to pay approximately $1,750, a savings of approximately $1,250.

Example 4:
Lisa, who resides in Iowa, wants to use her retirement funds to invest in tax liens and is debating between using a checkbook control self-directed IRA LLC and a self-directed IRA without checkbook control. Lisa expects to use approximately $125,000 of her retirement funds to purchase real estate.

If Lisa selects Custodian A as the custodian, Lisa will be paying approximately $450 each year for a custodian and will require custodian approval to make each tax lien purchase. Over a ten-year period, Lisa would pay approximately $4,500 to Custodian A for custodian services.

Alternatively, if Lisa elects to establish a self-directed IRA LLC checkbook control structure, Lisa would pay approximately $1,000 in year one. However, for every year thereafter, she would only be required to pay approximately $150 per year for maintenance of the checkbook control structure. Thus, over a ten-year period, Lisa would be required to pay approximately $2,500, a savings of $2,000.

Checkbook Control It Is

"Very interesting," Rich said. "It seems that not only will the checkbook control self-directed IRA LLC offer me the ability to have more control over my IRA investments and make investments quickly, it will also save me a good deal of money over the long run. And that will really pay off since the funds I would be saving are IRA funds and would be growing tax-deferred or tax-free in the case of a Roth IRA."

"You got it," John said. "I think that if you will be buying real estate as well as doing other types of alterative asset investments with your self-directed IRA, the checkbook control structure has more advantages."

Checkbook Control IRA Disadvantages

"So what are some of the disadvantages of using checkbook control? Rich asked.

"There always are some," John said. "The two main disadvantages of using checkbook control are the up-front costs and the level of control you gain over your retirement assets. We've already gone through a number of scenarios that showed an approximation of some of the up-front costs that you would likely need to incur if you elected to use a checkbook control self-directed IRA LLC structure. However, the scenarios also showed that after year one, if you expected to keep the checkbook control structure open at least a few years, it actually does pay for itself. In addition to the up-front costs, the checkbook control structure provides you an enormous amount of control and freedom over your retirement funds. Ultimately, after the self-directed IRA LLC structure has been set up, you, as manager of the LLC, will have control over your retirement assets and will be able to make an investment by simply writing a check or executing a wire transfer. In other words, you'll be able to make IRA LLC investments on your own without seeking the consent or approval or the IRA custodian or any person. What this means is that you will have total control over the investments you make. The custodian will not know if you are buying stocks, real estate, or precious metals with your IRA LLC assets."

"That part sounds great, but I bet that level of control also comes with a lot of responsibility," Rich said.

"It does," John answered. "The IRS has set forth numerous prohibited transaction rules that restrict an IRA holder or a disqualified person in making certain types of investments. I'll go through those rules with you in greater detail later on, but they are very important, and violating them can have severe tax consequences. In addition, recently the Securities and Exchange Commission (SEC) issued an investor alert to warn investors of the potential risks of fraud associated with investing through self-directed individual retirement accounts. The SEC notes that there has been a recent increase in reports or complaints of fraudulent investment schemes that utilized a self-directed IRA as a key feature. Because of the enormous amount of freedom and control the checkbook control self-directed IRA LLC provides you, it is important to do your due diligence and make sure you understand the types of investments you are considering and the risks associated with them. This is especially important if you will be investing with an investment promoter or marketer. I'll be happy to go through some tips I've learned to help protect your self-directed IRA funds from fraud."

Self-Directed IRS Reporting Requirements

"You mentioned that with the checkbook control self-directed IRA LLC structure," Rich said, "I'll be able to make investments without needing the consent of the custodian. So how does the custodian know what I am investing in and report it to the IRS?"

"It may be hard to believe," John said, "but as of 2014 the IRA custodian was not required to report to the IRS the type of investments you were making. When it comes to IRS reporting for a self-directed IRA, every IRA administrator or custodian is required to complete and file IRS Form 5498. That reports your total annual contributions to an IRA account and identifies the type of retirement account you have, such as a traditional IRA, Roth IRA, SEP IRA, or SIMPLE IRA. Form 5498 also reports the amounts that you roll over or transfer from other types of retirement accounts into your IRA. The custodian of your IRA, typically the bank or other institution that manages your account, will mail a copy of this form to both you and the IRS. Form 5498 requests information pertaining to the IRA account, including the name and address of the IRA custodian, the amount of any IRA contributions or distributions taken during the year, and most specifically, the value of the IRA account as of December 31 of the prior year. However, only as of 2015 does IRS Form 5498 request the category of investments being made with the IRA funds. I will address this new change in greater detail a bit later."

"Wow," Rich said. "So, based on Form 5498, the IRS doesn't know the exact IRA investment I am making, only a broad description of the investment category."

"Right," John said. "That's because the intent of the form is to provide the IRS with a summary and overview of the current value of your IRA as well as the amount of contributions and/or distributions taken during the year in order to match those amounts on your individual tax return."

"So," Rich said, "there's no reason the IRS would say, 'He's using a self-directed IRA LLC; let's audit him to see what he's up to.'"

"Not very likely," John said. "That argument against self-directed IRA LLCs doesn't hold water. The IRS has stated that the main purpose of this change is to get a better handle on valuations that are being used for distribution purposes for hard-to-value IRA assets, such as real estate. But it will certainly also provide the IRS with more insight than they have right now in terms of the types of assets that are being purchased with retirement funds. With over 47 million IRAs in the United States and over 90 percent of IRAs invested in traditional assets, such as stocks and mutual funds, coupled with the fact that IRAs do not pay tax, it is not expected that the IRS will begin targeting retirement accounts."

"Well, you've sold me," Rich said. "Based on this conversation, I feel comfortable that the checkbook control self-directed IRA LLC is the right solution for me. What steps should I take to move forward?"

Moving Forward

"The first thing you need to do is open your new self-directed IRA at the custodian of your choice. I'll go through the process in detail right away. Once your new self-directed IRA account has been opened, you then establish your new LLC, which will ultimately be 100 percent owned by your IRA. Once that LLC has been established, a tax ID number for your LLC will need to be acquired. At that point you then need to open a bank account for your new LLC at any local bank of your choice. Finally, once the LLC bank account has been established, your IRA funds can be transferred to the new LLC bank account in return for a 100 percent interest in the LLC. The ownership interest and operations of the LLC are outlined in the LLC operating agreement."

"Sounds very straightforward," Rich said.

"Great," John said. "So let's go through some of the process in more detail."

Establishing a Self-Directed IRA Account

John explained that the first question Rich will need to ask himself is what type of retirement funds he has. In general, it is possible to roll over or transfer any types of retirement funds to a self-directed IRA LLC, including:

- Traditional IRA
- Roth IRA
- SEP
- SIMPLE
- 401(k)
- 403(b)
- Plans for Self-Employed (Keoghs)
- ESOPs
- Money Purchase Pensions Plans

So, Rich will want to know what type of retirement account he will be looking to use in the self-directed IRA structure. For example, will it be a pretax IRA or a 401(k) plan, or is it a Roth IRA or an after-tax 401(k) plan? Also, Rich will need to know whether this is his retirement account or whether it is inherited by a spouse or nonspouse. All this information will be important in terms of helping Rich complete the self-directed IRA account application and open the right self-directed IRA account.

How to Fund a Self-Directed IRA LLC with a Traditional IRA Rollover

In general, a self-directed IRA LLC may be funded by a transfer from another IRA account or through a rollover from an eligible defined contribution plan. Eligible defined contribution plans include qualified 401(k) retirement plans under IRC Section 401(a), 403(a), 403(b), and governmental 457(b) plans.

What Is the Most Common Way to Fund a Self-Directed IRA?

Transfers and rollovers are types of transactions that allow movements of assets between like IRAs—traditional IRA to traditional IRA and Roth IRA to Roth IRA. An IRA transfer is the most common method of funding a self-directed IRA LLC or self-directed Roth IRA.

IRA Transfers to a Self-Directed IRA with a Traditional IRA

An IRA-to-IRA transfer is one of the most common methods of moving assets from one IRA to another. A transfer usually occurs between two separate financial organizations, but a transfer may also occur between IRAs held at the same organization. If an IRA transfer is handled correctly the transfer is not taxable. With an IRA transfer, the IRA holder directs the transfer but does not actually receive the IRA assets. Instead, the transaction is completed by the distributing and receiving financial institutions. In order for the IRA transfer to be tax-free and penalty-free, the IRA holder must not receive the IRA funds in a transfer. Rather, the check must be made payable to the new IRA custodian. Also, there is no reporting or withholding to the IRS on an IRA transfer.

Retirement tax professionals can assist you in funding your self-directed IRA LLC by transferring your current pretax or after-tax IRA funds to your new self-directed IRA or self-directed Roth IRA structure tax-free and penalty-free.

How the Self-Directed IRA Transfer Works

A retirement tax professional will work with you to establish a new self-directed IRA account at a new IRA custodian (i.e., bank or trust company). The new custodian will then, with your consent, request the transfer of IRA assets from your existing IRA custodian in a tax-free and penalty-free IRA transfer. Once the IRA funds are either transferred by wire or check tax-free to the new IRA custodian, the new custodian will be able to invest the IRA assets into the new IRA LLC checkbook control structure. Once the funds have been transferred to the new IRA LLC, you, as manager of the IRA LLC, will have checkbook control over your retirement funds so you can make traditional as well as nontraditional investments tax-free and penalty-free.

Moving 401(k) Plan and Qualified Retirement Plan Assets to a Self-Directed IRA

The 2001 Economic Growth and Tax Relief Reconciliation Act expanded the rollover opportunities between employer-sponsored retirement plans, such as 401(k) plans and IRAs. Since 2002, individuals may roll over both pretax and after-tax 401(k) plan fund assets from 401(a), 403(a), 403(b), and governmental 457(b) plans into a traditional IRA tax-free and penalty-free.

In general, in order to roll over qualified retirement plans to a traditional IRA there must be a plan-triggering event. A plan-triggering event is typically based on the plan documents, but it generally includes the following: (i) the termination of the plan, (ii) the plan participant reaching the age of 59½, or (iii) the plan participant leaving the employer.

A Direct Rollover to a Self-Directed IRA

DIRECT IRA ROLLOVER

Retirement account held at bank, financial institution, credit union, etc.

Retirement account held at bank, financial institution, credit union, etc.

A direct rollover occurs when a plan participant, who has access to his or her retirement funds, moves the eligible qualified retirement plan funds to an IRA custodian. In other words, a direct rollover is between a qualified retirement plan and an IRA, whereas a transfer is between IRA financial institutions. In general, employer 401(k) plan providers must offer the direct rollover option if it is reasonable to anticipate that the total amount of eligible rollover distributions to a recipient for the year would be more than $200.

How to Complete a Direct Rollover

A retirement tax professional will work with you to establish a new self-directed IRA account at a new IRA custodian. With a direct rollover from a defined contribution plan [i.e., 401(k) plan], the plan participant must initiate the direct rollover request. This means the plan participant must request the movement of 401(k) plan funds to the new IRA custodian, not the IRA custodian, as with an IRA transfer. A retirement tax professional will assist you in completing the direct rollover request form that will allow you to move your 401(k), 403(a), 403(b), 457(b), or defined benefit plan assets to your new IRA account.

A direct rollover may be accomplished by any reasonable means of direct payment to an IRA. Regulations state that the reasonable means may include wire, mailing check to new IRA custodian, or mailing check made out to new IRA custodian to plan participant.

Reporting a Direct Rollover

When an individual directly rolls over a qualified retirement plan distribution to a traditional IRA, the employer is generally required to report the distribution on IRS Form 1099-R, using Code G in Box 7, *Direct rollover and rollover contribution*. The receiving IRA administrator would then be required to report the amount as a rollover distribution in Box 2 of IRS Form 5498.

John handed Rich an IRS chart that summarized all the IRA rollover rules (see Exhibit E).

An Indirect Rollover to a Self-Directed IRA

An indirect rollover occurs when the IRA assets or qualified retirement plan assets are moved first to the IRA holder or plan participant before they are ultimately sent to an IRA custodian.

INDIRECT IRA ROLLOVER

Retirement account held at bank, financial institution, credit union, etc.

Retirement account held at bank, financial institution, credit union, etc.

Rollover to new IRA Custodian must be complete within 60 days – only can be done one time every 12 months for all IRA accounts in the aggregate

Sixty-Day Rollover Rule

An individual generally has sixty (60) days from receipt of the eligible rollover distribution to roll the funds into an IRA. The sixty-day period starts the day after the individual receives the distribution. Usually, no exceptions apply to the sixty-day time period. In cases in which the sixty-day period expires on a Saturday, Sunday, or legal holiday, the individual may execute the rollover on the following business day. However, to avoid abuse of the rule, the tax code prescribes that taxpayers can only complete an *indirect* IRA rollover once in a twelve-month period, which the IRS in the past has interpreted to apply to IRAs on an account-by-account basis. In turn, the "separate accounts" treatment of the IRA rollover rule potentially allows taxpayers to chain together multiple IRA rollovers in an attempt circumvent the one-year rule and gain "temporary" use of IRA funds for an extended period of time. Even though IRS Publication 590 seems to suggest that the sixty-day rule would apply to separate IRA accounts, many tax professionals have typically advised clients that the IRS could interpret the rule to apply to all IRAs because of the abuse of the sixty-day distribution rule that could potentially occur,

Low and behold, a recent Tax Court decision clarified how the IRS would interpret the sixty-day rollover rule and whether it would apply to all IRAs or to separate IRAs. In *Bobrow v. Commissioner*, the IRS has shut down the separate IRA rollover strategy altogether. That case arose because a taxpayer botched a version of the sequential separate accounts rollover strategy and drew the IRS's ire in the process. It ended with a finding of guilt for not only botching the rollovers but having the Tax Court (re-) interpret IRC Section 408(d)(3)(B) as well. In the decision, the Tax Court applied the one-year IRA rollover rule to apply *in the aggregate across all IRAs*, invalidating the separate IRA rollover treatment not only for Bobrow but *all taxpayers* as well!

The details are interesting. A tax attorney named Alvan Bobrow took $65,000 out of his traditional IRA account, intending to replace that money within sixty days, as the tax law states, in order to have the transaction treated as an IRA rollover rather than a taxable distribution.

Right before Bobrow repaid the $65,000 to his traditional IRA account, however, he took $65,000 out of a different IRA account. Then, just before the sixty-day period for *that* withdrawal expired, Bobrow's wife took $65,000 out of her traditional IRA, with a $65,000 repayment to Bobrow's second IRA account taking place just days later. Eventually, the Bobrows repaid the wife's IRA withdrawal and took the position that all of the transactions were tax-free IRA rollovers. The IRS disagreed, arguing in part that the nested withdrawals and repayments didn't line up the way the Bobrows contended.

It's also worth noting that Mr. Bobrow could have completed the transfer of funds without doing an indirect rollover. With an IRA transfer between institutions there's no annual limitation on the number of IRA transfers that can be done in a year.

Being a tax attorney, Bobrow chose to represent himself in the Tax Court after the IRS imposed taxes on him and his wife, in light of the multiple indirect IRA rollovers he did in the year in question. Rather than simply saying that Bobrow's serial withdrawals weren't eligible for tax-free IRA rollover status because they came in quick succession and were nested within each other, the Tax Court suggested that in *all* instances taxpayers are limited to one tax-free indirect IRA rollover per twelve-month period. That broader finding conflicted with the IRS's own guidance in its publication 590 on IRAs, which contemplates situations in which completely unrelated transactions using multiple IRAs *could* all qualify for tax-free IRA rollover treatment.

In the aftermath of the Bobrow case, the IRS has now issued IRS Announcement 2014–15, stating that it will acquiesce to the Tax Court decision, update its proposed regulations and publication 590, and issue new proposed regulations soon that will definitively apply the one-year IRA rollover rule on an IRA-aggregated basis going forward.

Now, an individual receiving an eligible rollover distribution may rollover the entire amount received or any portion of the amount received. The amount of the eligible rollover distribution that is not rolled over to an IRA is generally included in the individual's gross income and could be subject to a 10 percent early distribution penalty if the individual is under the age of 59½.

So what does all this mean? It is important to remember that this sixty-day rule applies only to indirect rollovers, in other words to funds that are not being transferred directly between retirement account custodians (i.e., financial institution, bank, trust company, etc.). When funds are moved from retirement account to retirement account, that's considered a direct rollover or IRA transfer and there is no sixty-day limit or limit on the amount of direct rollovers that can be done in a year.

John handed Rich a piece of paper that summarized the direct and indirect rollover rules:

The one-IRA-per-twelve-month (indirect rollover) limit does not apply to:

- rollovers from traditional IRAs to Roth IRAs (conversions)
- trustee-to-trustee transfers from one IRA another IRA
- IRA-to-plan rollovers
- plan-to-IRA rollovers
- plan-to-plan rollovers

How Does the Sixty-Day Rollover Work with a Self-Directed IRA?

If a plan participant ever elects to take a sixty-day rollover from a checkbook control self-directed IRA LLC, the funds would need to go from the LLC account to the IRA custodian and then he or she would request the rollover of the funds from the IRA custodian. This is important because if he or she took the funds from the LLC bank account directly and used them personally that would likely trigger a prohibited transaction, which would have a significant tax implication.

Sixty-Day Rollover from an Employer Retirement Plan

In general, when a plan participant requests a distribution from an employer qualified retirement plan, IRS rules require the employer to withhold 20 percent from the amount of the eligible rollover distribution. Just to be clear, the 20 percent withholding rule only applies to indirect rollovers and not direct rollovers. As a reminder, an indirect rollover occurs when plan funds are transferred directly to the plan participant first and not a financial institution. If an individual receives an eligible rollover distribution and then elects to roll over the assets to an IRA custodian within sixty days, the individual can make up the 20 percent withheld by the employer retirement plan provider for federal income tax purposes.

Employer-sponsored retirement plans are required to withhold at a rate of 20 percent on all eligible rollover distributions of taxable funds or assets, unless the participants elects to directly rollover the distribution to an IRA or to another eligible retirement plan. In other words, when taking an indirect rollover from an employer qualified retirement plan, the employer is required to withhold 20 percent of the eligible rollover distribution. The 20 percent withholding requirement is not applicable for IRA-to-IRA transfers or for direct rollover distributions (between financial institutions).

Reporting Indirect Rollovers

When an individual takes an indirect distribution from an employer-sponsored retirement plan, such as a 401(k) plan, the employer generally makes the check payable to the individual, even if the individual intends to roll the funds over to an IRA. The employer is required to withhold 20 percent from the eligible rollover distribution since the funds will be rolled to the plan participant and not directly to the IRA or qualified retirement plan custodian. The employer (payer) then reports the indirect distribution on IRS Form 1099-R, using the applicable distribution Code (1, 4, or 7). If the funds are deposited with an IRA custodian within sixty days, the receiving IRA custodian would report the rollover assets on IRS Form 5498 as a rollover contribution in Box 2.

In Rich's case, Rich will be doing a direct rollover as he will be transferring pretax retirement funds from an existing retirement account to a traditional IRA. Because these funds are Rich's, they will not be treated as an inherited IRA, which would require a separate IRA account application if the IRA was inherited from a nonspouse. On the other hand, if the inherited IRA were inherited from a deceased spouse, Rich would have the opportunity to turn the IRA into his own IRA. This information is relevant for purposes of completing the new self-directed IRA application process.

Establishing a Self-Directed IRA Account

In general, regardless of which self-directed IRA custodian you work with, you will need to complete several self-directed IRA account application documents. The following is a summary of the primary documents you will need to complete.

Self-Directed IRA Account Application Form

This form will help establish your self-directed IRA account with the IRA custodian you select. If you will be opening more than one IRA account— for example a Roth IRA or an inherited IRA from a nonspouse—you need to complete a separate application form. In the account application, you need to designate the type of IRA you will be opening as well as your personal information. Also, the application typically includes language acknowledging the custodian's limited responsibilities, including the fact that the account will be a self-directed account and that the custodian has no fiduciary responsibilities. You will also include details on how you will be funding your self-directed IRA, for example, whether it is via a contribution, rollover, or transfer. In addition, you will need to include a photocopy of your driver's license.

Expense Payment Request Form

The purpose of this form is so the IRA custodian you select can pay an adviser in connection with the establishment of your self-directed IRA LLC structure. Since the self-directed IRA LLC setup involves your IRA and not you, your IRA should pay all IRA establishment fees. No personal funds should be used for the payment of any self-directed IRA establishment fees, including the LLC fee, as well as the IRA account setup fee.

Representative Authorization Form

This form permits your tax adviser to contact the IRA custodian you select and discuss the status of your account (e.g., have they released your money to your LLC bank account?) on your behalf. Note: This authorization can be rescinded by you at any time and will not need to provide your tax adviser with access to the IRA custodian account.

Beneficiary Designation Form

This form allows you to designate a primary and contingent beneficiary for your IRA account in the case of your death. Note: Typically a spouse, if applicable, is designated as the primary beneficiary. In community property states, such as California, most custodians will require that a spouse be appointed as primary beneficiary of the account. To complete the beneficiary designation form:

- Include the name of the primary beneficiary and contingent beneficiary, if applicable
- Sign and date the designation (spouse signature is also required if spouse is not designated as primary beneficiary)

IRA LLC Agreement Form

This form is used exclusively for those who wish to do a checkbook control self-directed IRA LLC structure. Because of the amount of freedom the structure offers the IRA holder, it is important for the IRA custodian to have some protection in case the IRA holder engages in an IRS-prohibited transaction. In other words, since the IRA account holder will be the manager of the IRA LLC and will thus have checkbook control over the investment of the assets, the IRA LLC agreement form serves as a form of defense for the custodian against the IRA client claiming a prohibited transaction was the responsibility of the custodian.

Internet Access Request Form

This form allows you to check the status of your IRA services account online (i.e., to view funds).

Transfer Authorization Form

This form is used by the IRA custodian to request a transfer of your IRA funds from your current IRA custodian. For example, if your IRA is with Vanguard, the transfer authorization form will be submitted to Vanguard by the new IRA custodian. The form will let your old IRA custodian (i.e.,

Vanguard) know that you wish to transfer your IRA funds to a new custodian and will provide Vanguard with all the transfer information. The IRA transfer is a direct custodian-to-custodian transfer and there is no tax or penalty on the transfer. If you have non-IRA funds, such as a 401(k) plan or 403(b), the transfer authorization form is not required since, when it comes to non-IRA funds, you, as the plan participant, would need to initiate the rollover of the funds. You would likely need to contact the administrator of the plan and submit a document, which indicates the information necessary to move the funds to the new IRA custodian.

We will discuss the rollover rules in greater detail at a later point, but, typically, in order to get access to your non-IRA funds for rollover purposes, your plan must allow for the rollover of the funds out of the plan. For most 401(k)-qualified retirement plans, there needs to be a triggering even that allows the plan participant to gain access to the funds. In general, there are three main triggering events: (1) you leave your job with the company or agency that adopted the plan, (2) you reach the age of 59½, or (3) the plan is terminated by the adopting employer. In Rich's case, since he will just be moving IRA funds, he will not need to satisfy any 401(k) plan triggering rules and is free to transfer IRA assets tax-free, by way of a direct transfer to a new IRA custodian, at his convenience.

Also, it is possible to do as many direct IRA transfers as you want in a year. You are not restricted to the one-rollover-every-twelve-months rule because that only applies to indirect rollovers, which covers situations in which you take control of the IRA funds and the funds are not being transferred directly between IRA custodians. With most IRA custodians, you will need to attach a copy of your recent IRA statement from the IRA custodian where the IRA is being held. In general, the entire statement must be provided. The statement must have your name, account number, custodian name and address, and type of account.

Investment Authorization Form
This form authorizes the IRA custodian you have selected to release your IRA funds to your new IRA LLC checking account, which you will have

opened up by that time. Once your LLC account has been opened at the bank of your choosing and you have notified your tax adviser or the IRA custodian, you submit this form with the appropriate IRA LLC bank account information to the IRA custodian so that they can transfer your IRA funds by check or wire to your new LLC bank account. Since the IRA will be the sole owner(s) of your LLC, the investment authorization form serves as the form that documents the IRA's investment in the LLC. The LLC operating agreement will document the IRA's ownership in the LLC. We will discuss the IRA LLC operating agreement in more detail shortly.

Naming Your LLC

Rich leaned back in his chair and stretched, then got right back at it. He felt energized by the progress they were making.

"Okay, John," he said, "that sounds good. I'll get all my IRA account info and we can work together to complete my new self-directed IRA account application. I'm guessing the paperwork is pretty straightforward. So I assume that while we are completing the paperwork you'll be able to file the LLC articles of formation with the state?"

"Yes," John said. "While we're working on establishing the self-directed IRA custodian account, I'll work on establishing your self-directed IRA LLC. But in order for me to start working on establishing your LLC, I'll need answers to a few key questions."

He showed Rich a list.

Name of LLC

In general, a self-directed IRA LLC may use any permissible name that is not the same as or deceivingly similar to existing corporations, partnerships, limited partnerships, or other LLCs. When forming your self-directed IRA LLC, the state will notify you whether the name you have selected is available. Some states such as Utah even make you reserve the name of your LLC before proceeding with the LLC formation process.

Depending on the state statute, certain words or abbreviations (e.g., "limited liability company," "LLC") are generally required to be included in the name of the LLC. In selecting a name for your self-directed IRA LLC, be careful to include required language and avoid any prohibited language identified by the statute for the state in which the LLC is to be formed and the state in which the LLC is to operate.

Some statutes prohibit the use of certain words in the name of the LLC that indicate or imply that the LLC is organized for a purpose other than the purpose stated in its articles of organization. The name may not contain words stating or implying the LLC is connected with a government agency and may not suggest a charitable or nonprofit nature. Statutes often prohibit the use of specific words such as "corporation," "association," and "trust." A statute may also prohibit a name that misrepresents the geographic location or origin of the LLC. The use of a prohibited name will not violate the existence of the LLC, but the LLC may be blocked from using the name.

In the case of a self-directed IRA LLC, the question is often asked whether the name of the LLC must include the abbreviation "IRA." The answer is no—there are no federal or state rules that specifically govern the creation of self-directed IRA LLCs. Accordingly, you are not required to include the abbreviation "IRA" in the name of the self-directed IRA LLC, but you are permitted to do so. Most people tend to include the abbreviation "IRA" in the name of their self-directed IRA LLC as a means of identifying the entity for investment purposes. However, there is a group of people that would rather keep the identity of the owner of the LLC (the IRA) private. Therefore, it is also common for people to use generic names for their self-directed IRA LLC. For example, people will often use the street address of the investment property or other significant terms when naming their self-directed IRA LLC.

An LLC cannot infringe upon the name of another business entity or vice versa. Once a trade name establishes a special significance, the courts will protect the trade name either through common law trademark infringement or federal trademark law. The concern is whether the infringement name will cause confusion in the public mind with the protected name. The test is applied on a case-by-case basis, based on whether the public is likely to be deceived.

Registered Agent of LLC and Address of LLC

In general, an LLC is required to have and maintain a registered agent and/
or a registered office. A registered agent must be an individual residing in
the state, a domestic corporation, or a foreign corporation authorized to do
business in the state. The registered office is typically the business office of
the registered agent. It need not be the same office as the LLC's business
office.

The purpose of a registered agent is to accept any process, notice, or
demand required or permitted by law to be served upon the LLC. Anyone
with an address in the state of formation can serve as LLC registered agent.
In fact, there is an entire industry of companies that will serve as a registered
agent for a fee.

Rich finished reading the list of requirements and then looked up at John.

"Great," he said. "Is there any advantage to hiring a registered agent
company to serve as my registered agent?"

"In most cases," John said, "my clients who already have an address in
the state where the LLC will be formed serve as their own registered agent.
However, some clients find certain advantages to hiring a registered agent
company. A third-party registered agent can keep track of all legislative
changes and requirements within the state and provide timely notice of any
lawsuit or legal action against the corporation or LLC. Along those lines, a
third-party registered agent can also provide some confidentiality regarding
who the actual owner or managers of the LLC are. For a self-directed IRA
LLC structure, I don't see any issue with having your serve as your own
registered agent for the LLC and using your home address for the LLC's address since it does not involve actually providing any active services."

"Makes sense," Rich said.

"Great. I'll also need to know who will serve as manager of your LLC.
This is an important question because the whole idea behind doing the self-
directed IRA LLC checkbook control structure is to gain control over the
IRA funds via the LLC, and the manager or managers are the person(s) authorized to control the operations and activities of the LLC as per the operating agreement."

Serving as Manager of the IRA LLC

"I assume that I can serve as manager of my self-directed IRA LLC?" Rich asked.

"Yes, according to case law," John said. "Remember the Swanson case? That's probably the most important case in terms of understanding the legality of the self-directed IRA LLC structure because the court addressed the issue of the IRA holder serving as director/manager of the entity wholly owned by the IRA. The Swanson case makes it clear that an IRA holder may serve as manager, director, or officer of the newly established entity owned by his or her IRA. The Tax Court held that Mr. Swanson was not a disqualified person as president and director of Worldwide until after the stock was issued to IRA No. 1. In other words, by having the IRA invested in an entity such as an LLC of which the IRA owner is the manager, the IRA holder can serve as manager of the LLC and have checkbook control over his or her IRA funds. Then there's the Ellis case, which we looked at earlier. That also confirmed that the IRA holder can serve as the manager of the wholly owned IRA entity without triggering a prohibited transaction. Essentially what the Swanson and Ellis cases showed is that what counts is the IRA investment, not the investment vehicle being used to make the IRA investment."

"Remind me about *Swanson* again," Rich said.

"Well, the Tax Court in *Swanson* made it clear that it was only after Worldwide issued its stock to IRA No. 1 that Mr. Swanson held a beneficial interest in Worldwide's stock. Therefore, the Tax Court is arguing that only after the IRA funds have been invested in the newly established entity does the analysis begin about whether an IRA transaction is prohibited. Said another way, the Tax Court is contending that the use of an entity owned wholly by an IRA is not material in terms of whether a prohibited transaction occurred. The use of a wholly owned entity to make an investment is essentially no different than if the IRA made the investment itself with respect to the prohibited transaction rules. So what's important in determining whether a prohibited transaction occurred is not whether the IRA made the investment directly or via a wholly owned newly established special purpose entity but what investment was ultimately made using IRA funds.

So, yes, you can serve as manager of your self-directed IRA LLC without triggering a prohibited transaction. The key is going to be what type of activities you will be performing as manager of the LLC. And whether they rise to the level of a prohibited transaction. We will examine these rules in detail a little bit later."

"Okay," Rich said. "I remember that. Does that mean I can appoint my wife to serve as co-manager with me?"

John nodded. "There doesn't seem to be any issue with having a co-manager—even one that is a disqualified person. I have had clients elect to appoint a spouse as a co-manager of the LLC because that spouse had more experience in dealing with the investments that the LLC was going to make. The downside of having a co-manager is that you would need to have unanimous consent when making investments and both managers would need to sign all necessary transaction documents on behalf of the LLC. Of course, you could have a resolution drafted that would allow one of the managers to transact on behalf of both managers. One upside is that if one of the managers travels frequently, then having a co-manager could prove helpful. There's no right or wrong answer. The best choice is generally based on each client's individual facts and circumstance."

"Would it be safer to have a third-party nondisqualified person serve as manager of the self-directed IRA LLC?" Rich asked.

"I know some IRA custodians who allow for checkbook control self-directed IRA LLC structures but require that the manager of the LLC be a nondisqualified person," John answered. "There does not seem to be any legal foundation for this argument, especially based on the Swanson case. Although, I guess it would be somewhat safer from an IRS prohibited transaction standpoint to have a nondisqualified person serve as manager of the checkbook control self-directed IRA LLC. That being said, I don't think it's necessary or even advisable. Think about this: By granting a nondisqualified person discretion over all your LLC assets and investment decisions, you are essentially providing that person with 100 percent control over your hard-earned retirement funds. Now, sure, the person can be a sibling, friend, cousin, uncle, attorney, or CPA, but you better trust that person like you trust yourself. For me, that's just too much faith to have in someone and it's potentially very risky. On top of that, the person you appoint as manager may not want to serve as manager because that person would likely be treated as a fiduciary of your IRA, which can bring into play all kinds of liability risks. Based on the Swanson case and the fact that the majority of custodians allow for the IRA holder to serve as the manager of the IRA LLC, I would suggest that you serve as the sole manager of your LLC."

"Okay," Rich said. "Makes sense to me. But what happens if I die? What happens to the LLC?"

"What I like to do is draft a provision in the LLC operating agreement that states that upon your death, the LLC will be managed by your spouse or whomever you designate as the beneficiary of your IRA." John said. "It's important to nominate the successor manager in the case of your death to be the same person that you have appointed as your IRA beneficiary so that there is no conflict of interest. This way, the IRA beneficiary and successor manager will be one and the same and can make LLC investment decisions that are aligned and can also decide whether the IRA should be retitled into the IRA beneficiary's name or not."

"Who is qualified to serve as IRA LLC manager?"

"With a self-directed IRA, the manager (IRA holder) keeps most of this power. He or she directs the investment, instead of a broker or IRA custodian. Aside from life insurance, collectibles, and certain prohibited transaction investments outlined in Code Section 4975, a self-directed IRA can invest in most commonly made investments, including real estate, private business entities, public stocks, private stocks, and commercial paper."

"What qualities are you looking for in an IRA LLC manager?"

"Whoever is designated as manager of the LLC should be able to manage the daily operations of the business and should fully understand the responsibilities associated with that position. The manager will be required to make crucial business decisions. Since the manager will be making all LLC investment decisions and the LLC will be owned by your IRA, in almost all cases the IRA holder would want to serve as manager of the LLC. That being said, I have some clients who want their spouse or child to help them co-manage the LLC because of that person's high skill set or level of education."

"Right. Leverage the people you trust."

"If that's the best choice," John said. "Thanks to the Swanson case, we now know that the IRA holder can, in fact, serve as the manager of the self-directed IRA LLC. In *Swanson*, the Tax Court held that Mr. Swanson was not a disqualified person as president and director of Worldwide only until *after* the stock was issued to IRA No. 1. Furthermore, the Tax Court held that Mr. Swanson was not a disqualified person as an officer or director of Worldwide pursuant to IRC Section 4975(e)(2)(H) solely due to his shareholding in Worldwide as the constructive attribution rules provided under IRC Section 267 do not apply to someone in a nonshareholder capacity. In other words, by having the IRA invested in an entity such as an LLC of which the IRA owner is the manager, the Swanson case suggests that the IRA holder can serve as manager of the LLC and have checkbook control over his or her IRA funds."

"Right," Rich said.

"In addition to the IRA holder," John continued, "any third party who is not a minor can serve as a manager of a self-directed IRA LLC. Moreover, a self-directed IRA LLC can also have more than one person serve as manager of the LLC. Having more than one manager of an LLC is typically categorized as a board of management. Here's a tongue twister for you, though. Because the self-directed IRA LLC will be managed by a nonmember, the IRA is the member of the LLC, not the IRA holder or third party manager, and the self-directed IRA LLC will be considered a *manager-managed* LLC and not a *member-managed* LLC."

"I definitely want to serve as manager of my self-directed IRA LLC," Rich said. "Can you give me an idea of what of type of powers the manager would have?"

"Sure," Rich said. "The self-directed IRA LLC operating agreement describes the responsibilities and authority of the manager or the board of management. In most cases, the self-directed IRA LLC operating agreement will provide the manager with the authority to open a bank account on behalf of the LLC as well as have check-writing authority. In addition, the scope of any additional powers and responsibilities provided to the manager will be based on the contents of the self-directed IRA LLC operating agreement. For example, it is common for the manager to be given broad authority over the management and operations of the LLC since the member is an IRA, which is held in care of the IRA custodian. To this end, the manager of a self-directed IRA LLC is typically provided with the following powers and authority: (i) to determine if additional capital contributions can be made, (ii) whether to admit an additional member, (iii) the amount and timing of cash distributions to the members, (iv) the ability of the member to transfer its LLC interest to a third party, (iv) the ability to appoint officers and directors, (iv) and the ability to make investment decision on behalf of the LLC, which is checkbook control. In addition, the manager will typically be appointed as the tax matters partner [TMP] of the LLC. The purpose of a TMP is to provide a liaison between the LLC and the IRS during an administrative proceeding and to represent the LLC in judicial proceedings. Are you following?"

Rich nodded.

"As a result of the broad powers provided to the manager in connection with the self-directed IRA LLC structure," John continued, "including the checkbook control, it's important that the self-directed IRA LLC operating agreement be drafted by an attorney with expertise in the area so that the manager's responsibilities and powers are in line with the IRS prohibited transaction rules and IRS investment restrictions for an IRA. Since the manager in the self-directed IRA LLC structure will have the authority to make almost all LLC management decisions, including investment decisions, it's crucial that the self-directed IRA LLC operating agreement be drafted in a manner that includes the necessary prohibited transaction language to ensure that the investments made by the LLC will not violate IRS rules."

Prohibited Transaction Rules

"When I serve as manager of the LLC," Rich asked, "do I have to worry about the IRS prohibited transaction rules?"

John nodded. "Since the manager of the self-directed IRA LLC in most cases will be the IRA holder, and that person would be considered a disqualified person pursuant to the IRS prohibited transaction rules, a lot of discussion has been centered around the type of activities that can be performed by an IRA holder or other disqualified person serving as manager of the self-directed IRA LLC."

John got out his notepad again.

"First," he continued, "if an IRA holder or other disqualified person will be serving as manager of the LLC, that individual should not be compensated in any way by the LLC. Don't worry, I'll go through the IRA-prohibited transactions in greater detail the next time we meet, but as a summary, the definition of a disqualified person [IRC Section 4975(e)(2)] extends into a variety of related party scenarios, but generally includes the IRA holder, any ancestors or lineal descendants of the IRA holder, and entities in which the IRA holder holds a controlling equity or management interest. The receipt of any consideration or compensation by a disqualified person from the self-directed IRA LLC would trigger a prohibited transaction pursuant to the IRS rules."

"So a disqualified person can serve as the manager of a newly established entity owned by an IRA but not be compensated in any manner, directly or indirectly," Rich said.

"Correct," John agreed. "The next question that must be answered is what kinds of services the disqualified person can perform in his or her capacity as manager of the self-directed IRA LLC. The answer differs considerably based on whether the individual appointed as manager of the LLC is a disqualified person or not. If the person that will be assigned as manager of the LLC will *not* be a disqualified person, then technically that individual will be permitted to receive consideration for managing the LLC or providing certain services to the LLC. It's important to note that if that individual becomes the manager of the LLC and receives consideration for providing services to the IRA, he or she would likely become a disqualified person and that restricts the IRA from engaging in any other transactions with that person outside of the management relationship."

"Got it," Rich said.

"According to Code Section 4975(c)(1)(C)," John continued, "a prohibited transaction would involve the direct or indirect furnishing of goods, services, or facilities between an IRA and a disqualified person. We know that the IRA holder is considered a disqualified person under IRS rules. Therefore, the question is whether the IRA holder, in his or her capacity as the manager of the self-directed IRA LLC, is providing services to the IRA. It would seem clear that as manager of the LLC, the IRA holder or any disqualified person would be permitted to make investment decisions on behalf of the LLC. For example, if the IRA holder can direct and authorize the IRA custodian to make a particular investment, say, for example, to buy 100 shares of IBM, or a particular mutual fund, or even a specific piece of real estate, then the manager of the self-directed IRA LLC should have the same authority to make investment decisions on behalf of the self-directed IRA LLC. In addition to making investment decisions on behalf of the LLC, the manager of the self-directed IRA LLC will have the responsibility of managing the business and affairs of the LLC. To this end, the manager will be responsible of making sure the LLC remains in compliance with all accounting, tax, and reporting obligations. And the manager of the self-directed IRA LLC will have the responsibility of verifying that all federal and state income tax returns, if any, of the LLC have been filed and that all the necessary accounting and financial reporting has been completed."

"Just to be clear," Rich said, "I would serve as the manager of the LLC, but my IRA would be the member?"

"Correct," John said, "So to recap, in the case of an LLC, the manager is the person or persons responsible for making all LLC-related decisions, including how LLC funds are being used and whether distributions will be made. Whereas the member of the LLC is the owner of the LLC. In the case of a self-directed IRA LLC, the owner of the LLC would be the IRA. As we discussed, when completing the IRA custodian account setup paperwork, the investment authorization form will allow the IRA custodian to transfer IRA funds to the LLC in return for ownership in the LLC. The IRA would be the owner of the LLC. This means that all profits, losses, and income attributable to the IRA LLC will be allocated to the IRA as owner/ member and not the manager. The manager does not have any economic interest in the LLC; he or she just makes decisions on behalf of the LLC but does not share in any of the income or gains."

"Given what you've said about disqualified persons, I assume I can't earn any salary for serving as manager of the LLC?" Rich said.

"Yes," John said, "that's correct. We'll go through all this when we discuss the IRS prohibited transaction rules, but essentially because you are the IRA holder you are considered a disqualified person and thus are not able to transact in any way with your IRA and receive any compensation. In fact, IRC 4975(c)(1)(C) clearly states that a disqualified person is not allowed to furnish any services to the IRA."

"Okay," Rich said, "that makes sense. One thing, though: Since IRC 4975 does not allow me to provide services to my IRA, how can I make investments with the self-directed IRA without triggering a prohibited transaction?"

"Ah, a great question," John said with a smile. "We'll address most of this when we discuss in detail the IRS prohibited transaction rules. But here's a list of tasks that most tax professionals consider permissible for a manager of a self-directed IRA LLC to do":

- LLC activities and decisions that are required and necessary to further the purpose for which the self-directed IRA was established
- LLC and plan filing requirements that are necessary to keep the LLC and/or plan (as applicable) in good standing
- Tax filings that are necessary to comply with federal/state tax laws

"In general," John continued, "the less done by the IRA manager, the better. We will discuss all these rules in greater detail when we talk about the IRS prohibited transaction rules, but other than making investment decisions for the IRA LLC and other passive activities, the LLC should hire a third party to perform those tasks. This is especially important in the area of real estate."

"So who is responsible for assuring that the LLC remains in good standing?" Rich asked.

"Unlike a custodian-controlled self-directed IRA," John began, "with a self-directed IRA LLC with checkbook control the LLC manager and not the IRA custodian is the party that is responsible for maintaining the good standing of the LLC pursuant to the LLC operating agreement. Since the LLC manager is the party that is provided with the authority to make investment and other necessary decisions on behalf of the LLC, the LLC manager and not the IRA custodian is the party responsible for assuring that the LLC remains in full compliance with all state and federal filing and other requirements. The IRA custodian is simply serving as the administrator and trustee of the IRA in order to comply with IRS tax rules; once the IRA custodian transfers the IRA funds to the newly established LLC, the IRA custodian does not have any further responsibilities when it comes to the LLC. The IRA care of the custodian is just the LLC member (owner), while the LLC manager, the IRA holder, is the party that is granted management responsibility over the LLC pursuant to the LLC operating agreement. Therefore, the LLC manager, and not the IRA custodian, would be the party responsible for maintaining the good standing of the LLC, including all state and federal income tax filing requirements, as well as filing any necessary IRS 1099 forms."

IRA LLC Ownership

"So just to be clear," Rich said, "when the IRA LLC makes investments, I don't report the income or losses on my personal income tax return?"

"That's right," John said. "Remember, the LLC is owned by an IRA and not you. An IRA is treated as a tax-exempt trust pursuant to IRC 408 (IRC 408A in the case of a Roth IRA) and as a result does not file any income tax returns. Since you do not own any of the LLC and are just the manager, none of the income, gains, or losses from the IRA LLC will be reported by you on your personal income tax return (IRS Form 1040). Just like if you used you IRA funds to buy Apple or Google stock and you generated gains, the income would just flow back to your IRA and the gains would not be reported on your income tax return. The IRS would know that your IRA gained in value or not from IRS Form 5498 that the IRA custodian is required to file each year, but this would not be reported on your personal income tax return because you are not the owner of the IRA LLC. Really the only time you will report any IRA activity on your personal income tax return is if you take an IRA distribution or do a Roth conversion."

"So how do I show LLC ownership?" Rich asked.

"The LLC I will help you establish that will ultimately be owned by your IRA is newly established, and until the IRA funds have been transferred to the LLC and the operating agreement signed, the LLC is just a shell company with no ownership. The ownership of the LLC is documented by the LLC operating agreement, which will show the amount invested by the IRA member and the related ownership. As a result, the transfer of the IRA funds to the new LLC will begin the process of funding the LLC. The capital contribution table, typically shown on an LLC operating agreement exhibit at the end of the agreement, will show the member's name and the corresponding value of the cash or asset contributed along with the percentage of ownership. In the case of an LLC owned by one IRA, which is referred to as a single-member LLC or disregarded entity for tax purposes, the ownership is always 100 percent."

"I get that when investing IRA funds in cash the value of the amount transferred is clear," Rich said, "but what happens if I transfer IRA-owned assets like stocks or real estate?"

"When cash or property is contributed to an LLC, that's treated as a nonrecognition transaction for tax purposes under the partnership tax rules. When someone contributes cash or property in exchange for an interest in the LLC, that contributor does not recognize gain or loss on the contribution. The contributor will receive a basis in the cash or property transferred equal to the amount of cash transferred and the basis of the property contributed (including any liabilities associated with the property). In other words, the basis the contributor had in the property contributed becomes the LLC's basis in the property and the contributor's basis in the

LLC interest granted. Whereas the contributor's capital account will equal the amount of cash contributed and the fair market value of the property contributed to the LLC (net of liabilities)."

"Can you help me understand that more concretely?" Rich asked.

"Sure," John said. "Let's say Steve contributes a building owned by his IRA to the new IRA LLC. The building has a fair market value of $10,000, with a basis to Steve's IRA of $6,000 (what the IRA paid for the building). Steve's IRA receives a 100 percent interest in the LLC in exchange for contributing the building. Steve's IRA would have no gain on the contribution: His basis in his LLC interest is $6,000, and the LLC's basis in the building is $6,000 (a 'carryover basis'). However, Steve's IRA capital account in the LLC is $10,000 (the fair market value of the building on the date of contribution). These are very important partnership tax accounting principles, but because an IRA does not pay tax on any IRA LLC asset gains, focusing too much attention on the LLC tax basis and capital account rules are not particularly relevant. Alternatively, if Steve contributed $1,000 of IRA funds in cash to the LLC, Steve's IRA basis in the LLC interest he received and his capital account would be $1,000."

"Theoretically," Rich began, "can a self-directed IRA LLC be owned by multiple IRAs?"

"In the Swanson case, Mr. Swanson's IRA was the sole member of the newly established entity and, thus, was the only retirement account that purchased stock in the entity. As a result, it is quite clear that an IRA can own a wholly owned interest in a newly established entity. However, based on the Swanson case and the IRS field service advisory memorandum, a number of attorneys as well as IRA custodians have taken the position that more than one IRA, including traditional and Roth IRAs, as well as IRAs belonging to family members, can become owners of a newly established entity as long as the IRA funds were invested *simultaneously* into the new entity. The thinking behind this position follows the Tax Court's holding in Swanson that a new corporation without shares doesn't fit within the definition of a disqualified person under the prohibited transaction rules. Accordingly, only after one or more IRAs purchased an interest in the newly established entity would the entity become disqualified. In addition, since the only benefit the IRA holders would experience as a result of the investment in the new entity would be a benefit they would be entitled to as beneficiary of the IRA, which is exempted from the prohibited transaction rules pursuant to Code Section 4975(d)(9), the belief is that an investment by one or more IRAs into a newly established entity would not trigger a prohibited transaction."

"Well, if an entity becomes disqualified only when it is funded, why can't one contribute personal and IRA funds simultaneously to a newly formed entity?" Rich asked.

"That is a super question," John responded. "In general, you are correct, based on the Swanson case, when you make the statement that a newly established entity only becomes disqualified with respect to the IRA-prohibited transaction rules once it is funded. However, as we will soon discuss when examining the prohibited transaction rules under IRC 4975, the IRS could argue that the investment violates the self-dealing or conflict-of-interest prohibited transaction rules under IRC 4975(c)(1)(D)/(e) and could still make the argument the transaction is prohibited." Overall, like most tax professionals, I take the position that one should never commingle retirement and personal funds, no matter how minimal, in any transaction. Doing so could potentially open you and your IRA up to attack from the IRS.

"Okay, I understand," Rich said.

"So how would profits and losses be allocated?" Rich asked.

"Great question," John asked. "Computing the amount of LLC profits or losses is important in determining how much in profits or losses should flow through to the IRA members. In the case of an LLC owned by one member, the determination of the percentage of profits and losses allocated to the member is always 100 percent. However, when there are two or more members of an LLC, the determination of the amount of profits and losses allocated to each member is typically based on the economic arrangement between the members and is generally documented in the members' agreement or LLC operating agreement. The LLC operating agreement is the core document that will identify how profits, losses, and cash will be allocated or distributed to the members. The LLC operating agreement is also crucial for any LLC that will have more than one member."

"How does it usually work?" Rich asked.

"Typically, the profits and losses of an LLC are allocated based on the amount of cash contributed by the members to the LLC," John said. "For example, if John and Steve each contribute $1,000 to the LLC, they will typically each be provided a 50 percent interest in the profits, losses, and cash distributions of the LLC. This means that they each be allocated 50 percent of the LLC profits or losses in a year. So, if John and Steve's LLC generated $1,000 of profits in year one, they would each be allocated $500 of profits. In some cases, a member may receive an interest in the LLC for the performance of services (a profits interest) without contributing any cash to the LLC, or the members may have a more complex financial arrangement. But, in the case of a self-directed IRA LLC, the members' (IRA) ownership interest is typically based on the amount of IRA funds invested in the LLC."

"Got one of your great examples?" Rich asked.

"Sure," John said. "How about two examples? First, Jim has two IRAs, a traditional IRA and a Roth IRA. Jim wishes to use his retirement funds to invest in real estate, so Jim establishes an LLC and directs ABC Trust Company, his IRA passive custodian, to invest $80,000 from his traditional IRA and $20,000 from his Roth IRA into the LLC. The LLC then uses the $100,000 and purchases a home that is rented to a third-party tenant. The real estate investment generates a $10,000 net profit to the LLC in year one. Since the traditional IRA owns 80 percent of the LLC, the traditional IRA will be entitled to $8,000, or 80 percent, of the LLC profits. All $10,000 would be deposited in the LLC bank account since the LLC is the owner of the real estate. However, when the funds are ultimately distributed or the LLC is liquidated, the LLC funds would go to each IRA LLC owner (the IRAs) in proportion to their respective percentage interests in the LLC. The Roth IRA owns 20 percent of the LLC and will thus be entitled to $2,000 or 20 percent of the LLC profits. Assuming the state where John formed his LLC does not impose an entity level tax on a multiple-member LLC taxed as a partnership, the profits allocated to the IRAs would not be subject to tax since an IRA is a tax-exempt party pursuant to Code Section 408 and a partnership if treated as a flow-through entity for tax purposes."

"Okay, and what about your example number two?" Rich smiled.

"Let's say Jim and his wife Pam wish to each use their traditional IRA to invest in precious metals. Jim and Pam establish an LLC and they each direct ABC Trust Company, their IRA passive custodian, to invest $125,000 from Jim's traditional IRA and $125,000 from Pam's traditional IRA into the LLC. The LLC then uses the $250,000 to purchase precious metals. The precious metals investments generate a $30,000 net profit to the LLC in year one. Since Jim's IRA owns 50 percent of the LLC, Jim's IRA will be entitled to $15,000, or 50 percent, of the LLC profits. Pam's IRA also owns 50 percent of the LLC and will thus will be entitled to $15,000, or 50 percent, of the LLC profits. Again, all net profits of the LLC would be deposited in the LLC bank account since the LLC is the owner of the precious metals, but when the LLC is liquidated or there is a distribution of the IRA LLC funds to the LLC owners (the IRAs), each IRA will get a portion of the IRA LLC funds based on its percentage of interest ownership in the LLC. Assuming the state where Jim and Pam formed their LLC does not impose an entity level tax on a multiple-member LLC taxed as a partnership, the profits allocated to Jim and Pam's IRA would not be subject to tax because the IRA is a tax-exempt party pursuant to Code Section 408."

"So even though the IRA will own the LLC," Rich said, "the LLC will still operate like a typical for-profit LLC?"

IRA LLC Bank Account

"Right," John said. "Therefore, the manager of the LLC will have the authority to open a regular business checking account for the LLC at any local bank, credit union, brokerage house, or trust company. The LLC can also open a savings account, but in most cases involving a self-directed IRA LLC, a checking account will be required so that investments can be made using IRA funds. Just remember, when you're opening the LLC bank account, you want to open an LLC business checking account not an IRA account. You'll already have an IRA account with the IRA passive custodian so you won't need to open a new IRA. Opening a new IRA account will subject the IRA to the local bank's IRA investment restrictions and will eviscerate any of the benefits associated with establishing a self-directed IRA LLC with checkbook control."

"Right," Rich said. "I get it. I think I understand how the IRA LLC works. So once the LLC is established and you draft the LLC operating agreement, I assume I will need to open a bank account for my new self-directed IRA LLC."

"Yes," John said. "The whole beauty of the checkbook control self-directed IRA LLC structure is that all investment activity happens at the LLC bank-account level and not at the custodian level. This typically means lower custodian fees and quicker investment timing. In general, you can open the self-directed IRA LLC at any local bank or credit union. You would generally want to pick a bank or credit union you have researched and know and trust and remember to not deposit any personal funds into the account or sign up for a credit card."

"What am I looking for?" Rich asked.

"Each bank has its own internal rules concerning the documents you need to possess in order to open an LLC business checking account. The majority of banks will require the following documents."

John showed Rich a form with the list of documents:

LLC Articles of Organization

The LLC articles of organization is very similar to a corporation's certificate of formation. The LLC articles of organization is the document that establishes the LLC pursuant to state statute as well as identifying the name of the LLC, the LLC address, and the name of the registered agent. Before opening an LLC bank account, the majority of banks will require a copy of the LLC articles of organization and/or the LLC certificate of formation to ensure that the LLC is valid and has been established.

The LLC Tax Identification Number/
Employer Identification Number

The LLC tax identification number/employer identification number (EIN) is used to identify and collect information about the LLC. The EIN is comparable to a social security number. Most businesses are required to acquire an EIN for purposes of opening a business bank account.

In the case of a self-directed IRA LLC, an EIN would be required to open the LLC bank checking account since the IRA holder is not the owner of the LLC but just the manager. As your tax adviser, I would acquire a tax ID number for your IRA LLC from the IRS.

LLC Operating Agreement

In some cases, the bank may request a copy of the self-directed IRA LLC operating agreement. The LLC operating agreement is the core document referred to when issues concerning the self-directed IRA LLC need to be resolved. In addition, the LLC operating agreement is the document that identifies the member(s) and manager(s) of the LLC—which is especially important in the case of a self-directed IRA. This is because with a self-directed IRA LLC, the IRA holder is not a member/owner of the LLC but is typically just the manager. In other words, the IRA holder does not have any economic or financial interest in the LLC but is simply serving as the manager of the LLC. A properly drafted self-directed IRA LLC operating agreement will explicitly set forth the responsibilities and activities of the manager, which typically include the ability to open a bank account on behalf of the LLC as well as have check-writing authority over the LLC bank account.

"Does that cover it?" Rich asked.

"Pretty much," John said. "Most banks will typically require a copy of either the LLC articles of organization or the self-directed IRA LLC operating agreement; however, some banks will require a copy of both the LLC articles of organization and the LLC operating agreement in order to open the self-directed IRA LLC bank account. The determination of what documents are required in order to open a self-directed IRA LLC bank account is typically bank-specific."

"So it depends on my bank."

"Yes. Opening a bank account for a self-directed IRA LLC is a lot like opening a standard LLC bank account. The only difference is that in the case of a standard LLC, typically the manager is also a member (owner) of the LLC and in the case of a self-directed IRA LLC, the manager—the IRA holder—is not a member of the LLC. In fact, I have never had a client not be able to open the self-directed IRA LLC bank account at the bank of their choice."

"When you open a new bank account," Rich said, "you're usually required to put some money in the account. How does that work with a self-directed IRA LLC?"

"Most banks," John began, "will require an individual opening a new business bank account to deposit at least $100 into the account in order to maintain a minimum balance. This is not a problem for a standard LLC, since the individual opening the bank account is typically a member of the LLC and has the intention of making some future contribution to the business. But that's not how it works in the case of a self-directed IRA LLC. With a self-directed IRA LLC, the individual opening the bank account is typically the IRA holder who is not a member/owner of the LLC and who is solely serving as manager of the LLC. The IRA care of the IRA custodian will be the member/owner of the LLC. This presents a number of issues when it comes to opening and funding a new self-directed IRA LLC bank account. Since the IRA holder is a disqualified person with respect to his or her IRA pursuant to Code Section 4975, the IRA holder is not permitted to transfer any funds to the IRA. Therefore, the IRA holder is not permitted to deposit even one dollar into the self-directed IRA LLC bank account because doing so would likely trigger a prohibited transaction."

"So how can the IRA holder open a bank account for his or her new self-directed IRA LLC bank account?" Rich asked.

"Essentially," John said, "there are a number of ways that an IRA holder can fund his or new self-directed IRA LLC bank account."

1. Coordinate with Bank and IRA Custodian

The IRA holder can ask the bank to hold the opening of the new self-directed IRA LLC bank account until he or she has been notified by the

IRA custodian that the IRA funds will be transferred to the new LLC bank account. In effect, the IRA holder will complete all the necessary paperwork to open the bank account but will ask the banker to hold off processing the new bank account application until he or she has received confirmation from the IRA custodian that the funds will be transferred. Typically, a bank will allow a new account to be opened with no funds for twenty-four or forty-eight hours. This is sufficient time for the IRA passive custodian to wire the IRA funds to the new self-directed IRA LLC bank account.

2. Loan from a Nondisqualified Person

The IRA LLC can enter into a loan agreement with a nondisqualified person, such as a sibling, cousin, friend, or colleague to loan the LLC enough funds, which can be used to fund the new self-directed IRA LLC bank account. The IRA LLC can then repay the loan amount once the IRA funds have been deposited into the new IRA LLC bank account. For example, if Joe is trying to establish a self-directed IRA LLC bank account, he can ask his friend to lend his new LLC $100, which Joe can then use to fund his new LLC bank account. Once Joe's IRA custodian has transferred his IRA funds to the new LLC bank account, the LLC can then repay the loan with interest.

"When opening the self-directed IRA LLC bank account," John continued, "the most important thing to keep in mind is that no personal funds can be used when opening the self-directed IRA LLC bank account. Using personal funds when opening a bank account for a self-directed IRA LLC can potentially trigger a prohibited transaction, which could disqualify the entire IRA."

"So," Rich said, "once we establish the new self-directed IRA account with the new IRA custodian, establish the new LLC, and open the LLC bank account, how do I get the IRA funds to the new LLC bank account so I can make investments?"

"Once the retirement funds have been transferred to the new IRA custodian," John said, "the IRA holder will then have the ability to direct the IRA custodian to transfer the IRA funds to the new self-directed IRA LLC bank account. The IRA holder, as manager of the LLC, will provide the IRA custodian with the wiring instructions so that the IRA custodian can wire the funds to the new LLC bank account tax-free. Alternatively, the IRA holder can request that the IRA custodian issue a check made out to the new LLC, which the IRA holder will then be able to deposit into the new self-directed IRA LLC bank account. Upon transfer of the funds to the new self-directed IRA LLC bank account, the IRA care of the IRA custodian would become member/owner of the LLC."

"Just to confirm," Rich said, "the transfer of IRA funds to the new LLC will not be subject to tax?"

"That's right. The transfer of the retirement funds by the IRA custodian to the new self-directed IRA LLC bank account is made tax-free just as if an IRA custodian invested IRA funds to purchase IBM stock. As we have learned from the Swanson case, the investment of IRA funds into a newly established entity does not trigger a prohibited transaction pursuant to Code Section 4975. In essence, the transfer of the IRA funds into the new LLC by the IRA custodian is akin to the IRA holder directing an IRA custodian to buy Apple stock or a certain mutual fund. In the case of a self-directed IRA LLC, the only difference is that the IRA holder is directing the custodian to invest in a newly formed LLC instead of a public company, such as IBM or General Electric."

"In other words," Rich said, "the IRA funds being transferred or invested in the new self-directed IRA LLC are treated the same as if an individual invested or contributed funds to a new LLC that will be operating a for-profit business."

"Yup. Just like you would need to invest or contribute funds to a new business to get the business off the ground, the IRA custodian is investing the IRA holder's IRA funds into a new LLC."

Investment of IRA Funds into LLC

"Great," Rich said. So how is the investment of IRA funds into the new LLC treated for federal income tax purposes?"

"Based on the Swanson and Ellis cases," John began, "we know that the investment of IRA funds into a new entity is not treated as a prohibited transaction pursuant to Code Section 4975. But as far as how the IRS characterizes the investment of IRA funds into a new LLC for federal income tax purposes, in general, no gain or loss is recognized upon the contribution of money or property to an LLC in exchange for an LLC interest. For the most part, neither the contributing member (the IRA) nor the LLC is taxed."

"That sounds good," Rich said.

"So I have a better understanding of some of the taxation principles involving using a self-directed IRA LLC to make investments. But from a more practical standpoint, what stops the IRA custodian from just taking my money or investing the IRA funds without my consent?" Rich asked.

Trusting the IRA Custodian

"Fair question," John answered. "All IRA custodians have a number of insurance policies they subscribe to, but there are two major policies that would cover your IRA under the fact pattern you mentioned."

John pulled out a printed sheet.

Errors and Omission Insurance Policy:

This insurance policy is kept in the event of errors that may occur with processing any given transaction in which funds are lost and are not able to be recovered. This policy does not cover fraud or crimes committed by our employees. The errors and omission policy is coverage typically for up to $1 million.

Crime Insurance Policy:

This insurance policy is kept in the event of a malicious or deliberate removal of funds from the investor's account(s). This policy typically covers acts of up to $1 million.

"What happens if the IRA custodian goes out of business?" Rich asked.

"Since each IRA custodian is a trust company that is governed by a state banking division," John said, "if the IRA custodian goes out of business, the Division of Banking in the state where the custodian was licensed will come in and appoint a receiver—typically an attorney—to oversee at the point that the trust company fails."

"How does that work?" Rich asked.

"Typically, the receiver coordinates the sale of accounts to another qualified custodian. In this case, your funds would stay in IRA form—but with a different custodian. This is generally not a major issue for checkbook control self-directed IRA accounts because almost all your IRA funds will be at your local LLC bank account. Most IRA custodians only require you to keep between $300 and $800 in the IRA custodian account, so the bankruptcy of an IRA custodian is generally not a major issue for checkbook control IRAs. In contrast, if you had all your IRA funds at the IRA custodian and were using the IRA custodian as a full-service custodian, then the bankruptcy or governmental investigation of the IRA custodian could prove more stressful."

"I bet," Rich said. "Another reason to feel good about checkbook control. And another question. Once the IRA custodian transfers the IRA funds to the new LLC in return for a percentage interest in the LLC, how does the IRA custodian know what investments my LLC is making?"

"With a self-directed IRA LLC with checkbook control," John began, "all IRA investments are made via the LLC without custodian consent. This means that once the IRA custodian has invested the IRA holder's IRA funds into the new LLC, the LLC manager, and not the IRA custodian, becomes the party responsible for making and executing IRA investments. Accordingly, when an IRA investment is made, it will be made at the LLC level. In other words, the LLC manager, and not the IRA custodian, will be the party that makes the IRA investment determination. As a result, the IRA custodian will have no involvement in the investment.

New IRS Form 5498

John continued his explanation. "Starting in 2015 and beyond, the IRS updated IRS Form 5498 to include new Boxes 15a and 15b. The fair market value of investments in the IRA will be reported in Box 15a. Box 15b will be used to categorize the type of investments listed in Box 15a through the use of category code(s). Here are what the category codes will look like."

John produced a pamphlet.

A: Stock or other ownership interest in a corporation that is not readily tradable on an established US or foreign securities market

B: Short or long-term debt obligation that is not traded on an established securities market

C: Ownership interest in a limited liability company or similar entity (unless the entity is traded on an established securities market)

D: Real estate

E: Ownership interest in a partnership, trust, or similar entity (unless the entity is traded on an established securities market)

F: Option contract or similar product that is not offered for trade on an established US or foreign option exchange

G: Other asset that does not have a readily available fair market value

H: More than two types of assets (listed in A through G) are held in the IRA.

"Is that a big difference from previous years?" Rich asked.

"Somewhat," John answered. "The reporting change seems to signal an interest on behalf of the IRS to get a better handle on the type of IRA assets that are being purchased with IRA funds and get a better handle on what percentage of IRA assets should be considered 'hard-to-value' assets."

"Interesting," Rich said. "Does this new change mean that the IRS may be looking to start auditing IRAs more frequently?"

"It's hard to say," John said. "It seems clear that the IRS is trying to get a better handle of the amount of IRA assets that are being invested in alternative assets. I don't think this is a means for the IRS to try to find out whether an IRA engaged in a prohibited transaction but more about the IRS's concern that certain IRA assets fair market values are not being reported accurately. The fair market value of an IRA asset is very important to the IRS because that is what a tax would be imposed on. I don't think this is going to trigger an IRS witch hunt for self-directed IRA accounts, but it's clear that the IRS feel that certain IRA assets are not being valued accurately."

"So as long as I'm playing straight, I'll be fine. Same as with any other IRS matter."

"Yes. And as far as immediate concerns go, there's nothing to worry about with respect to the new IRS Form 5498 requirements if you are not engaging in any transaction that violates the IRS prohibited transaction rules. Using IRA funds to make alternative investments is perfectly legal, and we know from case law that it can be done via the use of a special purpose entity, such as an LLC, wholly owned by the IRA and even managed by the IRA holder."

"I get it," Rich said. "So once my IRA funds have been sent to the LLC I am free to start making investments with my self-directed IRA LLC."

"You sure are," John said. "As the manager of the self-directed IRA LLC, you will have the freedom to make all investment decisions for your self-directed IRA LLC. In other words, you will have checkbook control over your IRA funds, allowing you to make an IRA investment by simply writing a check or wiring funds directly from the IRA LLC bank account."

"I like the sound of that."

"You should. And since your IRA will become the owner(s) (member[s]) of the newly formed IRA LLC, all income and gains generated by an IRA LLC investment will generally flow back to your IRA tax-free. Because an LLC is treated as a pass-through entity for federal income tax purposes, all income and gains are taxed at the owner level, not at the entity level. However, since an IRA is a tax-exempt party pursuant to IRC Section 408 and, thus, does not pay federal income tax, all IRA LLC investment income and gains will generally flow through to the IRA tax-free!"

"Even better," Rich said. "Thanks for this explanation. It was thorough but critical."

"It was," John said. "And now that we've spent all this time going through the nuts and bolts of the checkbook control self-directed IRA LLC, let's spend some time next week on the features of the self-directed IRA LLC structure."

"I can't wait," Rich said.

V

The Features of the Checkbook Control
Self-Directed IRA LLC Structure

"All right," John said, "are you ready for some of the fun stuff?"

"I sure am," Rich said. "Let's get at it."

"Now that we've discussed the steps involved in establishing a check-book control self-directed IRA LLC structure," John began, "we'll get a better understanding of why the checkbook control IRA is turning into the most popular IRA investment platform for alternative asset investors, especially real estate investors. So let's explore all the features, such as the beauty of tax deferral, investment diversification, reduced annual fees, and greater control over IRA investment decisions."

"I got a fresh notepad," Rich said.

"Great," John said. "We'll start with a popular theme we've already touched on—the concept of tax-deferral or tax-free savings in the case of a Roth IRA."

Tax-Free Savings of a Roth IRA

"Americans love to spend and hate to save," John began.

"That's for sure," Rich agreed. "I read recently that Americans have one of the lowest savings rates for developed countries. We're the ultimate consumers."

"That definitely plays a role," John said. "However, I believe that education—or lack thereof—is a big factor. Most people don't understand the basic concepts of retirement planning and how crucial it is, largely because they're not taught any of that in our high schools or even our colleges and universities."

"Ideally, before they reach the age of 30," Rich said, "so they can start super-charging their retirement savings."

"Exactly," John said. "For example, if young workers begin funding an individual retirement account with $3,000 per year at age 20 and continued on through age 65, they will wind up with $2.5 million at retirement (assuming they earn the long-run annual compound growth rate in stocks, which was 9.88 percent from 1926 to 2011). Not a bad result for investing only $3,000 a year. Imagine if they learned that in school like we learn about history or English."

"I know," Rich said. "The entire country would be better off."

"And that's where a self-directed IRA can be so helpful. With a self-directed IRA, you have all the tax advantages of traditional IRAs, as well as tax deferral and tax-free gains. All income and gains generated by your IRA investment will flow back to your IRA tax-free. By using a self-directed IRA to make investments, as the IRA owner you will be able to defer taxes on any investment returns, thus, allowing you to benefit from tax-free growth. Instead of paying tax on the self-directed IRA returns of an investment, tax is paid only at a later date when a distribution is taken, leaving the investment to grow tax-free without interruption."

"It's incredibly powerful," Rich said.

"Okay, let's start with the basics for the traditional IRA and Roth IRA. I spent a lot of time earlier discussing the SEP IRA and SIMPLE IRA and will focus this recap mainly on the traditional and Roth IRA because of their popularity."

John pulled out a form.

"An individual retirement arrangement, or IRA, is a tax-favored personal savings arrangement that allows you to set aside money for retirement. There are several different types of IRAs, which you can set up with a bank, insurance company, or other financial institution. The original IRA is often referred to as a traditional IRA. You may be able to deduct some or all of your contributions to a traditional IRA. You may also be eligible for a tax credit equal to a percentage of your contribution. Amounts in your traditional IRA, including earnings, generally are not taxed until they are distributed to you. IRAs cannot be owned jointly. However, any amounts remaining in your IRA upon your death will be paid to your beneficiary or beneficiaries."

"So, how much can I contribute for 2015 to a traditional IRA?" Rich asked.

For 2015, John explained, the maximum you can contribute to all of your traditional and Roth IRAs is the smaller of:

- $5,500 ($6,500 if you're age 50 or older), or
- your taxable compensation for the year.

The IRA contribution limit does not apply to:

- Rollover contributions
- Qualified reservist repayments

"The same general contribution limit applies to both Roth and traditional IRAs," John continued. "However, your Roth IRA contribution might be limited based on your filing status and income, which we have previously discussed."

"Got it," Rich said.

"When you make a contribution to an IRA," John added, "you are putting a portion of your self-employment or W-2 income into an IRA. In this way, you avoid paying tax on that income in exchange for also putting off any personal immediate use of those funds."

"And when you take advantage of tax deferral by investing wisely with your IRA," Rich interjected, "you not only put off paying income taxes on the money you contribute, you may also save money on the taxes you eventually will pay."

"That's right," John said. "The money you contribute to a traditional IRA is pretax, which means that the contribution is deducted from your gross income and goes directly into your retirement savings plan, so you're left with a smaller dollar amount in your paycheck that can be taxed by the IRS. As a result, you'll pay less in your current income taxes for the year, because according to the IRS, you've earned less money. This can help you reduce your income tax liability."

"Speaking theoretically," Rich said, "why should I make IRA contributions? What is the main tax benefit?"

"The benefits of tax-deductible contributions are simple. For example, if you are in a 30 percent income tax bracket and contribute $5,000 to a traditional IRA in a year, that's $5,000 of your salary on which you're not paying taxes this year. So you will be able to reduce your annual income tax bill by approximately $1,500 ($5,000 x 30 percent). In other words, you will receive an income tax deduction for the $5,000 contribution, which will save you approximately $1,500 in tax payments. By making tax-deductible contributions, you're essentially paying yourself to save for your retirement. And best of all, the earnings generated from traditional IRA contributions are tax-deferred until distributed."

"What exactly does tax deferral mean?" Rich asked.

"Tax deferral literally means that you are putting off paying tax. The most common types of tax-deferred investments include those in IRAs or qualified retirement plans (i.e., 401(k)). Tax deferral means that all income, gains, and earnings, such as interest, dividends, rental income, royalties or capital gains will accumulate tax-free until the investor or IRA owner withdraws the funds and takes possession of them. As long as the funds remain in the retirement account, the funds will grow tax-free. This allows your retirement funds to grow at a much faster pace than if the funds were held personally—allowing you to build for your retirement more quickly. And when you withdraw your IRA funds in the form of a distribution after you retire, you will likely be in a lower tax bracket and thus be able to keep more of what you accumulated. So, with using a traditional IRA as a retirement savings vehicle, not only are you not paying taxes on the money you invested, you could be paying them at a lower rate when you finally do 'take home' your money."

"I just love that concept," Rich said.

"As long as the funds remain in the account, they grow without taxes eroding their value. This enables assets to accumulate at a faster pace, giving you an edge when saving for the long term. And when you withdraw funds after you retire, you'll likely be in a lower tax bracket and be able to keep more of what you've accumulated."

"What are the advantages of tax deferral?" Rich asked.

"By using an IRA to make investments," John said, "the IRA owner is able to defer taxes on any investment returns. This benefits the IRA owner in three ways. The first benefit is tax-free growth. Instead of paying tax on the returns of an investment, tax is paid only at a later date, leaving the investment to grow tax-free without interruption. The second benefit is that IRA investments are usually made when the IRA owner is in his or her highest income-earning years and is thus subject to tax at a higher tax rate. The third benefit is the ability to defer taxes on investments in the face of increased federal income tax rates."

"And tax rates are at historic lows right now," Rich said. "So the likelihood of higher federal income tax rates in the near future are significant, especially with the financial strain the baby-boomer generation is going to have on the federal budget."

"Very true," John agreed. "So the ability to defer tax on investments until the IRA owner is 70½ and likely in a low income tax bracket makes an IRA or 401(k) plan a highly attractive investment vehicle."

"And the returns keep growing too, right?" Rich said.

"Yes," John said. "Tax-deferred investments not only help investors avoid cash outflows for taxes in the immediate future, but they can help them generate higher returns, too. That's because the money that would normally be used for tax payments is instead allowed to remain in the account and earn a return. For example, if the IRA investor we talked about before is in a 33 percent tax bracket, she would have had to pay $3,333 in income taxes on the $10,000 earned on the IRA in 2011. That would have left $6,667 in the account. At a 10 percent annual return, those earnings would go on to produce $667 in 2012. However, because IRAs are tax deferred, the investor is able to earn a return on the full $10,000 rather than the $6,667 she would have had if she had to pay taxes that year. At a 10 percent annual return, she'd earn $1,000 in 2012. As you can see, the advantage of tax deferral compounds with each year."

"Do you have any other examples of the benefits of tax deferral?" Rich asked.

"You bet," John said. "Here are a few that illustrate the powerful advantage of tax-deferred contributions and compounding through a traditional IRA versus taxable-making contributions to a taxable account."

Example No. 1
Joe is forty years old and makes a $5,000 contribution to an IRA. Joe is in a 30 percent federal income tax bracket. Joe invests his IRA funds and receives a 6 percent annual return. When Joe retires at age seventy, his $5,000 contribution would be worth $21,609.71. If Joe invested the $5,000 personally, the account would only be worth $14,033.97.

Example No. 2
Jane is thirty-five years old and makes a $5,000 contribution to an IRA. Assume that Jane makes a $5,000 contribution to her IRA each year until she reaches the age of 70. Jane is in a 30 percent federal income tax bracket. Further assume that Jane was able to generate a 7 percent annual return on her investment. When Jane retires at the age of 70, her IRA account would be worth $792,950.21. If Jane made these $5,000 contributions through a taxable account, the account would only be worth $490,707.49.

Example No. 3
Ben is twenty-eight years old and has been working for a few years. Ben is in a 25 percent federal income tax bracket. Ben has been doing well at work and believes he can make a $2,500 annual IRA contribution. Ben spoke to

his CPA about this and his CPA ran some numbers and came back with some incredible numbers. Assuming Ben can generate a rate of return of 7 percent annually and he makes $2,500 contributions to the IRA until he reaches the age of 70, he would have almost $617,000 in his IRA. Ben's CPA then mentioned that if he was able to increase his contributions to $3,500 each year and was able to generate a 7 percent return, Ben would have almost $864,000 versus $734,160 if non-IRA funds were used. Ben thought that was a pretty impressive number for just putting away $3,500 a year in his IRA.

Example No. 4

Amy is twenty-five years old and just started her first job. Amy is in the 25 percent federal income tax bracket and was told about the IRA benefits. Amy thought that she would be able to make a $1,500 annual contribution. Amy's CPA ran some numbers and mentioned that if she was able to generate an 8 percent rate of return and kept making IRA contributions until she reached the age of 70 she would have a whopping $626,239 versus $469,604 if non-IRA funds were used.

"Those are great," Rich said, "and very helpful."

"It makes it clear that one of the key principles of tax deferral is starting early. The earlier you start making tax deferrals the better off you will be."

"Do I always have to make IRA contributions?" Rich asked.

John shook his head. "No, it's really important to remember that IRA contributions are flexible. Because an IRA is an individual retirement account, it is 100 percent up to you whether you want to make IRA contributions for the year. So if you have extra cash one year, you may wish to contribute to your allowable limit. However, if you have other needs for the money in another year, you can contribute less. In sum, you can change the amounts you contribute for any reason. Of course, it's in your interest from a long-term retirement standpoint to save as much as you can in your plan, but you are not required to do so."

"It's just good practice to make IRA contributions, though," Rich said.

"It really is," John agreed.

How Much Can I Contribute to an IRA?

"So how much can I contribute to an IRA?" Rich asked.

"I went over the IRA contribution rules in detail earlier, but as a recap, the contribution limit for 2014 and 2015 is $5,500, or $6,500 if you're age 50 or older. Your Roth IRA contributions may also be limited based on your filing status and income. The IRA contribution limit does not apply to (1) rollover contributions and (2) qualified reservist repayments."

"I assume I have to have income to make IRA contributions?" Rich said.

"Right," John said. "To contribute to a traditional IRA, you must be under age 70½ at the end of the tax year. You (and/or your spouse if you file a joint return) must have taxable compensation, such as wages, salaries, commissions, tips, bonuses, or net income from self-employment. Taxable alimony and separate maintenance payments received by an individual are treated as compensation for IRA purposes. Compensation does not include earnings and profits from property, such as rental income, interest, and dividend income, or any amount received as pension or annuity income, or as deferred compensation."

"Can I make IRA contributions after age 70½?" Rich said.

"You can't make regular contributions to a traditional IRA in the year you reach 70½ and older," John said. "However, you can still contribute to a Roth IRA and make rollover contributions to a Roth or traditional IRA regardless of your age as long as you have earned income during the year."

"I remember you saying that if one spouse doesn't have income and the other one does, the other spouse can use the first spouse's income to make IRA contributions," Rich said.

"If you file a joint return, you and your spouse can each make IRA contributions even if only one of you has taxable compensation. The amount of your combined contributions can't be more than the taxable compensation reported on your joint return. It doesn't matter which spouse earned the compensation. If neither spouse participates in a retirement plan at work, all of your contributions will be deductible."

"Can I contribute to an IRA if I participate in a retirement plan at work?" Rich asked.

"You can contribute to a traditional or Roth IRA whether or not you participate in another retirement plan through your employer or business. However, you might not be able to deduct all of your traditional IRA contributions if you or your spouse participates in another retirement plan at work. Roth IRA contributions might be limited if your income exceeds a certain level."

"Got any examples?"

"Sure," John said.

Example No. 1
Joe, an unmarried college student working part-time earns $2,500 in 2015. Joe can contribute $2,500, the amount of his compensation, to his IRA for 2015.

Example No. 2
John, forty-two, has both a traditional IRA and a Roth IRA and can only contribute a total of $5,500 to either one or both in 2015.

Example No. 3
Sarah, age fifty-two, is married with no taxable compensation for 2014. She and her husband reported taxable compensation of $60,000 on their 2014 joint return. Sarah may contribute $6,500 to her IRA for 2014 ($5,500 plus an additional $1,000 contribution for age fifty and over).

Claiming a Tax Deduction for Your IRA Contribution

"Your traditional IRA contributions may be tax-deductible," John said. "The deduction may be limited if you or your spouse is covered by a retirement plan at work and your income exceeds certain levels. Roth IRA contributions aren't deductible."

John showed Rich a chart:

Traditional IRAs

Retirement plan at work	Your deduction may be limited if you (or your spouse, if you are married) are covered by a retirement plan at work and your income exceeds certain levels.
No Retirement plan at work	Your deduction is allowed in full if you (and your spouse, if you are married) aren't covered by a retirement plan at work.

"These charts show the income range in which your deduction may be disallowed if you or your spouse participates in a retirement plan at work," John said. "For 2015, if you're not covered by a retirement plan at work, use this IRS table to determine if your modified adjusted gross income (AGI) affects the amount of your deduction."

YOUR FILING STATUS IS:	And Your Modified AGI Is...	Then You Can Take...
Single, head of household, or qualifying widow(er)	any amount	a full deduction up to the amount of your *contribution limit*.
Married filing jointly or separately with a spouse who is *not covered* by a plan at work	any amount	a full deduction up to the amount of your *contribution limit*.
Married filing jointly with a spouse who is covered by a plan at work	< $181,000	a full deduction up to the amount of your *contribution limit*.
	≥ $183,000 but < $193,000	a partial deduction.
	≥ $191,000	no deduction.
Married filing separately, with a spouse who is covered by a plan at work	< $10,000	a partial deduction.
	≥ $10,000	no deduction.

If you file separately and did not live with your spouse at any time during the year, your IRA deduction is determined under the "single" filing status.

Roth IRA

"Can you go over again how the Roth IRA contributions work?" Rich asked.

"Sure," John said. "The same general contribution limit applies to both Roth and traditional IRAs. However, your Roth IRA contribution might be limited based on your filing status and income. This table shows whether your contribution to a Roth IRA is affected by the amount of your modified AGI as computed for Roth IRA purposes for 2015."

YOUR FILING STATUS IS:	And Your Modified AGI Is…	Then You Can Contribute…
Married filing jointly or qualifying widow(er)	< $183,000	up to the limit
	≥ $183,000 but < $193,000	a reduced amount
	≥ $193,000	zero
Married filing separately, and you lived with your spouse at any time during the year	< $10,000	a reduced amount
	≥ $10,000	zero
Single, head of household, or married filing separately, and you did not live with your spouse at any time during the year	< $116,000	up to the limit
	≥ $116,000 but < $131,000	a reduced amount
	≥ $131,000	zero

Amount of Your Reduced Roth IRA Contribution

"For 2015," John continued, "if the amount you can contribute must be reduced, you can figure your reduced contribution limit according to this formula":

1. Start with your modified AGI.
2. Subtract from the amount in (1):

    a. $193,000 if filing a joint return or qualifying widow(er),
    b. $-0- if married filing a separate return, and you lived with your spouse at any time during the year, or
    c. $116,000 for all other individuals.

3. Divide the result in (2) by $15,000 ($10,000 if filing a joint return, qualifying widow(er), or married filing a separate return and you lived with your spouse at any time during the year).
4. Multiply the maximum contribution limit (before reduction by this adjustment and before reduction for any contributions to traditional IRAs) by the result in (3).
5. Subtract the result in (4) from the maximum contribution limit before this reduction. The result is your reduced contribution limit.

"Here's an example from IRS Publication 590 on how this works," John said.

Example

Joe, a forty-five-year-old, single individual with taxable compensation of $113,000, wants to make the maximum allowable contribution to his Roth IRA for 2013. Joe's modified AGI for 2013 is $113,000. Joe has not contributed to any traditional IRA, so the maximum contribution limit before the modified AGI reduction is $5,500.

Line	Description	Value
1)	Enter your modified AGI for Roth IRA purposes (Worksheet 2-1, line 12)	113,000
2)	• $178,000 if filing a joint return or qualifying widow(er). • $-0- if married filing a separate return and you lived with your spouse at any time in 2013, or • $112,000 for all others	112,000
3)	Subtract line 2 from line 1	1,000
4)	• $10,000 if filing a joint return or qualifying widow(er) or married filing a separate return and you lived with your spouse at any time during the year, or • $15,000 for all others	15,000
5)	Divide line 3 by line 4 and enter the result as a decimal (rounded to at least three places). If the result is 1.000 or more, enter 1.000	0.67
6)	Enter the lesser of: • $5,500 ($6,500 if you are age 50 or older), or • Your taxable compensation	5,500
7)	Multiply line 5 by line 6	369
8)	Subtract line 7 from line 6. Round the result up to the nearest $10. If the result is less than $200, enter $200	5,140
9)	Enter contributions for the year to other IRAs	0
10)	Subtract line 9 from line 6	5,500
11)	Enter the lesser of line 8 or line 10. This is your reduced Roth IRA contribution limit	5,140

"So, are you saying that if I earn more than $193,000 on my joint return I can't do a Roth IRA?" Rich asked.

"Yes and no," John answered. "One way for high earners to contribute to a Roth IRA is something called the 'backdoor' Roth IRA. The 'backdoor' Roth IRA approach allows a high-income earner (someone who makes over $193,000 in 2015) to make an after-tax IRA contribution, which has no income threshold, and then immediately convert the after-tax IRA to a Roth IRA. As of 2010, there is no longer any income level restrictions for making

Roth IRA conversions, hence a high income earner can do a conversion of the after-tax IRA funds to a Roth IRA immediately upon making the contribution. However, a tax could be due on the conversion under the pro rata rules if the IRA holder has other Traditional IRAs that have not been taxed. In general, the taxes owed on the conversion will depend on the ratio of IRA assets that have been taxed to those that have not making the "backdoor" IRA unattractive for some.

"When are Roth IRA contribution due?" Rich asked.

"You can make contributions for 2015 by the due date (not including extensions) for filing your 2015 tax return. This means that most people can make contributions for 2015 by April 15, 2016."

"The only thing I worry about, though, is what if I contribute too much to my Roth IRA since these Roth calculation limits are so complicated?"

"A 6 percent excise tax applies to any excess contribution to a Roth IRA. But don't worry—there is a way to correct any excess contributions made. Any contribution that is withdrawn on or before the due date (including extensions) for filing your tax return for the year is treated as an amount not contributed. This treatment only applies if any earnings on the contributions are also withdrawn. The earnings are considered earned and received in the year the excess contribution was made."

"Okay, that's a relief," Rich said.

"If you filed your 2014 tax return in a timely way," John continued, "without withdrawing a contribution that you made in 2014, you can still have the contribution returned to you within six months of the due date of your 2014 tax return, excluding extensions. If you do, file an amended return with 'Filed pursuant to section 301.9100-2' written at the top. Report any related earnings on the amended return and include an explanation of the withdrawal. And make any other necessary changes on the amended return."

Should I Make Roth or Pretax Contributions?

"I always wonder whether it makes sense to make a Roth after-tax contribution or a pretax contribution," Rich said.

"Tax professionals get that question all the time," John said. "The upside with Roth contributions is that your Roth withdrawals in retirement (including any earnings and gains on your Roth contributions) are completely federal income-tax-free if you meet certain requirements."

"That's great."

"Sure is," John agreed. "When deciding whether you should make Roth contributions, before-tax contributions, or a combination of the two, think about this: If you feel your tax rate in retirement will be higher than it is today, Roth contributions may make sense for you. If you expect your tax rate to be lower in retirement than during your working years, you may benefit more from making before-tax contributions and paying taxes when you withdraw your money."

"Like you said, it's hard to believe but we're currently in a historically low tax-rate environment," Rich said.

"I know," John said. "For most of the century, including some boom times, top-bracket income tax rates were much higher than they are today. In fact, during the 1950s and early 1960s, the top bracket income tax rate was over 90 percent. In light of our growing deficit, social security shortfall, and heavy government spending, it is not outlandish to suggest that income tax rates will be higher when you retire than they are now. That being said, no one knows what will happen tomorrow when it comes to Congress and taxes, and especially not in twenty or thirty years, so an educated guess is all one can make."

"So it comes down to how confident you are in your expected returns, I expect," Rich said.

"Exactly," John said. "If you are very confident that your investments and/or cash flow from your investments are relatively secure and will grow over time, a Roth account makes sense. Bear in mind that many people felt that Enron, Lehman Brothers, and Bear Stearns were safe investments and suitable for Roth funds, and we all know how those companies turned out...In general, Roth investments seem to work well with real estate income-producing investments as well as dividend growth investments in which the cash flows are generally perceived as stable."

"And once again, starting early is better," Rich said.

"Yes. The further away you are from retirement the greater opportunity you have for tax-free growth and the more potential you have for tax-free gains. Basically, if you will not be retiring in the near future, Roth contributions may make a good deal of sense, since your account has more time to potentially grow in value. This may make the tax advantages of Roth contributions even more important to you—although Roth dollars can benefit retirement savers of all ages."

John handed Rich a document that outlined some of the important considerations in determining whether to make pretax or after-tax (Roth) contributions to a solo 401(k) plan

Important considerations in determining whether to make pre-tax IRA or after tax (Roth) IRA contributions

	Pre-tax Contribution	After-Tax (Roth) contribution
Your age	Getting older potentially reduces the attractiveness of a Roth	The younger you are Roth offers greater advantages
Need for current income tax deduction	The greater the need the greater benefit for a pre-tax contribution	The less the need the more attractive the Roth contribution becomes
Future tax rates	The belief that tax rates will be lower when you retire increase the attractiveness of the pre-tax contribution	The belief that future tax rates will be higher increase attractiveness of Roth
Investment confidence	The less confident you are in the stock market or your IRA investment options the more attractive the pre-tax account will be because at least you will benefit from a current tax deduction	The more confident you are in your investment returns and their growth over the years, the more attractive the Roth account becomes because all future appreciation will be tax-free

What Is the Advantage of a Roth Contribution?

In order to get a better handle on the potential advantages of making after-tax Roth contributions, it is helpful to run several possible scenarios:

Starting Balance: $0
Annual contribution: $1,500
Current Age: 30
Age of retirement: 70
Expected rate of return: 9.77 percent
Marginal tax rate: 25 percent
Total amount of contributions: $60,000

At age 70 with a Roth IRA, the individual would have $684,646 tax-free, a taxable savings of $349,810 if non-IRA funds had been used.

Now let's assume the individual makes an annual Roth IRA contribution of $2,500 and earned a small annual rate of return.

Starting Balance: $0
Annual contribution: $2,500
Current Age: 30
Age of retirement: 70
Expected rate of return: 8 percent
Marginal tax rate: 30 percent
Total amount of contributions: $100,000

At age 70 with a Roth IRA, the individual would have $699,453 tax-free, a taxable savings of $369,700 if non-IRA funds had been used.

Let's further assume that the individual was able to make an annual Roth IRA contribution of $5,000 starting at age 35 until the age of 75 and was able to earn a modest 7 percent rate of return.

Starting balance: $0
Annual contribution: $5,000
Current age: 35
Age of retirement: 75
Expected rate of return: 7 percent
Marginal tax rate: 30 percent
Total amount of contributions: $200,000

At age 65 with a Roth IRA, the individual would have $1,068.048 tax-free, a taxable savings of $618,345 if non-IRA had been used.

"Those examples really show the enormous retirement benefits to making after-tax (Roth) contributions starting at a young age and on a consistent basis," Rich said.

"That being said," John amended, "there is certainly nothing wrong with having several million dollars in a pretax retirement account; although if your federal and state income tax rate was at 50 percent when you retired, that million-dollar-plus retirement account would still be nice, but definitely not as nice as being able to live off the money tax-free and without ever having to pay tax on the money again. Taking this a step further, you can argue, that with a 50 percent tax rate, having $1 million in a Roth IRA is like having $1.5 million in a pretax account."

"Numbers never lie," Rich said.

"They're very trustworthy," John agreed. "The hard part is turning down a CPA who is pushing for you to make the pretax contribution so it reduces your current income tax and also makes him or her look better in your eyes. You need to think long term by focusing on the advantages of tapping a tax-free account when you retire, especially if taxes are higher than now."

Reporting IRA Contributions to the IRS

"So how do you report IRA contributions on your income tax return?" Rich asked.

"Making a pretax IRA contribution is only half the battle," John said. "In order to get a tax deduction—in the case of a pretax contribution—or to notify the IRS—in the case of an after-tax (Roth) contribution—you must report the type and amount of the contribution on your individual tax return (IRS Form 1040) as well as the entity tax return, if applicable."

And if you made contributions to a traditional IRA for a taxable year, you may be able to take an IRA deduction, right?"

"Yes," John said. "But you, or your spouse if filing a joint return, must have had earned income to do so. You must file a joint return to deduct contributions to your spouse's IRA. Just enter the total IRA deduction for you and your spouse on line 32 of your personal income tax return (IRS Form 1040)."

"Any exceptions?"

"Well, if you were a member of the US Armed Forces, earned income includes any nontaxable combat pay you received. If you were age 70½ or older at the end of the year, you cannot deduct any contributions made to your traditional IRA for the taxable year in question or treat them as non-deductible contributions."

"What are the details?" Rich asked.

"In the case of a nondeductible IRA contribution, you must file Form 8606, Nondeductible IRAs, to report nondeductible contributions even if you do not have to file a tax return for the year. A nondeductible IRA contribution is a contribution in which you are not taking a tax-deduction for the IRA contribution. The after-tax IRA contribution is typically done by a high-income earner who wants to make a Roth IRA contribution but earns too much income, so he makes an after-tax IRA contribution then the funds are converted to an after-tax Roth IRA."

"What about a Roth IRA?" Rich asked. "How would your report that to the IRS?"

"You can't deduct contributions to a Roth IRA," John said. "If you are filing a joint return and you or your spouse made contributions to both a traditional IRA and a Roth IRA for a taxable year, you would likely be able to deduct the amount of the pretax contribution on your income tax return—IRS form 1040."

"Sounds simple," Rich said.

"Not too bad," John agreed. "When you're completing your income tax return, you would think the IRS would be interested in knowing the amount of your annual Roth IRA contributions since it is typically interested in gathering all sorts of financial and tax information about taxpayers. Interestingly though, one item you don't report on your Form 1040 tax return is your Roth individual retirement account contributions."

"Really?" Rich said.

"It's hard to believe, I know," John said. "You're not required to report your Roth IRA contributions anywhere on the tax return. Roth IRAs offer after-tax savings, which means your contributions won't get you a tax deduction when you make them, as traditional IRA contributions do. It would seem that the IRS's thinking is that since a Roth IRA contribution would not reduce one's taxable income, there is no need to report it on your tax return as a deduction. Instead, you'll report it when you take distributions, which, if qualified, will come out tax-free. Qualified distributions occur when the account is at least five tax years old and you're either 59½, permanently disabled, or taking out up to $10,000 for your first home. I will get into the Roth IRA distribution rules shortly," John said.

"If I was covered by a 401(k) plan at work, how would I report any IRA contributions I made during the year?" Rich asked.

"If you were covered by a retirement plan (qualified pension, profit-sharing [including 401(k)), annuity, SEP, SIMPLE, etc.] at work or through self-employment, your IRA deduction may be reduced or eliminated. But you can still make contributions to an IRA even if you can't deduct them and would report them on IRS Form 1040. In any case, the income earned on your IRA contributions is not taxed until it is paid to you."

"What about IRA rollovers?" Rich asked. "Would I report that on my tax return if I did an IRA rollover during the year?"

"The term *rollovers* means that you are moving money from one individual retirement account to another," John said. "Some people confuse the words *rollover* and *transfer*. A transfer is between IRAs only and a rollover is generally when a retirement account, other than an IRA is involved. For example, moving funds from a 401(k) plan to an IRA would be classified as a rollover, and moving IRA funds from one traditional IRA to another traditional IRA at another bank is typically known as a transfer. Regardless of what you are calling the movement of the retirement funds, even if you roll over retirement funds to a new IRA at the same bank, you'll still get a 1099-R showing a distribution. You have to report the rollover on your tax return so the IRS knows why you aren't paying taxes on the reported rollover withdrawal. How you report it depends on whether you rolled over the entire amount and whether you converted money to a Roth IRA. Here's a form that explains it all."

John handed Rich a pamphlet.

Tax-Free Rollover or Transfer

An eligible rollover of funds from one IRA to another is a nontaxable transaction. Rollover distributions are exempt from tax when you place the funds in another IRA account within sixty days from the date of distribution. Many plan administrators can even perform a direct rollover for you, which eliminate the risk of missing important funding deadlines. Even though you aren't required to pay tax on this type of activity, you still must report it to the IRS. Reporting your rollover is relatively quick and easy—the IRA custodian will report the IRA rollover on IRS Form 1099-R and you would report it on your personal income tax return (IRS Form 1040).

If you correctly completed a tax-free rollover or transfer whether retirement funds went directly from one retirement account to another retirement account (for example 401(k) plan to IRA, or IRA to IRA), you are still technically required to report it on your return with either Form 1040 or 1040A (short-form return if taxpayer meets certain requirements). On line 15a of Form 1040 or line 11a of Form 1040A, report the entire amount of the distribution. Then, report "$0" as the taxable portion of the distribution on line 15b of Form 1040 or line 11b of Form 1040A. To cap it off, write "Rollover" next to line 15b or line 11b if you are filing IRS Form 1040A so the IRS knows what you did.

Partial Taxable IRA Rollover

If you did not do a complete rollover or IRA transfer, for example, because you took a partial distribution and didn't roll over all of the funds, anything not rolled could be taxable and hit with the 10 percent early withdrawal penalty. If you're rolling money from one traditional IRA to the other, the portion not rolled over is fully taxable unless you've made nondeductible contributions. If so, use Form 8606 to figure out the taxable portion. On your taxes, report the entire amount on line 15a of Form 1040 or line 11a of Form 1040A, then enter the taxable portion on line 15b of Form 1040 or line 11b of Form 1040A. Finally, write "Rollover" next either line 15b or line 11b. If you're under 59½you also have to fill out Form 5329 to calculate the early withdrawal penalty.

Incomplete Roth IRA Rollovers

For Roth IRA rollovers, the portion that isn't rolled over is taxable only to the extent that it exceeds the contributions in your account. If you didn't roll over the entire amount, use Form 8606 to figure the taxable portion, then follow the reporting rules as incomplete traditional IRA rollovers. On your taxes, report the entire amount on line 15a of Form 1040 or line 11a of Form 1040A, then enter the taxable portion on line 15b of Form 1040 or line 11b of Form 1040A. Finally, write "Rollover" next to either line 15b or line 11b. If you're under 59½ or your Roth IRA hasn't been open for at least five years and a portion of your withdrawal is taxable, you also have to fill out Form 5329 to calculate the early withdrawal penalty.

IRA-to-IRA Transfer

Funds withdrawn from an IRA and redeposited into an IRA within sixty days (indirect rollover) may be eligible for treatment as a sixty-day rollover contribution. If eligible, this movement of funds may qualify as an IRA withdrawal of funds without any penalty or taxes.

The financial institution that you are transferring your retirement funds from will file IRS Form 1099-R and the institution that will be receiving the IRA transfer amount will file IRS Form 5498. US taxpayers do not include Form 5498 with their tax filing.

Direct Rollover

A direct rollover is the process by which retirement funds are received or withdrawn from an employer-sponsored retirement plan and deposited directly into an IRA. The 20 percent tax withholding of funds by the plan sponsor is waived when funds are rolled directly into an IRA.

The financial institution that you are transferring your retirement funds from will file IRS Form 1099-R and the IRA institution that will be receiving the rollover amount will file IRS Form 5498.

"So how does the IRS keep track of all IRA contributions besides the tax return?" Rich asked. "With millions of IRAs out there, and hundreds of thousands of IRA rollovers done each year, is there some type of form the IRS receives?"

"Yes," John answered. "IRS Form 5498 reports your IRA contributions to the IRS. Your IRA trustee or custodian (i.e., financial institution)—not you—is required to file this form with the IRS and a copy of the IRA holder by no later than May 31. IRS Form 5498 also helps the IRS keep track of any IRA rollovers or transfers."

"I think I've seen that form," Rich said.

"When you save for retirement with an individual retirement arrangement, you probably receive a Form 5498 each year," John said. "The institution that manages your IRA must report all contributions you make to the account during the tax year on the form. Depending on the type of IRA you have, you may need Form 5498 to report IRA contribution deductions on your tax return."

Administering the IRA

"How easy is the IRA to administer?" Rich asked.

"That's one of the great things about an IRA," John said. "It's so simple to administer. Let's just focus on the individual IRAs and not the SEP or SIMPLE plans, which need to be adopted by a business. Unlike a company 401(k), a traditional or Roth IRA is very simple to establish and maintain. An IRA can generally be opened at any local bank or financial institution, and other than reporting the pretax contribution amount or nondeductible contribution amount (remember, Roth IRA contributions are not reported on IRS Form 1040), there are really no other administrative matters to deal with in connection with having an IRA. Of course, IRA distributions need to be reported as well, but we will get to this in a little bit. The IRA custodian is required to file IRS Form 5498, which will show the IRA account value, and submit it to the IRS and, in the case of a rollover, the institution where the funds will be rolled over from will file IRS Form 1099-R."

"Okay," Rich said, "that's for an IRA but what about a checkbook control self-directed IRA?"

"As we discussed in detail in an earlier conversation," John said, "a self-directed IRA LLC structure that involves one IRA account owning the LLC will be treated as a disregarded entity for federal income tax purposes and, hence, no income tax return needs to be filed. What this means is that other than IRS Form 5498, which the self-directed IRA custodian is required to file with the IRS, you, as manager of the self-directed IRA LLC, will generally have no IRS or state filing requirements if your LLC is owned by one IRA."

"Right, I remember that," Rich said.

Establishing a Self-Directed IRA LLC

"I think this is a good time to expand on some of the benefits of establishing a self-directed IRA LLC, other than tax deferrals," John said. "Let's focus on the checkbook control self-directed IRA LLC and not the custodian-controlled self-directed IRA structure since you have decided to use the checkbook control IRA LLC to make your IRA investments."

"That sounds great," Rich said. "I think this will be very useful."

"According to the Investment Company Institute, a national association of US investment companies, traditional IRAs had $4.8 trillion in assets at year-end 2012. That makes them a key component of the US retirement system. Rollovers are the predominant way investors open traditional IRAs. In 2012, about seven in ten new traditional IRAs received rollovers. Because rollovers generally occur after job changes or retirement, which is a sporadic event for most people, in any given year only about one in ten traditional IRA investors made rollovers. In the aggregate, the data for rollover activity indicate that a large fraction of traditional IRA investors have had a rollover at some point."

"That's been my experience," Rich said.

"And it's widespread," John agreed. "In fact, the Investment Company Institute's March 2014 report said that 46.1 million, or 37.6 percent, of US households owned one or more types of IRAs in mid-2013. Households held $5.6 trillion in IRAs at year-end 2012, or more than one-quarter of the $19.9 trillion in total US retirement assets. IRAs accounted for 9.3 percent of US households' total financial assets."

"Wow," Rich said, "these numbers are astounding. I had no idea there was nearly $20 trillion is US retirement assets. Now I understand why the financial industry spends so much money targeting retirement accounts and why they are not inclined to offer self-directed retirement investment options."

And I presume traditional IRAs, the first type of IRA created, are the most common type of IRA," Rich said.

"Yes," John said, "but because almost all IRAs are set up with traditional financial institutions, such as Fidelity, Vanguard, Mass Mutual, etc., the investment opportunities offered to the millions of traditional IRA retirement holders are almost always equity-based investments, such as stock, mutual funds, ETFs, etc. There is really no financial incentive to offer IRA account holders the ability to make investments in which the financial institution holding the account does not make any money. For example, if you have $150,000 in an IRA account at a major financial institution and own a number of mutual funds, the financial institution will typically earn fees from facilitating these investments. If, however, you took your $150,000 and bought precious metals or real estate, the financial institution will no longer have use of those funds or the ability to generate any more fees on them."

"Follow the money," Rich said. "Why would a major financial institution spend millions of dollars on a TV, radio, or online media campaigns to educate the public about the fact that the IRS allows nontraditional investments?"

"That's why most Americans are not aware that the IRS allows retirement accounts to be invested in all sorts of different investment products, such as precious metals, real estate, private notes, loans, businesses, tax liens, currencies, options, and much, much more," John said.

"Then came the 2008 financial crisis," Rich said.

"Yes," Rich said. "If it had any positive effect it is that it resulted in many Americans asking about alternative investment options for their retirement accounts. It is believed that the financial crisis cost retirees almost 25 percent of their retirement assets, and many are still trying to get back to where they were prior to the crisis. The sudden and steep stock market fall coupled with the lack of faith in Wall Street and the global financial markets caused many Americans to seek a more balanced and diversified retirement portfolio. With this came a sharp increase in the number of Americans looking at a self-directed IRA as the vehicle for attaining a level of account diversification."

"And the answer was right there in front of them all along," Rich said.

"Exactly," John said. "Alternative investments such as real estate have always been permitted in IRAs. It even says so right on the IRS website.

"IRA law does not prohibit investing in real estate, but trustees are not required to offer real estate as an option."[2]

Yet, few people seemed to know about this option until recently. The nontraditional and self-directed retirement market was relatively small prior to 2008. Early adopters heard about the nontraditional asset option and took advantage of it to buy real estate and other nontraditional assets. This small group of retirees were on the cutting edge of investment options and largely did not have an impact on the larger retirement investment community. The crossover began after the 2008 financial crisis. Many people around the country—young, old, rich, middle-class, educated, even attorneys and CPAs—are now asking whether you can buy real estate with retirement money. And when they find out it's legal, they can't believe they haven't heard of it before."

"I would think the very people who are drawn to the self-directed IRA generally love the flexibility and opportunity it offers for using retirement funds for a wide range of investments," Rich said.

"Very true," John said. "Specifically, with the checkbook control feature. Unlike an IRA offered by most financial institutions or a custodian-controlled self-directed IRA, with a self-directed IRA LLC solution, the IRA-owned LLC account can be opened at most local banks in your community or town. The entire purpose of the checkbook-control structure is to allow the IRA holder the ability to make IRA investments more quickly and with fewer annual IRA custodian fees. With the self-directed IRA LLC structure, the manager(s) of the IRA LLC will have the authority to transact on behalf of the LLC. The powers and authorities of

---

2 http://www.irs.gov/Retirement-Plans/Retirement-Plans-FAQs-regarding-IRAs-Investments

the LLC manager(s) are outlined in the self-directed IRA LLC operating agreement. In general, the IRA LLC manager(s) will be provided broad powers to make investments on behalf of the LLC. The investments allowed to be made on behalf of the LLC are also broadly defined to allow the manager(s) to essentially make any investments not prohibited by IRS rules. Thus, with the self-directed IRA LLC solution, the manager(s) of the LLC, who is typically the IRA holder and/or close family members, has the ability to make nontraditional investments, such as real estate by signing a check or even executing a wire transfer. This is quite different from a regular IRA opened at a traditional financial institution, which will not allow you to make nontraditional investments, or a custodian-controlled self-directed IRA structure, which will not offer a checkbook with the account. The appealing aspect of having checkbook control by serving as manager of the IRA LLC held at a local bank is that you have the ability to make investments quickly, which can help get an offer accepted for a real estate investment property."

A World of Investment Opportunities

"So, what kind of investment opportunities are available for my self-directed IRA?" Rich asked.

"The IRS doesn't say what you can invest in only what you can't invest in," John said. "I'll go over those rules in detail later, but here are a few of the more popular investments allowed by the IRS."

John handed Rich a pamphlet.

- Residential or commercial real estate
- Domestic or foreign real estate
- Raw land
- Foreclosure property
- Mortgages
- Mortgage pools
- Deeds

- Private loans
- Tax liens
- Private businesses
- Limited liability companies
- Limited liability partnerships
- Private placements
- Precious metals and certain coins
- Stocks, bonds, mutual funds
- Foreign currencies

"Before we dive in and look at many of the popular investment options with a self-directed IRA, let's look at some of the reasons one would purchase nontraditional assets with a self-directed IRA LLC," said John.

1. Diversification

In general, most Americans have an enormous amount of financial exposure to the financial markets. Whether it is through retirement investments, such as IRAs or 401(k) plans, or personal savings, many of us have most of our savings connected in some way to the stock market. In fact, more than 90 percent of retirement assets are invested in the financial markets. With close to $20 trillion in retirement assets as of 2013, you can see the scope of that exposure. Investing in nontraditional assets, such as real estate, offers a form of investment diversification from the equity markets. In general, the belief is that the more diversified your retirement investment portfolio is, the greater chance that your asset movements will be subject to a lower correlation, meaning they are less likely to move in the same direction. However, diversification does not ensure profit or protect against loss or guarantee success, though history suggests that stocks are a solid investment over the long term. For example, according to historical records, the average annual return for the S&P 500 since its inception in 1928 through 2014 is approximately 10 percent. However, that number can be very misleading. Accurate calculations of average returns, taking all significant factors into account, can be challenging. Whereas, according to the S&P/Case-Shiller 20-City Composite Home Price Index, which seeks to measure the value of residential real estate in twenty major US metropolitan areas, as of 2015, the ten-year average return was 0.8 percent but was 7.06 percent over the last three years. Overall, the belief is that the use of nontraditional asset classes can help protect your portfolio when the market is down and help protect you from losing more than the market.

2. Invest in Something You Understand

Many Americans became frustrated with the equity markets after the 2008 financial crisis. Thankfully, we have seen the financial markets rebound since then and have even seen some years of over 20 percent growth in the equity markets. Nevertheless, many Americans are still somewhat shell-shocked from the market swings and not 100 percent sure what exactly goes on on Wall Street and how it all works. Real estate, in comparison, is often a more comfortable investment for the lower and middle classes because they grew up exposed to it, whereas the upper classes often learned about Wall Street and other securities during their younger years and college days. Everyone has heard someone talk about the importance of owning a home or the amount of money that can be made by owning real estate—from Donald Trump to reality TV stars. Real estate is fast becoming mainstream, and one of the most trusted asset classes for Americans. It is, of course, not without risk, but many retirement investors feel more comfortable understanding the real estate market and buying and selling real estate than they do stocks.

3. Inflation Protection

Rising food and energy prices, coupled with high federal debt levels and low interest rates, have recently fueled new inflationary fears. As a result, some investors may be looking for ways to protect their portfolios from the ravages of inflation. It is a matter of guesswork to estimate whether these inflation risks are real, but for some retirement investors, protecting retirement assets from inflation is a big concern. Inflation can have a nasty impact on a retirement portfolio because it means a dollar today may not be worth a dollar tomorrow. Inflation also increases the cost of things that are necessary for humans to live and enjoy life, such as food, gas, shelter, clothing, medical services, etc., decreasing the value of money so that goods and services cost more. For example, if someone has an IRA worth $250,000 at a time of high inflation, that $250,000 will be worth significantly less or have significantly less buying power. This can mean the difference between retiring and working the rest of your life. Buying hard assets is seen as one way of protecting your assets against inflation. Many investors have long recognized that investing in commercial real estate or precious metals can provide a natural protection against inflation, as rents tend to increase when prices do, acting as a hedge against inflation.

4. Hard Assets

Many nontraditional assets, such as real estate and precious metals, are tangible hard assets that you can see and touch. With real estate, for example, you can drive by with your family, point out the window, and say, "I own that." For some, that's important psychologically, especially in times of financial instability, inflation, or political or global upheaval.

"Let's go into a few of those opportunities in more detail so you understand the finer points," John said.

Real Estate

Real estate has become one of the most popular nontraditional investment options for IRA investors. We'll discuss the details in Chapter 6.

According to McKinsey & Company report *The Mainstreaming of Alternative Investments: Fueling the Next Wave of Growth in Asset Management,* by Onur Erzan, principal, dated June 2012, in the United States, institutional investors expect to have 28 percent of their portfolios allocated to alternative investments by the end of 2013, up from 26 percent in 2010. That quote was taken from a recent *Financial Advisor* magazine article. The same piece also referenced a multiyear McKinsey & Company study that noted year-end 2011 assets under management for global alternatives reached record levels of $6.5 trillion, having grown at a five-year rate of over seven times that of traditional asset classes.

Real estate offers diversification from overexposure to Wall Street for both personal and retirement funds. After the 2008 financial crisis, many retirement investors began to appreciate the importance of having a well-balanced and diversified retirement portfolio that can help protect against another financial crisis. People generally like to invest in something they know and understand. Real estate is reemerging as an asset class that more Americans have confidence and comfort in compared to the vagaries of the stock market. Buying tangible assets, such as real estate, is seen as a solid way of protecting retirement savings from the threat of inflation.

Plus, all income and gains from real estate owned in a self-directed IRA are exempt from tax, making real estate an even more powerful investment. For example, if you purchased a piece of property with your self-directed IRA for $100,000 and you later sold the property for $300,000, the $200,000 of gain appreciation would generally be tax-free. Whereas, if you purchased the property using personal funds (nonretirement funds), the gain would be subject to federal income tax and, in most cases, state income tax.

The IRS allows you to use a self-directed IRA to purchase real estate or raw land, as long as your plan does allow for it. Remember, it is up to the IRA custodian whether nontraditional investment options, such as real estate, are permitted to be made with IRA funds. In general, most financial institution–established IRAs do not allow for real estate investments, while a custodian-directed and checkbook control self-directed IRA will allow for the real estate investment option.

Since you are the manager of the self-directed IRA LLC, making a real estate investment is as simple as writing a check from your self-directed IRA LLC bank account.

Tax Liens and Tax Deeds

Tax lien and tax deed investments have become popular investment choices for many self-directed IRA investors. Beginning in 2009, as foreclosures continued to pile up, many properties were saddled with unpaid property taxes. For some investors, this created a great investment opportunity.

Tax collectors in twenty-nine states; Washington, DC; Puerto Rico; and the US Virgin Islands use tax lien sales to force owners to pay unpaid property taxes. The process varies by state, but here's how it generally works: When property owners don't pony up for their property taxes, tax collectors wait the time period required by state law and then put those unpaid property taxes up for auction. The time period varies from just a few months to several years depending on the state.

In most states, the person willing to pay the most cash for the tax lien wins the auction. Some states, however, have a bid-down process, in which investors' bids indicate how much interest they're willing to accept on their investment, and the lowest bidder wins. Whatever method is used, the tax collector takes the payment for the overdue taxes from the winning bidder. In exchange, the purchaser gets a lien on the property. As the winning bidder, you'd get a return on your investment in one of two ways: interest on your bid amount, or ownership of the property.

With a tax deed, on the other hand, you will actually own the property in which the owner has been delinquent in paying the property taxes. A tax deed sale generally involves property being sold by a taxing authority or the court to recover delinquent taxes.

The IRS permits the purchase of tax liens and tax deeds with a self-directed IRA. The advantage of purchasing tax liens or tax deeds with a self-directed IRA is that your profits are tax-deferred back into your retirement account until a distribution is taken. In the case of a self-directed Roth IRA, all gains are tax-free.

Once again, you have checkbook control and can make purchases on the spot without custodian consent.

Loans and Notes

The IRS permits using IRA funds to make loans or purchase notes from third parties. By using a self-directed IRA to make loans or purchase notes from third parties, all interest payments received are tax-deferred until a distribution is taken. In the case of a self-directed Roth IRA, all gains are tax-free. When engaging in private lending transaction or purchasing notes, it is important to make note of the IRS prohibited transaction and disqualified person rules, which are found in IRC 4975. A detailed description of the prohibited transaction and disqualified person rules can be found in the next chapter.

For example, if you used a self-directed IRA to loan money to a friend, all interest received would flow back into your self-directed IRA, whereas if you lent your friend money from personal funds (nonretirement funds), the interest received would be subject to federal and, in most cases, state income tax.

Private Businesses

With a self-directed IRA you are permitted to purchase an interest in a privately held business that is engaged in any type of business activity. The business can be established as any entity other than an S corporation (i.e., limited liability company, C corporation, partnership, etc.) because a retirement account cannot be a shareholder of an S corporation. When investing in a private business using retirement funds, it is important to keep in mind the disqualified person and prohibited transaction rules under IRC 4975 and the unrelated business taxable income rules under IRC 512. It is a good idea to consult a retirement tax professional to develop the most tax-efficient structure for using your self-directed IRA to invest in a private business. These rules will be explained in greater detail in the next chapter.

Precious Metals and Coins

You can also use your self-directed assets to make investments in precious metals and certain coins. The advantage of using a self-directed IRA to purchase precious metals and/or coins is that their values generally keep up with, or exceed, inflation rates better than other investments. In addition, in the case of a checkbook control IRA LLC, the metals and/or coins can be held in the name of the IRA LLC (for example, ABC, LLC) at your local bank's safe-deposit box, eliminating depository fees. A more detailed explanation of the rules involved in purchasing precious metals or IRS-approved coins can be found in Chapter 6.

Foreign Currencies and Options

There is no IRS prohibition against using retirement funds to purchase foreign currencies or engaging in option trading. Many investors believe that foreign currency investments offer liquidity advantages compared to the stock market as well as significant investment opportunities. With respect to option trading, there is a belief that it can potentially generate increased cost-efficiency, may be less risky than equities, and has the potential to deliver higher-percentage returns.

Again, all foreign currency gains and income from the lapse or termination of an option are generally tax-deferred until a distribution is taken, and in the case of a self-directed Roth IRA, all gains are tax-free.

Stocks, Bonds, Mutual Funds, CDs

In addition to nontraditional investments such as real estate, a self-directed IRA LLC may also purchase stocks, bonds, mutual funds, and CDs. According to the Investment Company Institute report titled *The IRA*

Investor Profile: The Traditional IRA Investors' Activity, 2007–2012, dated March 10, 2014, traditional IRA investors' allocation to equity holdings fell, on average, although some of the change merely reflects market movement rather than investors' rebalancing. For example, among consistent traditional IRA investors aged 25 to 59, about three-quarters of their traditional IRA assets were invested in equity holdings—which includes equities, equity funds, and the equity portion of balanced funds—at year-end 2007, and about two-thirds of their traditional IRA assets were invested in equity holdings at year-end 2012. Accordingly, it's easy to conclude that stocks, mutual funds, ETFs, and other equities are by far the most popular investment for retirement accounts.

The advantage of using a self-directed IRA LLC with checkbook control is that you are not limited to just making these types of investments. You can open a stock trading account with any financial institution.

No one is arguing against stocks as the best retirement investment. Indeed, history has shown that owning stocks is one of the easiest and most profitable ways to grow your wealth over the long term. From January 1, 1900, through December 31, 2013, for example, the average return of the S&P 500, which tracks the 500 largest stocks based on market capitalization, was 11.6 percent.

Stocks have proven to be a good investment over time. Could you do better with a different investment? Possibly. The bigger concern, however, is that such heavy exposure to the US equity markets carries some risk. Diversification is a must when it comes to retirement planning.

So How Much Does this Cost?

"I know we discussed fees earlier," Rich said, "but can you explain how all the fees work with a self-directed IRA when it comes to alternative asset investments, like real estate?"

"Absolutely," John said. "With a self-directed IRA LLC with checkbook control you can save a good deal of money on IRA custodian fees. In fact, you no longer have to pay high annual custodian fees based on account value and transaction fees. Instead, with a checkbook control self-directed IRA LLC, an FDIC-backed IRS-approved passive custodian is used. The custodian in the checkbook control self-directed IRA LLC structure is referred to as a passive custodian largely because the custodian is not required to approve any IRA-related investment and simply serves the role of satisfying IRS regulations. By using a self-directed IRA LLC with checkbook control, you can take advantage of all the benefits of self-directing your retirement assets without incurring excessive custodian fees and custodian-created delays since you, as manager of the IRA LLC, have checkbook control over your IRA funds."

"That sounds terrific," Rich said.

"Let's break down the fee discussion based on the type of self-directed IRA account established," John said.

Traditional Financial Institution Self-Directed IRA

The majority of Americans are able to invest their IRA funds in traditional types of investments, such as stocks, mutual funds, and ETFs, with very few fees, other than broker commissions. Most of the major financial institutions and brokerage houses will not charge annual fees for opening and operating a self-directed IRA. Essentially you will just pay fees based on the type of financial products you are purchasing, typically commissions. Some private wealth firms may charge an account valuation fee, but these types of accounts are quite rare when it comes to IRAs because of the amount of IRA assets needed to be a private wealth client.

"How are the financial institutions able to limit the investment options available?" Rich asked.

"A financial institution that offers IRA accounts is not required to offer its IRA investors the opportunity to make all allowable types of IRA investments," John explained. "For example, even though real estate is an IRS-approved investment, an IRA custodian is not required or obligated to offer that investment option. Remember the statement on the IRS website about IRAs making real estate investments:

"IRA law does not prohibit investing in real <u>estate, but trustees are not</u> <u>required to offer real estate as an option.</u>"

Accordingly, most financial institutions offering IRA accounts will restrict the IRA investment option to financial products offered by the financial institution. The reason behind this is quite clear—a financial institution earns fees from the sale of financial products, not by allowing its clients to pull money out of the IRA account to buy real estate from a third party."

Custodian-Controlled Self-Directed IRA

A custodian-controlled self-directed IRA offers an IRA investor more investment options than a financial institution self-directed IRA. With a custodian-controlled self-directed IRA, a special financial institution or IRA administrator will serve as the custodian of the IRA. Generally, all funds transferred to a custodian-controlled self-directed IRA are held in an omnibus custodial account at an FDIC-insured financial institution. Unlike a typical financial institution, most IRA custodians generate fees simply by opening and maintaining IRA accounts and do not offer any financial investment products or platforms. With a custodian-controlled self-directed IRA, the IRA funds are generally held with the IRA custodian and the IRA custodian, at the IRA holder's direction, will then invest those IRA funds accordingly.

Until the 1996 Swanson Tax Court case, which was previously discussed at length, the custodian-controlled self-directed IRA was the only way you could use IRA funds to make a nontraditional investment, such as real estate. In essence, with a custodian-controlled self-directed IRA, every step an IRA holder wanted to make had to be carried out through a custodian, which would involve high annual fees, transaction fees, and time delays. In other words, the IRA holder had limited control over the IRA investment process and could not take direct control. Every time the IRA holder needed to pay an IRA transaction expense, such as paying for someone to mow the grass or pay real estate taxes, the IRA holder had to have the IRA custodian do it.

The average full-service self-directed IRA custodian typically charges a flat annual account fee based on IRA account value as well as charging per transaction, in most cases. The average full-service self-directed IRA custodian charges anywhere between $350 and $1,500 for annual self-directed IRA full-service custodian services. The fees generally are based on the IRA holder's IRA account value and the number of and type of IRA transactions being performed during the year.

The Checkbook Control Self-Directed IRA LLC

One of the more popular reasons for selecting a checkbook control self-directed IRA LLC over a custodian-directed self-directed IRA to make alternative investments is the ability to reduce the annual IRA custodian fees. The reason behind this is quite simple. With a checkbook control self-directed IRA LLC, all the IRA investment activity is happening at the LLC level and not the IRA custodian level. In fact, the IRA custodian in a self-directed IRA LLC checkbook control structure is referred to as a passive custodian largely because the custodian is not required to approve any IRA-related investment and simply serves the role of satisfying IRS regulations. In large part, because all the IRA investments are occurring at the LLC level, from your local LLC bank account and not at the custodian level, the IRA custodian won't even know what investments your LLC will be engaged in once the IRA funds have been invested into the LLC. Remember, the self-directed IRA LLC operating agreement will provide for the manager of the LLC (typically the IRA holder) to have full authority over all LLC activities and investment decisions, which is where the term *checkbook control* comes from. This means that once the IRA custodian has transferred the IRA funds to the new IRA LLC the LLC manager is free to invest the funds as long as the investment does not violate the IRS prohibited transaction rules. Hence, all the IRA LLC manager needs to do is write a check or execute a wire transfer to make the LLC investment. No IRA custodian consent is required before making the investment. In fact, you don't need to even involve the IRA custodian in the investment as the investment will be made in the name of the LLC (i.e., ABC, LLC) and not the name of the custodian (IRA Custodian XYZ of the John Doe IRA). I will get into how to make investments with a self-directed IRA LLC shortly, but with a checkbook control self-directed IRA LLC, the IRA custodian is not involved in the investment process and this is why the fees associated with a self-directed IRA LLC checkbook control structure are typically less expensive than a full-service custodian-directed self-directed IRA account over a period of time. In essence, with a checkbook control self-directed IRA LLC, the custodian won't know if you are buying real estate in Texas, California, New York, or South Carolina. Since the IRA custodian is not involved in the transaction, all the IRA custodian will be involved in is the transfer of the IRA funds to the LLC. This is the main reason why the checkbook control self-directed IRA LLC is less expensive to administer than a full-service self-directed IRA account over the life of the structure.

LLC Filings

"What about the LLC filing fees and tax advisory fees to establish a self-directed IRA LLC?" Rich asked.

"That's a great question," John said. "The one downside to a checkbook control self-directed IRA LLC is the up-front fee for the establishment of the LLC and the need to engage a tax adviser to help with the establishment of the structure. The state filing fees for LLCs range from $50 to $600. In most cases, the average state-filing fee for establishing an LLC is somewhere close to $200. When you add the advisory fees and IRA custodian fees, the setup of a self-directed IRA LLC with checkbook control generally runs between $1,000 and $1,500 for the first year. This includes the LLC state filing fee, the fee for having a tax professional or facilitation firm establish your self-directed IRA LLC structure, and first-year IRA custodian fees, which generally cost between $150 and $300 for year one. After year one, the IRA custodian fee generally runs between $125 and $200 and most states impose an annual LLC state filing fee of anywhere from $0 to $800, in the case of California. The average state charges around $125 a year for annual filing fees."

"So not a ton of money, but not insignificant," Rich said.

"I gave you a chart earlier, outlined in Chapter 4, that describes the LLC establishment and annual fees for all fifty states. That should give you a better idea of annual fees involved in maintaining a self-directed IRA LLC," John said.

"Okay," Rich said, "it seems that if you look at the self-directed IRA LLC structure over a period of time, it generally makes cost-effective sense to establish a checkbook control self-directed IRA LLC structure, whereas if you are looking at a one- or two-year self-directed IRA LLC investment window, then maybe the full-service self-directed IRA model makes more financial sense. That being said, if you will be buying tax liens of engaging in multiple real estate transactions on a yearly basis, then the checkbook control IRA LLC would make your life much easier even if it cost a bit more money."

"Yes, I agree," John said. "One other thing to consider is that if you establish a self-directed IRA LLC that will be owned by two or more IRAs, the LLC will be treated as a partnership for federal and state income tax purposes and an IRS Form 1065 must be filed, even if no tax is due, as well as a state partnership return. Completing IRS form 1065—US Return of Partnership Income—is quite simple and can be done via an online tax return preparer provider or by using a tax professional. Accordingly, there will be some additional fees that will need to be incurred if one used a self-directed IRA LLC that will be owned by two or more IRAs to make investments since using a tax return preparation service will cost money. The cost generally could run anywhere from $50 to $500 depending on who you get to help you with filing the federal and state income tax returns. Of course, you can complete the form yourself for no cost, which some of my clients do. Also, it is important to remember that an LLC owned by one IRA, which makes up the majority of all self-directed IRA LLC structures, is treated as a disregarded entity for federal income tax purposes, and no federal income tax return is required to be filed. So no additional fees would be incurred is one established a self-directed IRA LLC owned by one IRA."

"Do I need to pay the self-directed IRA setup fees and annul account fees with retirement funds or can I use personal funds?" Rich asked.

"In general," John said, "since the establishment of an IRA is an expense associated with a retirement account and not a business or personal expense, the fees associated with establishing an IRA or for the facilitation of a self-directed IRA structure should be paid using IRA funds. It's my policy that my clients pay all IRA establishment fees, including the setup of the self-directed IRA account, LLC state filing fees, and any tax advisory service fees only with retirement funds. I think it is a good idea not to use any personal funds. First of all, the IRS could argue that by paying IRA-associated fees with personal funds you are somewhat benefiting directly or indirectly, which could violate the IRS prohibited transaction rules under IRC 4975. I will touch upon these rules in greater detail at a later point, but the premise of the IRS prohibited transaction rules is that one should not use IRA funds in any transaction that could directly or indirectly personally benefit the IRA holder or a disqualified person, which is essentially defined as the IRA holder and his or her lineal descendants. In addition to the IRS potentially arguing that using personal funds to pay for IRA-related expenses could be treated as a prohibited transaction, the IRS could also argue that the use of personal funds to pay IRA expenses allows one to potentially exceed the IRA contribution limitations by using funds in additional to IRA contributions to pay for IRA-related expenses. Again, I don't think it is worth the risk and strongly suggest that all my clients pay for IRA-related expenses, including establishment fees and, of course, investment-associated expenses with retirement funds."

"So what happens if you have no IRA funds and want to set up an IRA or pay annual LLC fees?" Rich asked.

"Another good question," John said. "The IRS allows an individual with earned income to contribute up to $5,500 if under the age of fifty and $6,500 if over the age of fifty for the 2015 taxable year. So, you can easily make a contribution to the IRA custodian in which their self-directed IRA account will be opened and then the IRA custodian can take the account-establishment fee from the IRA contribution or, alternatively, use those funds to pay annual IRA LLC–related expenses. This is done quite often with many IRA custodians. In addition, if you make a pretax IRA contribution, you will at least get a tax deduction for the IRA contribution and then the IRA account fees can be paid from the IRA contribution."

"Okay, I think I get it," Rich said. "All IRA setup fees should be paid with IRA funds and no personal funds should be used."

"Yes, and if you don't have IRA funds and want to set up a self-directed IRA, you should make an IRA contribution and use those funds to pay any IRA setup fees."

"You keep mentioning speed," Rich said. "How does a self-directed IRA LLC allow me to make investments more quickly?"

"With checkbook control, you, as manager of the IRA LLC, can act quickly on a great investment opportunity," John said. "When you have a self-directed IRA LLC and you find an investment that you want to make with your IRA funds, you simply write a check or wire the funds straight from your self-directed IRA LLC bank account to make the investment."

"So," Rich said, "the self-directed IRA LLC allows you to eliminate the delays associated with an IRA custodian, enabling you to act quickly when the right investment opportunity presents itself."

"Correct. As manager of the self-directed IRA LLC, all IRA investment decisions are truly yours."

Example No. 1:
Joe has a self-directed IRA LLC. Joe has established his self-directed IRA LLC bank account with Bank of America. The name of Joe's LLC is Joe Smith IRA LLC. Joe wishes to use his IRA funds to purchase a home from Steve, an unrelated third party (nondisqualified person). Steve is anxious to close the transaction as soon as possible. With a checkbook control self-directed IRA LLC, Joe can simply write a check using the funds from his IRA LLC account or can wire the funds directly from the account to Steve. Joe, as manager of the LLC, is no longer required to seek the consent of the IRA custodian before making the real estate purchase. In contrast, with a regular self- directed IRA *without* checkbook control

Joe may not be able to make the real estate purchase since seeking custodian approval as well as having the custodian execute all required transaction documents would likely take too much time.

Example No. 2:

Joe has a self-directed IRA LLC. Joe has established his self-directed IRA LLC bank account with Bank of America. The name of Joe's LLC is Joe Smith IRA LLC. Joe wishes to use his IRA funds to invest in tax lien certificates via auction. Purchasing tax lien certificates requires Joe to make the tax lien payment at the auction. With a checkbook control self-directed IRA LLC, Joe can simply bring his LLC checkbook to the auction or secure a certified check from the bank in order to make payments at the auction. In contrast, with a regular self-directed IRA without checkbook control, Joe would not be able to make tax lien certificate investments because he would need his IRA custodian to sign the check or make payment on the spot at auction, which would not be feasible.

Bankruptcy Protection

"I hear the self-directed IRA has really good asset protection from creditors inside and outside of bankruptcy," Rich said. "This is something I am really interested in. Can you explain further?"

"Retirement accounts have become many Americans' most valuable assets," John said. "That means it's vital that you have the ability to protect those assets from creditors, such as people who have won lawsuits against you. In general, the asset/creditor-protection strategies available to you depend on the type of retirement account you have [i.e., traditional IRA, Roth IRA, or 401(k) qualified plan, etc.], your state residency, and whether the assets are yours or have been inherited."

"I bet that because the self-directed IRA is set up using an LLC wholly owned by your IRA, you also gain another layer of limited liability protection," Rich said.

"That's right," John said. "In this regard, using a self-directed IRA LLC to make investments offers you far greater asset and creditor protection than making the investment personally."

"So growing and investing your retirement funds through a self-directed IRA LLC is a great tool to protect your retirement assets from creditors, inside or outside of bankruptcy," Rich said.

"You got it," John said, and he handed a pamphlet on bankruptcy protection for IRAs.

Federal Protection for IRAs for Bankruptcy

Like 401(k) qualified plans, The Bankruptcy Abuse Prevention and Consumer Protection Act of 2005 (BAPCPA or the Act) effective for bankruptcies filed after October 17, 2005, gave protection to a debtor's IRA funds in bankruptcy by way of exempting them from the bankruptcy estate. The general exemption found in Section 522 of the Bankruptcy Code, 11 USC Section 522, provides an unlimited exemption for IRAs under IRC Section 408 and Roth IRAs under IRC Section 408A. IRAs created under an employer-sponsored IRC Section 408(k) simplified employee pension (SEP IRA) or a IRC Section 408(p) simple retirement account (SIMPLE IRA), as well as pension, profit sharing, or qualified IRC Section 401(k) plan wealth transferred to a rollover IRA.

Traditional and Roth IRAs that are created and funded by the debtor are subject to an exemption limitation of $1 million in the aggregate for all such IRAs (adjusted for inflation and subject to increase if the bankruptcy judge determines that the "interests of justice so require"). It is understood that a rollover from a SEP or SIMPLE IRA into a rollover IRA receives only $1 million of protection since an IRC Section 408(d)(3) rollover is not one of the rollovers sanctioned under Bankruptcy Code Section 522(n).

Protection of IRAs from Creditors Outside of Bankruptcy

In general, ERISA pension plans, such as 401(k) qualified plans, are afforded extensive antialienation creditor protection both inside and outside of bankruptcy. However, these extensive antialienation protections do not extend to an IRA, including a self-directed IRA arrangement under Code Section 408. Therefore, since an individually established and funded traditional or Roth IRA is not an ERISA pension plan, IRAs are not preempted under ERISA. Thus, for anything short of bankruptcy, state law determines whether IRAs (including Roth IRAs) are shielded from creditors' claims.

Note: On June 12, 2014, the Supreme Court unanimously upheld a Seventh Circuit decision that said inherited IRAs do not enjoy the protections of IRAs in bankruptcy proceedings. "Many states do offer creditor protection outside of bankruptcy for IRAs, including Alaska, Arizona, Arkansas, Colorado, Connecticut, Delaware, Florida, Illinois, Iowa, Kansas, Kentucky, Louisiana, Maine, Maryland, Massachusetts, Michigan, Minnesota, Mississippi, Montana, Nebraska, Nevada, New Hampshire, New Jersey, New York, North Carolina, North Dakota, Ohio, Oregon, Pennsylvania, Rhode Island, South Carolina, Tennessee, Texas, Utah, Vermont, Virginia, Washington, and Wisconsin. However, some states do not offer Roth IRAs creditor protection outside of bankruptcy, such as Alabama, Georgia, Idaho, and Indiana. Whereas, some states, such as California and Wyoming seem to limit IRA protection from creditors outside of the bankruptcy context. I suggest you talk with a bankruptcy attorney if you need more info on this subject, because the rules can get quite complicated and trick." John said.

IRA Asset Protection Planning

The different federal and state creditor protection afforded to 401(k) qualified plans and IRAs, including self-directed IRAs, inside or outside the bankruptcy context, presents a number of important asset protection planning opportunities.

If, for example, you have left an employer where you had a qualified plan, rolling over assets from a qualified plan, like a 401(k), into an IRA may have asset protection implications. For example, if you live in or are moving to a state where IRAs are not protected from creditors or if you have in excess of $1 million in plan assets and are contemplating bankruptcy, you would likely be better off leaving the assets in the company qualified plan.

Note: If you plan to leave at least some of your IRA to your family members other than your spouse, the assets may not be protected from your beneficiaries' creditors, depending on where the beneficiaries live. IRA assets left to a spouse would likely receive creditor protection if the IRA is retitled in the name of the spouse. However, you will likely be able to protect your IRA assets that you plan on leaving to your family members other than your spouse by leaving an IRA to a trust. To do that, you must name the trust on the IRA custodian designation of beneficiary form on file. You should talk to an estate-planning attorney for more information on this.

The IRA Asset and Creditor Protection Solution

By having and maintaining an IRA, you will have $1 million of asset protection from creditors in a bankruptcy setting. However, the determination of whether your IRA will be protected from creditors outside of bankruptcy will largely depend on state law. As illustrated above, most states will afford IRAs full protection from creditors outside of the bankruptcy context.

Can I Take a Loan from My Self-Directed IRA?

"Can you take a loan from your self-directed IRA?" Rich asked.

"Unfortunately," John said, "you cannot borrow any funds from an IRA without triggering an IRS prohibited transaction. However, if you are a participant in an employer 401(k) plan or are self-employed and can adopt a solo 401(k) plan, you are able to borrow the lesser of $50,000 or 50 percent of the 401(k) plan account value and use the loan for any purpose."

"Oh, I didn't know that," Rich said.

"Yes," John nodded. "The loan feature is unique to a 401(k) plan, but the plan adoption agreement must include the option in the plan in order for the loan to be available to an eligible plan participant. The majority of employer 401(k) plans do include the loan feature, but an employer is not required to offer the loan feature. In the case of a Solo 401(k) plan, which is a 401(k) plan for a business with no full-time employees other than the owners or their spouses, most financial institution–provided plans, which are typically offered for no fee, usually do not offer the loan feature because these institutions only make money when the 401(k) plans are being invested and not when they are being pulled out for personal purposes. In contrast, most of the custodian-directed and open architecture solo 401(k) plan document providers will offer the loan feature."

"Okay, so that's something to look into if I had a solo 401(k)."

"Right," John said. "With a 401(k) plan loan, you can access your retirement funds without tax or penalty by taking a loan using the accumulated balance of your solo 401(k) plan as collateral. Such a loan is permitted at any time, and you can borrow up to either $50,000 or 50 percent of your account value—whichever is less."

"Is that different from other retirement savings plans?" Rich asked.

"Yes, that 401(k) loan feature is unique among retirement savings plans and makes the solo 401(k) plan particularly attractive to many sole proprietorships and small-business owners with no full-time employees other than the owner(s)/spouse(s). There is no loan feature available with any type of IRA, including a SEP IRA or SIMPLE IRA. The solo 401(k) loan feature is really the only way you can use retirement funds for personal use without triggering a tax or penalty. The loan feature is truly helpful because it allows you to use the retirement funds and do a prohibited transaction and not pay a tax or penalty."

"And you still pay it back, right?" Rich said.

"The 401(k) plan loan must be paid back over a five-year period (fifteen years if you will be using the loan proceeds to purchase a primary residence), at least quarterly, but can be paid back more quickly (i.e., weekly, biweekly, monthly) and at an interest rate of at least prime per the *Wall Street Journal*. As of July 1, 2015, the prime interest rate is 3.25 percent."

"Why are those kinds of plan loans legal?" Rich asked.

"Plan loans from a 401(k) are legal," John said, "because of a limited statutory exception to the prohibited transaction rules as stated in IRC 4975(d)(1). Specifically, IRC 72(p) and the 2001 EGGTRA rules allow you to borrow money from your solo 401(k) plan tax-free and without penalty. As long as the plan documents allow for it and the proper loan documents are prepared and executed, you can take such a loan for any reason. If the loan payments are made on time, there are no penalties or taxes due."

"There must be thousands of ways to use a 401(k) plan loan," Rich said.

"There are," John agreed. "In fact, you can use the 401(k) loan for practically anything as long as that activity is not illegal—you can do it. There is no need to worry about IRS prohibited transactions because the 401(k) loan is exempt from the reach of the prohibited transaction rules."

"What could you possibly do with such a loan?" Rich asked.

"Well," John answered, "There are a number of popular ways to use the 401(k) loan proceeds":

- To obtain immediate funds for your business
- To help pay personal expenses
- To lend to a third party at a higher interest rate
- To invest in a real estate project that offers a higher rate of return than prime plus 1 percent
- To consolidate your debt and help pay it off
- To pay for college expenses
- To pay for unexpected emergencies
- To avoid distribution penalties while using up to $50,000 immediately without restrictions
- To invest in a new franchise or business
- Take an investment—such as a tax lien, private placement, or mortgage pool—that will generate a higher rate of return than prime plus 1 percent
- To invest in some transaction that would otherwise be prohibited under IRC 4975

"It sounds like you can have quick, easy, and inexpensive access to $50,000 for any reason," Rich said.

"That's true," John said. "And you are not limited to taking or making only one loan, but those loans together must not exceed $50,000 or 50 percent of your account value, whichever is less, with some stipulations. Specifically, the total amount you can borrow can't, when added to the balance of all other outstanding loans, exceed the lesser of:

- $50,000 that is reduced by the highest loan outstanding balance (HLOB) of any other loans during the plan
- More than half of your vested current plan outstanding balance (POB) or $10,000."

"What happens if I miss a loan payment?" Rich asked.

"Loan payments must be made in a timely manner or they will be considered delinquent and will become subject to tax as well as 10 percent penalty if the borrower is under the age of 59½," John answered. "A delinquent loan is not the same as a defaulted loan. A defaulted loan is an IRS-defined term, and a 401(k) plan loan is deemed to be in default when it no longer meets the requirements found in Treasury Regulation 1.72(p)-1. In general, there is no prepayment penalty for paying back a 401(k) loan early."

"Too bad I am not self-employed," Rich said. "The loan feature seems really attractive and I understand I would be able to do the same investments I would be able to do with a self-directed IRA. What I am curious about is how does the solo 401(k) plan match-up with the SEP IRA?"

"Prior to 2002," John said, "there was no compelling reason to establish a solo 401(k) plan because you would essentially get the same retirement and investment benefits by establishing a SEP IRA, and a SEP IRA was easier and less costly to establish. However, the Economic Growth and Tax Relief Reconciliation Act of 2001 (EGTRRA) changed all of this. After 2002, EGTRRA paved the way for an owner-only business to put more money aside for retirement and to operate a more cost-effective retirement plan than a SEP IRA or 401(k) plan."

The SEP IRA vs. the Solo 401(k) Plan

"What's the difference with a SEP?"

"The SEP is a pure profit-sharing employer-sponsored retirement plan that allows for a tax-deductible contribution equal to the smaller of $53,000 or 25 percent of compensation for 2015."

"And the solo 401(k) is better?"

"I think so," John said. "The solo 401(k) has the following advantages":

1. Higher maximum contribution

A solo 401(k) plan allows you to make an employee salary-deferral contribution and an employee profit-sharing deferral contribution. A SEP IRA, on the other hand, only allows for a profit-sharing contribution for 2015 equal to the lesser of $53,000 or 25 percent (20 percent in the case of a sole proprietorship or single-member LLC) of the earned income or compensation earned via the business, and it does not have an employee salary-deferral contribution. Whereas, with a solo 401(k) plan you are able to make an employee-deferral contribution of $18,000 ($24,000 if over the age of 50), in either pretax or Roth, as well as a profit-sharing contribution for 2015 equal to the lesser of $53,000 or 25 percent (20 percent in the case of a sole proprietorship or single-member LLC) of the earned income or compensation earned via the business.

So, if you are sixty years old and have an S corporation from which you earn $100,000 in self-employment wages according to your W-2 form, then you can put in approximately $24,000 plus $25,000 (which is 25 percent of $100,000) or $49,000 into your solo 401(k), whereas, if you had established a SEP IRA you could only defer 25 percent of $100,000 or $25,000.

2. Catchup contributions

With a solo 401(k) you can contribute an extra $6,000 if you are over 50 years of age. The SEP IRA does not allow a catchup contribution.

3. Roth feature

A solo 401(k) plan can be made in either pretax or after-tax (Roth) formats. A SEP IRA only permits pretax contributions.

4. Tax-free loan option

As we just discussed, a solo 401(k) permits you to borrow up to $50,000 or 50 percent of your account value, whichever is less. This loan can be used for any purpose. A SEP IRA does not allow you to borrow any money from your account without triggering a prohibited transaction.

5. Invest in real estate and use leverage with no additional tax

With a solo 401(k) you can make a real estate investment using nonrecourse funds without triggering the Unrelated Debt Financed Income Rules and the Unrelated Business Taxable Income Tax (IRC 514). These rules will be discussed in greater detail in Chapter 7. This is not possible with a SEP IRA as using SEP IRA funds to purchase real estate using a nonrecourse loan would trigger the (Unrelated Business Taxable Income (UBT) tax rules.

Solo 401(k) Plan vs. the SIMPLE IRA

"I have a few friends that have adopted a SIMPLE IRA over a SEP IRA and solo 401(k) plan," Rich said, "but now I am not sure that was a smart move."

"A SIMPLE IRA plan can be established by an employer who has fewer than a hundred employees who will receive at least $5,000 in compensation from the employer in the preceding calendar year."

"Oh," Rich said. "How are they different?"

"A SIMPLE IRA plan is similar to a solo 401(k) plan," John continued. "Both are funded by employee deferrals and additional employer contributions. However, a SIMPLE IRA has a lower deferral limit and uses an IRA-type trust to hold contributions for each employee, rather than a single plan."

"Does it have the same issues, then?"

"Mostly," John said, "the SIMPLE IRA has all of the same disadvantages as the SEP IRA relative to the solo 401(k) with one big exception. The SIMPLE IRA has an even lower deferral limit of $12,500 (for 2015) and a catchup contribution that is just $3,000. In addition, the employer must provide:

1. A dollar-for-dollar match of up to 3 percent of compensation to all who defer; or

2. A 2 percent nonelective contribution to all employees who are eligible to participate in the plan

"That's a knock against it I would think."

"For someone who's a sole proprietor, yes," John said. "In essence, the solo 401(k) plan is the most attractive retirement plan for the self-employed and has become the best retirement plan for the self-employed over the SEP IRA and SIMPLE IRA. If all things are equal and one is self-employed, the solo 401(k) plan offers the greatest retirement and investment opportunities over any other IRA. Unfortunately, not all of us are self-employed and for you, Rich, and for all the other non-self-employed folks, including W-2 employees, retirees, etc., the self-directed IRA and particularly the checkbook control IRA LLC is the best and most popular retirement vehicle for making alternative investments, such as real estate, tax liens, precious metals, private business investments, third-party loans, and much more."

"I get it. So now do we get to talk more about those alternative investments?"

"You read my mind, Rich. Let's do it."

VI

The Prohibited Transaction Rules

The next time they met, Rich was ready with the question that was first and foremost on his mind.

"I'd really like to talk about prohibited transactions," Rich said. "When I think of that word *prohibited* in relation to the IRS, I definitely feel the need to pay close attention and get the facts straight. Can you go through the rules that govern IRA investments in greater detail?"

"You bet," John said. "Now's a perfect time."

John pulled out some notes and dug in.

The Basics of Prohibited Transactions

"Even though it sounds daunting," John said. "It's really not. But it is a little fuzzy. The IRC doesn't describe what a self-directed IRA can invest in, only what it *cannot* invest in. Specifically, IRC Sections 408 & 4975 prohibit disqualified persons from engaging in certain types of transactions. The purpose of these rules is to encourage the use of IRAs for the accumulation of retirement savings and to prohibit those in control of IRAs from taking advantage of the tax benefits for their personal account."

"So it's sort of protecting my account from me?" Rich asked.

"In a way. Prohibited transaction rules are based on the premise that investments involving IRAs and related parties should be handled in a way that benefits the retirement account and not the IRA owner."

"Would the IRS prohibited transaction rules be different if I did a custodian-controlled self-directed IRA instead of a checkbook control self-directed IRA LLC?" Rich asked.

"Not at all," John said. "The IRS prohibited transaction rules are triggered when IRA funds are used to make an investment, whether or not the investment is made directly by a custodian or via a special purpose entity, such as an LLC wholly owned by an IRA. The checkbook control self-directed IRA LLC solution does not allow any IRA holder to circumvent the IRS prohibited transaction rules, it simply allows the IRA holder to make investments more quickly and, in most cases, for fewer annual fees."

"So if no harm would be coming to anyone except me, by my own hand, why should the IRS be so concerned about investments involving my IRA and my family members?" Rich asked.

"Basically," John answered, "that's the only way the IRS can protect its very important revenue-generating distribution rules. It needs to make sure that if people want to use their IRA funds for personal purposes, they pay tax and a penalty if they are under the age of 59½. In other words, it's the IRS's position that if you want to use retirement funds for personal purposes, that's okay as long as you pay the appropriate tax and penalty."

"Fair enough, I guess," Rich said. "I'd want to protect my revenue too."

"Exactly," John said. "So, in developing the disqualified person rules, the IRS is basically saying that it believes an IRA holder and his or her lineal descendants are one and the same, and if IRA funds are being transferred directly or indirectly to a disqualified person, it is the same as if the IRA holder him- or herself were personally benefiting."

"That position makes sense," Rich said.

John nodded. "Yes. If you think about it—by giving money to your parents or children, you are clearly benefiting to some degree because of the close family relationship, For example, using your IRA to pay your children's tuition or your parents' mortgage is either directly or indirectly benefiting you because if your parents or kids benefit, you are benefiting to some degree. The IRS's position is that if you were able to transact with a disqualified person and use IRA funds you could simply transfer the IRA funds to a child or parent and that would be just like them taking the money personally, which would eliminate the need to take a taxable distribution. This is something the IRS would definitely not appreciate."

"I think I get it," Rich said. "So if I could take some of my IRA funds and give them to my wife and kids, it would be pretty much the same as if I got to use the money personally."

"Right," John said. "The IRS was concerned that if they allowed this, people would be able to circumvent the distribution rules and avoid paying tax on their IRS accounts while simultaneously receiving some degree of benefit from the funds because they were used to help a close family member, such as a parent, child, or spouse."

"Ah, because I wouldn't have paid tax on that money otherwise, and I would still get to use it for my personal benefit."

"Remember, in the case of a traditional pretax IRA, you were granted a tax-deduction for the IRA contribution on the expectation that you would eventually pay tax on the accumulated IRA account value," John said. "If you were able to take the IRA funds and give them to a parent, spouse, or child, it would be like you were gaining use of the IRA funds without having to pay any tax or the 10 percent penalty, if applicable."

"And if that were possible, everyone would do it to avoid paying some taxes on that money," Rich said.

"Sure," John said. "And the IRS would be left with very little tax revenue from the IRA account and it would also lose tax revenue because of the use of the IRS deduction in the year of contribution—a double whammy."

"So prohibited transaction rules are actually very important for the IRS," Rich said.

"The bottom line," John said, "is that most Americans' largest asset by the time they retire is their IRA. The self-directed IRA structure has become so popular over the last several years because the 2008 financial crisis hit those retirement assets so hard and showed people how important it is to diversify their retirement investments. The IRS has actually granted retirement investors with a wide array of investment options when using retirement funds, but there are a number of important rules the IRS has codified that govern how IRA retirement funds are to be used."

"I never thought of the IRA as being the most important tool in America for retirement," Rich said.

"It really is," John said. "According to the Investment Company Institute November 2013 publication, IRAs represent more than one-quarter of US total retirement market assets, compared with 17 percent two decades ago, with $5.7 trillion in assets at the end of the second quarter of 2013. And they've only risen in importance on household balance sheets. In June 2013, IRA assets were 9 percent of all household financial assets, up from 4 percent of assets two decades ago. In May 2013, 46.1 million, or 38 percent of US households reported they owned IRAs. IRAs are such an important asset for retirees that it makes navigating the IRS prohibited transaction rules even more crucial."

"But like you said," Rich added, "the tricky part is that the IRS doesn't tell you what you can invest in or how you should use your IRA assets, it only tells you what you can't invest in or how you can't use those assets."

"Exactly," John said. "So prohibited transactions are important to follow if you want to gain maximum advantage from the work you are doing to create and grow your IRA retirement assets."

"Are the penalties for violating prohibited transaction rules harsh enough to be worth worrying about?" Rich asked.

"Yes," John said, "they're steep. And if your IRA is your most valuable asset, as it is for most Americans, it will trigger a hefty tax and penalty with significant financial ramifications to your retirement."

"Are the prohibited transaction rules the same for traditional and Roth IRAs?" Rich asked.

John nodded. "The same rules apply to all retirement accounts, including IRAs, Roth IRAs, SEP IRAs, SIMPLE IRAs, and 401(k) qualified retirement plans. The one main difference between the application of the prohibited transaction rules for IRAs and 401(k) plans is that an IRA cannot purchase life insurance, but a 401(k) plan can. I'll expand on the rules shortly."

"I wonder why I never heard of prohibited transaction rules before we started talking."

"You're not alone," John said. "Most Americans have never heard of the prohibited transaction rules for good reason. After all, most retirement investors use their retirement funds to buy traditional financial assets, such as stocks, mutual funds, and ETFs. With those investments, the chance of engaging in a prohibited transaction is slim to none. For people who make nontraditional investments with their self-directed IRA such as real estate, the prohibited transaction rules become very important. The good news is that the harsh penalties are easily avoidable. As long as you stay away from breaking the rules, you have no reason to fear the IRS when making self-directed IRA investments."

"Okay," Rich said. "So what areas do we need to discuss?"

"Let's look at prohibited transactions that are restricted because they pertain to disqualified persons, conflicts of interest, and self-dealing," John said. "And we should also look at exceptions and exemptions to the restrictions, as well as certain categories of transactions that are not allowed with a self-directed IRA, such as the purchase of collectibles. Though there are many different scenarios stipulated in IRC Section 4975, and extensive case law clarifying those scenarios, the restrictions themselves are not complicated, and I can simplify them as much as possible to make them easier to follow. Even so, it can be helpful to get advice from a tax professional just to make sure you're on the straight and narrow path."

John then explained everything Rich needed to learn about disqualified persons.

Disqualified Persons

If a self-directed IRA transaction is restricted, it is likely because it pertains to a disqualified person. Who does the IRS consider a disqualified person?

Generally, this is referring to *you* (the IRA holder) and most of *your immediate family*, including your direct lineal ancestors or descendants as well as *any business* entities that hold a controlling equity or management interest in your self-directed IRA.

Specifically, a disqualified person is:

A) **You**, as the IRA holder, or any person with authority for making IRA investments

B) **A trustee or custodian**, or a person providing services to the self-directed IRA

C) **The owner**: This is generally not applicable to IRAs and only really covers 401(k) plans.

D) **An employee organization**: This is generally not applicable to IRAs and only really covers 401(k) plans.

E) **A 50 percent owner** of C or D

F) **A family member** of A, B, C, or D, which includes your spouse, your parents and grandparents, your children and grandchildren, and their spouses, but not brothers, sisters, aunts, uncles, cousins, step-siblings, or friends

G) **A partnership, corporation, trust, or estate** more than 50 percent owned or controlled by A, B, C, D, or E

H) **A 10 percent owner, officer, director, or highly compensated employee** of C, D, E, or G

I) **A 10 percent or more partner or joint venture** of C, D, E, or G.

In order to determine whether a proposed transaction is a prohibited transaction and violates IRC 4975, it is important to examine all the parties engaged in the proposed transaction rather than just the IRA owner.

According to IRC Section 4975, a self-directed IRA is prohibited from engaging in certain types of transactions. The types of prohibited transactions can be best understood by dividing them into three categories: (1) direct prohibited transactions, (2) self-dealing prohibited transactions, and (3) conflict-of-interest prohibited transactions.

Direct or Indirect Prohibited Transactions

What is a direct or indirect prohibited transaction? Essentially, it is a transaction between the self-directed IRA and a disqualified person, which either directly or indirectly personally benefits that disqualified person. It is important to remember that the IRS prohibited transaction rules are primarily in place to ensure that the use of retirement funds is in no way directly or indirectly personally benefiting the plan participant or any of his or her lineal descendants. The reason is clear. The IRS holds that if you wish to make personal use of your retirement funds to help yourself or a close family member, doing so is essentially like helping yourself. Accordingly, you must take a distribution and pay the tax and penalty, if you are under 59½ years old. Those prohibited transaction rules are basically the way the IRS polices and protects their distribution rules—a significant revenue source for the IRS and Treasury. In addition, when it comes to accumulating 401(k) and IRA funds, most of the funds are in pretax form, meaning the IRS provided the 401(k) plan participant or IRA holder with a tax deduction with the anticipation that the benefit provided to the taxpayer would be paid back in the form of taxation on the appreciated assets of the retirement account at a later time. It makes sense, then, that the IRS is so concerned with making sure that retirement funds are not used for any personal purpose that would allow someone to circumvent the distribution rules and taxation on the funds used. The IRS and Department of Labor need to protect their distribution rules because that is how they ensure that the IRS and Treasury will receive the taxes they believe they deserve from retirement distributions.

Direct and indirect prohibited transactions are different. A direct prohibited transaction is the simplest type of prohibited transaction to uncover because it deals with scenarios involving a disqualified person and the retirement account directly. In contrast, an indirect prohibited transaction concerns transactions that do not appear to directly benefit a disqualified person but could do so indirectly based on certain facts and circumstances. For example, using your self-directed IRA to pay your personal credit card bill would be a clear direct prohibited transaction. However, using your self-directed IRA to invest in a company in which you own 15 percent might be considered an indirect prohibited transaction based on certain facts and circumstances.

For example, you cannot use your self-directed IRA to do the following with a disqualified person:

- Sell, exchange, or lease property
- Lend money or extend credit
- Furnish goods, services, or facilities
- Transfer income or assets

John handed Rich a copy of IRC 4975 for his review. Here are some scenarios pertaining to IRC 4975(c)(1)(A) that illustrate prohibited transactions to do with directly or indirectly selling, exchanging, or leasing property to a disqualified person:

4975(c)(1)(A): The direct or indirect sale, exchange, or leasing of property between an IRA and a disqualified person

- Joe sells an interest in a piece of property owned by his self-directed IRA to his son—PROHIBITED
- Beth leases real estate owned by her self-directed IRA to her daughter—PROHIBITED
- Mark uses his self-directed IRA funds to purchase an LLC interest owned by his mother—PROHIBITED
- Victor leases an interest in a piece of property owned by his self-directed IRA to his son—PROHIBITED
- Tracy sells real estate owned by her self-directed IRA to her father—PROHIBITED
- Ben sells real estate he owns personally to his self-directed IRA—PROHIBITED
- Jason transfers property he owns personally to his self-directed IRA—PROHIBITED
- Katy purchases real estate with her self-directed IRA funds and leases it to her son—PROHIBITED

- David uses his self-directed IRA funds to purchase an interest in an entity owned by his father—PROHIBITED
- Ted transfers property he owns personally subject to a mortgage to his self-directed IRA—PROHIBITED
- Sally uses personal funds to pay expenses related to her self-directed IRA real estate investment—PROHIBITED
- Jane uses personal funds to pay taxes and expenses related to her self-directed IRA real estate investment—PROHIBITED

Here are other scenarios pertaining to IRC 4975(c)(1)(B) that illustrate prohibited transactions to do with directly or indirectly lending money or extending credit to a disqualified person:

4975(c)(1)(B): The direct or indirect lending of money or other extension of credit between an IRA and a disqualified person

- Ted lends his wife $70,000 from his self-directed IRA— PROHIBITED
- Mary personally guarantees a bank loan to her self-directed IRA to purchase real estate—PROHIBITED
- Dan uses his self-directed IRA funds to lend an entity owned and controlled by his father $18,000—PROHIBITED
- Ken lends his son $4,000 from his self-directed IRA—PROHIBITED
- Rick uses the assets of his self-directed IRA as security for a loan—PROHIBITED
- Brandon uses his personal assets as security for a self-directed IRA investment—PROHIBITED
- Chuck uses self-directed IRA funds to lend an entity owned and controlled by his father $45,000—PROHIBITED
- Eric acquires a credit card for his self-directed IRA bank account— PROHIBITED

Real-Life Examples

Here is a real example of how the self-directed IRA-prohibited transaction rules work:

Peek v. Commissioner, 140 TC 12 (2013)

In *Peek*, the Tax Court held that a personal guarantee by an IRA owner of a loan to the owner's IRA is a prohibited transaction [since it is a loan of money or extension of credit between a plan and a disqualified person under Code Sec. 4975(c)(1)(B)].

However, what if the loan was not made directly to the IRA but was made instead to an entity owned by the IRA? Is a personal guarantee by the IRA owner of such a loan a prohibited transaction? That was the subject of the Peek case. *Peek* involved two IRA owners (Mr. Fleck and Mr. Peek) who jointly invested in a corporation (FP) formed by them to acquire the assets of another company (AFS). The IRAs were the only shareholders of FP.

FP acquired the assets of AFS in exchange for a combination of cash and notes, including a promissory note from FP to the sellers secured by personal guarantees from both IRA owners. Fleck and Peek were fiduciaries of their respective IRAs due to retaining authority and control over such IRAs and thus were disqualified persons under Code Sec. 4975(c)(1)(A), and each IRA constitutes a "plan" under 4975(e)(1).

Nevertheless, they argued that because their personal guarantees did not involve the plan itself—i.e., since the guarantees were between disqualified persons (Fleck and Peek) and an entity (FP) other than the IRAs themselves—the guarantees were not prohibited.

This argument was flatly rejected by the Tax Court, which noted that 4975(c)(1)(B) also prohibits indirect loans and/or extensions of credit between a plan and a disqualified person and that the "obvious and intended meaning" of (c)(1)(B) "prohibited Mr. Fleck and Mr. Peek from making loans or loan guarantees either directly to their IRAs or indirectly to their IRAs by way of the entity owned by the IRAs."

It is also prohibited, according to IRC 4975(c)(1)(C), to use your self-directed IRA to directly or indirectly furnish goods, services, or facilities to a disqualified person:

4975(c)(1)(C): The direct or indirect furnishing of goods, services, or facilities between an IRA and a disqualified person

- Andrew buys a piece of property with his self-directed IRA funds and hires his father to work on the property—PROHIBITED
- Rachel buys a condo with her self-directed IRA funds and personally fixes it up—PROHIBITED
- Betty owns an apartment building with her self-directed IRA and hires her mother to manage the property—PROHIBITED
- Bill purchases a condo with his self-directed IRA funds and paints the walls without receiving a fee—PROHIBITED
- Henry buys a piece of property with his self-directed IRA funds and hires his son to work on the property—PROHIBITED
- Mary buys a home with her self-directed IRA and her son makes repairs for free—PROHIBITED
- Beth owns an office building with her self-directed IRA and hires her son to manage the property for a fee—PROHIBITED
- Jackie owns an apartment building with her self-directed IRA funds and has her father manage the property for free—PROHIBITED
- Doug receives compensation from his self-directed IRA for investment advice—PROHIBITED
- Matt acts as the real estate agent for his self-directed IRA—PROHIBITED

Indirect Prohibited Transactions

Indirect prohibited transactions inspire a lot of debate because the determination of whether a prohibited transaction occurred is largely based on the facts and circumstances.

Indirect prohibited transactions are transactions that may not violate any of the direct prohibited transaction rules on their face, but still may be considered a prohibited transaction by the IRS. For example, when an individual uses an IRA to invest in a company in which he owns a 15 percent share, this would not seem to be a prohibited transaction because the individual IRA holder owns less than 50 percent of the entity and the entity does not seem to be a disqualified person under IRC 4975. However, if it turned out that the company needed the funds to avoid bankruptcy or the investment was made to secure a job within the company, the IRS could argue that the investment directly or indirectly helped the IRA holder personally.

Many tax professionals fail to focus on the indirect prohibited transaction rules outlined in IRC 4975 and just focus on the direct prohibited transaction rules. The IRS seems to be using the indirect prohibited transaction rules as a tool for scrutinizing IRA transactions that seem to personally benefit the IRA holder but don't violate the direct prohibited transaction rules under IRC 4975.

The following examples below will help illustrate.

Subject to the exemptions under IRC Section 4975(d), an indirect prohibited transaction generally involves one of the following:

4975(c)(1)(D): The direct or indirect transfer to a disqualified person of income or assets of an IRA

- Ken is in a financial jam and takes $32,000 from his self-directed IRA to pay a personal debt—PROHIBITED
- John uses his self-directed IRA to purchase a rental property and hires his friend to manage the property. The friend then enters into a contract with John and transfers those funds back to John—PROHIBITED
- Melissa invests her self-directed IRA funds in a real estate fund and then receives a salary for managing the fund—PROHIBITED
- Jim uses a house owned by his self-directed IRA for personal use—PROHIBITED

- Seth deposits self-directed IRA funds into his personal bank account—PROHIBITED
- Spencer buys precious metals using his self-directed IRA funds and uses them for personal gain—PROHIBITED
- Bryan purchases a vacation home with his self-directed IRA funds and stays in the home on occasion—PROHIBITED
- Elliot buys a cottage with her self-directed IRA funds on the lake and rents it out to her daughter and son-in-law—PROHIBITED
- Allison purchases a condo using her self-directed IRA on the beach and lets her son use it for free—PROHIBITED
- Kelly invests her self-directed IRA funds in an investment fund and then receives a salary for managing the fund—PROHIBITED
- Larry uses his self-directed IRA funds to purchase real estate and earns a commission as the real estate agent on the sale—PROHIBITED
- Steve uses his self-directed IRA funds to lend money to a company he owns and controls—PROHIBITED
- Gordon invests his self-directed IRA funds into a business he owns 75 percent of and manages—PROHIBITED

Self-Dealing Prohibited Transactions

Self-dealing is a term for a situation that arises when someone benefits on both sides of a deal. According to 4975(c)(1)(E), self-dealing, which is a form of an indirect prohibited transaction, occurs when you directly or indirectly use the income or assets of your self-directed IRA to further your own interests or benefit your own accounts.

4975(c)(1)(E): The direct or indirect act by a disqualified person who is a fiduciary whereby he/she deals with income or assets of the IRA in his/her own interest or for his/her own account

- Debra, who is a real estate agent, uses her self-directed IRA funds to buy a piece of property *and* earns a commission from the sale—PROHIBITED

- Ben wants to buy a piece of property for $120,000 and would like to own the property personally but does not have sufficient funds. As a result, Ben uses $110,000 from his self-directed IRA *and* $10,000 personally to make the investment—PROHIBITED
- Nancy uses her self-directed IRA funds to invest in a real estate fund managed by her son, *and* Heidi's father receives a bonus for securing Nancy's investment—PROHIBITED
- Karen makes an investment using her self-directed IRA funds into a company she controls that will benefit her personally—PROHIBITED
- Brett uses his self-directed IRA funds to invest in a partnership with himself personally in which he and his family will own more than 50 percent of the partnership—PROHIBITED
- Pam uses her self-directed IRA funds to invest in a business she and her husband own and operates and she and her husband earn compensation from the business—PROHIBITED
- Rick uses his self-directed IRA funds to lend money to a business that he controls and manages—PROHIBITED
- Lance invests his self-directed IRA funds in a trust in which Lance and his wife would gain a personal benefit—PROHIBITED
- Helen uses her self-directed IRA funds to invest in a real estate fund managed by her son, who receives a bonus for securing her investment—PROHIBITED
- Stanley invests his self-directed IRA funds into a real estate project in which his development company will be involved in order to secure the contract—PROHIBITED
- Warren uses his self-directed IRA funds to invest in his son's business that is in financial trouble—PROHIBITED
- Alex uses his self-directed IRA funds to buy a note on a piece of property for which he is the debtor personally—PROHIBITED

Real-Life Examples

Here's a real-life example of a self-dealing prohibited transaction:

Rollins v. Commissioner, T.C. Memo 2004-60

Rollins v. Commissioner is an important case in the self-directed IRA LLC context because it illustrates how one can engage in a prohibited transaction with an entity even if the entity is not a disqualified entity per se. The Rollins case also is important for examining whether a potential transaction could be considered an indirect prohibited transaction under IRC 4975.

The facts in *Rollins* are as follows: Mr. Rollins owned his own CPA firm. He was sole trustee of its 401(k) plan. Mr. Rollins caused his plan to lend funds to three companies in which he was the largest stockholder (9 percent to 33 percent), but not controlling, stockholder. The companies had twenty-eight, seventy, and eighty other stockholders respectively. Mr. Rollins made the decision for the companies to borrow from his 401(k) plan. The loans were demand loans, secured by each company's assets. The interest rate was market rate or higher. Mr. Rollins signed loan checks for his plan and signed notes for borrowers. All loans were repaid in full.

Mr. Rollins acknowledged that he is a disqualified person with regard to the plan because he owns Rollins, the CPA firm, but he contends that (1) none of the corporations that were the borrowers was a disqualified person, (2) none of the loans was a transaction between him and the plan, and (3) he "did not benefit from these loans, either in income or in his own account."

The Tax Court held that a Code Section 4975(c)(1)(D) indirect prohibition did not require an actual transfer of money or property between the plan and the disqualified person. The fact that a disqualified person could have benefited as a result of the use of plan assets was sufficient. The Tax Court held that the transactions were uses by Rollins or for his benefit, and were assets of the plan. These assets of the plan were not transferred to Rollins. For each of those transactions, however, Rollins sat on both sides of the table. Rollins made the decisions to lend the plan's funds, and Rollins signed the promissory notes on behalf of the borrowers.

One of the more interesting parts of the Rollins case was the Tax Court's emphasis that as the taxpayer, the burden of proof is the responsibility of the taxpayer. In other words, at its core, the Rollins case is a burden-of-proof case that illustrates the breadth of the application of 4975(c)(1)(D) as well as the difficulty of meeting that burden of proof. Mr. Rollins was not a majority owner of any of the borrowers, but he was the largest shareholder for each company. And he also signed the notes for each borrower.

Would the same decision have been made if Mr. Rollins was not the largest shareholder or had not, as the court put it, "sat on both sides of the table" (e.g., by not signing the notes on behalf of the borrowers)? It's not entirely clear if that would have influenced the court since it was still Mr. Rollins's burden (as the disqualified person) to prove that the transaction did not enhance or was not intended to enhance the value of his investments in the borrowers. That seems to be a very tough burden to meet. Moreover, as the court noted, the fact that a transaction is a good investment for the plan has nothing to do with the problem.

The lesson is that caution should be exercised whenever a disqualified person is sitting "on both sides of the table."

"Here is another real-life example," John said.

T.L. Ellis, TC Memo-2013-245

On October 29, 2013, the Tax Court in *T.L. Ellis*, TC Memo. 2013-245, Dec. 59,674(M), held that establishing a special purpose limited liability company to make an investment did not trigger a prohibited transaction, as a newly established LLC cannot be deemed a disqualified person pursuant to IRC Section 4975.

In T.L. Ellis, TC Memo. 2013-245, Mr. Ellis retired with about $300,000 in his 401(k) retirement plan, which he subsequently rolled over into a newly created self-directed IRA.

The taxpayer then created an LLC taxed as a corporation and had his IRA transfer the $300,000 into the LLC. The LLC was formed to engage in the business of used-car sales. The taxpayer managed the used-car business through the IRA LLC and received a modest salary.

The IRS argued that the formation of the LLC was a prohibited transaction under IRC Section 4975, which prohibits self-dealing. The Tax Court disagreed, holding that even though the taxpayer acted as a fiduciary to the IRA (and was therefore a disqualified person under IRC Section 4975), the LLC itself was not a disqualified person at the time of the transfer. After the transfer, the LLC was a disqualified person because it was owned by Mr. Ellis's IRA, a disqualified person. Additionally, the IRS also claimed that the taxpayer had engaged in a prohibited transaction by receiving a salary from the LLC. The court agreed with the IRS. Although the LLC (and not the IRA) was officially paying the taxpayer's salary, the Tax Court concluded that since the IRA was the sole owner of the LLC, and that the LLC was the IRA's only investment, the taxpayer (a disqualified person) was essentially being paid by his IRA.

The Ellis case is the first case that directly reinforces the legality of using a newly established LLC to make IRA investments without triggering an IRS prohibited transaction. The Tax Court ruled that a prohibited transaction had occurred because Mr. Ellis received a salary from the LLC, which was wholly owned by his IRA. Of note—the Tax Court confirmed that using a newly established LLC, wholly owned by an IRA and managed by the IRA holder does not in itself trigger a prohibited transaction. In addition, we will soon discuss how using a 401(k) plan to purchase corporate stock could have allowed Mr. Ellis to make the business investment without triggering a prohibited transaction.

ERISA Advisory Opinion Letter 93-33A

In this advisory opinion, an IRA owner proposed to use his IRA to buy land and a building at a high school founded by his daughter and son-in-law and to lease the property back to the school at either fair market rent or lower rent depending on the school's ability to pay. Presumably, this school was a nonprofit organization, without stockholders.

The IRA owner, having discretion to invest the IRA's assets, was a fiduciary and a disqualified person. The IRA owner's daughter and son-in-law were the sole directors and officers of the school. As such, by virtue of 4975(e)(2)(F), they also were disqualified persons. Consequently, the Department of Labor concluded that the proposed sale-leaseback transaction would constitute the use of IRA assets for the benefit of disqualified persons (i.e., the IRA owner's daughter and son-in-law) in violation of

4975(c)(1)(D). It seemed that the major factor here was the arrangement to lease back the property at a rent dependent on the school's ability to pay. In fact, the Department of Labor took the broad view that either 4975(c)(1)(D) or (E) would be violated if a transaction were part of an agreement, arrangement, or understanding in which the fiduciary caused plan assets to be used in a manner designed to benefit any person in whom such fiduciary had an interest that would affect the exercise of his or her best judgment as a fiduciary.

Conflict-of-Interest Prohibited Transactions

According to 4975(c)(i)(F), a prohibited transaction also occurs when a disqualified person is connected to a transaction involving the income or assets of the self-directed IRA. This is called a conflict-of-interest prohibited transaction. For example:

4975(c)(i)(F): Receipt of any consideration by a disqualified person who is a fiduciary for his/her own account from any party dealing with the IRA in connection with a transaction involving income or assets of the IRA:

- Jason uses his self-directed IRA funds to loan money to a company that he manages and controls and also owns a small ownership interest in—PROHIBITED
- Cathy uses her self-directed IRA to lend money to a business that she works for in order to secure a promotion—PROHIBITED
- Eric uses his self-directed IRA funds to invest in a fund that he manages and where his management fee is based on the total value of the fund's assets—PROHIBITED

Real-Life Examples

And here's a real-life example:

Technical Advice Memorandum 9118001

In this Technical Advice Memorandum, the IRS concluded that loans made by a law firm's pension and profit-sharing plans to its clients to provide those clients with financial support while they were awaiting settlement on their lawsuits were prohibited transactions under both IRC Sections 4975(c)(1)(D) and 4975(c)(1)(E) of the code.

The law firm's partners, who were fiduciaries with authority over plan assets, directed a bank, as the plan trustee, to lend clients money pending the outcome of their suits. The district office contended that this is a transaction prohibited by IRC Section 4975(c)(1)(D) since the partners of the law firm were acting as a lending institution and the law firm was indirectly using and benefiting from plan assets. The taxpayer disagreed, arguing that the loans were made to clients from the plan assets solely to benefit plan participants, and that it is a common business practice in personal injury law firms to advance funds to clients who are awaiting settlement.

The IRS determined that the loans were prohibited under IRC Section 4975(c)(1)(D) because the employer, who is a disqualified person under IRC Section 4975(e)(2)(C), benefited from the use of plan assets. As the IRS stated, the parties benefiting from the loans (i.e., the party whose business object is being served) were the partners in the law firm. It did not matter that the clients could have received loans elsewhere or that the loans were good investments, nor did it matter that it was common practice for law firms to advance funds to clients pending the conclusion of their lawsuits. As long as a benefit is derived by a disqualified person through the use of a plan asset, a transaction is prohibited under IRC Section 4975(c)(1)(D).

In addition, the IRS found that the loans were also prohibited under IRC Section 4975(c)(1)(E). The partners of the law firm were fiduciaries since they exercised their authority with respect to the management of plan assets by directing the trustee (the bank) to enter into loans with their clients in conjunction with their legal representation. As such, the partners, in their capacity as plan administrators, dealt with the assets of the plan in their own interest.

Statutory Exemptions to the Prohibited Transaction Rules

Rich was doing a good job taking in all the information that John was giving him.

"There are a lot of situations to consider," Rich said.

"Yes," John said. "Like I said, the IRS doesn't tell you what you can do, only what you can't, and that understanding develops like any tax law."

"But I don't need to be an expert and know everything," Rich said. "I just need to start by thinking about my particular situation or the investments I want to make."

"Exactly," John said. "And then check with a tax attorney or CPA who understands self-directed IRAs to make sure."

"That way I'll have a pretty good idea whether the IRS would be interested in what you want to do."

"Exactly. And Congress has also created several ways to grant exemptions from the very broad prohibited transaction rules. This allows some wiggle room when it comes to navigating prohibited transaction rules for certain specific circumstances."

"Oh," Rich said. "Tell me more."

"The most popular way for satisfying a prohibited transaction exemption is the statutory exemption because anyone who complies with the terms of the statute will be able to benefit from the exemption."

John continued to explain:

In IRC 4975(d), Congress created certain statutory exemptions from the prohibited transactions outlined in 4975(c). These exemptions were made because Congress believed there is a legitimate reason to permit them, as long as certain specified requirements are satisfied. In such situations, Congress has decided to issue blanket prohibited transaction exemptions permitting certain types of transactions, as long as certain requirements prescribed in the statute are met.

The most common prohibited transaction exemption involves participant loans from a 401(k) plan, which, unfortunately, do not apply to IRAs. IRC 4975(d)(1) describes conditions under which loans are allowable. The majority of the statutory exemptions found under IRC 4975(d) are not commonly applied because of their specific application, such as the ability to invest plan assets in bank deposit accounts where the bank is the employer, or to invest plan assets in life insurance company products where the company is the employer. However, besides the 401(k) loan exemption, the other common prohibited transaction exemption often used is the ability for a disqualified person to contract with the plan in order to provide office space, legal, accounting, or other services *necessary* for the operation of the plan as long as reasonable compensation is paid.

This exemption is often cited as a source of potential abuse because it allows certain services and fees to be paid from the plan to a disqualified person. The exemption refers specifically to "necessary" services, which seems to mean only those required types of services that must be performed in order to maintain the legality of the IRA, such as legal or accounting. The exemption does not, on the other hand, allow one to provide services to a plan asset, such as would be the case if a disqualified person were serving as real estate agent for a plan's real estate purchase, being paid to paint the walls of an investment property owned by the plan, or taking a salary to manage the plan's investments.

"So in a perfect world," Rich said, "you'd just avoid this exemption and pay people who aren't disqualified persons for any necessary services that must be performed in connection with the plan."

"Yes," John said. "Taking advantage of this statutory exemption could create some level of scrutiny from the IRS. They might ask you to prove that the service and/or fee received in connection with the service performed was really *necessary*. The burden would then be on the IRA holder to prove this to the IRS. So it's generally believed that hiring nondisqualified third parties to perform all services in connection with the plan, including any "necessary" expenses, is the best course of action."

John continued. When it comes to the self-directed IRA, the statutory exemptions pertain to three areas:

- You can contract with a disqualified person for office space, legal, accounting, or other services that are necessary for the operation of your self-directed IRA as long as reasonable compensation is paid. You can't, however, contract with yourself for such services.
- A bank trustee can provide ancillary services to your self-directed IRA.
- A disqualified person can receive benefits to which he or she may be entitled as a participant or beneficiary of the self-directed IRA, as long as those benefits are consistent with the way the plan pays benefits to all other participants and beneficiaries. As we discussed, this exemption is used to allow additional contributions made to the self-directed IRA LLC.

"How popular are these prohibited transaction rule exceptions to a self-directed IRA LLC investor?" Rich asked.

"Unfortunately the exceptions to the prohibited transaction rules are so narrow and limited in scope that most self-directed IRA investors are not able to take advantage of any of them when making self-directed IRA investments."

"That's what I figured," Rich said.

"Yes," John agreed. "Navigating IRS prohibited transaction rules is complex and requires a thorough examination of the facts and circumstances involved in the IRA transaction before determining whether a prohibited transaction had occurred."

The Prohibited Transaction Rules and the Self-Directed IRA LLC

"So let's cut to the chase," John said. "You're interested in the self-directed IRA because it gives you the checkbook control that allows you to serve as manager of the self-directed IRA LLC structure. And you want to be manager because that allows you to make alternative investments that can strengthen and grow you retirement funds better than putting everything into the stock market."

"That sums it up," Rich said.

"Well," John continued, "the fact that the IRA holder will be serving as manager of the LLC potentially brings to light several questions about the scope of services that the IRA LLC manager can provide to the LLC and to the LLC investment."

"Our good old prohibited transaction rules and the famous disqualified persons."

"Right," John said. "So in light of that, I think it would be helpful to quickly review the IRS rules concerning a disqualified person providing services to an IRA."

"Necessary" Fiduciary Services to a Self-Directed IRA LLC

IRC Sec. 4975(c)(1)(C): Furnishing of goods, services, or facilities between a plan and a disqualified person is a prohibited transaction.

IRC Sec. 4975(e)(2): Disqualified person includes (among others):

(A) a fiduciary
(B) a person providing services to a plan
(C) an employer who has any employees are covered by the plan

IRC Sec. 4975(e)(3): A fiduciary is any person who:

(A) exercises any discretionary authority or discretionary control respecting management of such plan or exercises any authority or control respecting management or disposition of its assets
(B) renders investment advice for a fee or other compensation, direct or indirect, with respect to any moneys or other property of such plan, or has any authority or responsibility to do so
(C) has any discretionary authority or discretionary responsibility in the administration of such plan.

Therefore, an IRA holder who also serves as a manager of the self-directed IRA LLC is a fiduciary as well as a disqualified person relative to the IRA.

John continued, "Now let's look at the statutory exception language from in the tax code concerning a disqualified person providing services. IRC Sec. 4975(d)(2) states that 'any contract, or reasonable arrangement, made with a disqualified person for office space, or legal, accounting, or other services necessary for the establishment or operation of the plan, if no more than reasonable compensation is paid therefore, is not a prohibited transaction.'"

"Now let's examine Treasury Regulation 54.4975-6(a)(2) to learn more about what is a 'necessary service,' John said. John handed Rich another document containing Treasury Regulation 54.4975-6(a)(2).

"Under the Treasury regulation, a service is necessary for the establishment and operation of the plan if the service is appropriate and helpful to the plan obtaining the service in carrying out the purposes for which the plan is established or maintained. A person providing such a service may also furnish necessary goods in the course of, or incidental to, the furnishing of such service.

"Looking at this one step further, Treasury Regulation Section 54.4975-6(a)(5)(i) provides further limits on a disqualified person's ability to provide necessary services to a retirement account. Under this Treasury regulation, a fiduciary may not use the authority, control, or responsibility that makes such person a fiduciary to cause a plan to pay an additional fee to such fiduciary to provide a service. Nor may a fiduciary use such authority, control, or responsibility to cause a plan to enter into a transaction involving plan assets whereby such fiduciary will receive consideration from a third party in connection with such transaction. Therefore," John continued, "it would appear that an IRA holder who is also the LLC's manager may provide 'necessary' services to the plan as long as it is not provided without additional compensation."

"So it comes down to necessary services and additional compensation," Rich said.

"In my experience," John agreed, "necessary services are generally any services that must be performed in order to keep the IRA or LLC in good standing and satisfy all applicable rules, for example, filing required tax returns, annual filings, and other administrative functions relating to the IRA and the LLC. I think you would be hard-pressed to argue that making improvements on the real estate owned by the IRA LLC or acting as the real estate agent on your IRA LLC real estate purchase is a necessary service."

"Got it," Rich said.

"The determination of whether a service is 'necessary' should be as narrow as possible and the service should be one that is appropriate and helpful to the IRA for the IRA carrying out the purpose for which it was established or maintained. The IRS has not issued detailed guidance regarding the type of service that would fit into this definition, but it is generally believed that the types of services covered by the definition are limited to a certain category of services necessary for the establishment or operation of the IRA. Some of these services are fleshed out in further detail below."

"Will do," Rich said.

"As manager of the LLC, the IRA holder will be responsible for making all IRA investment decisions as well as validating that the LLC remains in compliance in connection with all state and federal reporting and filing requirements. To this end, it would seem that any service that allows the manager to perform such tasks should be treated as a necessary service since it can arguably be considered appropriate and helpful in carrying out the purpose for which the plan has been established—using the LLC to make IRA investments. In this regard, it would appear that if the LLC manager had the knowledge and ability to perform accounting, legal, consulting, investment, or other services involving the operation and management of the IRA-owned LLC, the service performed would be considered necessary and could be performed by the fiduciary for no compensation or other consideration."

Providing Services to Your IRA LLC Investment

"What about providing services to my self-directed IRA LLC investment assets?" Rich asked.

"One of the most popular questions that arises in connection with the self-directed IRA LLC structure is whether the IRA holder as LLC manager is permitted to provide services to a self-directed IRA LLC investment asset (again, without compensation)," John said. "Can the LLC manager, for example, provide improvement or repair services to real estate acquired by the self-directed IRA LLC? Breaking down this question even further, can the LLC manager fix a toilet, paint a wall, repair a stove, or even purchase materials for the property? Assuming these services are performed for no compensation, are they necessary within the meaning of the Treasury regulations—i.e., are they appropriate and helpful to the plan obtaining the service (meaning the IRA) in carrying out the purposes for which the plan is established or maintained?"

"I think I know, but please go on," Rich said.

"An IRA is a retirement account, an obvious purpose of which is to accumulate as many funds as possible to benefit the holder's retirement. To achieve this end, the IRA will therefore need to invest wisely. You can certainly make the argument that an LLC manager providing investment, accounting, or legal services to the self-directed IRA LLC is providing a service that is appropriate and helpful in carrying out the purpose for which the IRA was established—to make investments. However, it's a much more difficult argument to make that the LLC manager fixing a toilet, painting a wall, or installing a sink on a real estate asset owned by the self-directed IRA LLC is a service that is appropriate and helpful in carrying out the purpose for which the IRA was established. In addition, the plan asset rules would prevent a disqualified person from providing services to an IRA LLC investment as it would treat the services being performed as being performed to the IRA directly, which would directly violate IRC Section 4975."

"That's along the lines of what I imagined," Rich said.

"Most practitioners in the area, including me, take the position that the LLC manager should provide no services to any self-directed IRA LLC investment or asset—even for free. It's one thing to argue that providing accounting services to the LLC—so that the LLC satisfies its annual filing requirements or filing the annual LLC report with the applicable state or federal authority—should be considered a necessary service, whereas painting a wall, installing a floor, or repairing a roof on a real estate investment owned by the self-directed IRA LLC is a much more difficult argument to make—one the IRS would likely not accept."

"Yes," Rich said. "It's more of a luxury than a necessity, no matter how important you might think it is."

Plan Asset Rules

"Right," John said. "So now would be a good time to introduce the plan asset rules."

"What are those?" Rich asked.

"The plan asset rules," John answered, "are a group of rules that work to extend the prohibited transaction rules and certain ERISA fiduciary standards, which are not relevant to IRAs, to certain types of investments. The Plan Asset Rules are generally designed to apply 'look-through' rules to interests held by a retirement account in an investment fund, such as a hedge fund."

"Such as?"

"Let's assume that you have looked at all the prohibited transaction rules under IRC 4975 and 408, and feel pretty comfortable that your transaction would not be treated as a prohibited transaction and then are told that there are another set of rules—called the plan asset rules—that you may need to look at before being totally comfortable that the transaction would not violate the prohibited transaction rules."

"Great," Rich said sarcastically.

"Better to know than to be surprised," John said.

"Absolutely," Rich agreed.

"In late 1986," John continued, "the Department of Labor issued regulations relating to the definition of plan assets. The plan asset rules were developed in order to examine situations when a 401(k) plan or IRA was invested in a pass-through entity, such as an LLC or partnership. They were put in place to determine the assets of the plan for the purpose of applying the prohibited transaction and ERISA rules."

"How do they work?" Rich asked.

"The plan asset regulation describes circumstances in which there is a 'look-through,' which, if applicable, treats not only the interests in an investment fund owned by retirement accounts as 'plan assets' but also the assets of the investment fund as 'plan assets.' If the look-through applies, the retirement account fiduciary and prohibited transaction sections apply to parties dealing with the assets of the investment fund, such as the investment fund's investment manager."

"Okay," Rich said.

"Under the plan asset rules, if the aggregate self-directed IRA ownership of an entity is 25 percent or more of all the assets of the entity, then the equity interests and assets of the 'investment entity' are viewed as assets of the investing self-directed IRA for the purposes of the prohibited transaction rules, unless an exception applies."

"Got it," Rich said.

"Also, if a self-directed IRA or group of related qualified plans owns 100 percent of an 'operating company,' the operating company exception will not apply and the company's assets will still be treated as plan assets."

"I see," Rich said.

"So in summary," John continued, "the plan asset rules can be triggered if:

- 100 percent of an 'operating company' is owned by one or more IRAs and disqualified persons, in which case all the assets of the 'operating company' are deemed plan assets (assets of the IRA), or,
- If 25 percent or more of an 'investment company' is owned by IRAs/401(k) plans and disqualified persons, in which case all the assets of the 'investment company' are deemed plan assets [assets of the IRA/401(k)].

"In determining whether the 25 percent threshold is met," John continued, "all IRA and 401(k) owners are considered, even if they are owned by unrelated individuals."

"So why do we care about the plan asset rules?" Rich asked. "What's the big deal for a self-directed IRA LLC?"

"The big deal is that if an IRA owns 100 percent of an LLC, any services being provided to the LLC or its asset will be attributable to the IRA and could trigger a prohibited transaction."

Exceptions to the Plan Asset Regulations

"Are there exceptions?" Rich asked.

"Yes," John said. "The plan asset look-through rules do not apply if the entity is an operating company or the partnership interests or membership interests are publicly offered or registered under the Investment Company Act of 1940 (e.g., REITs). They also do not apply if the entity is an 'operating company,' which refers to a partnership or LLC that is primarily engaged in the real estate development, venture capital, or companies making or providing goods and services, such as a gas station, unless the 'operating company' is owned 100 percent by a plan and/or disqualified persons."

"Can you explain that a little more?" Rich said.

"In other words, if an IRA or 401(k) plan owns less than 100 percent of an LLC that is engaged in an active trade or business, such as a restaurant or manufacturing plant, the plan asset rules would not apply. However, the IRA or 401(k) P\plan investment may still be treated as a prohibited transaction under IRC Section 4975."

"I see," Rich said.

"In addition," John continued, "the UBTI rules, which we go through in detail shortly, may apply to the IRA or 401(k) plan, subjecting it to tax on the income or gains generated from the operating business, specifically if the business is being operated though a pass-through entity, such as an LLC."

"How can the plan asset rules affect my IRA/401(k) plan investments?" Rich asked.

"The plan asset rules are typically only triggered if your IRA/401(k) plan assets will own greater than 25 percent of an investment company (i.e., a passive investment fund) or will own 100 percent of an operating company (i.e., a gas station)."

"Does that come into play much?" Rich asked.

"In general, the majority of investments involving IRA/401(k) plan funds will not cause the plan asset rules to trigger a prohibited transaction. For example, any direct purchase of real estate, precious metals, tax liens, or lending transaction not involving a disqualified person will likely not trigger the prohibited transaction rules or plan asset rules."

"That's good to know," Rich said.

Consequences of a Transaction Falling Under the Plan Asset Rules

"So what happens if a transaction falls under the plan asset rules?" Rich asked.

"Let's say," John began, "your self-directed IRA LLC investment is involved in an investment in either an 'operating company' that your IRA will own 100 percent of, or an investment company in which 25 percent of more of the 'investment company' is owned by retirement accounts and disqualified persons..."

"Okay," Rich said. "What then?"

"Then all assets of the entity," John continued, "are deemed owned by the IRA and 401(k) and all transactions between the investment entity or its assets and a disqualified person may be prohibited. It is important to remember that the fact that a transaction does not trigger the plan asset rules does not mean that the transaction may not be deemed a prohibited transaction under IRC Section 4975. In other words, a transaction that does not fall under the plan asset rules can still be treated as a prohibited transaction."

"How about some examples to show me the scope of the plan asset rules?" Rich asked.

So John spelled them out but reinforced that the rules generally apply to investment funds, such as hedge funds:

Example No. 1:
A general partner of a hedge fund wishes to invest his self-directed IRA LLC in the hedge fund he manages. If the percentage of IRA ownership, including what it would be after the general partner invests his IRA in the fund, equals or exceeds 25 percent of the equity interests, then the fund's assets are considered "plan asset." That means that a transaction between the general partner, as a disqualified person, and the fund, could be deemed a prohibited transaction because the assets of the fund are viewed as assets of his IRA, since a disqualified person cannot transact with the assets of his plan or IRA. Accordingly, the general partner cannot receive benefits from his IRA investment into the fund. Thus, the general partner would not be permitted to receive any management fees associated with the IRA's ownership interest in the fund because he would be receiving a personal benefit from his IRA. (Note: The general partner's IRA investment in the fund may also be deemed a direct or indirect prohibited transaction under IRC Section 4975.)

Example No. 2:
Jane's self-directed IRA LLC owns 100 percent of ABC, LLC, which operates a retail store. ABC, LLC makes a loan to Jane. The loan is subject to the plan asset rules and will also be considered a prohibited transaction pursuant to IRC Section 4975. (**Note:** Any income generated by ABC, LLC that is allocated to the self-directed IRA LLC would also likely be subject to the unrelated business income tax.)

Example No. 3:
Steve's self-directed IRA LLC owns 15 percent of ABC, LLC, an investment company. Allan's IRA owns 20 percent of ABC, LLC. Steve and Allan are unrelated. Since IRAs (plans) own greater than 25 percent of ABC, LLC, an "investment company," assets of ABC, LLC are plan assets and deemed owned by each IRA. Thus, if ABC, LLC makes a loan to Steve's father, the loan would be a prohibited transaction under IRC Section 4975.

"So," Rich said, "failing the plan asset rules could potentially trigger some unexpected prohibited transaction rule exposure and could cause some unexpected tax implications."

"Absolutely," John agreed. "Now that you have some understanding of how the plan asset rules work and how they can potentially trigger the IRS prohibited transaction rules, let's look at some types of services that a self-directed IRA LLC manager may be required to perform in the context of managing a self-directed IRA LLC and consider whether the service could potentially trigger the IRS prohibited transaction rules."

"Sounds good," Rich said.

"These examples," John continued, "are based on real-life situations involving my clients. My conclusions come from my research and from various conversations I've had with employees of the Department of Labor and IRS."

John put a chart before Rich to look at.

"This is a guide, and you should think about the examples in that context. Generally, the less you do as the IRA holder and manager of the LLC vis-à-vis your IRA LLC investments, the less you will have to worry about the IRS prohibited transaction rules. But as a rule of thumb, other than making investment decisions for the IRA LLC and taking care of all administrative functions regarding the IRA and the LLC, such as filing LLC annual reports, tax returns, and filing IRS Form 1099, when appropriate, the IRA holder or any disqualified person should not provide any additional services to the IRA or the IRA LLC investments."

John handed Rich a chart that offered some helpful tips in determining whether a certain self-directed IRA-related service was necessary and, thus, potentially exempted from the prohibited transaction rules.

Type of Service	Is it Necessary?	Rationale
Establishing an IRA account	YES	Appropriate and helpful to the formation of the IRA
Managing an LLC owned by an IRA	YES	Appropriate and helpful to further the purpose for which the self-directed IRA was established - i.e., LLC is necessary to allow the IRA to be self-directed by the IRA holder
Making investment decisions as LLC manager	YES	One purpose of the plan is to invest wisely in order to increase the value of plan assets. Thus investment decisions are appropriate and helpful to the plan in carrying out this purpose.
Complying with annual filing requirements	YES	LLC and plan filing requirements are necessary to keep the LLC and/or plan (as applicable) in good standing.
Complying with tax reporting rules (i.e. Filing IRS Form 1099, when appropriate)	YES	Complying with all IRS tax reporting rules is necessary and required by law
Complying with filing federal and state income tax returns and related tax filings	YES	Completely consistent with the Code and Treasury Regulations as a "necessary" service.
Providing accounting or legal services to the LLC	YES	The younger you are Roth offers greater advantages
Selecting a property management company	YES	If a plan will invest in real estate, it may be necessary to retain a property management company in order for the plan to make prudent investments.
Selecting a tenant for the investment property	YES	If a plan invests in real estate, it may earn rental income. To maximize rental income, it is important to lease the property out to tenants with good credit histories.
Making improvements or repairs to the property	NO	While improvements/repairs undoubtedly improve the value of invested property, it would seem to be a stretch to deem it a necessary service in furtherance of the purposes for which the plan was established.
Serving as real estate agent for the investment property	NO	A real estate agent would help sell or lease invested property, but it would seem to make sense to delegate this responsibility to a third party that is not a disqualified person as it is arguably not a necessary service.

"Okay, I think I get it," Rich replied. Rich then said, "So what about any expenses I incur as manager of the self-directed IRA LLC, are they reimbursable?"

John handed Rich another chart that outlined his thoughts on seeking reimbursement for self-directed IRA LLX expenses incurred as manager of the IRA LLC:

REIMBURSABLE EXPENSES TO AN IRA HOLDER/MANAGER OF A SELF DIRECTED IRA LLC

(It is best practice to pay all IRA LLC related expenses with IRA funds and not use any personal funds)

Type Service	Reimbursable	Rationale
Establishing an IRA Account?	YES	In order for the fiduciary to effectively manage the IRA's assets, an essential first step is opening an account with the custodian (e.g. a bank) to hold the IRA funds. The IRA holder/LLC manager may need to pay expenses out-of-pocket in order to set up the account. Thus, this expense is direct and also properly and actually incurred in the performance of the fiduciary's services as LLC Manager.
Paying a Self-Directed IRA facilitator a consulting fee	YES	The payment of a consulting fee may be necessary to set up the IRA account and also assist the LLC Manager in making prudent (and legal) investment decisions.
Paying for investment advice for an LLC investment	YES	The objective of the IRA is to increase the value of its funds. Therefore, anything the IRA invests in– either directly or through a wholly- owned LLC – should be done with an eye toward appreciation in value. Paying for investment advice is directly related to these IRAs purposes.
Paying for an investment course to facilitate IRA investments	YES	An investment course may help educate the LLC Manager to make more prudent investments, and thus this expense should be reimbursable by the Note- one should be careful about reimbursement as the burden would be on the IRA holder to prove no personal benefit was derived from the expense incurred.
Incurring travel expenses to scout property for potential IRA investment	Yes but be cautious	The LLC manager may not truly know if a property is worth investing in until he/she actually sees and inspects the property. This expense should be reimbursable. Note- one should be careful about reimbursement in this case, as the burden would be on the IRA holder to prove no personal benefit was derived from the expense incurred.

Other Prohibited Assets

"There are a number of other investments," John continued, "that are not permitted. These investments do not fall under the prohibited transaction rules under IRC Section 4975 but are outlined under IRC 408. I talked about those in detail already. But just to review, a self-directed IRA LLC can't invest in life insurance contracts or collectibles such as:

- any work of art
- any metal or gem
- any alcoholic beverage
- any rug or antique
- any stamp
- most coins."

"Right," Rich said, "I remember being surprised by that."

"Well," John explained, "the basic reason these types of assets are prohibited from being purchased with retirement funds is that they are generally hard to value and difficult to sell."

"Makes sense," Rich said.

"Remember, though, that 0.99 percent pure gold, silver, or platinum bullion as well as American Eagle and state-minted coins are approved investments for your self-directed IRA and will not trigger a prohibited transaction."

"Yes, interesting," Rich said.

S and C Corporation Investments

"In addition to the IRS prohibited transaction rules outlined in the IRC Section 4975," John continued, "a self-directed IRA can't own stock in an S corporation."

"Why is that, again?" Rich asked.

"Because of the shareholder restrictions imposed on S corporations," John answered. "S corporations are C corporations that elect to pass corporate income, losses, deductions, and credits through to their shareholders for federal tax purposes. To qualify for S corporation status, the corporation must meet the following requirements:

- be a domestic corporation
- have only allowable shareholders, including individuals, certain trusts, and estates and
- not include partnerships, corporations, or nonresident alien shareholders
- have no more than a hundred shareholders
- have only one class of stock."

"Because an IRA is considered a trust for federal income tax purposes," John said, "which is not treated as a permitted shareholder for an S corporation, having a self-directed IRA invest and become a shareholder would violate the S corporation rules and cause the S election to be invalid, making the entity a C corporation again for tax purposes."

"But a self-directed IRA plan can own stock in a C corporation, right?" Rich asked.

"That's right."

"Okay," Rich said, "I understand I can't engage in four categories of transactions with my self-directed IRA":

(1) collectibles, with a special carve-out for precious metals and IRS-approved coins
(2) life insurance contracts
(3) S corporation stock, and
(4) any transaction that directly or indirectly personally benefits me or any other disqualified person—the IRC 4975 prohibited transactions."

"You got it," John said.

"I was just wondering something," Rich said. "Who determines whether I've engaged in a prohibited transaction?"

"That's actually a good question," John said. "Through an arrangement between the IRS and the Department of Labor (DOL), it's the DOL's responsibility to determine whether a specific transaction is a prohibited transaction and to issue prohibited transaction exemptions. When the IRS discovers what appears to be a prohibited transaction in an individual's IRA, it turns the matter over to the DOL to make the determination. The DOL reviews the situation and responds to the IRS, which in turn responds to the taxpayer. If the IRA grantor wants to apply for a prohibited transaction exemption, he or she must apply to the DOL."

"So does the DOL issue the exemptions?" Rich asked.

"It does have that authority," John said. "What's known as 'prohibitive transaction class exemptions,' or PTCEs, are available for anyone, while another class of exemptions, called individual prohibited transaction exemptions, or PTEs, are issued only to the applicant."

Penalties for Engaging in a Prohibited Transaction

"This makes sense to me," Rich said, "but I was wondering, what are the IRS penalties if someone does engage in any IRS prohibited transaction?"

"As you can imagine," John said, "the penalties are quite steep. The IRS needs to make them painful in order to protect the distribution taxation rules, which are a big revenue source for the government."

"I get it," Rich said.

"In general," John continued, "the penalty under IRC Section 4975 generally starts out at 15 percent for most types of retirement plans."

"Wow," Rich said, "that is harsh."

"Actually," John said, "it's even harsher for self-directed IRAs. In general, if the IRA holder (IRA owner) or IRA beneficiary engages in a transaction that violates the prohibited transaction rules set forth under IRC Section 4975, the individual's IRA would lose its tax-exempt status and the entire fair market value of the IRA would be treated as a taxable distribution, subject to ordinary income tax. In addition, the IRA holder or beneficiary would be subject to a minimum penalty of 15 percent as well as a 10 percent early distribution penalty if the IRA holder or beneficiary is under the age of 59½."

"Holy smokes," Rich said.

"Yeah," John said. "Although the penalty for engaging in a prohibited transaction generally starts out at 15 percent for most types of retirement plans, the penalty is more severe for IRAs. The initial tax on a prohibited transaction is 15 percent of the amount involved for each year (or part of a year) in the taxable period. If the transaction is not corrected within the taxable period, an additional tax of 100 percent of the amount involved is imposed. Both taxes are payable by any disqualified person who participated in the transaction (other than a fiduciary acting only as such). If more than one person takes part in the transaction, each person can be jointly and severally liable for the entire tax. According to Code Section 408(e), when an IRA is involved in a transaction that is prohibited under Code Section 4975, the IRA loses its tax-exempt status and the IRA holder is treated as receiving a distribution on the first day of the tax year in which the prohibited transaction occurred. The distribution amount that the IRA holder is deemed to have received is equal to the fair market value of the IRA as of the first day of such tax year. In other words, the entire IRA is blown up and no longer treated as an IRA as of the first day of the taxable year in which the prohibited transaction occurred."

"I want to avoid that," Rich said. "Can you give me some examples?"

"Sure," John said. "Let's say Jim, who is fifty-two, decides to borrow $25,000 from his traditional self-directed IRA for personal use on May 15 of Year X. Jim's self-directed IRA account has a value of $100,000 on January 1 of Year X. The Department of Labor reviews the transaction and holds that Jim engaged in a prohibited transaction. Jim's IRA would be deemed immediately disqualified as of January 1 of the year in which the prohibited transaction occurred (Year X), resulting in current income tax treatment (ordinary income tax) and an excise tax penalty of 10 percent for a premature withdrawal from an IRA based on the fair market value of Jim's IRA on January 1 of Year X, $100,000."

"Poor Jim," Rich said.

"X was not a good year for him," John agreed. "So let's say Jim used his IRA to invest in collectibles or life insurance, prohibited transactions under

Code Section 408 of the code, not Code Section 4975. In that case, only the assets used to purchase the investment would be considered distributed for purposes of imposing ordinary income tax or an excise tax penalty, not the entire IRA as it would have been in the case of a prohibited transaction under 4975. Therefore, assuming the same facts as the first example, if Jim purchased antiques for $25,000 instead of making a loan with his self-directed IRA, Jim's IRA would be deemed immediately disqualified as of January 1 of the year in which the prohibited transaction occurred (Year X), resulting in current income tax treatment (ordinary income tax) and an excise tax penalty of 10 percent for a premature withdrawal from an IRA in the amount of $25,000—the cost of the antiques."

"Still hurts," Rich said.

"Yes, and the pain is spread around," John said. "For the disqualified person involved in the transaction, the initial tax on a prohibited transaction is 15 percent of the amount involved for every year (or portion thereof) in the taxable period, which is the period beginning when the transaction occurs and ending on the date of the earliest of either (1) the mailing of a notice of deficiency for the tax, (2) assessment of the tax, or (3) correction of the transaction. The 15 percent excise tax is followed by an additional tax of 100 percent if the disqualified person is recalcitrant."

"Ouch," Rich said.

"The good thing when it comes to prohibited transaction penalties," John said, "is that they are easily avoidable."

"Basically," Rich said, "just don't engage in a prohibited transaction and you have nothing to worry about."

"Exactly," John said. "For most retirement investors who will be investing in stocks and other traditional financial products, there is really not much to worry about when it comes to a prohibited transaction. The likelihood of engaging in a prohibited transaction in such circumstance is almost impossible, especially if you are buying stocks, mutual funds, and ETFS from a major financial institution. But, for a self-directed IRA investor looking to make nontraditional investments, such as real estate, private loans, and precious metals, you really need to make yourself aware of the prohibited transaction rules because of the harsh penalties."

"I get it," Rich said. "Investor beware."

"The prohibited transaction rules are extremely broad," John noted. "So a self-directed IRA investor looking to engage in certain nontraditional investments must be especially cautious and should consult a tax attorney or CPA with specific questions."

"I promise," Rich said.

"It's critical to understand what you can't do when it comes to the IRS," John said. "We need this information in advance before making important decisions about how we will invest or allocate our self-directed IRA plan assets. But I think it's time we start talking about what you *can* do with your self-directed IRA plan assets. Specifically, let's talk about the investments you can make and how those decisions will help grow your retirement assets and meet your individual needs and life goals."

"I can't wait," Rich said.

VII

Making Investments with
Your Self-Directed IRA

"All right," John said. "We've now spent a lot of time discussing the different types of self-directed IRA accounts, with specific focus on the checkbook control self-directed IRA LLC. And we've also examined all the features of the self-directed IRA LLC structure in depth. So now I think it's a good time to focus on how to make investments with a self-directed IRA, what types of investments can be made, and which investments are popular. Once we review the types of investments that are typically made with a self-directed IRA, the IRS prohibited transaction rules we discussed will make a lot more sense.

"Okay," Rich said. "That makes sense. I'm particularly interested in real estate, so I hope we'll cover how to make real estate investments with a checkbook control self-directed IRA LLC.

"Absolutely," John agreed. "In addition, we'll talk about some of the other popular self-directed IRA investments, such as precious metals, hard money lending, tax liens, and private business investments."

"Whenever I talk about retirement funds with friends now, they are all convinced that their retirement funds must be invested in bank CDs, the stock market, or mutual funds. Amazing, isn't it?"

"As I've mentioned a few times now," John said, "traditional financial institutions have no incentive to publicize the advantages of self-directed

IRA accounts or inform people that IRA account holders have the ability to make nontraditional investments with their retirement funds. In fact, the IRS does give retirement account holders the ability to make all sorts of traditional as well as nontraditional investments using IRA funds; you just need to make sure your plan documents allow for it. The IRS can't force any of the major financial institutions to allow you to buy gold, real estate, or make private loans, but you do have options to go elsewhere."

"I love that," Rich said.

"That's the main advantage of the self-directed IRA," John agreed. "You gain tremendous latitude and freedom to invest your plan assets and grow them in the way that suits your needs, interests, and personal expertise."

'Dos and Don'ts

"I know we spent a lot of time discussing prohibited transaction rules," John said, "but for now when you're thinking about the type of investments that are permitted with a self-directed IRA, it's important to remember that the IRC does not describe what a self-directed IRA can invest in, only what it *cannot* invest in. As a reminder, IRC Sections 408 & 4975 prohibit disqualified persons from engaging in certain types of transactions. The purpose of these rules is to encourage the use of IRAs for accumulation of retirement savings and to prohibit those in control of IRAs from taking advantage of the tax benefits for their personal account. The foundation of the prohibited transaction rules are based on the premise that investments involving IRAs and related parties are handled in a way that benefits the retirement account and not the IRA owner. The rules prohibit transactions between the IRA and certain individuals known as disqualified persons. The outline for these rules can be found in IRC Section 4975."

"So the IRS is mainly worried about you or a close family member taking personal advantage of the funds in your IRA for reasons other than accumulating retirement savings," Rich said.

"Correct," John said.

Popular Self-Directed IRA Investments

"So what kind of investments can you make?" Rich asked.

John passed Rich a piece of paper.

"Here's a list of a handful of the most popular types of investments available for retirement accounts. Remember, as long as your IRA custodian allows it, or—in the case of a checkbook control IRA LLC—the investment does not violate IRS prohibited transaction rules under IRC 4975 or is not a collectible or life insurance contract pursuant to IRC 408(m), you can enjoy the benefits of tax-deferred or (in the case of a self-directed Roth IRA) tax-free income and gains."

- Domestic or foreign real estate
- Residential or commercial real estate
- Raw land
- Foreclosure property
- Mortgages
- Mortgage pools
- Deeds
- Private loans
- Tax liens
- Private businesses
- Limited liability companies
- Limited liability partnerships
- Private placements
- Precious metals and certain coins
- Stocks, bonds, mutual funds
- Foreign currencies

"That's quite a range of options," Rich said.

"It is," John agreed. "So let's look more closely at the main groups. I want to paint you a clear picture of what you can do, and provide you with some helpful tips for making investments that can enable you to achieve your investment goals."

"Thanks," Rich said.

"Let's start with using a self-directed IRA to purchase real estate," John said. "Most people mistakenly believe that their IRA funds must be invested in bank CDs, the stock market, or mutual funds. Few investors realize that the IRS has always permitted real estate purchases with IRA funds. Investments in real estate with an IRA are fully permissible by the IRS and it is even stated right on its website as we discussed previously. Of course, the IRS cannot force an IRA custodian to offer real estate as an investment option, but real estate is an allowable investment to be made with retirement funds. Basically, IRS rules permit you to engage in almost any type of real estate investment, aside from any investment involving a disqualified person."

"What are the advantages of using retirement funds to buy real estate?" Rich asked.

"In general," John said, "income or gains generated by an IRA generate tax-deferred/tax-free profits. Using a self-directed IRA to purchase real estate allows the IRA to earn tax-free income/gains and pay taxes at a future date, rather than in the year the investment produces income. For example, if you purchased a piece of property for $100,000 with your IRA and later sold the property for $200,000, all $100,000 would go back to your IRA without tax."

"That's really powerful," Rich said.

"It is. When I tell people about this, some wonder about the advantages and disadvantages. They say, 'Well if I bought the property personally and held the property for at least twelve months, I would only have capital gains tax of 15 percent, which is not so bad.' And that's true, but it's still 15 percent more than you would have to pay if you bought the real estate with your self-directed IRA. And if you sold the real estate that you owned personally within twelve months, then the gain would count as a short-term capital gain and the ordinary income tax rate would apply, which can be as high as 39 percent without including state tax. Clearly, not paying tax on real estate income or gains provides far more advantages than even paying 15 percent tax, let alone ordinary income tax rates.

"What about getting depreciation deductions?" Rich asked. "Aren't deductions tax beneficial? If I used my self-directed IRA I wouldn't receive a tax deduction because a self-directed IRA is a tax-exempt plan."

"No doubt," John said. "Getting depreciation for buying real estate has its advantages, since it does reduce the amount of tax you pay. But people forget that when you sell property you will have to pick up the depreciation taken as ordinary income. This is referred to as depreciation recapture. Tax deductions are swell, but they are certainly not as good as not paying tax. Ask any CPA or tax attorney which would be better—getting a tax deduction or not paying tax on gains. I would be shocked if anyone answered that a tax deduction would be preferred. That answer could change if the investment lost money—because when one makes a bad investment and loses money with a retirement account there is no net operating loss (NOL) benefit that can help reduce past or future income. However, the retirement account simply decreases in value and you have less money for retirement."

"No risk, no reward," Rich said. "But it sounds like the key is the taxes. With a self-directed IRA you can invest without paying tax and you will not have to pay taxes right away—or in most cases for many years to come. This allows your retirement funds to grow tax-free. And all the income or gains from your real estate deals flow though to your self-directed IRA account without tax!"

"You got it," John said.

"So what types of real estate investments can I make with a self-directed IRA?" Rich asked.

"Here's a partial list of real estate–related investments that you can make with a self-directed IRA."

- Raw land
- Residential homes
- Commercial property
- Apartments
- Duplexes
- Condos/townhomes
- Mobile homes

- Real estate notes
- Real estate purchase options
- Tax liens certificates
- Tax deeds

"Great," Rich said. "But how do I actually buy the real estate with my self-directed IRA?"

"Let's assume you'll be using a checkbook control self-directed IRA LLC," John said. "The steps for buying real estate are typically the same for any IRS-approved investment made via a checkbook control self-directed IRA LLC."

Steps for Establishing a Self-Directed IRA LLC

1. Establish your IRS-compliant self-directed IRA LLC.

You should use a tax professional or self-directed IRA facilitation company to establish your new self-directed IRA structure, including the IRA account. If an LLC will be used to make investments, you must complete all the necessary steps to establish the LLC, tax identification number, and LLC operating agreement.

2. Tax-Free Transfer of Retirement Funds

Once the self-directed IRA account has been opened with an IRA custodian, it's time to either transfer existing retirement funds to the IRA account or make contributions to the IRA account so funds are available for investment. In general, as long as the funds are coming from a retirement account, pretax or after-tax (Roth IRA), the funds can be rolled into the IRA account without tax or penalty. The transfer of IRA accounts to your new self-directed IRA account is often referred to a transfer, and the movement of qualified retirement funds from a 401(k) plan, 457(b), or other non-IRA account is referred to as a direct rollover. In both cases the movement of funds from one retirement account to another is tax- and penalty-free.

"I assume the pretax retirement funds I'll be transferring would go to a pretax IRA and my after-tax IRA funds would go into a Roth IRA?" Rich asked.

"Yes," John said, "that's correct. IRS rules require that pretax retirement funds be rolled into or transferred into a pretax IRA, whereas your Roth funds from your retirement accounts would be rolled into a Roth IRA. That's why, if you had pretax and after-tax retirement funds from either a 401(k) plan or IRA, you would have to establish two self-directed IRA accounts, one pretax and one after-tax (Roth)."

"Makes sense," Rich said.

"In most cases, the rollover of funds from a non-IRA account [i.e., 401(k) plan] to an IRA must be initiated by the plan participant typically via a rollover request or distribution form, whereas, IRA funds transferred to an IRA can be initiated by the new IRA custodian. So, whether it's an IRA, SEP IRA, SIMPLE IRA, 401(k) plan, 403(b), 457(b), or defined benefit plan fund, the retirement assets, in cash or property (in-kind), can be rolled tax-free and penalty-free into a self-directed IRA."

"How do you do it?" Rich asked.

"For cash, the transfer can typically be done by cash or wire, whereas property is typically transferred by retitling the asset to show the change of ownership of the asset to the new IRA custodian. It's advisable to work with a tax professional to assist in completing the rollover and ensuring that the paperwork is completed properly so that the transfer is done without tax. Also, there is typically no withholding that occurs on a transfer of retirement funds to the new plan.

"Can personal nonqualified retirement funds be transferred into the new self-directed IRA?" Rich asked.

"Unfortunately, no," John said. "Only retirement funds from an IRA or a qualified retirement plan, such as a 401(k) plan, 457(b), 403(b), defined benefit plan, etc., whether pretax or after-tax, can be transferred into a self-directed IRA. Unfortunately, some people believe that because they have some funds in a bank account or an annuity that they have earmarked for their retirement, those can be rolled into a retirement account."

IRA LLC Bank Account

"Not so?" Rich asked.

"If the funds in the bank account or annuity are not titled in the name of a retirement account [i.e., IRA or 401(k) plan], they are not considered eligible to be rolled into an IRA," John said. "Of course, as we discussed, you can always make contributions to an IRA from personal funds up to your annual limitation, which is based on your income level, for example $5,500 if you are under fifty and $6,500 if you are over the age of fifty for 2015."

Real Estate Investments with Your Self-Directed IRA LLC

"Okay, so you've touched on getting retirement funds in a self-directed IRA vehicle so that they are ready for investment," Rich said, "but how are real estate investments made with a self-directed IRA?"

"As soon as the rollover retirement funds have been deposited into the IRA LLC bank account via investment by the IRA custodian, either by check or wire, the manager of the LLC is now ready to make an investment. Hopefully, the LLC manager has performed the necessary due diligence required in order to have a high degree of confidence that the real estate investment will be a good one for the IRA."

"Can you explain how real estate investments are made with a custodian-controlled self-directed IRA?" Rich asked.

"With a custodian-controlled self-directed IRA account (without the use of an LLC)," John said, "the IRA investment is made by the IRA custodian for the benefit of the IRA holder. What this means in practice is that you don't have a checkbook or wire transfer abilities to make an investment even if it is your IRA."

"So how do you buy real estate?" Rich asked.

"Essentially, you work with the custodian where the self-directed IRA is held to make the purchase. The IRA holder would communicate to the IRA custodian, typically in writing via an investment authorization form or some similarly titled form, the details of the transaction, including the amount and the appropriate payment instructions whether by check or wire. The custodian would be required to review and execute all required real estate purchase documents and cut the check or execute the wire transfer so that the IRA could purchase the real estate. Since the self-directed IRA is a custodian-directed plan, the custodian is typically in control of the retirement funds and would need to be directed by the IRA holder to make the investment."

Custodian-Controlled IRA vs. Checkbook Control IRA for Real Estate

"That doesn't mean the custodian can just invest in anything he or she wants, right?" Rich asked.

"Absolutely not," John said. "The IRA holder directs all IRA investments and the custodian is not allowed by law to make any investment without that direction. Title to the property is typically in the name of the IRA custodian for the benefit of the IRA holder. Therefore, if you established an IRA with XYZ Trust Company and purchased a piece of real estate, the title would generally be as follows: "'XYZ Trust Company custodian of the Rich Smith IRA.'"

"Does it make sense to do it that way?" Rich asked.

"Using a custodian-controlled self-directed IRA is a common way to buy real estate, but it's not the most convenient or, in most cases, the most cost-effective. The custodian will generally help you make sure your IRA remains in IRS compliance, by filing IRS Form 5498, for example, while at the same time helping you facilitate traditional as well as nontraditional investments, such as real estate."

"How do you know if it's the way to go?" Rich asked.

"To determine whether it's a viable option for you, closely examine the fees involved in maintaining the self-directed IRA with the custodian as well as any annual fees or transaction-specific fees for facilitation of self-directed IRA investments."

"What about making real estate investments with a checkbook control self-directed IRA LLC?" Rich asked.

"Unlike the custodian-controlled self-directed IRA, which requires that the IRA investment be made and held at the IRA custodian, a checkbook control self-directed IRA gives you, as manager of the IRA LLC, greater control over the account and investments. As we discussed in detail, the self-directed IRA account could be opened at any number of IRA custodians, often referred to as passive custodians since they are not actively involved in the investment of the IRA assets. Once the self-directed IRA account has been opened, a tax professional or IRA facilitation firm will establish an LLC, typically in the state where you will be buying the real estate. The LLC account can generally be opened at most local banks, credit unions, and a majority of financial institutions, such as Fidelity. It's important to emphasize that you will be opening up a regular LLC business account, just like you would if you owned the LLC personally and were starting a new business. Remember you already have an IRA account, so there is no need to open another IRA account with the bank. The whole point of the structure is to have an investment vehicle, the LLC, that will allow you to make investments more quickly and with less cost involved. So, you would just need to open a regular LLC checking account at the bank of your choice."

"That sounds simple," Rich said.

"It is," John agreed. "But some of my clients get confused and open another IRA account since they tell the banker that the LLC will be owned by an IRA or because the banker reads the LLC operating agreement and notices that the LLC is owned by an IRA."

"And that's not correct," Rich said.

"Right. A plain old regular LLC business banking account is all that is needed since you already have an IRA account setup. Think about it this way: If you use your IRA to buy Google stock, Google doesn't have a separate bank account for your IRA funds. Your IRA funds will go directly into the Google business banking account in return for the shares you will receive. The same holds true for your LLC. Your LLC will be used for investment purposes and your IRA will be investing funds in return for ownership of the LLC, the same way it would work if you bought Google shares."

"When you open a bank account," Rich said, "most banks ask that you deposit at least $100 to set up the account. How does that work with an IRA?"

"That is a great question," John said. "As we discussed, when IRA funds are used to make investments, no personal funds should be commingled with the IRA funds. So, no personal funds should be deposited into the IRA LLC account. Also, you should not apply for a credit card associated with the LLC account, as that could trigger a prohibited transaction," John said. "A pure debit card could work, but make sure you, as the IRA holder, are under no obligation to personally guarantee an obligation of the IRA LLC account," John added.

"Got it," Rich said.

"The question then becomes how do you open the LLC account that will be owned by IRA funds? In general, there are a few ways you can open an LLC bank account, which will be owned by an IRA. The first and most common approach is to just tell the bank to keep the LLC account information on hold and when you bring in the IRA custodian check you receive, the bank can open the LLC account and then you can deposit the check. The second way to open an LLC account, which will be owned by your IRA, is to have a nondisqualified person (i.e., a nonlineal descendant), for example, a sibling, friend, cousin, aunt, or uncle, lend the LLC enough funds to open the account, and once the LLC account has been funded with IRA funds, the LLC can pay back the disqualified person, along with a small interest payment. For example, you can have your brother, a nondisqualified person, lend your LLC $100, which you can then deposit into your LLC bank account. Once the IRA custodian wires the IRA funds into the LLC account, the LLC can then pay back your brother with the IRA funds that have been deposited into your LLC account."

"Neat," Rich said.

Buying Real Estate with a Checkbook Control Self-Directed IRA

"Okay," John said, "now that we've briefly talked about how the self-directed IRA account is established and the LLC account has been opened at a local bank, let's jump into buying real estate with a checkbook control self-directed IRA LLC."

"I'm ready," Rich said.

"So, you've established your LLC bank account at the local bank of your choice and your IRA funds have been deposited into the LLC account, either by check or wire. Now, you, as manager of the LLC, assuming the LLC operating agreement has been drafted properly, have control over all LLC activities."

"In other words, you have checkbook control," Rich said.

"Correct," John said. "In practice, this means that when you open your IRA LLC bank account you will receive a checkbook and wiring transfer authority so you can make an investment by simply writing a check or executing a wire transfer."

"And like you said," Rich said, "one of the main reasons for establishing a checkbook control self-directed IRA LLC is the ability to make investments quickly, conveniently, and cost-effectively."

"That's right," John said. "Making investments with a self-directed IRA LLC is generally quick and easy. This is one of the primary advantages. As the manager of the LLC, you will have the freedom to make all investment decisions for your IRA LLC. The impetus behind the checkbook control self-directed IRA LLC solution is that it allows you to eliminate the expense and delays associated with an IRA custodian so you can act quickly when the right investment opportunity presents itself. As manager of the IRA LLC, you will be able to write a check or wire money from the IRA-owned LLC bank account to make an investment. In addition, you will not need to get your real estate investment documents signed by the IRA custodian as you can sign all real estate–related transaction documents for as manager of the LLC, since title to the real estate will be purchased in the name of the LLC and not in the IRA custodian name."

"That sounds so much easier," Rich said.

"It is," John agreed. "And when a real estate or other investment is made with your checkbook control assets, the investment is made in the name of the LLC. For real estate titling purposes, the common practice is for the real estate to be titled in the name of the LLC because the LLC will be the legal owner of the real estate."

"What about a single-member LLC?" Rich asked. "You mentioned it would be treated as a disregarded entity for tax purposes."

"Yes," John said. "That's correct from a tax perspective. However, as a corporate and legal matter, a single LLC is respected as an entity for corporate limited liability purposes and, accordingly, would hold title in the LLC name and not the name of the LLC owner (member). The owner would report the income of the LLC since it is a flow-through entity for tax purposes and the single-member LLC does not file a federal income tax return. It is still respected for corporate purposes and is recognized as an entity separate from its owner."

"So, for example, if my IRA established an LLC and named the LLC ABC, LLC, then ABC, LLC would be owned 100 percent by my IRA care of XYZ Trust Company. And title to real estate purchased by ABC, LLC will be in the name of ABC, LLC and not XYZ Trust Company, Custodian of the Rich Smith IRA."

"Right," John said. "I'll spend a considerable amount of time going through some helpful tips for buying real estate with a self-directed IRA LLC with checkbook control later. But I think it's helpful to go through the actual procedures of buying real estate with a self-directed IRA LLC with checkbook control."

"How about an example?" Rich asked.

"Good idea," John said. "Let's assume Rich Smith, who resides in Texas, has $275,000 in a rollover IRA held at a major bank. Rich previously worked at a Fortune 500 Company for over twenty years and recently left his job for a new opportunity. Upon leaving his employer, Rich elected to move his employer 401(k) plan funds into a traditional IRA at a local bank. Because Rich left his employer, he satisfied the plan triggering-event rules and was permitted to roll over his 401(k) funds to an IRA. Over the last few years, Rich invested his IRA in traditional stocks, mutual funds, and ETFs but was not satisfied with his returns and felt somewhat insecure about what was happening on Wall Street, so he decided to look for alternative asset investment options for his IRA funds. He did some research on the Internet and found that the IRS permits one to use IRA funds to buy real estate along with an array of other interesting asset classes, such as precious metals, tax liens, hard money loans, etc. Rich spoke with his accountant and they discussed some of the pros and cons of taking retirement funds out of the equity markets and putting them into real estate. Although Rich was not a seasoned real estate investor, as he has an engineering background, his father did own a number of rental real estate properties and so did his brother-in-law. Rich felt more comfortable buying hard assets and something he can see and touch. Rich worked with a real estate agent and started looking around for real estate investment opportunities. Although the real estate market in Texas has been relatively strong, he was able to find a number of interesting investment opportunities. Rich did some additional diligence on the property, spoke to some real estate investor friends about the property, location, and price, and he received favorable feedback. The next step was to put an offer down on the property. The problem is that Rich wanted to use his retirement funds and was not sure how to proceed. Rich then called his accountant, who gave him the name of a tax attorney: John. Rich then called John, the tax attorney, and told him about his plans to use IRA funds to buy the real estate property. Luckily for Rich, John did have experience in that area and had actually helped a few people use a self-directed IRA to buy real estate. The first thing John told Rich is not to use any personal funds when making a deposit for the IRA investment. Rich mentioned that he had not yet signed the purchase agreement and wanted to talk with an attorney to figure out how he would even sign the real estate purchase agreement since his self-directed IRA was not even set up. John was happy to hear this and told Rich that the first question that needs to be addressed is what type of self-directed IRA he wanted to establish, the custodian-controlled self-directed IRA or the checkbook control self-directed IRA LLC."

"Boy that sounds familiar," Rich said with a laugh.

"Fortunately," John said, "the story has a happy ending! Here's some paperwork on the details."

Choosing the Right Self-Directed IRA for Real Estate Investments

The self-directed IRA is a type of IRA structure that allows the IRA holder (you) to have more control over your retirement funds. Unknown to some, not all self-directed IRAs are the same. It is well known that the IRS allows you to use your IRA funds to make traditional investments, such as stocks and mutual funds, it is not as well known that the IRS also allows you to use IRA funds to invest in real estate, precious metals, tax liens, private business, and much more tax- and penalty-free! In fact, the IRS only prescribes a few restrictions on the type of investments that can be made using IRA funds.

Types of Self-Directed IRA Accounts

Since we have examined the three types of self-directed IRA accounts in detail when we first met, as a reminder, I will just briefly touch on them again:

I. Financial Institution Offered Self-Directed IRA

FINANCIAL INSTITUTION OFFERED SELF-DIRECTED IRA

STEP 1
Transfer of retirement funds to U.S. bank, financial institution, credit union, etc.

Investment

STEP 2
Investment is made into assets marketed by the bank or financial institution where the IRA is held – no alternative asset investments are generally permitted

Current custodian holding retirement funds

The most popular self-directed IRA account offered is the financial institution self-directed IRA. The reason that this type of self-directed IRA is so popular is because it is generally offered by the major financial institutions, such as Bank of America, Wells Fargo, Fidelity, Vanguard, etc. With this type of self-directed IRA, the IRA holder is generally able to make only IRA investments offered by the financial institution, which typically only include financial-related investments, such as stocks, mutual funds, and ETFs. Even though these types of IRA accounts are called self-directed IRA accounts, they are very limited in their investment scope and do not allow IRA investors to make any nontraditional investments, such as real estate.

Why do the financial institutions limit the investment options available?

A financial institution that offers IRA accounts is not required to offer its IRA investors the opportunity to make all allowable types of IRA investments. For example, even though real estate is an IRS-approved investment, an IRA custodian is not required or obligated to offer that investment option—remember the language on the IRS website I highlighted earlier? Accordingly, most financial institutions offering IRA accounts will restrict the IRA investment option to financial products offered by the financial institution. The reason behind this is quite clear—a financial institution earns fees from the sale of financial products not by allowing its clients to pull money out of the IRA account to buy real estate from a third party.

2. Custodian-Controlled Self-Directed IRA

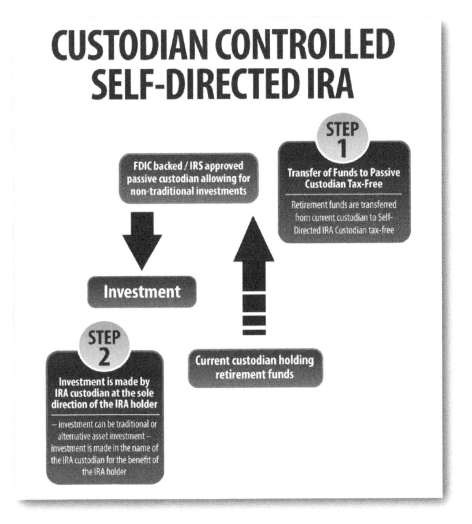

A custodian-controlled self-directed IRA offers an IRA investor more investment options than a financial institution self-directed IRA. With a custodian-controlled self-directed IRA, a financial institution or special trust company will serve as the custodian of the IRA. Generally, all self-directed IRA custodians offer FDIC protection for IRA funds held. Unlike a typical financial institution, most IRA custodians generate fees simply by opening and maintaining IRA accounts and do not offer any financial investment products or platforms. With a custodian-controlled self-directed IRA, the IRA funds are generally held with the IRA custodian and the IRA custodian, at the IRA holder's direction, will then invest those IRA funds accordingly.

Until the 1996 Swanson case, which I went through in detail earlier, the custodian-controlled self-directed IRA was the only way one was able to use IRA funds to make a nontraditional investment, such as real estate. In essence, with a custodian-controlled self-directed IRA, every investment step an IRA holder wanted to make had to be carried out through the IRA custodian, which would typically involve high annual fees, transaction fees, and time delays. In other words, the IRA holder could not take direct control of his or her IRA funds in connection with making an IRA investment. Every time the IRA holder wanted to make an IRA investment or pay an IRA transaction expense, for example, mowing the lawn or paying the bills on a real estate IRA investment, the IRA holder had to request that a custodian do it.

3. Checkbook Control Self-Directed IRA LLC

In the 1996 case of *Swanson v. Commissioner*, 106 T.C. 76 (1996), the Tax Court gave its blessing to a new type of self-directed IRA structure—the self-directed IRA with checkbook control, also known as the checkbook IRA—that is much simpler than investing through a regular custodian-controlled self-directed IRA account.

With a checkbook control self-directed IRA, the IRA holder (you) will have total control over your IRA funds, and you will no longer have to get each investment approved by the IRA custodian of your account as in a custodian-controlled self-directed IRA. Instead, all IRA LLC decisions are truly yours. When you find an investment that you want to make with your IRA funds, as manager of the LLC, simply write a check or wire the funds straight from your self-directed IRA LLC bank account to make the investment.

Under the checkbook IRA format, the IRA is set up with a passive IRA custodian. The self-directed IRA account is then typically funded either by retirement funds rolled over or transferred from a current retirement account or via direct contribution. Then, an LLC is created in which your new IRA, care of the IRA custodian, purchases all the membership units/interests. Now, the IRA funds are at an account in the name of the LLC at a local bank or credit union. When you find an investment that you want to make with your IRA funds, as manager of the LLC, simply write a check or wire the funds straight from your self-directed IRA LLC bank account to make the investment. The self-directed IRA allows you to eliminate the delays associated with an IRA custodian, enabling you to act quickly when the right investment opportunity presents itself.

"Rich, I have put together the following diagram that I think will help you better understand how the checkbook control self-directed IRA LLC works.

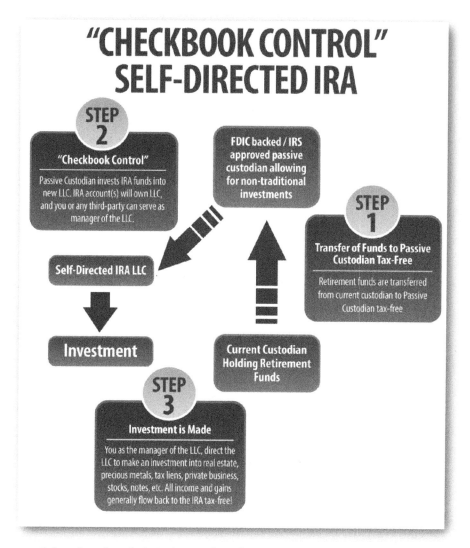

John then handed Rich another document that highlighted some of the main differences between the checkbook control self-directed IRA LLC and the custodian-controlled self-directed IRA.

Main Differences Between Custodian-Controlled IRA and Checkbook Control IRA LLC

Checkbook Control

With a self-directed IRA LLC, you have even more advantages than using a custodian-controlled IRA, including what's called checkbook control. As manager of the self-directed IRA LLC you will have the ability to make IRA investments without seeking the consent of a custodian. Instead, all decisions are truly yours.

Access

With a self-directed IRA LLC, you will have direct access to your IRA funds, allowing you to make an investment quickly and efficiently. There is no need to obtain approvals from your IRA custodian or deal with time delays in waiting for the custodian to execute all investment documentation. Your IRA funds will be held at a local bank instead of at a custodian you have never worked with before.

Speed

With a self-directed IRA LLC, as manager of the LLC, when you find an investment that you want to make with your IRA funds, simply write a check or wire the funds straight from your self-directed IRA LLC bank account to make the investment. The self-directed IRA LLC allows you to eliminate the delays associated with a custodian-controlled self-directed IRA account, enabling you to act quickly when the right investment opportunity presents itself.

Lower fees

Another advantage to a self-directed IRA LLC account is that over the long term you will save money on IRA custodian fees versus with a custodian-controlled IRA. With the checkbook control self-directed IRA LLC structure, you will not be required to seek IRA custodian consent when making

IRA investments, allowing you to eliminate IRA custodian-related transaction fees and account valuation fees associated with a custodian-controlled self-directed IRA. With a self-directed IRA LLC with checkbook control," in general, you no longer have to pay custodian fees based on IRA account value as well as transaction fees.

Limited liability protection

By using a self-directed IRA LLC with checkbook control, your IRA will benefit from the limited liability protection afforded by using an LLC. By using an LLC, all your IRA assets held outside the LLC will be shielded from attack. This is especially important in the case of IRA real estate investments in which many state statutes impose an extended statute of limitations for claims arising from defects in the design or construction of improvements to real estate.

Asset and Creditor Protection

By using a self-directed IRA LLC with checkbook control the IRA holder's IRA will generally be protected for up to $1 million in the case of personal bankruptcy under the 2005 Federal Bankruptcy Act. In addition, most states will shield a self-directed IRA from creditor attack against the IRA holder outside of bankruptcy. Therefore, by using a self-directed IRA LLC, the IRA will be generally protected against creditor attack against the IRA holder.

Privacy Protection

With a self-directed IRA LLC, the investment will be made in the name of the LLC, whereas, with a custodian-controlled self-directed IRA, the name of the IRA owner will be in the name of the investment, allowing the public to easily locate the asset's owner. For example, if an IRA LLC is established in a state such as Nevada or Delaware, which offer strong privacy protection, identifying the owner of the LLC would be extremely difficult.

John handed Rich a chart that summarized the differences between all three types of self-directed IRA structures:

	Financial Institution Offered Self-Directed IRA	Custodian Controlled Self-Directed IRA	"Checkbook Control" Self-Directed IRA
Ability to take control of your retirement funds	YES	YES	YES
Ability to make annual IRA contributions	YES	YES	YES
Ability to accept rollover or transfer of retirement funds	YES	YES	YES
Ability to make traditional investments, such as stocks	YES	YES	YES
Ability to make alternative asset investments, such as real estate	NO	YES	YES
Limited Liability Protection	NO	NO	YES
Ability to hold IRA funds at local bank	NO	NO	YES
Ability to use LLC managed by IRA holder to make investments	NO	NO	YES
$1,000,000 of personal bankruptcy protection	YES	YES	YES

"Thanks, John," Rich said, "this is really helpful. I really like the idea of using an LLC to buy real estate from a limited liability standpoint. In addition, the fact that I will be saving IRA custodian fees in the long run as well as the ability to have more control over my IRA investments makes the checkbook control structure a no-brainer for me.

John nodded. "Most people mistakenly believe that their IRA must be invested in bank CDs, the stock market, or mutual funds. Few investors realize that the IRS has always permitted real estate to be held inside IRA retirement accounts. IRS rules permit you to engage in almost any type of real estate investment, aside from any investment generally involving a disqualified person. Here are some more documents on that."

Advantages of Using a Self-Directed IRA LLC to Purchase Real Estate

Income or gains generated by an IRA generate tax-deferred/tax-free profits. Using a self-directed IRA LLC to purchase real estate allows the IRA to earn tax-free income/gains and pay taxes at a future date (in the case of a Roth IRA, the income/gains are always tax-free), rather than in the year the investment produces income.

"Let me jot down the main advantages of using a self-directed IRA to buy real estate," John said.

- Gains are tax-free
- Positive cash flow is tax-free
- No time limit for holding property
- IRA can borrow money—leverage your investment with nonrecourse financing
- Potential to earn a larger rate of return on invested capital

"When purchasing real estate with a self-directed IRA LLC, in general, all income and gains generated by your pretax retirement account investment would generally flow back into the retirement account tax-free. Instead of paying tax on the returns of a real estate investment, tax is paid only at a later date, leaving the real estate investment to grow unhindered. Generally, self-directed IRA real estate investments are usually made when a person is earning higher income and is taxed at a higher tax rate. Withdrawals are made from an investment account when a person is earning little or no income and is taxed at a lower rate."

"Do you have an example?" Rich asked.

"For example, Joe established a self-directed IRA LLC with $100,000 to purchase real estate and make other investments. Assume Joe kept his self-directed IRA LLC open for twenty years. Further assume that Joe was able to generate an average annual pretax rate of return of 8 percent and the average tax rate was 25 percent. By using a tax-deferred self-directed IRA

LLC strategy, after twenty years Joe's $100,000 investment would be worth $466,098, whereas, if Joe made the investments with taxable funds (non-retirement funds), he would have accumulated only $320,714 after twenty years, a difference of $145,384."

"What about other benefits?" Rich asked.

"In addition to tax benefits," John said, "there are also several potential investment advantages to buying real estate with a self-directed IRA. Real estate offers diversification from overexposure to Wall Street from both personal and retirement funds. After the 2008 financial crisis, many retirement investors began to appreciate the importance of having a well-balanced and diversified retirement portfolio that can help protect against another financial crisis. Also, people tend to like to invest in something they know and understand. Real estate has fast become an asset class that more and more Americans have confidence in and have a greater comfort level with than trying to guess why stocks go up or down. And real estate is a hard asset you can touch and see and it offers a level of confidence against any potential US inflation. Buying hard assets, such as real estate, is seen as a solid way of protecting retirement assets from the threat of inflation."

"I get it," Rich said. "And combined with the fact that all income and gains from real estate owned in a self-directed IRA are exempt from tax makes real estate an attractive investment for retirement investors."

"Exactly," John said. "Now that I've covered some of the advantages of using a self-directed IRAs to buy real estate, here are some ways you can structure a real estate investment using a self-directed IRA." He handed Rich a pamphlet.

Different Ways to Structure a Self-Directed IRA Real Estate Investment

When using a self-directed IRA LLC to make a real estate investment, there are a number of ways you can structure the transaction:

1. Use Your Self-Directed IRA LLC Funds to Make 100 Percent of the Investment

If you have enough funds in your self-directed IRA LLC to cover the entire real estate purchase, including closing costs, taxes, fees, and insurance, you may make the purchase outright using your self-directed IRA LLC. All ongoing expenses relating to the real estate investment must be paid out of your self-directed IRA LLC bank account. In addition, all income or gains relating to your real estate investment must be returned to your self-directed IRA LLC bank account.

2. Partner with Family, Friends, Colleagues

If you don't have sufficient funds in your self-directed IRA LLC to make a real estate purchase outright, your self-directed IRA LLC can purchase an interest in the property along with a family member (nondisqualified person: any family member other than a parent, child, spouse, daughter-in-law, son-in-law), friend, or colleague. As a reminder, a disqualified person would be you as the IRA holder and any of your lineal descendants, parents, children, spouse, daughter-in-law, son-in-law, as well as any entity controlled by such persons (50 percent or greater ownership). I explained earlier why you should avoid investing IRA funds with any disqualified person including any entity a disqualified person has any personal ownership of vested interest in, even if less than 10 percent.

How an LLC Can Make Your Life Easier

"Does an LLC really make a difference?" Rich asked.

"Definitely," John said. "Investing with a nondisqualified family member, friend, or colleague does present several nice benefits, including securing the necessary funds to take advantage of an attractive real estate investment opportunity. But it also comes with some risks, which exist any time a joint venture arrangement is entered into. The main type of risk presented by a joint venture–type of arrangement is making sure each partner lives up to the intended deal agreed upon by the partners, including profit split and sharing of expenses, as well as the determination of when to sell or not. In addition, there is the risk of potentially being personally responsible for any claim or liability arising out of the property, assuming sufficient property insurance was not acquired. One popular way of removing a good chunk of the risks involved with making co-investments is the use of the LLC."

The LLC Explained

"So what exactly is an LLC?" Rich asked.

"An LLC is a legal entity that is treated as a pass-through entity for tax purposes but offers limited liability protection for corporate purposes. In other words, all profits and losses are 'passed through' the business to each member of the LLC without any corporate tax, such as the case with a corporation. LLC members then report profits and losses on their personal federal tax returns. When partnering up with a nondisqualified person to make real estate investments, using an LLC presents a number of advantages. I think it will be helpful to touch on a few of the important advantages the LLC can offer when using multiple IRAs to make investments."

1. Titling of real estate

Since the self-directed IRA LLC and other nondisqualified investor(s) will invest in the LLC and the LLC will be the party ultimately buying the real estate, the title of the real estate is in the LLC, which makes things a lot cleaner than having multiple parties on the deed.

2. Papering the Terms of the Investment

When establishing an LLC, the members (owners) of the LLC should prepare and execute an LLC operating agreement, which sets forth the specific terms in connection with the investment. The document should be prepared by an attorney who is familiar with the joint venture arrangement in order to make sure that the agreed-upon terms are properly reflected in the LLC operating agreement. Having the operating agreement should reduce any future misunderstandings and conflicts with the joint venture partners. Also, it is much easier to share the profits and gains associated with the investment because they will be allocated to the LLC bank account and then can be sent to each partner's bank account as necessary.

3. Limited Liability Protection

Members of an LLC are protected from personal liability for business decisions or actions of the LLC. This means that if the LLC incurs debt or is sued in connection with any of its activities or investments, members' personal assets are usually exempt. This is particularly important when it comes to retirement accounts, since many Americans' largest asset is their retirement account. That being said, limited liability protection would not prove very valuable if all the IRA assets were tied up in the self-directed IRA LLC investment since limited liability protection only protects assets outside of the LLC, not within the LLC. For example, Ben had $100,000 in his self-directed IRA LLC and wanted to buy a piece of real estate for $200,000. Ben approached Doug, a friend who is quite well off, about partnering to buy the property. Doug agrees to invest the $100,000 along with Ben's $100,000 to buy the property. Doug recommends they form an LLC that would be owned proportionally by Ben's self-directed IRA LLC and Doug personally. The LLC operating agreement will show that Ben's IRA and Doug personally each own 50 percent of the LLC and also will set forth all the terms they agreed upon with respect to the management of the LLC and real estate project. Because Ben invested all his self-directed IRA funds into the LLC to buy the real estate, if there was a claim or liability against the LLC, Ben self-directed IRA funds in the LLC could be subject to attack because the LLC only protects assets held outside of the LLC. Whereas if Ben had IRA funds outside of the LLC that were either in the self-directed IRA account or invested elsewhere, those funds would be protected by using an LLC, if any liability issues arose.

"Are there any negatives?" Rich asked.

"In general," John said, "using the LLC as an investment entity has some big advantages when buying real estate with a self-directed IRA, but there are some potential negatives. The first is cost. In most cases it costs anywhere from $50 to $500 to form the LLC and most states have annual fees of anywhere from $25 to $800. So, you must weigh the advantages of using an LLC as a self-directed IRA investment vehicle against the cost of doing so. In addition, because the LLC will be owned by two or more persons and the real estate investment will be a joint venture between the self-directed IRA and at least one other person or entity, the LLC will need to file a partnership income tax return (IRS Form 1065) for federal and state income tax purposes. No federal income tax will be due, but a return must still be filed by April 15 of each year."

"Seems like with the "checkbook control" IRA I will have a lot of control over the LLC assets to make investments and pay IRA LLC related expenses?" Rich stated

"Yes, like all things, sometimes a positive can turn into a negative without much warning." John said. "Because you as manager of the IRA LLC will have total control over the LLC bank account, you will have ultimate control over the LLC's funds. With such control comes a high degree of responsibility. I know we spent a considerable amount of time going through the prohibited transaction rules, but I do want to stress them again. As manager of your LLC, it is imperative that the funds are used for only IRA LLC related activities; including paying any and all IRA LLC related expenses. The funds must not be used for any personal benefit, which includes paying personal expenses or taking a small loan. There is no exception to this rule. Not one cent of IRA LLC funds should be used for any personal activity or connected to any disqualified person. I know I may be coming across as quite direct, but this is a very important point and the IRS is very strict on these rules. For example, I have a client that has over $600,000 in his IRA LLC and he mistakenly issued an IRA LLC check to pay for a personal business expense of just $400, and the IRS argued prohibited transaction and is pursuing this position quite forcefully." John added. "So to be clear, all funds in the IRA LLC bank account should be used 100% for LLC related activities. In no event should any of the IA LLC funds be used for any personal purpose or in any way that directly or indirectly benefits a disqualified person. Even one dollar of IRA LLC funds used for a personal expense can trigger a prohibited transaction and invalidate your entire IRA. The IRS is very serious about these rules, as my example hopefully shows. " John said.

"I understand," Rich responded.

"The "checkbook control" Self-Directed IRA brings with it many attractive features, but it also comes with great responsibility." John added. "Before establishing a "checkbook control" Self-Directed IRA LLC is it important to make sure you are confortable working in a very loose and free environment and trust yourself to respect the IRS prohibited transaction rules and make 100% sure that the IRA LLC funds are never used for any personal purpose, not even $1 and not even for one day.

"Got it," Rich said.

Using an LLC to Buy Real Estate with a Self-Directed IRA

"By using a self-directed IRA LLC," John continued, "you can partner with any nondisqualified person using personal or retirement funds and either invest in the real estate property together, where the self-directed IRA LLC and the other partner(s) are identified on the title, or you can establish a new LLC, we can call the new LLC Newco, and the LLC would be owned proportionally by your self-directed IRA LLC and the other nondisqualified person based on the amount invested. The advantages of using a separate investment LLC is that the title to the property would be in the name of the new LLC and it makes operating the property easier because the business terms of the arrangement can be properly documented in the LLC operating agreement. The downside of using a separate LLC is that there is a fee for establishing an LLC and having a tax professional draft the LLC operating agreement. In addition, an LLC owned by two or more persons is treated as a partnership for tax purposes and an IRS partnership tax return (IRS Form 1065) and state partnership would be required to be filed. Even though the partnership does not pay taxes, there would still be a cost to filing the partnership return. Something to consider, but I believe the advantages of using an investment LLC to make a real estate investment with a nondisqualified person outweighs the negatives because it is so much cleaner and easier to operate."

"Can you give me an example?" Rich said.

"Let's say your self-directed IRA LLC could partner with a family member (nondisqualified person: any family member other than a parent, child, spouse, daughter-in-law, son-in-law), friend, or colleague—to purchase a piece of property for $150,000. Your self-directed IRA LLC could purchase an interest in the property (i.e., 50 percent for $75,000) and your nondisqualified family member, friend, or colleague could purchase the remaining interest (i.e., 50 percent for $75,000)."

"Okay."

"So, all income or gains from the property would be allocated to the parties in relation to their percentage of ownership in the property. Likewise, all property expenses must be allocated in relation to the parties' percentage of ownership in the property. So, for a $2,000 property tax bill, the self-directed IRA LLC would be responsible for 50 percent of the bill ($1,000) and the family member, friend, or colleague would be responsible for the remaining $1,000 (50 percent). The LLC would ultimately pay the property expense but it would be treated as though it had been paid by each of the LLC members in proportion to their ownership in the LLC. Using the LLC versus a joint venture arrangement in which multiple parties are listed on the title as the owner makes it much easier to keep track of all expenses and income associated with the asset. Using a joint venture arrangement would likely require each joint venture member to cut a check to pay their allocated portion of any property expenses or even require the tenant to issue multiple rent checks, splitting the aggregate rental amount among the owners."

"Just to confirm," Rich said, "I don't need an LLC to buy real estate with an IRA, but it does make things easier."

"That's correct. Remember what I said about the custodian-controlled self-directed IRA vs. the checkbook control self-directed IRA LLC. And remember that I said many thousands of IRA investors use a full-service IRA custodian to purchase real estate and are quite happy with this arrangement. In that case, the IRA custodian purchases the asset for the benefit of the IRA and the IRA custodian is more formally involved in the real estate acquisition, maintenance, and divestiture process. This could cause some delays, inconveniences, as well as in some case higher annual custodian fees. This has led to the growing popularity of the checkbook control self-directed IRA LLC solution. With the checkbook control IRA LLC, you'll be able to make the real estate investment from a local bank in the name of the LLC and be able to make the real estate purchase, operate and maintain the property, as well as sell the property by simply writing a check or executing a wire transfer, as manager of the LLC, straight from the IRA LLC bank without ever having to include the IRA custodian. Also, the checkbook control self-directed IRA offers limited liability protection."

"That sounds perfect," Rich said.

"By using a self-directed IRA LLC with checkbook control, your IRA will benefit from the limited liability protection afforded by using an LLC. By using an LLC, all your IRA assets held outside the LLC will be shielded from attack. This is especially important in the case of IRA real estate investments in which many state statutes impose an extended statute of limitations for claims arising from defects in the design or construction of improvements to real estate."

"And there's the liability protection."

"Yup. Using an LLC as an investment vehicle instead of using a custodian-controlled self-directed IRA offers the owner of the LLC—the IRA—limited liability protection. What limited liability protection means is that the IRA, as owner of the LLC, would generally be protected from any debt, liabilities, or obligations of the LLC. In other words, limited liability protection will protect all IRA funds held outside of the LLC from attack based upon a liability, debt, or obligation of the LLC. Therefore, the LLC will not protect your IRA funds held inside the LLC but will protect your IRA assets held outside of the LLC. This could prove valuable to a number of retirement investors seeking to make nontraditional investments, such as real estate with IRA funds, as often your retirement account may be the most valuable asset. Protecting that from attack by creditors could be essential."

"What else does it do for you?" Rich asked.

"Along with limited liability protection, the LLC offers its owner(s) privacy, confidentiality, and discretion when making investments. Because most states do not require the name(s) of the member(s) of the LLC to be made publicly available when forming an LLC, by using an LLC, the IRA holder can shield his or her identity when making an investment, whereas, if the IRA custodian made the investment directly (without using an LLC), the IRA holder's name would likely be included on all the real estate and title-related documents and would be publicly available. For example, if John Doe used ABC Trust Company to buy real estate, title to the real estate would most likely be ABC Trust Company, Custodian of the John Doe IRA. In the case of an LLC, only the name of the LLC would be included, and identifying the owner of managers of the LLC could provide difficult, depending on the state."

Choosing a Partner for Your Self-Directed IRA Investment

"Isn't partnering with a family member in a real estate transaction a prohibited transaction?" Rich asked.

John shook his head. "Not always, as long as the transaction is structured correctly. Investing in an investment entity with a family member and investing in an investment property directly are two different transaction structures that affect whether the transaction will be prohibited under Code Section 4975. The different tax treatment is based on who currently owns the investment. Using a self-directed IRA LLC to invest in an entity that is owned by a family member who is a disqualified person will likely be treated as a prohibited transaction. However, partnering with a family member who is a nondisqualified person directly into an investment property would likely not be a prohibited transaction. But if you, a family member, or other disqualified person already owns a property, then investing in that property with your self-directed IRA LLC would be prohibited."

"Can I partner with myself to do a self-directed IRA real estate investment?" Rich asked.

"That's one of the most popular questions I get from prospective real estate investors seeking to use retirement funds to make real estate investments," John said. "Can I use some personal funds to co-invest with my self-directed IRA funds? The majority of Americans have anywhere between $65,000 and $150,000 in a retirement account. A single-family home could easily exceed the amount of retirement funds held by that individual. With most banks not overly eager to make real estate–related loans, especially nonrecourse loans, using personal funds along with your retirement funds to make an investment is very appealing. The problem with commingling retirement and personal funds to make an investment is that the IRS could argue that the transaction violates the IRS self-dealing and conflict-of-interest prohibited transactions pursuant to IRC 4975(c)(1(D),(E), and (F). The IRS could easily make the case that using your retirement funds to make the real estate investment personally benefited the individual because without the retirement funds the real estate investment could not have been made personally."

"Got it," Rich said.

"On the flip side," John continued, "the IRS could also argue that using retirement and personal funds in the same real estate transaction could be considered the transfer or use by or for the benefit of a disqualified person of the income or assets of a plan. The analysis generally depends on the facts and circumstances involved in the transaction at issue, but any time personal and retirement funds are used together in one investment the door is open for the IRS to argue that a prohibited transaction occurred. With the burden of proof on the taxpayer for proving a prohibited transaction did not occur, I always advise clients not to use any personal funds in connection with an investment involving retirement funds."

"What if I have enough in my self-directed IRA to make the investment but I still think it's a good investment for my self-directed IRA and personal funds?"

"That's another question I get often," John said. "The scenario is typically as follows: You are looking to buy a property and can make the investment personally or via your retirement account since both include ample funds. But you want to own the property through some shared percentage of retirement account and personal funds."

"Is that permitted?"

"The problem is that any time retirement funds and personal funds are mixed in an investment, there's no guarantee that the IRS could not try to argue that it's a self-dealing or conflict-of-interest prohibited transaction pursuant to IRC 4975. With the burden of proof falling on the taxpayer to prove otherwise and with that burden of proof being difficult to meet, it's best practice to stay away from using a combination of personal and retirement funds in a single real estate transaction. Overall, I suggest never commingling self-directed IRA and personal funds in one transition. I think it's highly risky and it opens the door for the IRS to argue that a prohibited transaction has occurred by arguing that the IRA investment in some way directly or indirectly personally benefited a disqualified person. The repercussions can be very steep and painful."

How to Borrow Money for Your Self-Directed IRA LLC

"You can, however," John said, "obtain financing through a loan or mortgage to finance a real estate purchase using a self-directed IRA LLC. However, two important points must be considered when selecting this option:"

The loan must be nonrecourse

Pursuant to IRC 4975(c)(1)(B), a prohibited transaction is a transaction that, directly or indirectly, involves the loan of money or other extension of credit between a plan and a disqualified person. Normally, when an individual purchases real estate with a mortgage, the traditional loan provides for recourse against the borrower (i.e., personal liability for the mortgage) as the borrower typically has to personally guarantee the loan. The issue with this is that the act of personally guaranteeing a loan would be considered an extension of credit between an IRA and a disqualified person and would violate the rules under IRC 4975(c)(1)(B). However, if the IRA purchases real estate and secures a mortgage for the purchase, the loan must be nonrecourse; otherwise there will be a prohibited transaction. A nonrecourse loan only uses the property for collateral and there is no personal guarantee associated with the loan. In the event of default, the lender can collect only the property and cannot go after the IRA itself.

Using Leverage to Buy Real Estate with a Self-Directed IRA

Pursuant to Code Section 514, if your self-directed IRA LLC uses nonrecourse debt financing (i.e., a loan not personally guaranteed by the borrower) on a real estate investment, some portion of each item of gross income from the property is subject to the UBTI rules as the income is considered unrelated debt-financed income (UDFI). "Debt-financed property" refers to borrowing money to purchase the real estate. In such cases, only the income attributable to the financed portion of the property is taxed; gain on the profit from the sale of the leveraged assets is also considered UDFI (unless the debt is paid off more than twelve months before the property is sold). There are some important *exceptions* from UBTI: those exclusions relate to the central importance of investment in real estate and other passive re-lated categories of income, such as dividends, interest, annuities, roy-alties, most rentals from real estate, and gains/losses from the sale of real estate. However, rental income generated from real estate that is "debt financed" loses the exclusion, and that portion of the income becomes subject to UBTI. Thus, if the IRA borrows money to fi-nance the purchase of real estate, the portion of the rental income attributable to that debt will likely be taxable as UBTI.

"I hope these rules haven't scared you too much," John joked. "Don't worry, although the application of the UBTI rules to a self-directed IRA real estate transaction could be quite complex, I will go through the rules in detail and will do my best to provide a clear overview."

"Great," Rich said.

"For example," John said, "if the average acquisition indebtedness is $50 and the average adjusted basis of the asset is $100, 50 percent of each item of gross income from the property is included in UBTI. I'll explain the UBTI and UDFI rules as they pertain to real estate investments and other investments made with a self-directed IRA shortly."

"Can I borrow money for my self-directed IRA from a nondisqualified person?" Rich asked.

"When it comes to using a self-directed IRA to buy real estate, the IRS allows you to seek outside financing from a nondisqualified person as long as the loan is not personally guaranteed by the IRA holder or another disqualified person. "

"Can you please go over what a nonrecourse loan is in a bit more detail?" Rich asked.

"A nonrecourse loan is a type of loan that is secured by collateral, which is usually property, such as real estate acquired by the self-directed IRA" John said. "If the borrower defaults, the issuer can seize the collateral but cannot seek out the borrower for any further compensation, even if the collateral does not cover the full value of the defaulted amount. This is one instance in which the borrower does not have personal liability for the loan."

"Why does the loan have to be nonrecourse?" Rich asked.

"A prohibited transaction is a transaction that, directly or indirectly, involves the loan of money or extension of credit between a plan and a disqualified person. Normally, when an individual purchases real estate with a mortgage, the traditional loan provides for recourse against the borrower (i.e., personal liability for the mortgage). However, if the self-directed IRA purchases real estate and secures a mortgage for the purchase, the loan must be nonrecourse; otherwise there will be a prohibited transaction. A nonrecourse loan only uses the property for collateral. In the event of default, the lender can collect only the property and cannot go after the self-directed IRA itself."

Getting a Nonrecourse Loans

"How hard is it to get a nonrecourse loan a potential self-directed IRA investment?" Rich asked.

"Nonrecourse loans are not especially common because of the added risk imposed on the lender in the case of a failure to pay. Unlike a traditional mortgage that you acquire when purchasing a home or commercial building, in the case of a default, the bank or lender could go after the individual borrower personally, which provides added security to the lender. Whereas, in the case of a nonrecourse loan, the lender's only recourse against the nonpayment of the loan is to take the property that secured the loan back, which in a falling real estate market is not very attractive to banks or lenders. That being said, depending on your personal relationship with a bank or particular lender, it may be possible to get a nonrecourse loan. In general, most banks and financial institutions will require at least 35 percent equity in the project before they will consider a nonrecourse loan. Of course, the more funds you are investing in cash, the easier it will be to secure a nonrecourse loan. Because of the limited number of banks that offer nonrecourse loans, there is a small industry of lenders that have emerged over the past ten or so years that specialize in nonrecourse lending. The terms of the nonrecourse loan are generally more expensive than a standard mortgage because of the risk the nonrecourse lender is taking with no personal guarantee. Also, most nonrecourse loans are for under five years and typically are for income-producing properties only and not raw land. In addition, some nonrecourse lenders will not lend to a real estate transaction in certain states or if the investment involves raw land."

The Unrelated Business Taxable Income Rules Explained

"Is there taxation on the use of a nonrecourse loan by a self-directed IRA to buy real estate?" Rich asked.

"Before I jump into how using a nonrecourse loan for a real estate purchase can trigger a tax, I want to mention that this area is complex and not well known by many tax professionals and Cpas. The rules and calculations can get complicated so I will do my best to provide a very basic overview of how a self-directed IRA LLC using a nonrecourse loan can trigger a tax. Before I do, I think it's important that I discuss the UBTI/UBITs in some detail. I know I touched on them before, but now I'll spend some time diving into the intricacies of the rules."

"Terrific," Rich said.

"The tax advantage of an IRA," John began, "is that income is essentially tax-free until distributed. By way of background, in general, an exempt organization, like the Red Cross, is not taxed on its income from an activity that is substantially related to the charitable, educational, or other purpose that is the basis for the organization's exemption. Such income is exempt even if the activity is a trade or business. However, to prevent tax-exempt entities from competing unfairly with taxable entities, tax-exempt entities are subject to the UBTI rules when their income is derived from any trade or business that is unrelated to its tax-exempt status."

"And what exactly is UBTI?"

"UBTI is defined as 'gross income derived by any organization from any unrelated trade or business regularly carried on by it' reduced by deductions directly connected with the business. An exempt organization that is a limited partner, member of a LLC, or member of another noncorporate entity will have attributed to it the UBTI of the enterprise as if it were the direct recipient of its share of the entity's income, which would be UBTI had it carried on the business of the entity. As I'll explain shortly, UBTI is not triggered if the investment is made into a C corporation as a C corporation acts as a blocker so that the corporation income is trapped in the corporation and does not flow to the shareholder. That is why when a charity or a retirement account buys public stocks, such as Apple or IBM, there is no UBTI triggered as almost all public companies are C corporations, one notable exception being the private equity fund Blackstone, which is why most retirement investors have never heard of UBTI. UBTI also applies to unrelated debt-financed income (UDFI) relating to 'debt-financed property.' The term *debt-financed property* refers to borrowing money to purchase the real estate (i.e., a leveraged asset that is held to produce income). In such cases, only the income attributable to the financed portion of the property is taxed; gain on the profit from the sale of the leveraged assets is also UDFI (unless the debt is paid off more than 12 months before the property is sold).

"There are some important exceptions from UBTI: those exclusions relate to the central importance of investment in most of the popular types of passive income investments, such as real estate, dividends, interest, annuities, royalties, most rentals from real estate, and gains/losses from the sale of real estate. However, rental income generated from real estate that is 'debt financed' loses the exclusion, and that portion of the income becomes subject to UBTI. So, if the IRA borrows money to finance the purchase of real estate, the portion of the rental income attributable to that debt will be taxable as UBTI. I will explain this further soon."

"I follow," Rich said.

"Great," John said. "For an IRA, any business regularly carried on or by a partnership or LLC of which it is a member is an unrelated business. For example, the operation of a shoe factory, the operation of a gas station, or the operation of a computer rental business by an LLC or partnership owned by the self-directed IRA LLC would likely be treated as an unrelated business and subject to UBTI."

"Okay," Rich said.

"Although there's little formal guidance on UBTI implications for self-directed real estate IRAs," John said, "there's a great deal of guidance on UBTI implications for real estate transactions by tax-exempt entities. In general, gains and losses on dispositions of property (including casualties and other involuntary dispositions) are excluded from UBTI unless the property is inventory or property held primarily for sale to customers in the ordinary course of an unrelated trade or business or involves leverage. I'll get into some factors that the IRS looks at in determining whether an activity should be treated as a business that is regularly carried out. This exclusion covers gains and losses on dispositions of property used in an unrelated trade or business, as long as the property was not held for sale to customers. In addition, subject to a number of conditions, if an exempt organization acquires real property or mortgages held by a financial institution in conservatorship or receivership, gains on dispositions of the property are excluded from UBTI, even if the property is held for sale to customers in the ordinary course of business. The purpose of the provision seems to be to allow an exempt organization to acquire a package of assets of an insolvent financial institution with assurance that parts of the package can be sold off without risk of the resales tainting the organization as a dealer and thus subjecting gains on resales to the UBIT."

Types of Self-Directed IRA Investments that Can Trigger the UBTI Tax

"So what types of self-directed IRA transactions can trigger the UBTI tax?"

John nodded. "I know I started talking about using a nonrecourse loan with a self-directed IRA to buy real estate and a potential tax, and you are probably wondering why I started talking about the UBTI tax and investing IRA funds in an active trade or business via a pass-through entity, such as an LLC. But I believe it's important to understand the UBTI rules in some basic form before tacking how to calculate the tax imposed on a self-directed IRAs using a nonrecourse loan to buy real estate."

"I'm ready," Rich said.

"One of the advantages of using retirement funds through your self-directed IRA to make investments is that—in most cases—all income and gains from the investments flow back to your IRA LLC tax-free. This is because an IRA is exempt from tax, pursuant to IRC 408. Pursuant to IRC 512, most of the popular forms of income generated by a retirement income will be exempt from tax. This is why most American investors look at you funny when you start telling them about the Unrelated Business Taxable Income rules, also known as UBTI or UBIT."

"I know, I never hear about it," Rich said.

"Okay, makes sense," Rich said. "The good thing about the UBTI rules is that they won't apply to over 90 percent of American retirement investors because most types of income and gains generated by a retirement account are exempt from the UBTI rules. The IRC exempts dividends, interest, capital gains, royalties, and rental income from being subject to the UBTI tax rules. Even so, the UBTI rules are new and somewhat intimidating to most people when learning about them for the first time. For example, buying public stocks and mutual funds with a self-directed IRA will not trigger the UBTI; neither would receiving a dividend from a public stock, or interest from a bond, or even rental income from an investment property. In the case of a self-directed IRA, the UBTI tax is essentially triggered in three main types of investments:

1. Investing in an active trade or business via a pass-through entity, such as an LLC
2. Using margin when buying stock
3. Using a nonrecourse loan to buy real estate

"Before I go through the three ways the UBTI tax can be triggered when using a self-directed IRA, I think it is helpful to examine why the UBTI tax came into law," John said.

"What's the backstory on that?" Rich asked.

"It's pretty interesting," John said. "Back in the 1950s Congress was concerned that for-profit companies would set up a charity and run their business through a charity and escape taxation forever, thus providing them with an unfair advantage because of their tax-exempt status. With that in mind, they created the UBTI rules under IRC 512. These rules can be found under IRC Sections 511-514 and have become known as the Unrelated Business Taxable Income rules or UBTI or UBIT. If the UBTI rules are triggered, the income generated from those activities will generally be subject to a tax of approximately 35 percent. Of note, a self-directed IRA investing in an active trade or business using a C corporation, which consists of almost all public stock companies and mutual funds, will not trigger the UBTI tax. The reason is that a C corporation is not a pass-through entity and so the C corporation essentially 'blocks' the income from traveling to the shareholders, thus blocking the active trade or business income from flowing to the IRA. You can think of a C corporation as a box and an LLC or partnership as a funnel, which I think helps to explain why the UBTI tax would not apply to a retirement account owning shares in a C corporation."

What Is Unrelated Business Taxable Income?

"So what is unrelated business taxable income?" Rich asked.

"UBTI is defined as 'gross income derived by any organization from any unrelated trade or business regularly carried on by it; reduced by deductions directly connected with the business.' The UBTI rules apply only to exempt organizations such as charities, IRAs, and 401(k) plans. With the enactment of ERISA in 1974, IRAs and 401(k) plans, which are considered tax-exempt parties pursuant to IRC 408 and 401 respectively, became subject to the UBTI rules. As a result, if an IRA or 401(k) plan invests in an active business through an LLC or partnership, the income generated by the IRA or 401(k) from the active business investment will be subject to the UBTI rules."

"Okay," Rich said.

"In the case of a self-directed IRA, a transaction would not trigger the UBTI or UBIT rules if the transaction is not considered a trade or business that is regularly carried on. This typically involves passive types of activities that generate capital gains, interest, rental income, royalties, and dividends, the categories of income exempt according to IRC 512. However, if the tax-exempt organization (your self-directed IRA) engages in an active trade or business that is regularly carried on, such as a restaurant, store, or manufacturing business, the IRS will tax the income."

The UBTI Tax Rate

"What's the UBTI tax rate?" Rich asked.

"IRC 511 taxes 'unrelated business taxable income' (UBTI) at the rates applicable to corporations or trusts, depending on the organization's legal characteristics. In general, a self-directed IRA subject to UBTI is taxed at the trust tax rate because an IRA is considered a trust. For 2015, a self-directed IRA subject to UBTI can pay close to 40% in taxes. There is an exemption if the UBTI income for the year is under $1,000" John said.

Rich looked up. "Pretty steep."

"Yes. In fact, they're higher than most individual's income tax rates as well as the corporation income tax rate. This is one of the main reasons the UBTI tax rules are so important to understand and avoid if possible. In essence, the UBTI tax is imposed on the self-directed IRA investment and actually creates a double tax regime since the UBTI tax will apply in the year the income or gain is realized and then also when the plan participant takes a distribution or is required to take a distribution after the age of 70½ (in the case of a pretax IRA). This is just another reason why it is important to be aware of the UBTI tax rules and their potential application to self-directed IRA plan investments."

Applying the UBTI Rules to Your Self-Directed IRA Investment

"So how do you know if UBTI will apply to your self-directed IRA investment?" Rich asked.

"The UBTI generally applies to the taxable income of 'any unrelated trade or business…regularly carried on' by an organization subject to the tax. The regulations separately treat three aspects of the quoted words— 'trade or business,' 'regularly carried on,' and 'unrelated.'"

1. Trade or Business
In defining "unrelated trade or business," the regulations start with the concept of "trade or business" as used by IRC 162, which allows deductions for expenses paid or incurred "in carrying on any trade or business." The idea of "trade or business" is generally defined by the IRS to include any activity carried on for the production of income from selling goods or performing services. The IRS took the position that income generated as dividends, interest, royalties, rental income, or capital gains should not be treated as "trade or business" income and, thus, should not be subject to the UBTI tax rules.

2. Regularly Carried On

The UBTI applies only to income of an unrelated trade or business that is "regularly carried on" by an organization. Whether a trade or business is regularly carried on is determined in light of the underlying objective to reach activities competitive with taxable businesses. Short-term activities are exempt if comparable commercial activities of private enterprises are usually conducted on a year-round basis. In the case of a self-directed IRA, the IRS generally takes the position that any income generated by an investment in a "trade or business" via a pass-through entity would likely be treated as UBTI even if it is not regularly carried on because any business activity for a self-directed IRA will be treated as "regularly carried on."

3. Unrelated

In the case of a self-directed IRA, any business activity will be treated as "unrelated" to its exempt purpose.

"Is real estate a trade or business that is regularly carried on?" Rich asked.

"When it comes to determining whether real estate activity rises to the level of an active trade or business, the IRS generally takes the position that a passive real estate activity is a real estate activity without material participation by the IRA holder. For example, a limited partner or LLC member of a real estate project who is not personally involved and is simply investing in the project will likely be considered passive, which would not rise to the level of active participation. Clearly, purchasing a home to sell or rental property would not be considered an active trade or business. But what about if you purchase five homes or a tract of land that you intend to develop? These are activities the IRS could argue rise to the level of an active trade or business regularly carried on. Unfortunately, it all comes down to the facts and circumstances involved, but there is some IRS guidance and case law that can help make a more comprehensive determination of whether the UBTI rules would apply."

Factors the IRS May Look at When Determining if the UBTI Rules Apply to a Self-Directed IRA Investment

"What are some of the factors the IRS or the courts may consider when determining whether a real estate transaction may be subject to UBTI?" Rich asked.

"One of the foundation cases for examining the application of the UBTI rules in connection with making real estate transactions with tax-exempt funds is *Mauldin v. Comr.* 195 F.2d 714 (10th Cir. 1952). In *Mauldin*, the court explained that there is no fixed formula or rule of thumb for determining whether property sold by a taxpayer was held by him primarily for sale to customers in the ordinary course of his trade or business. Each case must rest upon its own facts. The court identified a number of helpful factors to point the way, among which are the purposes for which the property was acquired, whether for sale or investment, and the continuity and frequency of sales as opposed to isolated transactions."

"I get it," Rich said.

"But the Tax Court case of *Adam v. Comr.* 60 T.C. 996 (1973), acq., 1974-1 C.B. 1.," John continued, "is probably the most helpful case in trying to determine whether the UBTI rules would apply to a real estate transaction involving a tax-exempt organization, such as a charity or IRA. The Tax Court analyzed the following factors in determining whether the taxpayer was engaged in the operation of a trade or business":

1. The purpose for which the asset was acquired
For example if you can show that the real estate was purchased solely for investment purposes and not for any ongoing business purpose, that would help your argument that the real estate transaction should be excluded from the reach of the UBTI rules.

2. The frequency, continuity, and size of the sales
This factor is particularly significant in determining whether the sale constitutes a trade or business that is regularly carried on, within the

meaning of IRC Section 512. It may range from a onetime sale of a parcel of land to many sales over a long period. If sales are infrequent, not continuous, and small, the organization will not likely be viewed as similar to a taxpayer engaged in a real estate trade or business. Conversely, as sales become more frequent, more continuous, and larger, they are more likely to be considered a trade or business that is regularly carried on, comparable to the commercial activity of a taxpayer in the trade or business of selling real estate.

"In Private Letter Ruling (PLR) 9247038," John continued, "the IRS issued a favorable ruling to an organization that planned to sell land in up to fifteen sales spread over a five- to ten-year period. The reason for the number of sales over the time period was that the value of the land was such that it was unlikely a single purchaser would be able to acquire the entire parcel. Also, market conditions dictated this sales process for the organization to receive maximum value, and keep control of the pace and type of development that would occur after the sales. Similarly, in PLR 9017058, where the exempt organization was engaged in selling forty-five of sixty-eight lots, such sales were deemed to meet the exception from unrelated business income under IRC 512(b)(5). Although this quantity of sales is admittedly significant, external forces essentially dictated the high number of sales. The organization first tried to sell the property in one block but was unsuccessful due to the high cost of developing the property in order to comply with local ordinances. According to the IRS, had the organization attempted to sell the entire property as a whole, and had local ordinances required certain development prior to sale as residential property, it is possible that the high number of sales in this case would have resulted in unrelated business taxable income. Of course, the cases I just referred to involve charities, however retirement accounts and charities are both subject to the UBTI taxing regime."

"So, a limited number of sales is usually a 'good fact' for purposes of the facts and circumstances test?" Rich said.

"Yes," John agreed, "however, you shouldn't assume that any set limit applies. Instead, you should remember that factors such as frequency of sales and cost of the property to be sold and other market conditions play a part in the number of sales allowed and the time frame of the sales allowed. If the real estate investment has significant amounts of acreage, or the cost of the property precludes finding one purchaser, then it is more likely that the organization will be permitted to sell the property in more than one transaction and still comply with the requirements of IRC 512(b)(5)."

Flipping Real Estate and UBTI

"What about flipping real estate?" Rich asked.

"I get that a lot," John said. "Clearly one or two flipping transactions would not be considered an active trade or business and would not trigger the UBTI or UBIT tax, as it would be hard to argue that the activity rises to the level of an active trade or business. The question then becomes what happens if you do three, four, or even ten flipping transactions in a year—would that be considered an active trade or business that triggers the UBTI tax? I can't tell you how many people I have talked to who have been frustrated by the lack of clarity over the number of real estate–flipping transactions that would trigger a prohibited transaction. Again, you need to examine all the facts and circumstances surrounding the multiple house-flipping transactions in order to determine whether the transactions as a whole would constitute an active trade or business. It is important to work with a tax professional who can help you evaluate the transaction in that light. Here are some considerations":

The activities of the seller in the improvement and disposition of the property

The less extensive the improvements by the organization to the property, the more likely the sale will fall under the exclusion for unrelated business income under IRC 512(b)(5). In PLR 8043052, an organization proposed selling a parcel of undeveloped raw land. The fact that the land had remained undeveloped was significant in determining that gains from the proposed transaction would not constitute unrelated business taxable income. Whereas, in PLR 8522042, the property in question consisted of both developed and undeveloped lands, these developed lands included residential land improved with single-family dwellings or condominium apartments. However, based on the facts presented, all the improvements were constructed by unrelated third parties. The absence of development activity by the organization demonstrated that it was not holding property for sale to customers in the ordinary course of trade or business. This PLR could seemingly help self-directed IRA investors involved in flipping real estate, since all development activity must be completed by nondisqualified persons in order to not trigger the prohibited transaction rules.

The extent of improvements made to the property

The more minimal the activities of the owner in improving and disposing of property, the more likely its sale will meet the exclusion from unrelated business taxable income under IRC 512(b)(5). Of course, the greater the number of improvements allowed, the greater the likelihood of maximizing gains from the sale. So there is a balancing act that organizations must exercise when preparing land for disposition in order to maximize its return, while not acting too much like a dealer and triggering UBIT. The rationale here is that the more improvements you are doing to the property, the more the activity looks like a real estate development business versus a passive real estate investment.

"The IRS has ruled favorably on improvements made to property in accordance with city or local ordinances requiring the organization to construct a street as well as curb, gutter, sidewalk, drainage, and water supply improvements in order to subdivide the property for sale," John said.

"What else should I be concerned about?" Rich asked.

"Retaining limited control of the redevelopment project before the land is eventually sold also has been an acceptable activity by a tax-exempt organization when the organization is not involved in any way with advertising, marketing, or otherwise attempting to sell the lots. In PLR 200544021, an organization maintained control over the development process to ensure a compatible environment for the adjoining high school. The IRS recognizes that even though an organization is concerned with receiving a high yield from the sale, it may be equally concerned that the property be developed in keeping with the surrounding features of the property. In addition, an organization's interest in preserving the natural beauty of a tract of land to be developed is not generally indicative of a normal sales transaction."

"Right, okay," Rich said.

"In PLR 8950072, a tax-exempt foundation's largest asset was a parcel of unimproved real estate. The foundation was examining four ways of using the property: (1) continue leasing the property, (2) sell the property as is, (3) complete some preliminary development work—obtaining permits and approvals—and sell the property, or (4) completely develop the property before sale. The last alternative would provide the highest return. The IRS ruled that the first three alternatives would not subject the foundation to UBIT or adversely affect its exempt status. However, the last alternative, to assume all the responsibilities of development, would result in UBTI."

"Definitely want to watch out for that," Rich said.

"Aside from development activities, the lack of marketing of the property by the organization helps differentiate it from a taxpayer in the trade or business of selling real estate. For example, in PLR 8522042, an organization's lack of promotional or development activity in connection with the proposed sale demonstrated that it was not holding property for sale to customers in the ordinary course of a trade or business. Moreover, the use of real estate brokers or other independent contractors is not determinative. Rather, the pertinent facts involve the extent of the activities of the organizations themselves in promoting and marketing the property. Here's what you should think about":

The proximity of sale to purchase

In evaluating this factor, generally the longer the period between purchase and sale, the more likely the sale will be excluded from UBTI. For example, buying a home and then selling it thirty days after and then repeating this process several times in a year can give the impression that you are in the real estate–flipping business rather than a passive investor. In contrast, buying a home and then selling it thirty days later but not buying another home for ten to fifteen months would make it much harder for the IRS to argue that the retirement account is engaged in a trade or business and, thus, subject to the UBTI tax rules.

The purpose for which the property was held during the taxable year

In evaluating this factor, generally the longer the period between purchase and sale, the more likely the sale will be excluded from UBTI. For example, in PLR 9505020, the fact that a school received land by bequest and held it for a significant period of time was considered a favorable factor, and the IRS did not impose UBTI on the sale of the land when the school was facing condemnation proceedings and it did not actively advertise the sale.

"And here are several real-life examples that shed some light on how the IRS treats certain real estate investments for purposes of determining whether they rise to the level of an active trade or business and, hence, should be subject to the UBTI tax rules."

- In *Brown v. Comr.*, 143 F.2d 468 (5th Cir. 1944), the exempt taxpayer owned 500 acres of unimproved land used for grazing purposes within its tax-exempt mission. The taxpayer decided to sell the land and listed it with a real estate broker. The exempt organization instructed the broker to subdivide the land into lots and develop it for sale. The broker had the land plotted and laid into subdivisions with several lots. Streets were cleared, graded, and shelled; storm sewers were put in at street intersections; gas and electric lines were constructed; and a water well was dug. Each year twenty to thirty properties were sold. The court held that the taxpayer was holding lots for sale to customers in the regular course of business. The court identified the sole question for its determination as to whether the taxpayer was in the business of subdividing real estate. The fact that the taxpayer did not buy additional land did not prevent the court from finding that the sales activities resulted in an active trade or business.
- In *Farley v. Comr.*, 7 T.C. 198 (1946), the taxpayer sold twenty-five lots out of a tract of land previously used in his nursery business but now more desirable as residential property. Because the

taxpayer made no active efforts to sell and did not develop the property, the court described the sale as "in the nature of the gradual and passive liquidation of an asset." Therefore, the income derived from the sales represented capital gains income rather than ordinary income from the regular course of business as in the Brown case.

- Dispositions of several thousand acres of land by a school over a period of twenty-five years does not constitute sale of land held primarily for sale to customers in the ordinary course of business and thus gains are excludable under IRC Section 512(b)(5) [Priv. Ltr. Rul. 9619069 (Feb. 13, 1996)].
- Developing or subdividing land and selling a large number of homes or tracts of land from that development in a given period would likely be considered an active trade or business for UBTI purposes. "That's really helpful," Rich said.

The UBTI Rules and the Self-Directed IRA in a Nutshell

"In general, if you make passive investments with your self-directed IRA, such as stocks, mutual funds, precious metals, foreign currency, rental real estate, and so on, the income generated by the investment will not be subject to the UBTI tax. Only if your self-directed IRA makes investments into an active business, such as a retail store, restaurant, real estate development, or software company using a pass-through entity such as an LLC or partnership will your self-directed IRA likely be subject to the UBTI tax."

"Can you give me another example?" Rich asked.

"Let's say a self-directed IRA invests in an LLC that operates an active business such as a restaurant or gas station; the income or gains generated from the investment will generally be subject to the UBTI tax. However, if the self-directed IRA invested in an active business through a C corporation, there would be no UBTI since the C corporation acts as a blocker, blocking the income from flowing through to the self-directed IRA. This is why most Americans have never heard of the UBTI rules and why you can invest your IRA funds in a public company, such as IBM, without triggering the UBTI tax. Remember that if an IRA makes a passive investment, such as rental income, dividends, and royalties, such income would not be subject to the UBTI rules.

"Do you mind expanding on how the UBTI tax could apply to flipping real estate?" Rich said.

"With a self-directed IRA with checkbook control, flipping homes or engaging in a real estate transaction is as simple as writing a check. As manager of your self-directed IRA LLC, you will have the authority to make real estate investment decisions on behalf of your IRA on your own without needing the consent of an IRA custodian. One of the true advantages of a checkbook control IRA is that when you want to purchase a home with your self-directed IRA, you can make the purchase, pay for the improvements, and even sell or flip the property on your own without involving the IRA custodian."

"And the best part is that all gains generated from the house-flipping transaction will flow back to the IRA LLC tax-free!" Rich said.

"So the question is, what level of real estate transaction must you cross before triggering the UBTI or UBIT tax? Unfortunately, there is no clear test for how many house-flipping transactions or the number of real estate transactions one must engage in in a given year in order to trigger the UBTI or UBIT tax. In general, the IRS has a number of factors it will examine to determine whether one has engaged in a high enough volume of real estate transactions, such as home flipping, to trigger the UBTI tax. First, the IRS will examine the frequency of the transactions—how many flipping transactions are done in a year. Second, the IRS will examine the intent of the person—was the person intending to engage in an active trade or business. Third, the IRS will look at the scope of other activities of the retirement account to determine whether the activity is part of a business activity or an investment. Fourth, the IRS will look at the personal business activities of the IRA investor to help determine whether the IRA investment is part of an overall business model. So for example, several real estate flips by Donald

Trump's self-directed IRA could look more like a business than if they were made by a teacher or an accountant."

"So the determination of whether an activity is an active trade or business and will, thus, trigger the UBTI or UBIT tax, which is taxed at a rate of approximately 35 percent, depends on the facts and circumstances," Rich said.

"Yes," John agreed. "Clearly one or two flipping transactions would not be considered an active trade or business and would, thus, not trigger the UBTI or UBIT tax. The question then becomes what happens if you do three, four, or even ten flipping transactions in a year—would that be considered an active trade or business and, hence, trigger the UBTI tax? Again, you must examine all the facts and circumstances surrounding the multiple house-flipping transactions in order to determine whether the transactions in the aggregate would constitute an active trade or business. Some of the factors that would likely be considered by the IRS would be the total amount of flips done in a year, the frequency of the flipping transactions, the level of improvement made to the properties, the personal activities of the IRA holder (i.e., does the individual do real estate flips full-time personally), as well as the intent of the IRA holder. Therefore, it is important to work with a tax professional who can help one evaluate the transaction to determine whether the flipping transaction will trigger the UBTI tax."

Calculating the UBTI Tax on a Self-Directed IRA Investment

"So how do you calculate and pay the UBTI tax if it applies to a self-directed IRA investment?" Rich asked.

"Once you've determined that the UBTI tax rules will apply to a self-directed IRA investment, the next part is figuring out how much tax will be due. This an important point, you, as the IRA holder, and not the IRA custodian, are responsible for determining whether the UBTI rules would apply. If an IRA generates gross income subject to UBTI of more than $1,000 during the taxable year, the retirement account must file IRS Form

990. Form 990-T is the tax form on which a charitable organization or re-tirement account, such as an IRA, reports income that would be subject to UBTI tax. In general, only income generated from an active trade or busi-ness via a pass-through entity, margin, or real estate acquisition indebted-ness would be subject to the UBTI/UBIT tax."

"When does all this have to happen?" Rich asked.

"For a retirement account, IRS Form 990 is due on the fifteenth day of the fourth month following the end of the organization's taxable year. You can also elect to file an extension with the IRS for filing Form 990, which would allow you an extra three months to complete the form. It is impor-tant to note that IRS Form 990 is not part of your personal income tax return and, in the case of a self-directed IRA, is only being filed because a retirement account has generated UBTI. The UBTI tax is typically paid by the retirement account. It is a good idea to work with a CPA or tax profes-sional to complete IRS Form 990-T."

"Can you pay in installments?" Rich asked.

"Generally, a self-directed IRA filing Form 990-T must make installment payments of estimated tax if its estimated tax (tax minus allowable credits) is expected to be $500 or more. The organization must pay any tax due in full by the due date of the return without extensions. I'll get into how to calculate the tax imposed on using a nonrecourse loan to buy real estate shortly."

Exceptions to the UBTI Tax

"I assume there are exceptions to the UBTI rules?" Rich said.

"As I mentioned before," John said, "there are some important excep-tions to UBTI. Thankfully, the exceptions generally include the majority of the most popular categories of income-generating investment activities, such as dividends, interest, annuities, royalties, most rentals from real estate, and gains/losses from the sale of real estate. Because the majority of those income categories reflect the most popular investments made using retire-ment funds, almost all retirement account investors will never have to worry about the UBTI rules. Investments such as stocks, mutual funds, ETFs, precious metals, real estate, interest from a loan or bond, and dividends from a stock would be exempt from the UBTI tax and flow back to the retirement account without tax."

"Now that I have a good understanding of how the UBTI tax can be triggered by business-type activities, can you please expand on how using a nonrecourse loan to buy real estate with a self-directed IRA can trigger a tax," Rich said.

Applying the UBTI Tax When Using a Nonrecourse Loan for Real Estate

"Okay, we spent some time earlier discussing what a nonrecourse loan is and how it could trigger the UBTI tax rules, but I will get more into the details now.

"IRC Section 514 requires debt-financed income to be included in unrelated business taxable income. It was enacted in 1969 for reasons best understood in their historical context. Under IRC Section 514, if an exempt organization owns 'debt-financed property,' some portion of each item of gross income from the property, and a like portion of all related deductions, are included in unrelated business taxable income, whether the income is in the form of rent, interest, gain on disposition of the property, or some other character. Property is debt-financed if it is held for the production of income, its use is not substantially related to the organization's exempt purposes, and there is acquisition indebtedness with respect to the property. The term *acquisition indebtedness* generally includes any liability incurred before, contemporaneously with, or after the acquisition or improvement of the property if it arose because of the acquisition or improvement or if the need for the indebtedness was foreseeable at the time of the acquisition or improvement."

"I get it," Rich said.

"Under IRC Section 514(b)(1), property is 'debt-financed property' if it is held to produce income and 'acquisition indebtedness' with respect to the property exists at any time during the taxable year (or, in the case of a disposition, at any time during the preceding twelve months). The application of IRC Section 514 has a wide application. For example, it has been held that securities purchased on margin can be debt-financed property."

Calculating the UBTI Tax When a Nonrecourse Loan Is Used for an IRA Real Estate Investment

"How is UDFI calculated on the sale of a debt-financed asset?" Rich asked.

"When a debt-financed asset is sold, a special rule applies for the purpose of calculating the taxable gain. The property's average adjusted basis is the average of the adjusted basis as of the first day during the year in which the property is held by the organization and on the day the property is sold or disposed of. The percentage of gain taxed is the percentage that the average adjusted basis on sale or other disposition of debt-financed property is of the highest amount of acquisition indebtedness with respect to the property during the twelve-month period ending with the date of the sale or other disposition. The regulations permit adjustments to basis that include decreases in basis for depreciation for periods since the acquisition of the property and increases in basis for capitalized improvements or additions."

"Can you give me an example of how you would calculate the UBTI tax using a nonrecourse loan to buy real estate with a self-directed IRA?" Rich asked.

"Okay, here is how the formula works. Gross income 'derived…from or on account of' debt-financed property is unrelated business income in an amount equal to the income multiplied by the following fraction (the debt/basis percentage):

$$\frac{\text{Average acquisition indebtedness}}{\text{Average adjusted basis}}$$

"For example, if the average acquisition indebtedness is $50 and the average adjusted basis is $100, 50 percent of each item of gross income from the property is included in UBTI.

"The debt/basis percentage is recomputed annually. Normally, the average acquisition indebtedness for any taxable year is the average of the acquisition indebtedness during the portion of the year when the organization owns the property. The average is computed by determining the amount of acquisition indebtedness on the first day during each month on which the organization holds the property, adding these amounts together, and dividing by the number of months and partial months during the year when the property is held.

"For example, assume a self-directed IRA LLC borrows $300 to purchase a building on July 10 of year one and makes principal payments on the debt of $20 on July 20 and on the twentieth day of each succeeding month during the year. Average acquisition indebtedness is $250 (sum of $300, $280, $260, $240, $220, and $200, divided by six). However, in determining the includable portion of gain or loss on a disposition of the property, the average acquisition indebtedness is the highest amount of acquisition indebtedness during the 12-month period ending with the date of the disposition."

Getting Around the UBTI Tax

"Is there any way to avoid or minimize the UBTI tax?" Rich asked.

"That is a good question, and I am happy you brought that up," John replied. "First, you can avoid the investment, which would clearly allow you to sidestep the UBTI tax rules, but that is probably not the answer you are looking for. Second, and the more popular option, is to establish a C corporation, which acts as a blocker to any UBT income, blocking the application of the UBTI rules. The income would be subject to corporate income tax, but for profits under $50,000, the corporate tax rate is 15 percent. However, the corporate tax rate would increase to 35 percent for profits above $50,000, which would reduce the tax advantage of using a C corporation as a blocker.

Third, if the LLC or pass-through entity you will be investing in with your retirement account will be making tax distributions to its owners, then the UBTI tax bite will not be material. A tax distribution provision assists the members in meeting their federal and state income tax obligations with respect to their allocated net profits. Hence, if the LLC operating agreement or partnership agreement contained a tax distribution provision, then the entity, not your IRA, would be paying the UBTI tax."

"That is really helpful. Obviously, I need to speak with a tax professional about potential ways to minimize the impact of the UBTI tax rules if I think the rules could apply to my self-directed IRA investment," Rich said. "I really appreciate the options you presented; it makes having to potentially deal with the UBTI tax rules much more palatable," he added.

IRS Form 990-T

"Can you explain how you actually calculate the UBTI tax and report it on IRS Form 990-T?" Rich asked.

"Sure thing," John said. "This may be overly complex for you, so just bear in mind that you can always hire a tax professional or CPA to take care of this for you, but I want to provide you the information just in case you are interested."

"Thanks," Rich said.

"When a tax-exempt organization like an IRA or charity borrows money for a transaction on a nonrecourse basis, the IRA or charity must complete IRS Form 990-T and Schedule E and report the income, as the income is likely subject to tax, assuming there is greater than $1,000 of income. In general, a tax-exempt organization like a charity or IRA is permitted to borrow funds on a nonrecourse basis (a loan that is not personally guaranteed by the borrower); however, a pro-rata percentage of the income or gains associated with the nonrecourse loan will be considered unrelated debt financed income, which will likely trigger the unrelated business taxable income tax, assuming the interest earned is greater than $1,000 for the year. Note: A recourse loan, a loan that the IRA holder will be required to personally guarantee, is not a permitted transaction and is treated as a prohibited transaction pursuant to IRC Section 4975, as the loan would require the IRA holder to personally guarantee the obligation of the IRA. IRS Form 990-T Schedule E applies to all organizations except IRC Sections 501(c)(7), (9), and (17) organizations. So, the Schedule E would apply to IRAs."

"What about debt-financed property?" Rich asked.

"When debt-financed property is held for exempt purposes and other purposes, the IRA must allocate the basis, debt, income, and deductions among the purposes for which the property is held. It is important to remember to not include in Schedule E amounts allocated to exempt purposes. With respect to an IRA, income considered exempt is all passive categories of income, such as interest, capital gains, rental income, royalties, dividends, and interest. So, the majority of transactions involving IRAs are not subject to tax and Schedule E reporting."

John handed Rich a copy of IRS Form 990-T along with some examples explaining how the UBTI tax would apply to a self-directed IRA transaction involving a nonrecourse loan.

Example No. 1

An IRA, via a self-directed IRA LLC, owns a four-story building, and is subject to a nonrecourse loan. The building generates $10,000 of rental income. Expenses are $1,000 for depreciation and $5,000 for other expenses that relate to the entire building. The average acquisition indebtedness is $6,000, and the average adjusted basis is $10,000. Both apply to the entire building.

To complete Schedule E of IRS Form 990-T for this example, describe the property in column 1. Enter $10,000 in column 2 (since the entire amount is for debt-financed property), $1,000 and $5,000 in columns 3(a) and 3(b), respectively, $6,000 and $10,000 in columns 4 and 5, respectively, 60 percent in column 6, $6,000 in column 7, and $1,800 in column 8 (60 percent of $1,000 and $5000 of depreciation/expenses). Thus, the IRA holder would be subject to tax on unrelated business taxable income of $2,400. So, $10,000 of income multiplied by 60 percent—the amount of average acquisition indebtedness of debt-financed property ($6,000) over the average adjusted basis of average debt-financed income ($10,000), minus $3,600 (60 percent of $6,000 expenses), equals $2,400.

Example No. 2

Assume the same facts as in *Example 1*, except the building is rented out as an unrelated trade or business for $20,000. To complete Schedule E for this example, enter $20,000 in column 2, $1,000 and $5,000 in columns 3(a) and 3(b) respectively (since the entire amount is for debt-financed property), $6,000 and $20,000 in columns 4 and 5 (since the entire amount is for debt-financed property), 30 percent in column 6, $6,000 in column 7, and $1,800 in column 8. Thus, the IRA holder would be subject to tax on $3,200 of unrelated business taxable income: $20,000 of income multiplied by 30 percent minus the amount of average acquisition indebtedness of debt financed property ($6,000) over the average adjusted basis of average debt-financed income ($20,000), minus $1,800 (30 percent of $6,000 of expenses), equals $3,200.

"Obviously," John said, "calculating the amount of the UBTI tax on the use of a nonrecourse loan to buy real estate by a self-directed IRA is quite complex and one should consult with a tax professional or CPA for guidance when determining whether any tax would apply as well as the filing of the IR Form 990-T."

Foreign Currencies

"You can also use your self-directed IRA to purchase foreign currencies, from any country in the world. Many people believe that such investments offer liquidity advantages compared to the stock market and represent significant investment opportunities in and of themselves."

"How does that work?" Rich said.

"As with real estate investments, all gains generated from your currency investments are tax-deferred until a distribution is taken. Pretax distributions are not required until you turn 70½ years old, and in the case of a self-directed Roth IRA, all gains are tax-free."

"That appeals to me," Rich said.

"If so," John said, I recommend that you have a solid background in trading currencies, as such investments can be highly volatile and may carry significant risk. If you're investing through a third party, please make sure that this group or individual has the knowledge to trade foreign currencies and that all securities licenses are in good standing."

"Will do."

"You must also make sure that all gains or losses from foreign currency transactions are allocated to your self-directed IRA and keep excellent records. You should also beware of leverage or use of margin. It is allowable but would trigger the application of the UBTI under IRC 512, and subject you to a corresponding tax. No personal guarantee of any leverage or loan obligation is permitted."

Stocks, Bonds, Mutual Funds, IRS-Approved Precious Metals and Coins

"Naturally, in addition to nontraditional investments like real estate or foreign currencies, you may also use your self-directed IRA to purchase stocks, bonds, mutual funds, and CDs. Again, with checkbook control you can open a stock trading account with any financial institution."

"I'm sure stocks and mutual funds continue to be the most popular investment for retirement accounts," Rich said.

"This is especially true in the case of a financial institution–type self-directed IRA, which make up the most popular category of self-directed IRAs being used today. These types of self-directed IRAs, which essentially only allow you to buy the investment products offered by the financial institution, are typically quite restrictive and only permit the plan participant to make limited investments, such as stocks and mutual funds. The reason behind this is quite simple. Financial institutions make money when you hold funds at their institution and buy financial products, such as stocks and mutual funds, which generate fees for them. With close to $20 trillion in retirement funds available for investment as of 2015, you can imagine the enormous impact retirement funds have on the equity markets."

"But when purchasing stocks or securities with a self-directed IRA, all income and gains, including dividends, flow back to the plan without tax, correct?" Rich asked.

"Yes. With a self-directed IRA, all gains are tax-deferred (tax-free in the case of a Roth IRA). Whereas, if you purchased stocks with personal funds, all income and gains would be subject to federal and in most cases state income tax. As with foreign currency investments, if you will be investing with a third party, perform adequate diligence on the individual and make sure he or she has the knowledge to trade stocks or securities and that all securities licenses are in good standing. And please beware of promoters promising high returns, especially those who do not work at reputable financial institutions."

"Will do," Rich said.

"All income, gains, or losses from stock investments should be allocated to the self-directed IRA account. And leverage is allowable but would compel you to pay a tax since it would trigger the application of the UBTI rules under IRC 512."

"What about precious metals and coins?" Rich asked.

"Definitely," John said. "If you've watched enough late-night commercials, you may already know that precious metals such as gold, silver, platinum, and palladium can be purchased with retirement account funds. Precious metals and coins actually make excellent investment opportunities because their values generally keep up with or exceed inflation rates better than other investments. This should be no surprise since precious metals are the original currencies of civilization and have been leveraged or exchanged throughout history. Of course, like any market, the precious metal markets has its ups and downs, but it is still believed to be a really good hedge against a financial meltdown, high inflation, or a weakening US dollar. The purchase of bullion, in particular, is viewed as a surprisingly safe investment. Using a self-directed IRA can be one of the most tax-efficient ways to finance a precious metals purchase."

"Not too common though," Rich said.

"Right. Only a handful of financial advisers are skilled in these specialized account structures, however, so you should seek the right level of guidance and expertise. There are a number of basic details to understand from the outset. For example, only IRS-approved metals and coins may be purchased. Moreover, these metals and coins must be purchased by your self-directed IRA using plan funds or funds from a nondisqualified third party. As with other investments you make with your self-directed IRA funds, all income, gains, or losses incurred should flow through your self-directed IRA account."

Determining Whether a Metal or Coin Is IRS-Approved for an IRA

"What type of metals and coins are IRS-approved?" Rich asked.

John handed Rich a copy of IRC 408(m), which outlines the categories of approved precious metals and coins. "

These are described in IRC 408(m). They include:

- One, one-half, one-quarter, or one-tenth ounce US gold coins (American Gold Eagle coins are the only gold coins specifically approved for IRAs). Other gold coins, to be eligible as IRA investments, must be at least 0.995 fine (99.5 percent pure) and be legal tender coins.
- One-ounce silver coins minted by the Treasury Department
- Any coin issued under the laws of any state
- A platinum coin described in 31 USCS 5112(k)
- Gold, silver, platinum, or palladium bullion of a certain finesse that is in the physical possession of a trustee, as defined in IRC 408(a).

- "Essentially, you can purchase gold, silver, or palladium bullion if they are at least 0.99 percent pure as well as American Eagle and state-minted coins."

"Here are the relevant sections in IRC Section 408(m) that relate to purchases of IRS-approved coins for retirement funds, "John said.

John handed Rich a list that detailed the types of coins approved by the IRS for purchase by retirement accounts.

- Exception for certain coins and bullion: for purposes of this subsection, the term *collectible* shall not include—
  - Any coin which is—
    - A gold coin described in paragraph (7), (8), (9), or (10) of section 5112 (a) of title 31, United States Code
    - A silver coin described in section 5112 (e) of title 31, United States Code
    - A platinum coin described in section 5112 (k) of title 31, United States Code
    - A coin issued under the laws of any state
- 31 USC § 5112 refers to denominations, specifications and design of coins.
  - The secretary of the Treasury may mint and issue only the following coins:
    - A dollar coin that is 1.043 inches in diameter
    - A half-dollar coin that is 1.205 inches in diameter and weighs 11.34 grams
    - A quarter-dollar coin that is 0.955 inch in diameter and weighs 5.67 grams
    - A dime coin that is 0.705 inch in diameter and weighs 2.268 grams
    - A five-cent coin that is 0.835 inch in diameter and weighs 5 grams

- A one-cent coin that is 0.75 inch in diameter and weighs 3.11 grams (exceptions to this are described in the next section)
- A fifty-dollar gold coin that is 32.7 millimeters in diameter, weighs 33.931 grams, and contains one troy ounce of fine gold
- A twenty-five dollar gold coin that is 27 millimeters in diameter, weighs 16.966 grams, and contains one-half troy ounce of fine gold
- A ten-dollar gold coin that is 22 millimeters in diameter, weighs 8.483 grams, and contains one-fourth troy ounce of fine gold
- A five-dollar gold coin that is 16.5 millimeters in diameter, weighs 3.393 grams, and contains one-tenth troy ounce of fine gold
- A fifty-dollar gold coin that is of an appropriate size and thickness, as determined by the secretary, weighs 1 ounce, and contains 99.99 percent pure gold.
- A twenty-five-dollar coin of an appropriate size and thickness, as determined by the secretary, that weighs 1 troy ounce and contains 0.9995 fine palladium.

- Notwithstanding any other provision of law, the Secretary shall mint and issue in quantities sufficient to meet public demand, coins that—
  - Are 40.6 millimeters in diameter and weigh 31.103 grams
  - Contain 0.999 fine silver
  - Have a design—
  - Symbolic of Liberty on the obverse side; and
  - Of an eagle on the reverse side.
  - The secretary may mint and issue platinum bullion coins and proof platinum coins in accordance with such specifications, designs, varieties, quantities, denominations, and inscriptions as the secretary, in the secretary's discretion, may prescribe from time to time.

"In addition, legislation in 1997 (Technical and Miscellaneous Revenue Act of 1988—TAMRA) further liberalized the rules for retirement accounts investing in IRS-approved metals and coins. This legislation made reference to specific definitions of acceptable coins in USCS, title 31; sections 5112(a), (e) and (k): the Commodity Exchange coins that would not be treated as a collectible to "certain gold and silver coins issued by the US government," John mentioned.

"Wait," Rich said, "I heard you can buy Canadian Maple Leafs and Krugerrands."

"In order for coins to be held inside an IRA, coins must be satisfy a certain level of pureness in their mineral content so that they are not viewed as a type of collector's coin. As a result, Krugerands and the old Double Eagle gold coins are disallowed because they do not meet this standard. When it comes to coins or metals, IRC Section 408 is generally the provision that applies. In general, collectibles such as artwork, rugs, stamps, certain coins, beverages, and antiques, etc., are not allowed within a self-directed IRA LLC pursuant to IRC Section 408."

"Okay," Rich said.

"IRC Section 408 is specific about what it defines as a collectible. Some notable exceptions are allowed for certain gold (such as American Eagle) and silver coins and any coins issued by a state."

"Okay," Rich said, "I understand now that I can buy pure gold, silver, and palladium, as well as American Eagle and state-minted coins, but how can a self-directed IRA hold these assets?"

Holding IRS-Approved Metals and Coins

"This is a great question that I get asked a lot by my clients and I wish had more guidance from the IRS. IRC 408(m) and the Technical and Miscellaneous Revenue Act of 1998 allowed retirement account holders to invest their retirement assets in precious metals, as long as they are held in the 'physical possession' of a US depository or at a US bank in the name of the self-directed IRA. The IRS has not offered crystal clear guidance on this issue, but their regulations do imply that precious metals should not be stored in the home or possession of the IRA holder or any person who does not satisfy the definition of a trustee pursuant to the IRC."

Holding IRS-Approved Bullion in a Self-Directed IRA

"How do you hold physical gold in a self-directed IRA LLC?" Rich asked.

"IRC Section 408(m) identifies what types of coins and precious metals are permitted to be purchased using a retirement account, such as a self-directed IRA. IRC Section 408(m) also states that bullion (IRS-approved gold, silver, or palladium) must be held in the physical possession of a trustee described under subsection (a)."

"And what's a trustee?"

"A trustee is defined in IRC Section 408(a) as a bank [as defined in subsection (n)] or a person who demonstrates to the satisfaction of the secretary that the manner in which that person will administer the trust will be consistent with the requirements of this section."

"And a bank?"

"IRC Section 408(n) defines a bank as any bank (as defined in IRC Section 581) or an insured credit union [within the meaning of paragraph (6) or (7) of section 101 of the Federal Credit Union Act]. IRC Section 581 defines a bank as a bank or trust company incorporated and doing business under the laws of the United States (including laws relating to the District of Columbia) or of any state, a substantial part of the business of which consists of receiving deposits and making loans and discounts, or of exercising fiduciary powers similar to those permitted to national banks under authority of the comptroller of the currency, and which is subject by law to supervision and examination by state, territorial, or federal authority having supervision over banking institutions.

That also means a domestic building and loan association. The code seems to suggest that metals cannot be held in a foreign bank account since it would not satisfy the definition of a bank."

"And what does 'physical possession' mean?"

"IRC Section 408(m) clearly states that gold, silver, or palladium bullion must be held in the physical possession of a US trustee, otherwise known as a US bank or financial institution."

"Here is the exact language from the tax code under IRC 408(m)(3) (B)," John said. "'Any gold, silver, platinum, or palladium bullion of a fineness equal to or exceeding the minimum fineness that a contract market (as described in section 7 of the Commodity Exchange Act, USC) requires for metals, which may be delivered in satisfaction of a regulated futures contract, if such bullion is in the physical possession of a trustee described under subsection (a) of this section.'"

"Interesting," Rich said.

"The tax code clearly states that any IRS-approved metals (bullion) must be held in the physical possession of a trustee, which we now know means a US bank."

"So," Rich said, "if a self-directed IRA account holder holds precious metals in a safe deposit box at a US bank in the name of the self-directed IRA LLC, that would be considered to be in the 'physical possession' of a US trustee or bank and satisfy the definition under IRC 408(m)?"

"It appears an argument can then be made that precious metals held in a US bank safe deposit box are certainly not in the physical possession of the IRA holder since the metals will physically be held in a safe deposit box of the bank in the name of the IRA LLC and not with the IRA holder personally. However, the safe deposit box is in the constructive control of the self-directed IRA LLC manager, the IRA holder. That being said, the IRC under Section 408 clearly states 'physical possession' and not 'constructive control.' From a legal standpoint, possession is not defined to represent control, meaning you can be in possession of an item but not in control or ownership of it. Therefore, many tax practitioners take the position that holding precious metals in a safe deposit box in the name of the self-directed IRA would satisfy the 'physical possession' requirement under IRC Section 408(m)."

"What's the IRS guidance on that?"

"Not clear," John said. "What is clear is that IRS-approved precious metals should not be stored in the home or in possession of the self-directed IRA holder or any person that does not satisfy the definition of a trustee according to the IRC. It is good practice to hold precious metals owned by a self-directed IRA at an IRS-approved depository, where it is clearly in the 'physical possession' of a US trustee."

"Here are some helpful tips for holding IRS-approved precious metals in a self-directed IRA," John said.

- The purchase of the metals should be made in the name of the LLC.
- Only self-directed IRA LLC funds should be used to make the purchase.
- It is preferred to hold the metals at a US depository or US bank, which satisfies the definition of "Trustee" under the IRC.
- IRS-approved precious metals should not be held in your personal possession.
- If holding the metals at a US bank safe deposit box, account should be in name of LLC.
- Do not hold the precious metals in any foreign bank.
- An affidavit should be signed by the LLC manager and notarized describing how the metals will be purchased solely for the benefit of the IRA LLC and not for any personal purpose.
- A full inventory of the purchased metals should be kept and updated when necessary.
- Pictures of the metals should be taken to show that the metals held are what has been purchased.
- Try to limit your personal contact with the metals held in the safe deposit box.

Holding IRA-Owned Metals in a Safety Deposit and Potential Audit Risk?

"Does holding IRS-approved precious metals purchased by my self-directed IRA LLC at a safe deposit increase my audit risk?"

"I wish I knew," John said. "No one really knows what triggers an IRS audit. That being said, holding the metals at a US depository is your safest best. If, for whatever reason, you really want to hold the metals at a safe deposit box at a US bank, the IRS could potentially argue that this does not satisfy the 'physical possession' requirement, but as we discussed earlier, that may prove difficult. The IRS could also try to make you prove as the IRA holder that you have used the precious metals for some personal purposes and thus have triggered a prohibited transaction. This goes back to the tips I just referred to for holding precious metals with a self-directed IRA. The onus is always on the taxpayer to prove his or her innocence, so keeping good records of the metals that have been purchased will help you show the IRS that the metals were purchased solely for the benefit of the IRA and there has been no direct or indirect personal benefit that was derived. I think it would be hard for the IRS to argue that someone personally benefited from buying precious metals when the metals simply sat in a safe deposit box."

"Great," Rich said.

"Okay, now that we've discussed how to purchase IRS-approved precious metals, let's move on to coins," said John.

How to Hold IRS-Approved Coins with a Self-Directed IRA

"How can I hold IRS-approved Coins with my self-directed IRA without violating IRS rules?" Rich asked.

"Most people don't realize that a coin can be treated as bullion. As a result, based on the language in IRC 408(m)(3)(B), all coins defined in IRC 408(m), including American Eagle and state-minted coins must be held in the physical possession of a US trustee, just like gold and silver bars," John said.

"I have read on the Internet that there is some debate as to whether IRS-approved coins must be held in the 'physical possession' of a US bank," Rich added.

"Although bullion may be cast into bars or minted into coins, the defining attribute of bullion is that it is valued by its mass and purity rather than by face value as money. Hence, I think the answer is that the physical possession requirement outlined for bullion in IRC 408(m)(3)(B) does pertain to coins, such as American Eagle coins, defined in IRC 408(m)(3)(A), since they can be defined as bullion. That being said, it is best for retirement account holders to hold all IRS-approved coins outlined in IRC 408(m) at a depository or bank safe deposit box and not in their personal possession. In addition, it may be wise to have some type of legal document or affidavit drafted stating that the IRS-approved coins are being held for the benefit of the self-directed IRA LLC and not for any personal or other benefit. I believe it is best practice to hold all IRS-approved coins at a bank or depository, including the American Eagle and state-minted coins," John added.

"Most importantly," Rich agreed, "the freedom to buy precious metals and coins provides you with one more valuable tool in your retirement wealth-building portfolio."

"The following are some helpful tips for holding IRS-approved coins outlined in IRC 408(m) in a self-directed IRA," John said.

- The purchase of the coins should be made in the name of the LLC.
- Only self-directed IRA LLC funds should be used to make the purchase.
- IRS-approved coins should be held at a depository of US bank that satisfies the definition of "Trustee" under the IRC.
- If holding the coins at a US bank safe deposit box, account should be in name of LLC.
- Do not hold coins in your personal possession.
- Do not hold the coins in any foreign bank.

- An affidavit should be signed by the LLC manager and notarized describing how the coins will be purchased solely for the benefit of the IRA LLC and not for any personal purpose.
- A full inventory of the purchased coins should be kept and updated when necessary
- Pictures of the coins should be taken to show that the metals held are what has been purchased.
- Try to limit your personal contact with the coins.

"What is the point of these tips?" Rich asked.

"The main purpose behind the tips just described is that it all goes back to the concept that we want to be able to show that the purchase and holding of the IRS-approved coins is solely for retirement purposes and there is no personal benefit. That is the reason for signing an affidavit that shows that you are holding the coins as manager of the IRA LLC solely for the benefit of the IRA. Also, keeping a detailed inventory of the coins purchased as well as photos of the coins only helps to show that the coins being held are what was purchased by the IRA LLC and there has been no personal benefit."

Tax Liens

"What about using a self-directed IRA LLC to buy tax liens and deeds?" Rich asked.

"They've become popular investments for a number of my self-directed IRA clients," John said. "Real estate has long been considered one of the best areas of investment available to anyone. In a down market, such as the one we have just experienced, many savvy investors make money in real estate by purchasing properties for a fraction of their value."

"How do they do this?"

"By investing in tax lien and tax deed sales. When a property owner falls behind on his taxes and fails to pay for one or more years, the local tax-ing authority has the legal right to plan a lien or repossess the property and sell it at auction to recoup the lost tax revenue. Lien laws vary in different areas; however, in many cases properties may be acquired for a few thousand dollars, regardless of actual worth. At the same time, paying off the lien may cost more than the property is actually worth."

"I guess it's important then to take the time to research each property carefully prior to sale day."

"Tax lien sales usually happen at public auctions once or twice a year, although large urban areas may hold monthly auctions. There are two types of lien sales that happen at auctions: the tax lien certificate and the tax lien deed. Both can offer safe but profitable investment opportunities."

"Right," Rich said.

"Tax lien certificate sales offer the delinquent homeowner one last chance to retain ownership of the property by using third-party investment money to pay off the taxes. This gives the homeowner more time to collect the money needed to pay his debt without losing his home. As an investor, if you bid on a tax lien certificate, you are essentially agreeing to loan the homeowner the money needed to pay all taxes due, and the homeowner, in turn, is agreeing to pay back the tax lien certificate holder, with interest, by a specified date. If the homeowner fails to pay the debt on time, the deed to the property is transferred to the investor for the amount paid on the taxes."

"In either case, you make a profit, either on the interest earned on the loan or by obtaining the property for a fraction of its value and reselling it," Rich said.

"Tax lien deeds sales are handled a bit differently, since the investor is actually bidding (or buying), the property at the time of auction, with no responsibility to give the homeowner more time to pay the tax debt. Once the selling price is approved, the deed is automatically transferred to its new owner, giving the investor full reign over what to do with the property next. You can renovate it, sell it as is, or raze the existing house and build anew."

"What are the advantages and disadvantages?" Rich asked.

"Investors usually pay more for properties in this type of tax lien sale, which may lower their profit margins compared to the acquisition of tax lien certificate properties. But many investors prefer outright purchases to eliminate problems with current homeowners. Either way, investing in tax liens is a profitable and easy way to enter the real estate market in virtually any area."

"That interests me," Rich said.

"As an investment, tax liens offer significant returns for a surprising amount of security. In fact, you can quickly double your money through such opportunities. For example, a tax lien certificate can earn up to 16 percent annually in your self-directed IRA. When you buy tax lien investments you generally receive the amount invested plus interest within twelve months. If you continue to reinvest in tax liens year after year at 16 percent, you can double your money in about 4.4 years."

"Just as important, your money grows tax-free," Rich said.

"Correct. You avoid all taxes until the money is withdrawn from your self-directed IRA, usually when you are around age 59½. The money can be invested once, twice, or a thousand times and continue to grow tax-free, as long as it is not withdrawn for personal use. You should not use personal checks, credit cards, or cash for such purchases; indeed, the deposit and purchase price for the tax lien or deed should be paid using your self-directed IRA LLC or funds from a nondisqualified third party—never personal funds or funds from a disqualified person. And, of course, all gains or losses from your tax lien or tax deed investments should be allocated to your solo 401(k) plan."

"And tax liens are relatively safe," Rich said.

"Yes, because they are backed and leveraged by real estate and guaranteed by the governmental taxing authority. In most states, all junior liens, including mortgages, are wiped out when a property is foreclosed. This allows you to potentially receive a valuable piece of real estate for pennies on the dollar! There are risks, however, to any investment, so it is important to have a clear and detailed understanding of the process involved before engaging. But a well-educated investor can do very well, and you can use that knowledge to build your retirement wealth very quickly.

"One thing to remember when buying tax liens or tax deeds with a self-directed IRA LLC, is that if liens are purchased, the IRA LLC can generally be established in any state since owning a lien or deed would not rise to the level of a trade or business. However, in the case of a foreclosure of the underlying property, if one elected to take title to the foreclosed property, the LLC would need to be filed in the state where the property was located. As we discussed earlier on, almost all states deem the ownership of real estate as creating a nexus with the state, which would require the filing of the LLC to do business in the state in order to take advantage of the limited liability protection.," John concluded.

Loans and Notes

"What about loans and notes?" Rich asked. "Can I use my self-directed IRA LLC to make these types of investments?"

"The IRS also allows you to use self-directed IRA funds to make loans or purchase notes from third parties. By doing so, all interest payments received are tax-deferred until a distribution is taken, and in the case of a self-directed Roth IRA, all gains are tax-free. For example, if you used a self-directed IRA to loan money to a friend, all interest received would flow back into your self-directed IRA tax-free, whereas, if you lent your friend money from personal (nonretirement) funds, the interest you received would be subject to federal and, in most cases, state income tax. When it comes to making hard money loans to friends, colleagues, or any third parties, it is very important to be mindful of the IRS prohibited transaction rules, which do not allow you to lend money to any disqualified person or disqualified entity."

"Okay," Rich said.

"Once again, the loan or note amount should be paid using self-directed IRA funds or funds from a nondisqualified third party, and no personal funds or funds from a disqualified person should be used in the loan transaction, nor should a disqualified person be directly or indirectly involved. The loan or note should also have a stated interest rate of at least prime as per the *Wall Street Journal*. Recently, that has been around 3.25 percent interest."

"And all interest and principal associated with the loan or note should be allocated to your self-directed IRA," Rich said.

"Exactly," John said. "It's good practice to have the loan terms documented in a promissory note or loan agreement, even if you are dealing with a friend. And if you are acting as the lender, you should consider securing the loan with an interest or lien in an asset owned by the borrower. Additionally, read up on the prohibited transaction rules to make sure you will not be engaging in any self-dealing loan transaction, which would involve a loan or note that will personally benefit you or a disqualified person."

Using a Self-Directed IRA to Buy a Business or Franchise

"I've read on the Internet and heard that you can use a self-directed IRA to buy a business or franchise without tax or penalty and even earn a salary," Rich asked. "Is this true?"

"That's another question that I get a lot," John said. "Yes, there is a way you can use retirement funds to buy or finance a new business or franchise that you would be involved in personally with a 401(k) plan and not an IRA."

"How does that work?" Rich said.

"The legality of using retirement funds to purchase employer corporate stock is firmly established in the IRC and under ERISA law. IRC Section 4975(c) includes a list of transactions that the IRS deems prohibited. However, IRC Section 4975(d) lists a number of exemptions to the prohibited transaction rules. Specifically, IRC Section 4975(d)(13) lists an exemption for any transaction, which is exempt from Section 406 of ERISA by reason of Section 408(e) of such act. Section 408(e) provides that Section 406 of ERISA shall not apply to the acquisition or sale by a plan of qualifying employer securities (as defined in ERISA Section 407(d)(5), provided that: (1) the acquisition or sale is for adequate consideration, (2) no commission is charged with respect to the acquisition or sale and (3) the plan is an eligible individual account plan [as defined in ERISA Section 407(d)(3)]. A 401(k) plan fits into this definition."

"So what does all this mean?" Rich said.

ROBS

"When it comes to using retirement funds to buy or finance a business that you or another disqualified person will be involved in personally, there is only one legal way to do it and that is through the Business Acquisition Solution, also known as a Rollover Business Start-Up solution (ROBS). The ROBS solution takes advantage of an exception in the tax code under IRC Section 4975(d) that allows one to use 401(k) plan funds to buy stock in a C corporation, which is known as qualifying employer securities. The exception to the IRS prohibited transaction rules found in IRC 4975(d)(13) requires that a 401(k) plan buy qualifying employer securities, which is defined as stock of a C corporation. This is the reason one cannot use a self-directed IRA LLC to invest in a business the IRA holder or a disqualified person will be personally involved in or why a 401(k) plan cannot invest in an LLC in which the plan participant or disqualified person will be involved without triggering the prohibited transaction rules. Hence, in order to use retirement funds to invest in a business in which a disqualified person will be personally involved, one needs a C corporation to operate a business and adopt a 401(k) plan.

"How does the ROBS arrangement work?" Rich asked.

"The ROBS arrangement typically involves rolling over a prior IRA or 401(k) plan account into a newly established 401(k) plan, which either an already existing or newly established C corporation business sponsored, and then investing the rollover 401(k) plan funds in the stock of the C corporation. The funds are then deposited in the C corporation bank account and are available for use for business purposes."

"How about some examples?" Rich asked.

"Here you go," John said.

Examples:1. Jim, an entrepreneur or existing business owner establishes a new C corporation in the state where the business will be operating. The ROBS structure must involve a C corporation and not an LLC or S corporation because the exemption to the IRS prohibited transaction rules under IRC 4975(d) involves the purchase of qualifying employer securities, which is defined as stock of a corporation. Using an LLC would not satisfy this definition and only individuals can be shareholders of an S corporation and a 401(k) plan is a trust.

- 2. The C corporation adopts a prototype 401(k) plan that specifically permits the plan participants, including Jim, to direct the investment of their plan accounts into a selection of investment options, including employer stock, also known as qualifying employer securities.
- 3. Jim elects to participate in the new 401(k) plan and, as permitted by the plan, directs a rollover of a previous employer's 401(k) plan funds into the newly adopted 401(k) plan.
- 4. Jim then directs the investment of his or her 401(k) plan account to purchase the C corporation's newly issued stock at fair market value (i.e., the amount that Jim wishes to invest in the new business). The value of the stock is established by an appraiser or qualified tax professional.
- 5. Jim also invests personal funds equal to more than 1 percent of the purchase price so that the structure is not considered an Employee Stock Option Plan (ESOP).
- 6. The C corporation utilizes the proceeds from the sale of stock (the amount of rollover funds and personal funds used) to purchase the assets for the new business.
- 7. Joe would be able to earn a salary from the revenues of the business.

The Self-Directed IRA vs. ROBS

"So what is the difference between using a self-directed vs. ROBS structure to buy a business?" Rich asked.

"In a lot of respects, using a self-directed IRA LLC or a 401(k) plan to purchase stock in a corporation would seem to be subject to the same rules. However, as described above, using 401(k) plan funds and not IRA funds allows one to take advantage of the prohibited transaction exemption under IRC 4975(d)(13) for qualifying employer securities. In essence, if one used an IRA to buy an interest in a new business that he or she was personally involved in, that transaction would likely violate the IRS prohibited transaction rules and would not satisfy the exception in the tax code since the exception would only apply if a 401(k) plan and C corporation is used and the 401(k) plan purchased stock in the adopting employer C corporation stock."

"That's helpful," Rich said.

"The recent US Tax Court case *T.L. Ellis*, TC Memo. 2013-245, Dec. 59,674(M) highlights the risk and limitations involved when using a self-directed IRA to purchase business assets. In the Ellis case, the taxpayers used IRA funds to invest in a corporation that ultimately purchased business assets. Because Mr. Ellis used an IRA and not a 401(k) plan to purchase the C corporation stock, Mr. Ellis was not able to earn a salary or personally guarantee a business loan, which ultimately was the cause of the IRS prohibited transaction rule violation."

"Okay," Rich said.

"The limitation of using a self-directed IRA LLC to buy a business is that the individual retirement account business owner would not be able to be actively involved in the business, earn a salary, or even personally guarantee a business loan, whereas, if the business owner used a ROBS strategy, that individual would be able to be actively involved in the business and earn a salary without triggering the IRS prohibited transaction rules."

Any Downside to Using ROBS?

"The ROBS solution sounds pretty good, what are some of the downsides?"

"In my opinion, there are basically four disadvantages of establishing a ROBS."

1. **The C Corporation Requirement**
    Although there are advantages to establishing a C corporation, such as owner's liability protection from the actions of the company, there are several disadvantages as well.
    A. Double Taxation: Corporations, unlike other companies that are considered sole proprietorships and partnerships, file their own taxes separately from their owners at their own tax rates.

After the company's profits are taxed at the corporate level, they are then distributed to the shareholders who have to report the amount received on their individual tax returns. The corporate tax rate is generally 15 percent for corporate profits under $50,000 and 35 percent for profits above $50,000. This isn't the case for Subchapter S corporations or LLCs, in which the profits bypass being taxed at the corporate level and are distributed and taxed at the shareholder's level. That is called pass-through taxation. For example, if we assume a 20 percent income tax rate for both corporation and individuals and a C corporation earned $100 of profits, the C corporation would be required to pay tax of $20 (20 percent of $100) and then the shareholder would be required to pay tax of $16 (20 percent of $80) on any dividend issued by the C corporation to the shareholder, whereas, in the case of an LLC or S corporation, there is no entity level tax so the $100 would flow directly to the shareholder or LLC member and a tax of only $20 would be imposed at the shareholder level. Comparing this with the C corporation example, by using a pass-through entity such as an S corporation or LLC, the individual would save $16 in our example (total tax of $36 with a C corporation versus $20 in the case of an LLC or S corporation).

"It's important to note that it can be argued that the disadvantage of double taxation bite does not affect retirement accounts [i.e., 401(k) plans] as much as individuals, since the dividend from the C corporation to the 401(k) plan shareholder would be exempt from tax since a 401(k) plan is a tax-exempt retirement account (IRC 512). However, the double taxation is not eliminated but simply deferred until the 401(k) plan participant elects to take a 401(k) plan distribution, which would generally be subject to a second tax (the first tax would be applied at the C corporation level). In contrast, if a 401(k) plan invested in an LLC, a pass-through entity for taxation, the income or gains from the LLC would generally flow back to the 401(k) plan without tax, and the 401(k) plan participant would only be required to pay one tax when a distribution is taken."

"Okay, that's good to know," Rich said.

"Unfortunately, the IRS rules require a C corporation be used when a retirement account holder wishes to use retirement funds to invest in a business he or another disqualified person will be involved in personally. The issue of double taxation is certainly one disadvantage of the ROBS solution, but it is generally perceived as better than paying tax and potentially a 10 percent early distribution penalty on a distribution from your retirement account. Here are a few of the negative features of using a ROBS solution to acquire or invest in a business or franchise":

B. Regulations and Formalities

Subchapter C corporations generally involve more corporate formalities than LLCs, for example. In general, C corporations have to report annually to the states in which they're incorporated, and the states in which they do a lot of business, on an annual basis. Also, C corporations must observe certain formalities to be considered corporations. This includes holding regular board and shareholder meetings and issuing stock. Also, the names of corporate officers are made public, which is not required by businesses formed under different organizational structures.

2. 401(k) Plan Administration

Even though 401(k) plan administration costs have come down significantly over the years, there is still a cost of offering a 401(k) plan to employees. In addition to having to make a 3 percent safe harbor contribution, which will be discussed below, 401(k) plans cost money to administer because there are many compliance issues that have to be monitored, there are many ongoing service and administration functions that have to be provided, and there are a host of education and communication services that are required to be offered to plan participants. It is not uncommon for a small business 401(k) plan to cost anywhere from $750 to $1,500 annually for a third-party administration company to administer as well as file the annual IRS Form 5500.

A. Matching Contributions: A "safe harbor" 401(k) plan, which is a popular type of 401(k) plan for small businesses, offers employees who participate in the plan a 3 percent matching contribution made by the employer.

Starting in 1999 a new twist on the traditional 401(k) plan is available for plan sponsors, the "Safe Harbor 401(k) Plan." This twist on the traditional 401(k) plan promised to be a simpler plan to administer. If an employer adopted this type of 401(k) plan there would be no need to worry about complex testing at the end of each year, and, in some cases, no need to make top-heavy contributions (since 2002, safe harbor plans satisfy top-heavy requirements). All this in exchange for a commitment to make a minimum level of contributions that many sponsors make anyway. Thus, for example, if the employee earns $40,000 in salary during the year and contributes 3 percent of the salary or $1,200 to the 401(k) plan, the employer would contribute an additional $1,200 (3 percent of the salary) to the individual 401(k) plan account. Taking this a step further, if the business has five employees and each employee makes $40,000 a year, the employer now has to make $6,000 in employer safe harbor matching contributions. Although the contributions are tax-deductible to the employer, it is still additional funds that are being removed from the company and could affect the cash flow of a new small business.

3. Potential IRS Audit

"What about a potential IRS audit?" Rich asked.

"Dating back to 2005 or so, the IRS started focusing some attention on the ROBS solutions and some of the abuses they perceived were occurring."

"And what happened?"

"On October 31, 2008, Michael Julianelle, director, Employee Plans, signed a memorandum approving IRS ROBS examination guidelines. The IRS stated that while this type of structure is legal and not considered an abusive tax-avoidance transaction, the execution of these types of transactions, in many cases, have not been found to be in full compliance with IRS and ERISA rules and procedures. In the memorandum, the IRS highlighted two compliance areas that they felt were not being adequately followed by the promoters implementing the structure during this time period. The first noncompliance area of concern the IRS highlighted in the memorandum was the lack of disclosure of the adopted 401(k) plan to the company's employees, and the second noncompliance area was establishing an independent appraisal to determine the fair market value of the business being purchased. The memorandum also went into detail describing some other ROBS problem areas that the IRS was concerned with, such as lack of plan notification to eligible employees, inadequate stock valuation, and failure to purchase business assets. In sum, the IRS was concerned that people were using their retirement funds to buy a business and either the business was not being purchased and the individual then used the funds for personal purposes, thus avoiding tax and potential penalties, or the business that was purchased closed, and the retirement account liquidated, thus leaving the IRS without the potential to tax the retirement account in the future."

"And how did it turn out?"

"The IRS did not publicly comment on the ROBS solution again until August 27, 2010, almost two years after publishing the memorandum. The IRS held a public phone forum that covered transactions involving using retirement funds to purchase a business. Monika Templeman, director of employee plans examinations and Colleen Patton, area manager of employee plans examinations for the Pacific Coast, spent considerable time discussing the IRS's position on this subject. Monika Templeman began the presentation reaffirming the government's position that a transaction involving the use of retirement funds to purchase a new business is legal and not an abusive tax-avoidance transaction as long as the transaction complies with IRS and ERISA rules and procedures. The concern the IRS has had with these types of transactions is that the promoters who have been offering these transactions have not had the expertise to develop structures that are fully compliant with IRS and ERISA rules and regulations. The IRS added that a large percentage of the transactions they reviewed were in noncompliance largely due to the following non-compliance issues: (i) failure by the promoters to develop a structure that requires the new company to disclose the new 401(k) plan to the company's employees, and (ii) the failure to require the client to secure an independent appraisal to determine the fair market value of the company stock being purchased by the 401(k) plan. The IRS concluded by stating that a transaction using retirement funds to acquire a business is legal and not prohibited as long as the transaction is structured correctly to comply with IRS and ERISA rules and procedures."

Does ROBS Trigger an IRS Audit?

"So, does the ROBS solution trigger an audit?" Rich asked.

"No one knows what factors trigger an IRS audit, but although legal, the ROBS solution is something the IRS and Department of Labor are looking at. As we learned from October 31, 2008, the IRS has been looking at the ROBS transaction closely for a number of years and even examined a number of well-known promoters in the area. Yet still, they clearly state the ROBS solution is 100 percent legal if established properly. Again, if your structure is set up properly and the funds are used to buy a business, the 401(k) plan is being offered to all eligible employees, a valuation of the stock purchased is performed, and the plan is compliant with all annual testing and IRS filing requirement, there is nothing to be concerned with if your plan was audited by the IRS or DOL."

"That sounds good," Rich said.

"But I'd say if you want to use retirement funds to invest in a business that you will be personally involved in, the ROBS solution should be your last resort.

Options for Funding a Business with Retirement Funds

There are a few options you should consider before jumping in and doing a ROBS transaction. Using personal funds would be generally more tax-efficient and will let you keep your retirement funds invested in a generally safer investment environment. Second, your new business can adopt a 401(k) plan and you can use the 401(k) loan feature to borrow $50,000 or 50 percent of your account value, whatever is less and use that loan to fund your new business. Third, taking a taxable distribution from your retirement account could be painful but if the amount needed for the business is not significant, or you have net operating losses you can use, paying the tax and potential 10 percent early distribution penalty is something to consider."

"Okay," Rich said. "But it's still a loan that has to be paid back."

"Yes, but at least you are paying your own plan back and not a bank. In general, the lowest interest rate you can use is the prime rate as per the *Wall Street Journal*, which has been 3.25 percent for some time. Also, loan payments, must be paid back at least quarterly. The loan is a straight-line loan of interest and principal and no balloon payments are allowed, although there is no prepaying penalty for paying back the loan early. The loan does give you tax-free and penalty-free use of up to $50,000 to use for any purpose, including funding a new business, but you are capped at that amount which may not be enough for you. So, if you can't make it work with your personal funds or by taking a taxable distribution, and the $50,000 loan is not enough, then the ROBS option may make sense. I would certainly advise you to talk this over with your CPA or tax adviser, as there are costs to set up the structure as well as ongoing fees. In addition, you are putting your hard-earned retirement funds at risk since the majority of all new businesses tend to fail. Although the ROBS solution is legal and the IRS has repeatedly stated publicly that they will not treat it as a tax shelter or reportable transaction, they are not in love with the structure because of the high likelihood that the retirement funds being invested will be lost, which ultimately means less tax money for the IRS when you eventually would have taken taxable distributions."

"I know I can't use my self-directed IRA to invest in my own business, but what about a friend's business?"

"With a self-directed IRA LLC you are also permitted to purchase an interest in a privately held business not owned by you or a disqualified person. The business can be established as any entity, such as an LLC, a C corporation, or partnership, but not an S corporation since only individuals can generally be S corporation shareholders. When investing in a private business using self-directed IRA funds, it is particularly important to keep in mind the disqualified person and prohibited transaction rules, and it's a good idea to consult with a tax or retirement expert."

"Will do," Rich said.

"In order to avoid triggering the prohibited transaction rules when making investments in a private business, you should be careful not to invest any retirement funds in any business in which you get a direct or indirect personal benefit, including ownership, serving as office or manager, and even being an employee in some cases. I know we discussed the Rollins case in great detail when we discussed the IRS prohibited transaction rules, but I wanted to just briefly reference it again when looking at how the IRS looks at investments in a business owned by a disqualified person, even if the ownership is less than 50 percent. Mr. Rollins owned a small percentage of a company and served as officer of the company without being an employee, and the Tax Court still ruled that the loan from his 401(k) plan to the company was a prohibited transaction. It's all about the facts and circumstances. How big is the company? Is it a public or private company? How many shareholders? Do you have any personal role in the company? Would the retirement investment personally benefit you in any way, directly or indirectly?"

"And what about those prohibited transaction rules we discussed earlier?" Rich asked.

"Certainly using a self-directed IRA to invest in a private business of a friend in which you have no involvement and the investment is 100 percent passive would not violate the IRS prohibited transaction rules. Also, an employee of IBM or another large public company can use 401(k) funds to buy stock in the company they work for without triggering a prohibited transaction because of the size of the company and number of shareholders. Remember, a retirement account, including a self-directed IRA or 401(k) plan cannot purchase the stock of an S corporation. Therefore, since almost all public corporations are C corporations, you can generally purchase qualifying employer securities of the company you work for."

"But what about a private company in which you already own a small percentage or that you are an employee of, would that violate the IRS prohibited transaction rules?" Rich asked.

"Unfortunately, there's no clear answer and you must examine the facts and circumstances in relation to the prohibited transaction rules under IRC 4975 to see if a prohibited transaction would occur. Even if you own less than 50 percent of the private business and on its face the entity does not seem to be a disqualified person under IRC 4975, remember, the self-dealing and conflict-of-interest prohibited transaction rules could still trigger a prohibited transaction—ask Mr. Rollins about that. Of course, if you work for a public company, like Apple, using your IRA to buy stock would not trigger a prohibited transaction because of the size of the company."

"So," Rich said, "the safest approach is not to invest retirement funds in any private business in which you have a personal ownership or are an employee of, or have any direct or indirect personal relationship with. That being said, depending on the facts and circumstances, it still could be possible to invest retirement funds in a private business in which you or a disqualified person owns a small percentage, serves as director, or works for. "The problem is that anytime such a transaction is done, one potentially opens themselves up to IRS attack and the burden then falls on the IRA holder to prove that a prohibited transaction did not occur."

"Right," John said. "Once again, the deposit and purchase price for the business should be paid using self-directed IRA funds or funds from a non-disqualified third party, and no personal funds or funds from a disqualified person should be used. The purchase of the stock or assets of the business should not directly or indirectly benefit you personally or any disqualified person, to avoid self-dealing or issues with prohibited transactions."

"And the UBTI?" Rich asked.

"As we have discussed, the purchase of a business operated via an LLC or partnership will potentially trigger the unrelated business taxable income rules under IRC 512, and a corresponding tax of approximately 35 percent would be applied. But the purchase of stock in a C corporation would not trigger UBTI rules. Most importantly, make sure you perform adequate diligence on the business you will be purchasing or investing in, especially if you will be buying the stock or an interest and not the actual assets of the business."

Option Trading

"What about option trading with my self-directed IRA?" Rich asked.

"When it comes to making investments with a self-directed IRA LLC," John said, "the IRS generally does not tell you what you can invest in, only what you cannot invest in. The types of investments that are not permitted to be made using retirement funds is outlined in IRC Section 408 and 4975."

"Our prohibited transaction rules," Rich said.

"When it comes to investing in options with a self-directed IRA LLC, the question then becomes whether the investment would trigger the UBTI rules. An option is a contract that gives the buyer the right, but not the obligation, to buy or sell an underlying asset at a specific price on or before a certain date. An option, just like a stock or bond, is a security. It is also a binding contract with strictly defined terms and properties."

"And what does the IRS say?" Rich asked.

"According to the IRS, any gain from the lapse or termination of options to buy or sell securities is excluded from unrelated business taxable income. Note: The exclusion is not available if the organization is engaged in the trade or business of writing options or the options are held by the organization as inventory or for sale to customers in the ordinary course of a trade or business. So, if option trading is not being done as an active trade or business, then using a self-directed IRA LLC to invest in options would not trigger the UBTI tax rules."

Hedge Funds/Private Equity Funds/Venture Capital Funds

"What about hedge funds or private equity investments with my self-directed IRA?" Rich asked.

"There is generally no issue with using a self-directed IRA to invest in a hedge fund or private equity fund," John said. "A hedge fund is an alternative investment vehicle available only to sophisticated investors, such as institutions and individuals with significant assets. In general, retirement funds are permitted to invest in hedge funds. If you will be looking to make an investment in a fund in which you or any disqualified person has any personal interest in or relationship with, you will not have to worry about the IRS prohibited transaction rules. However, if the fund will be using margin, leverage, or will be investing in companies that operate through an LLC or other pass-through entity, then you will need to consider the potential tax ramifications of the UBTI tax rules. Since most funds are set up as pass-through entities, i.e., LLCs or partnerships, if the fund will be using any margin, leverage, to buy real estate for example, or investing in companies that will operate through a pass-through entity, then the UBTI tax rules could kick in and turn your tax-friendly investment into a very tax-inefficient investment because of the potential for a 35 percent tax. In general, a number of hedge funds investing in equities do use margin, which could trigger the UBTI, so that is something to consider. The same would go for hedge funds investing in real estate or real estate–type funds that generally use leverage to acquire the real estate. In other words, they don't use all cash and borrow funds to complete their real estate transactions, whereas, in the case of venture capital firms that invest in start-ups, a lot of these firms actually require that the target companies be C corporations and not LLCs, so in a lot of cases venture capital investments with a self-directed IRA would not trigger the UBTI tax rules. Most large funds have a solid understanding of the UBTI rules because, typically, pension funds are large investors in these funds, so they will generally be able to tell you whether any UBTI would be triggered, and in some cases they may actually have a special fund for retirement investors."

"What about if I wanted to use my self-directed IRA to invest in a new real estate–type fund I want to start?" Rich asked.

"The same principles that apply to using retirement funds to invest in your own business will apply to using a self-directed IRA to invest in your own real estate fund," John said, "since the real estate fund will likely be considered an active business for UBTI purposes. So, when it comes to using retirement funds to invest in a hedge fund, it is important to be mindful of the IRS prohibited transaction rules under IRC Section 4975. In general, the IRS has restricted certain transactions between the IRA and a disqualified person. As a reminder, the definition of a disqualified person [IRC Section 4975(e)(2)] extends into a variety of related-party scenarios but generally includes the IRA holder, any ancestors or lineal descendants of the IRA holder (i.e., parents, children, spouse, daughter-in-law, or son-in-law), and entities in which the IRA holder or a disqualified person holds a controlling or management interest. Furthermore, IRC Section 4975(c)(1)(D) and (E) outlines rules that relate to self-dealing or conflict-of-interest transactions that involve an investment that could directly or indirectly personally benefit a disqualified person. The self-dealing or conflict-of-interest prohibited transaction rules have the broadest application especially when it comes to hedge fund–type investments."

"And once again how do prohibited transaction rules play in?"

"The prohibited transactions rules tend to become more of an issue when the person using the IRA funds or any disqualified person related to the IRA owner has a personal interest or relationship with the hedge fund investment. In other words, an IRA can generally make an investment into a hedge fund in which neither the IRA holder nor any disqualified person has any personal ownership or relationship with. The issues begin to arise from an IRS prohibited transaction standpoint when the IRA owner wishes to use retirement funds to invest in a hedge fund in which he or she or a disqualified person is either an owner or employee or, in some cases, has a professional relationship with the fund in question."

"Got it," Rich said.

"In general, if structured correctly, there may be a way for you to use your retirement funds to invest in a hedge fund that one is personally involved in. The key is to make sure that the IRA investment in the hedge fund will not directly or indirectly personally benefit the IRA owners since that type of investment would likely trigger a prohibited transaction."

Using Retirement Funds to Invest in My Own Investment Fund—Is It Possible?

"Okay," Rich said. "And how are they structured?"

"Generally, hedge funds are structured as limited partnerships or LLCs. In the case of a limited partnership, a general partner (GP) is created who tends to perform all the hedge fund management tasks. The GP generally owns a small percentage of the partnership. The investors are limited partners (LP) of the partnership. A typical fee structure for a hedge fund is the two-and-twenty model, which means the hedge fund manager will take a 2 percent management fee of all assets under management and then take 20 percent of the profits generated by the fund after the LP investors have received the money they invested back and, in some cases, a preferred return on the money invested is also returned to the investor."

"If you're a principal or in a management position with the hedge fund, can you use your retirement funds to invest in the fund?" Rich asked.

"I get that a lot," John said. "To begin with, the use of the retirement funds cannot be invested into the GP entity since that is the entity in which the services are generally being performed on behalf of the hedge fund and where the management fee and carried interest are typically being directed because investing IRA funds in a company in which the IRA holder has a personal ownership or is performing services as an employee would likely violate the IRS prohibited transaction rules. Therefore, the question then becomes can the IRA holder who has some personal ownership in the hedge fund use retirement funds to invest as an LP of the fund? The answer generally depends on the facts and circumstances involved in the transaction. However, in general, there are ways that one can properly structure an investment of retirement funds into a hedge fund in which the IRA holder has some personal interest. The main question that needs to be asked and answered positively is if the IRS looked at the transaction, could they argue that the IRA owner has in any way directly or indirectly personally benefited from the IRA investment. If the IRA owner cannot prove that he or she did not receive any direct or indirect personal benefit from the IRA investment in the hedge fund, then the IRS would likely argue that the investment triggered a prohibited transaction. Since the onus is always on the taxpayer to disprove a claim made by the IRS, it is crucial that the IRA owner who is seeking to make a retirement investment in a hedge fund in which he or she has some personal connection be extremely confident that he or she can prove, if requested, that no personal benefit was derived from the retirement account investment, either directly or indirectly. Accordingly, when it comes to using retirement funds to make investments in a hedge fund in which the IRA owner has a personal relationship, issues such as the management fee and carried interests are items that need to be taken into account when structuring the self-directed IRA hedge fund investment."

"And how does the IRS look at it?"

"The Tax Court in *Rollins v. Commissioner*, a 2008 Tax Court case, offers some insight into how the IRS looks at transactions that involve investments into entities in which the IRA owner has a small ownership interest. Even though the Rollins case did not involve using retirement funds to invest in a hedge fund, it nevertheless offers some insight into the IRS's thoughts on the application of the IRA self-dealing and conflict-of-interest rules. The Rollins case is especially helpful in examining how the IRS could look at a transaction involving the use of retirement funds into a hedge fund in which the IRA owner has some personal relationship or ownership interest. Mr. Rollins was a CPA who had an ownership in several companies.

One of the companies, in which he owned less than 10 percent, served as a director but received no compensation, was in financial trouble, and needed additional funds. Mr. Rollins decided to use his 401(k) plan funds to lend the company money at prevailing interest rates. The IRS audited the transaction and argued that the loan from Mr. Rollins's 401(k) plan to the company was a prohibited transaction as the loan personally benefited him. The Tax Court agreed and basically stated that even though the company was not itself a disqualified person because Mr. Rollins owned less than 50 percent of the company, nonetheless he could not provide that he did not directly or indirectly personally benefit from the loan made to the company by his 401(k) plan. Clearly the Tax Court felt that Mr. Rollins personally benefited from the loan since without the loan his personal investment would have been lost. The Rollins case is a good illustration of how the IRS could view an investment in a hedge fund by an IRA owner who has some personal interest in the hedge fund below the 50 percent ownership threshold."

"Can you give me some examples?" Rich asked.

"Sure," John said. "Here are a few that highlight the complexities involved in structuring an investment of retirement funds in a hedge fund in which the IRA owner has some personal relationship or ownership":

1. Joe is looking to start a hedge fund and needs $100,000 to begin operations. The hedge fund would be a limited partnership and Joe would be charging a traditional 2 percent management fee and 20 percent carried interest on fund profits. Joe will own 100 percent of the general partner of the hedge fund and is looking for investors to invest in the hedge fund. Joe wishes to use his IRA funds to invest in his hedge fund.

    Issues for Joe to consider: Joe would clearly not be able to use his IRA funds to invest in the general partner since he will own 100 percent of that entity personally and that would likely trigger a prohibited transaction. What if Joe wanted to invest the funds as a limited partner of the fund? Unfortunately, there is no clear answer to this question as the answer is generally dependent on the facts and circumstances involved in the transaction. For example, if the only way Joe could attract investors to the fund is to show he also has invested in the fund and the only funds he had available to invest were IRA funds, the IRS could argue that the use of his IRA funds would personally benefit him since without his IRA funds being used he would not be able to attract investors to his fund and derive a personal financial return from owning the fund.

2. Ben is a 2 percent partner at a hedge fund that has $500 million under management. The hedge fund is set up as a limited partnership. The hedge fund has a traditional fee model of 2 percent management fee and 20 percent carried interest. The hedge fund is looking to raise an additional $250 million and Ben is seeking to use $250,000 from his IRA to invest as a limited partner of the fund. His limited partnership interest would be 2.5 percent of the total fund.

   Issues for Ben to consider: Ben is clearly a disqualified person because he is the IRA holder, but the hedge fund he is a partner in would likely not be since he owns just 2 percent of the fund, pursuant to IRC Section 4975(e)(2). However, the self-dealing or conflict-of-interest rules under IRC Section 4975(c)(1)(D) and (E) could treat Ben's investment in the fund as a prohibited transaction. The question Ben must ask himself is whether he would receive any personal benefit, either directly or indirectly, from making the fund investment with his IRA funds. For example, would the fund be in financial trouble without Ben's investment? Will Ben receive a salary bonus if he invests in the fund? Or, what if Ben is required to invest in the fund in order to maintain his position as partner of the fund? These are some of the facts that would need to be examined before determining whether Ben's investment would rise to the level of a prohibited transaction.

3. Steve is a 99 percent owner of hedge fund A, which has over $750 million in assets under management. The hedge fund is set up as a limited partnership. The hedge fund has a traditional fee model of 2 percent management fee and 20 percent carried interest. The hedge fund is looking to create fund B, which will be exclusively investing

in a pool of loans. Fund B will be looking to raise $500 million from outside investors. Steve and a number of hedge fund A executives want to invest their retirement funds into fund B, but expect to own less than 5 percent of fund B. Fund A will be charging a management fee and carried interest on the limited partners of fund B.

Issues for Steve to consider: Since Steve owns 99 percent of hedge fund A and hedge fund A will be receiving a fee from the limited partners of fund B, a management fee and carried interest allocated to Steve's IRA and potentially his executives could violate the prohibited transaction rules under IRC Section 4975. Fees paid by Steve's IRA to a company he owns 99 percent of could be considered a prohibited transaction. What if Steve and his executives were able to have their IRAs exempted from the management fee and carried interest going to the general partner of fund A or were able to buy a different membership class of fund B, which did not have to pay any fees to hedge fund A. Because of Steve's large ownership interest in hedge fund A, it is especially important that he focuses on the self-dealing and conflict-of-interest prohibited transaction rules to make sure his IRA investment into fund B could not be viewed as personally benefiting him directly or indirectly.

Oil and Gas Investments

"What about oil and gas investments? I hear a lot about this category of investment. Can I make an oil and gas–related investment with a self-directed IRA?" Rich asked.

John explained that over the last several years, a number of self-directed IRA investors have turned to oil and gas partnerships, which provide investors the opportunity of participating in the oil and gas industry and balance their portfolios, increase the rate of return, and reduce risks through diversification. These drilling funds are often registered with the Securities Exchange Commission and are registered in all the states they are sold in (Blue Sky registration with your State Securities Department within fifteen business days) and are also designed to accept accredited investors.

"In most cases, royalties generated by the oil and gas investment project would be exempt from tax, as IRAs are not subject to tax pursuant to IRC 408. However, if the IRA invests in an active trade or business through a pass-through entity, such as a partnership, or used leverage, income from that investment could be subject to the UBTI tax. Pursuant to IRC Section 512, royalties, including overriding royalties, and all deductions directly connected with such income shall be excluded in computing UBTI.

"The general rule under Treasury Regulation Section 1.512(b)-1(b) provides that mineral royalties are excluded from the computation of unrelated business taxable income. However, mineral royalties are included in such computation if an organization (1) owns a working interest in a mineral property, and (2) is not relieved of its share of development costs.

"The key in determining whether income from an oil and gas project would be subject to the UBIT tax is whether the income would be treated as royalty for income tax purposes. The IRS addressed this is IRS Revenue Ruling 69-179. In IRS Revenue Ruling 69-179, a tax-exempt organization owned a working interest in oil and gas–producing property. Under the terms of an agreement with an independent operator, it was relieved of any liability for the development costs associated with the interest but remained liable for operating expenses. The IRS held that the income from the mineral interest was not a 'passive' royalty and therefore not excluded from unrelated business taxable income under the Section 512(b)(2) exclusion for passive royalty income. The revenue ruling notes that a royalty interest is a right to a mineral in place that entitles its owner to a specified fraction of the total production from the property free of expense of *both* development and operation. Although the regulations are silent about the effect of liability for operating costs, the reference to relief from development costs is only by way of illustration, and to be a royalty interest, the right to payment must be free of both development and operating costs.

"So, your self-directed IRA oil and gas investment will be exempt from the UBTI tax if the investment generates pure royalty income whereby the IRA does not own an interest in the mineral property and is not responsible for its share of any development or operating costs of the underlying mineral investment. In other words, as long as the royalty income from the mineral investment is measured by the accurate oil and gas measurement from the lease and is relieved of its share of the development costs, the royalty income would not be subject to the UBTI tax, whereas, if the exception pursuant to IRC 512 is not satisfied, the income from the oil and gas investment partnership would likely be subject to the UBTI tax.

"The majority of oil and gas investments marketed to retirement investors require that the investor (1) own a working interest in a mineral property (a K-1 is issued), and (2) is not relieved of its share of development costs. As a result, oil and gas investments are not the most popular self-directed IRA investment and it is generally more tax-efficient to make the investments using nonretirement funds, as most oil and gas investments, especially those structured as MLPSs, tend to trigger the UBTI tax, which is approximately 35 percent."

"Great," Rich said. "That's really helpful. You make it concrete and I can follow you. It's pretty amazing what you can do on your own with some knowledge."

"It sure is," John said. "A self-directed IRA LLC offers you the ability to use your retirement funds to make almost any type of investment on your own without requiring the consent of any custodian or person. The IRS only describes the type of investments that are prohibited, which are very few. Using a self-directed IRA LLC to make investments offers the investor the ability to make traditional as well as nontraditional investments, such as real estate, in a tax-efficient manner."

"I know we have spent a considerable amount of time discussing the types of investments that are allowed and not allowed with a self-directed IRA under the IRS rules but really didn't focus on whether you use pretax or Roth (after-tax) IRA funds to make the investment. The next time we meet I think it will be very beneficial if I spend some time unlocking the secret world of the self-directed Roth IRA."

VIII

The Self-Directed Roth IRA Strategy

"Many tax practitioners like me make the argument that the self-directed Roth IRA is the last best legal tax shelter out there for the American individual taxpayer," John said. "I'm a huge believer in the enormous tax advantages the Roth IRA offers retirement account holders from both a savings, wealth accumulation, and estate-planning perspective. I'm pretty confident that after we finish talking about the self-directed Roth IRA, you will be mouthing the same saying I do, 'In Roth We Trust.'"

"So how different are the self-directed IRA and the self-directed Roth IRA?" Rich asked.

"I get that question a lot," John said. "The answer is that they are essentially the same except that a pretax IRA is used in one case and an after-tax Roth IRA is used in another."

"I don't have a Roth IRA," Rich said.

John nodded. "I know. A lot of my clients are like you," John said. "So why are we spending time talking about the self-directed Roth IRA? Well, I really believe that if more people understood the benefits of having a Roth IRA and using Roth IRA funds to make investments, it would greatly enhance their financial future and retirement."

"Well, in that case," Rich said, "I don't mind spending some time learning more about the self-directed Roth IRA solution."

"Great," John said. "I've already touched briefly on the basics of the Roth IRA some time ago, but let me review the features of a Roth IRA."

The Features of a Roth IRA

"I know we discussed the Roth IRA at the outset when we first met, but I thought it would be helpful if I went through a few of the key points again," John started. "In 1997," John continued, "Congress, under the Taxpayer Relief Act, introduced the Roth IRA to be like a traditional IRA but with a few attractive modifications. The big advantage of a Roth IRA is that if you qualify to make contributions, all distributions from the Roth IRA are tax-free—even the investment returns—as long as the distributions meet certain requirements. In addition, unlike traditional IRAs, you may contribute to a Roth IRA for as long as you continue to have earned income (in the case of a traditional IRA, you can't make contributions after you reach age 70½). The rules for the Roth IRA are found in the IRC under Section 408A."

"And what exactly is a Roth IRA?" Rich asked.

"A Roth IRA is an IRA that the owner designates as a Roth IRA," John said. "A Roth IRA is generally subject to the rules of traditional IRAs. For example, traditional and Roth IRAs and their owners are identically affected by the rules treating an IRA as distributing its assets if the IRA engages in a prohibited transaction or the owner borrows against it. The reporting requirements for IRAs also apply to Roth IRAs. However, several rules, described below, apply uniquely to Roth IRAs."

"Got it," Rich said.

"The most attractive feature of the Roth IRA is that even though contributions are not deductible, all distributions, including the earnings and appreciation on all Roth contributions, are tax-free if certain conditions are met."

"And what are the characteristics of a Roth IRA?" Rich asked.

"Here's a table that briefly outlines the differences between a traditional pretax IRA and an after-tax Roth IRA," John said.

Pre-tax Contribution	After-Tax (Roth) contribution
Tax deductible contributions	Contributions are not tax deductible – contributions made to a Roth IRA are from after tax dollars
Distributions may be taken by age 59½. and are mandatory by 70 1/2.	No Mandatory Distribution Age – with a Roth IRA you are not required to ever take distributions
Taxes are paid on amount of distributions (10% excise tax may apply if withdrawn prior to age 59½.)	No taxes on distributions if rules and regulations are followed
Available to everyone; no income restrictions with earned income	• For 2015, subject to adjustments each year, Single filers, Head of Household or Married Filing Separately (and you did not live with your spouse during the year) with modified adjusted gross income up to $131,000 can make a full contribution. Contributions are phased-out starting at $116,000 and you cannot make a contribution if your adjusted gross income is in excess of $131,000. • Joint filers with modified adjusted gross income up to $193,000 can make a full contribution. Once again, this contribution is phased-out starting at $183,000 and you cannot make a contribution if your adjusted gross income is in excess of $193,000.
Funds can be used to purchase a variety of investments (stocks, real estate, precious metals, notes, etc.)	Funds can be used to purchase a variety of investments (stocks, real estate, precious metals, notes, etc.)
IRA investments grow tax-free until distribution (tax deferral)	All earnings and principal are 100% tax free if rules and regulations are followed – No tax on distributions so maximum tax-deferral
Income/gains from IRA investments are tax-free	Income/gains from IRA investments are tax-free
Purchasing a real estate property than taking possession of the property after 59½. would be subject to tax	Purchasing a domestic or foreign real estate property then taking possession after 59/1/2 would be tax-free

"In general," John said, "the main reason people establish Roth IRAs is to generate tax-free income and gains from the investment. Remember, as long as the Roth IRA has been opened at least five years and you are over the age of 59½, all income and gains from your Roth IRA are tax-free."

"That's what they call a qualified Roth IRA distribution, correct?" Rich said.

"Correct," John said. "The advantage of contributing to a self-directed Roth IRA is that income and gains generated by the Roth IRA investment can be tax-free and penalty-free as long as certain requirements are satisfied. Unlike with a traditional self-directed IRA, contributions to a self-directed Roth IRA are not tax-deductible."

"Are there other differences?" Rich asked.

"Yes. Unlike the self-directed traditional IRA, there is no 70½ age limit on making contributions. Individuals of any age with compensation are eligible to contribute to a self-directed Roth IRA. The total amount you may contribute to a self-directed Roth IRA for 2015 cannot exceed the lesser of $5,500 ($6,500 if over the age of 50) or 100 percent of compensation ($11,000 for married couples, $13,000 if over the age of 50). If you maintain a traditional self-directed IRA, the maximum contribution to your self-directed Roth IRA is reduced by any contributions made to your traditional self-directed IRAs."

"I remember you saying that if you make too much money you can't have a Roth IRA," Rich said. "Is that true?"

"Pretty much. The same general contribution limit applies to both Roth and traditional IRAs. However, your Roth IRA contribution might be limited based on your filing status and income. You can consult the chart I gave you earlier that detailed the Roth IRA income level limitations for 2015," John said.

"I heard there is still a way to have a Roth IRA even if you make too much money," Rich said. "How does that work?"

"You're right," John said. "It's called the backdoor Roth IRA. Higher-income investors who want access to Roth IRAs may need to use the back door. The back-door Roth IRA works as like this:

(1) The high earner would make a nondeductible contribution to a traditional IRA

(2) The individual would then convert the nondeductible traditional IRA to a Roth IRA. No tax would be due on the conversion because the initial IRA contribution was nondeductible."

"What's the difference between a nondeductible IRA and a Roth IRA?" Rich asked.

"The main difference between a nondeductible IRA and a Roth IRA," John said, "is that in the case of a nondeductible IRA, there would be no deduction when your money goes in and when you money comes out; only the contributions would be tax-free and all the income and appreciation on the amount contributed would be subject to tax. In contrast, with a Roth IRA, there would be no tax deduction when your money goes in, but when your money comes out, it's all tax-free as long as the Roth IRA has been open at least five years and you are over the age of 59½ (a qualified distribution). In other words, with a Roth IRA, all contributions, appreciation, and income are tax-free as long as there is a qualified distribution. My recommendation is that funds in a nondeductible IRA should be converted to a Roth IRA as soon as feasible so that the appreciation could be tax-free."

"Great," Rich said. "So, you keep mentioning this five-year rule and being over the age of 59½ to take a tax-free Roth IRA distribution. Can you explain this in more detail?"

"Sure," John said. "You can withdraw contributions you made to your self-directed Roth IRA any time, tax- and penalty-free. However, you may have to pay taxes and penalties on earnings in your Roth IRA."

The Roth IRA Distribution Rules

"I know we covered the Roth IRA distribution rules way back when we first started talking, but I think it would be helpful if we revisited the rules again, just briefly," said John. "In general, distributions from a Roth IRA that are not qualified may be subject to income tax and an additional 10 percent early distribution penalty."

"Can you please remind me what a qualified distribution is?" Rich asked.

"A qualified distribution is a distribution from a Roth IRA that meets both of the following two categories of requirements:

1. It occurs at least five years after the Roth IRA owner established and funded his or her first Roth IRA. *Remember, all Roth IRAs of an individual are counted for determining the five-year period.*
2. It is distributed under one of the following circumstances:
   * The Roth IRA holder is at least age 59½ when the distribution occurs.
   * The Roth IRA holder becomes disabled before the distribution.
   * The beneficiary of the Roth IRA holder receives the assets after his or her death.
   * The distributed assets will be used toward the purchase or re-building of a first home for the Roth IRA holder or a qualified family member. This is limited to $10,000 per lifetime.

"So what about distributions that are nonqualified? How are they taxed?" Rich asked.

"The IRS categorizes withdrawals from a Roth IRA in a specific order," John explained. "When you make a withdrawal from any of your Roth IRAs, you may have several accounts. The first withdrawals you make are considered to be your contributions. This allows you the most flexibility and saves you from taxes and potential penalties when you start withdrawing your money from a Roth IRA."

"Good to know," Rich said.

"After you have exhausted the limits of your contributions, the IRS considers withdrawals to be conversion contributions from a traditional IRA or a 401(k) retirement plan. These contributions are calculated on a first-in, first-out basis. And, finally, any other withdrawals that are made are then considered to be from your Roth IRA's earnings and income, which must be a qualified withdrawal unless it falls into an exemption or you are 59½ years old or older. Here is the breakdown of the Roth IRA distribution ordering rules:

1. Regular Roth IRA contributions
2. Taxable conversion and rollover amounts
3. Nontaxable conversion and rollover amounts
4. Earnings on all Roth IRA assets

"Don't worry," John said. "I'll go through all these rules again and give examples of how a nonqualified Roth IRA distribution is taxed when we talk about the taxation of self-directed IRA distributions."

"Okay," Rich said.

IRA Roth Conversion and the Roth IRA Distribution Rules

"What about if I do a Roth conversion?" Rich asked. "How do the early distribution penalties work?"

"The penalty rules regarding conversions are a bit different from those for annual contributions, which may be taken at any time for any purpose free of income taxes and penalty. An early withdrawal of a conversion contribution has a different twist. The early withdrawal penalty applies to a distribution of conversion money from a Roth IRA from an individual under the age of 59½ in a few situations.

1. The distribution is made within the five-tax-year period starting with the year that the conversion was distributed from a traditional IRA.
2. Only to the extent that the distribution is attributable to amounts that were includable in gross income as a result of the conversion.

"In general," John said, "when doing a Roth conversion, you can take a distribution of the funds that were converted at any time without tax. However, an early distribution penalty of 10 percent would apply if the five-year holding period from date of conversion was not satisfied and you are under the age of 59½."

"How about an example?" Rich said.

"Let's say Joe made a $20,000 conversion from his regular IRA to a Roth IRA in 2008. The entire amount converted was includable in Joe's income for 2008. Joe made no additional contributions or conversions to a Roth IRA in 2008 or in later years. In 2011, before he is age 59½, Joe withdraws $10,000 from the Roth IRA. Joe will have no tax to pay on this withdrawal because he paid income taxes on the full $20,000 he converted in 2008; however, he will have to pay a 10 percent penalty (or $1,000) unless one of the IRA early withdrawal exceptions apply. Why? Because Joe was under the age of 59½ when he took the distribution. If Joe, had been over the age of 59½ when he took the distribution, there would have been no tax or 10 percent penalty since the amount distributed was part of the taxable Roth IRA conversion. Also keep in mind, the income or gains generated from the Roth IRA conversion amount would be subject to the regular Roth IRA distribution rules."

"So, if you are going to take funds early from your Roth IRA, weigh your conversion decision very carefully," Rich said.

"That's the lesson," John agreed.

"The Roth IRA sounds really good," Rich said. "Can I move from a traditional IRA to a Roth IRA if I am a high-income earner?"

"Beginning in 2010," John said, "the modified adjusted gross income (AGI) and filing status requirements for converting a traditional IRA to a Roth IRA were eliminated. This means that no matter what you income level is, you can do a Roth conversion any time. When you do a Roth IRA conversion, you must pay tax on the amount converted. Tax is due when you file your income tax return for the year the conversion was taken and the amount converted is added to your income to determine your applicable income tax rate. So, if you elected to do a Roth IRA conversion in January 2014, you would not have to pay tax on the amount converted until April 15, 2015. You can convert pretax IRA funds in cash or in-kind, such as stocks or real estate, but you will be required to pay tax on the fair market value of the asset and not what you paid for the asset."

"What's the reason behind the Roth IRA conversion rule change?" Rich asked.

"Really it goes back to the 2008 financial crisis," John said, "which significantly reduced the government's revenues. In response, the IRS loosened its Roth IRA conversion rules and actually encouraged people to make Roth IRA conversions in order to generate immediate tax revenue for the Treasury even if it would ultimately cost them tax dollars in the future."

Things to Consider When Contemplating a Roth IRA Conversion

"What should you think about when deciding whether to convert your traditional IRA to a self-directed Roth IRA LLC?" Rich asked.

"Most importantly, do you have the ability to pay income taxes on the money you convert from your traditional IRA?" John said. "Based on your income tax bracket, does it make sense to pay the entire tax due in 2015? If you expect your rate to go up, converting may be for you. If you think it will go down, then the opposite holds true. Do you anticipate withdrawing Roth IRA funds for personal use within five years of conversion? If so, you may face taxes and penalties if you withdraw within five years of a conversion. Converting a traditional IRA to a Roth self-directed Roth IRA LLC has a number of tax advantages and can offer you multiple retirement and estate-planning benefits."

Roth IRA Discount Valuation Strategy

"I've heard of some people trying to get a discount on the value of property being converted," Rich said. "How risky is that?"

"The amount of taxable income on a Roth conversion is based on the fair market value of the IRA assets subject to the conversion," John answered. "So, the lower the fair market value of the IRA assets, the lower the taxes that will be due on the Roth conversion. In general, according to case law, the standard of fair market value is an objective test using hypothetical buyers and sellers. Furthermore, in determining the valuation of an LLC, the assets to be valued must be the interests in the entity. Certain retirement tax professionals and valuation experts have helped clients in specific situations take a discount when determining the fair market value of the IRA assets subject to the Roth conversion, thus reducing the amount of tax one would have to pay on the conversion."

"How does that work?" Rich asked.

"The Roth conversion valuation discount strategy is based on techniques used in the context of family limited partnerships looking to take gift tax discounts of certain assets for estate-planning purposes. The valuation discounts applicable to an LLC with IRA assets typically fall into two categories: (1) a discount for lack of control, and (2) a discount for lack of marketability. I have had a number of clients use this discount valuation strategy for their Roth IRA and were able to take a discount of anywhere from 15 percent to 35 percent on the value of the IRA assets subject to the Roth conversion. I did not recommend this and really don't think it makes much sense, especially if you only have a few hundred thousand dollars in funds being converted. For example if you have $200,000 and want to try to get 20 percent discount valuation on the funds being converted, that means that you would be paying tax on $160,000 and not $200,000. If you assume a 30 percent income tax rate, that is only a savings of $12,000 ($60,000 tax on $200,000 vs. a $48,000 tax on $160,000)."

"Is that really worth it?" Rich asked.

John nodded. "You have to ask yourself whether it's worth potentially triggering an IRS audit for such a small tax savings. And the IRS does not have to accept your appraisal of discounted position, so the onus is on you as the taxpayer to provide the discounted valuation."

"How has that played out?" Rich asked.

"I've had clients that had a traditional IRA and want to convert to a self-directed Roth IRA LLC to purchase raw land, real estate, precious metals, or invest in an investment fund and used a type of Roth conversion valuation discount strategy to save thousands in taxes."

"But using a Roth discount strategy for taking a Roth conversion is highly risky and not recommended," Rich said.

"Right," John said. "Remember, you're playing with the IRS's tax money, and unless you are really confident in your discounted position in connection with the Roth IRA conversion, I would stay away from this strategy."

Roth IRA Tax Strategies

"What are some examples of tax strategies using a self-directed Roth IRA LLC?" Rich said.

"Using a self-directed Roth IRA LLC presents a number of exciting tax planning opportunities. The primary advantage of using a self-directed Roth IRA LLC to make investments is that all income and gains associated with the Roth IRA investment grow tax-free and will not be subject to tax upon withdrawal or distribution. This is because unlike traditional IRAs, you are generally not subject to any tax upon taking Roth IRA distributions once you reach the age of 59½ and the Roth IRA has been opened for five years. This presents a number of exciting tax strategies:

- Purchasing a vacation home with Roth IRA funds and moving in tax-free at age 59½
- Purchasing a retirement home with Roth IRA funds and moving in tax-free at age 59½
- Purchasing an office building with Roth IRA funds and then using the building for your own business after you turn 59½
- Investing in precious metals and then taking possession of the metals once you reach the age of 59½
- Investing in tax deeds and then taking possession of the property personally once you reach the age of 59½
- Investing in a distressed property—generating large gains and then withdrawing the funds tax-free for personal use upon reaching the age of 59½
- Investing in an investment fund—generating large gains and then withdrawing the funds tax-free for personal use upon reaching the age of 59½

Self-Directed Roth IRA Investments

"I assume if you can generate strong returns with your self-directed Roth IRA investments, you can build up a nice tax-free retirement nest egg pretty quickly," Rich said.

"Using a self-directed Roth IRA to purchase real estate or make other alternative-asset investments is the most tax-beneficial way to make such investments. With federal and state income tax rates expected to increase in the future, gaining the ability to generate tax-free returns from your retirement investments when you retire is the last surviving legal tax shelter. With a self-directed Roth IRA you can make almost any investment tax-free, including real estate, tax liens, precious metals, currencies, options, and private business investments, and once you hit the age of 59½ you will be able to live off your Roth assets without ever paying tax. Imagine if someone told you that if you started making Roth IRA contributions in your forties and by just generating a modest rate of return on your real estate investments, you could have over a million dollars tax-free when you retire. Once you have reached the age of 59½ and have had the Roth IRA plan opened for at least five years, all income and gains from your self-directed Roth IRA can be used tax-free and penalty-free. You can also pass the Roth IRA funds to your spouse or children upon your death, allowing them to use the Roth funds for any purpose without paying tax."

"Sounds great," Rich said. "What are some of the tax advantages of buying real estate or making alternative assets with a self-directed Roth IRA?"

Tax-Free Growth

"The primary benefit lies in the power of tax-free investing," John said. "One of the main attractions to the self-directed Roth IRA is that qualified distributions of Roth earnings are tax-free. As long as certain conditions are met and the distribution is a qualified distribution (the Roth IRA holder is over the age of 59½ and any Roth IRA account has been open for at least five years), the Roth IRA holder will never pay tax on any Roth distributions received."

"How about an example to show the power of tax-free investing?" Rich said.

Example 1:

Joe, a self-employed consultant began funding a self-directed Roth IRA with $3,000 per year at age twenty and would continue on through age sixty-five. At age sixty-five Joe would wind up with $2.5 million at retirement (assuming they earn the long-run annual compound growth rate in stocks, which was 9.88 percent from 1926 to 2011). Not a bad result for investing only $3,000 a year.

Example 2:

Ben, who is thirty years old, began funding a Roth IRA with $4,000 and wanted to know how much he would have at age seventy if he continued to make $4,000 annual contributions and was able to earn at an 8 percent rate of return. Ben did some research and was astonished that at age seventy he would have a whopping $1,119.124 tax-free, which he could then live on or pass to his wife or children tax-free.

Example 3:

Mary, who is thirty-five years old, began funding a Roth IRA with $5,000 and wanted to know how much she would have at age seventy if she continued to make $5,000 annual contributions and was able to earn at a 10 percent rate of return, which she felt was possible based on her past investment returns. Mary did some research and was astonished that at age seventy she would have a whopping $1,490.634 tax-free, which she could then live on or pass to her husband and children tax-free.

Example 4:

Steve, who is eighteen years old, began funding a Roth IRA with just $1,200 and wanted to know how much he would have at age seventy if he continued to make just a $1,200 annual contributions and was able to earn at an 8 percent rate of return. Steve did some research and was astonished that at age seventy he would have a whopping $870,038 tax-free, which he could then live on or pass to his wife or children tax-free. By just saving $100 a month, Steve would be able to have close to $900,000 tax-free when he retired.

"It's hard to comprehend that putting away just a few thousand dollars a year in a Roth IRA can leave you with millions of dollars tax-free," Rich said.

"I know," John said, "But it's as simple as making annual contributions to your self-directed Roth IRA and then generating tax-free returns from making real estate or other investments with your self-directed Roth IRA. The earlier you start making contributions to your IRA, the better. Of course, starting at any point is good. Take the example of Ron, who is forty-five years old, and began funding a Roth IRA with $5,500 and wanted to know how much he would have at age seventy if he continued to make $5,500 annual contributions and was able to earn an 8 percent rate of return. At age seventy, Ron would have $434,249 tax-free, which he could then live on or pass to his wife or children tax-free."

"What about a self-employed person? Is the Roth IRA the best option?" Rich asked.

"If you're self-employed, I certainly recommend the solo 401(k) plan because of the high contribution options, especially in the case of Roth contributions. A solo 401(k) plan is a 401(k) qualified retirement plan that is established by any business that has no full-time employees (over 1,000 hours) other than the business owner(s) and spouse(s). It is far more robust than a SEP IRA, which is another popular retirement plan for a small business and does not include a Roth feature, because the solo 401(k) plan has an employee deferral feature, loan feature of $50,000, and high Roth contribution options."

"Can you touch on the Roth contributions benefits again?" Rich asked.

John nodded. "A Roth solo 401(k) combines features of the traditional 401(k) with those of the Roth IRA. Like a solo 401(k) plan, the Roth solo 401(k) plan is perfect for any self-employed individual or small-business owner with no employees. The Roth solo 401(k) plan contains the same advantages of a solo 401(k) plan, but as with a Roth IRA, contributions are made with after-tax dollars. While you don't get an up-front tax-deduction, the Roth 401(k) account grows tax-free, and withdrawals taken during retirement aren't subject to income tax, provided you're at least 59½ and you've held the account for five years or more. For the 2015 taxable year, an individual under the age of fifty can make an after-tax Roth solo 401(k) plan contribution of up to $18,000, whereas an individual over the age of fifty can make Roth solo 401(k) plan contributions of up to $24,000 for the 2015 taxable year. As for the employer profit-sharing contributions, the employer may make contributions equal to 25 percent (20 percent in the case of a sole proprietorship or single-member LLC) of the plan participant's W-2 or self-employment income amount up to $53,000 ($59,000 for individuals over the age of fifty), including any employee deferrals made by the employee during the year. The employer profit-sharing contributions must be made pretax, but as of 2013, those employer contributions can be converted immediately to Roth as long as the solo 401(k) plan allows for in-plan Roth conversions. A tax would have to be paid on the Roth conversion amount, but one would technically be able to make Roth contributions of up to $53,000 ($59,000 if over the age of fifty) for the 2015 taxable year, almost ten times the amount of an IRA."

Making Investments with a Self-Directed Roth IRA

"I assume you make self-directed Roth IRA investments the same way you would make investments with a traditional pretax self-directed IRA," Rich said.

"Absolutely," John said. "The only difference lies in the type of IRA being used and the taxation of the income and appreciation. In the case of a pretax IRA, just like a Roth IRA, all income and gains would flow back to the IRA without tax. The difference lies in the distribution rules. In general, with a pretax IRA, distributions prior to the age of 59½ are subject to income tax and a 10 percent early distribution penalty, and distributions after the age of 59½ are just subject to income tax. In contrast, with a Roth IRA, as long as the Roth IRA has been open at least five years and the individual is over the age of 59½, there is generally no tax on any distributions from the Roth IRA. This obviously leads to a number of exciting tax-planning opportunities and strategies."

Using a Self-Directed Roth IRA to Invest in a Business

"Can I use my Roth IRA to invest in my business and shelter all income from tax?" Rich asked.

"Unfortunately, no," John said. "The same prohibited transaction rules that apply to traditional IRAs also apply to Roth IRAs. So, just as you are not permitted to invest your traditional IRA in your own business as it would violate the prohibited transaction rules under IRC 4975, the same rules would apply to Roth IRAs. Imagine if you can invest your Roth IRA funds in your own business and shelter all the income tax for your business. That would be pretty nice, but unfortunately the IRS doesn't feel the same way. In fact, the IRS has issued a number of letter rulings outlining this exact type of situation, so it is highly risky to try to use a Roth IRA to shelter personal or business income. Not only could it trigger civil penalties, but the IRS could also pursue criminal charges."

"What about investing a Roth IRA in a friend's business. Can I shelter all income from tax?"

"Yes and no," John said. "On the yes side, just like with a traditional IRA, you could use a self-directed Roth IRA to invest in a friend's business or any nondisqualified person's business. However, if the business is being conducted via an LLC or other flow-through entity, the UBTI tax would kick in and could potentially impose a 35 percent tax on the business income allocated to your Roth IRA. So, it would turn your potentially tax-free investment into a very tax-unfriendly investment. You would need to run the numbers and see how the UBTI tax would affect your expected returns and would need to determine whether using personal funds instead of Roth IRA funds would make more sense."

"What about using a nonrecourse loan?" Rich asked. "Do the UBTI tax rules apply to Roth IRAs?"

"Unfortunately, the UBTI tax rules apply to all IRAs, including Roth IRAs," John said. "So, using a nonrecourse loan when buying real estate with a self-directed Roth IRA would trigger the UBTI tax just as it would for a pretax traditional IRA. The only difference is that with a Roth IRA you have the potential to generate tax-free returns, so using a nonrecourse loan to buy real estate is something that must be closely examined as it could potentially impose a 35 percent tax or so on your Roth IRA returns."

"Are there any differences in the types of investments I can make with a Roth IRA vs. a traditional IRA?" Rich asked.

"No," John said. "You can make the same types of investments as you can make with a traditional IRA. The same restrictions against purchasing life insurance and collectibles still apply to a Roth IRA as well as the prohibited transaction rules under IRC 4975. The main differences between a pretax traditional IRA and a Roth IRA from an investment perspective is that with a Roth IRA all income and gains generated by the investment can be taken tax-free as long as the Roth IRA holder is over the age of 59½ and the Roth IRA has been open at least five years, whereas, in the case of a pretax IRA, income and gains would be subject to tax after the IRA holder reached the age of 59½ and an additional 10 percent prepayment penalty would apply for an IRA holder who takes a pretax IRA distribution under the age of 59½."

Self-Directed Roth IRA Estate-Planning Opportunities

"I've heard that the Roth IRA also offered some estate-planning opportunities," Rich said. "What about that?"

"In addition to the significant tax benefits in using a self-directed Roth IRA LLC to make investments," John said, "the Roth IRA also offers a number of very exciting estate-planning opportunities."

"Such as?"

"In general," John said, "in addition to tax-free growth and no tax on qualified Roth IRA distributions, a Roth IRA holder would not be subject to the required minimum distribution rules (RMD)."

"What about when it comes to estate taxes?" Rich asked.

"In general, an IRA, whether a traditional or a Roth, is included in the owner's gross estate," John said. "You can't avoid that. But when a traditional IRA is inherited, the beneficiary must include all distributions in gross income just as the original owner would have. The distributions are taxed at the beneficiary's ordinary income tax rate. The beneficiary is able to stretch out the distributions over his or her life expectancy, but annual distributions are required and will be taxed. So, when passing a traditional IRA to a spouse or child, the beneficiary is required to pay ordinary income tax on the IRA distribution amount taken, which would reduce the amount of traditional IRA funds available to spend, whereas a Roth IRA that is left to a beneficiary would not be subject to tax when a distribution is taken."

"What are the estate-planning benefits of converting a traditional IRA to a Roth IRA?" Rich asked.

"In a conversion of a traditional IRA to a Roth IRA, the IRA converted amount is as though it were taken as a distribution. So, you would be subject to ordinary income taxes on the converted amount. Of course, there's no restriction on the amount of IRA funds that can be converted at one time."

"What are the estate tax benefits of a Roth IRA conversion?" Rich asked.

"Mostly that the Roth IRA holder's estate is reduced by the income taxes paid on the amount of the Roth IRA conversion. There are several estate-planning benefits to paying tax on the Roth conversion while you are alive."

"How do you turn taxable distributions into tax-free distributions?" Rich asked.

"Doing a Roth IRA conversion is, in effect, paying the taxes on the IRA funds for your heirs. They would have owed the taxes in the future when they were required to take a distribution from the inherited IRA. Instead, the Roth IRA holder would be paying the tax now, out of his/her taxable estate, and avoid estate and gift taxes on that amount. Thereafter, when your beneficiary would take a distribution from the inherited Roth IRA, those Roth IRA distributions would be tax-free."

"Can you pay tax and reduce estate taxes?" Rich asked.

"Paying the taxes now reduces the size of your estate and any estate tax bill. This isn't a factor for estates below the taxable level ($5.43 million for 2015), but it could be important for taxable estates."

"What are the tax benefits for a lifetime?" Rich asked.

"A Roth IRA conversion can provide lifetime income tax benefits to the Roth IRA holder and it can also benefit your beneficiaries. When you maintain a traditional IRA, after age 70½ you're required to take minimum annual distributions, which would be subject to income tax. If it turned out that you didn't need this money for spending or living purposes, it simply increases the taxes you would be required to pay. In addition, being required to take a traditional IRA distribution could increase your income enough to push you into a higher tax bracket, reduce itemized deductions, increase taxes on social security benefits, and have other effects. The older you become, the higher the required distributions and taxes become. With a Roth IRA, you or your beneficiaries could benefit from tax-free appreciation of the Roth IRA assets as well as generating tax-free income to live off of."

"What about tax-free growth and tax-free income?" Rich asked.

"Once the traditional IRA has been converted to a Roth IRA, the Roth IRA holder and his or her beneficiaries would be able to benefit from tax-free growth and income generated by the Roth IRA. In other words, the assets of the Roth IRA will be able to grow tax-free and all qualified distributions from the Roth IRA would be tax-free, allowing the Roth IRA holder or his or her beneficiaries to live off of the Roth IRA funds without ever having to pay tax on the income."

"So it's an opportunity to take advantage of historically low tax rates," Rich said.

"Even though a lot has been made of the increasing Obamacare tax rates, our current income tax rates are still at historical lows. It is conceivable that income tax rates will rise in the future, especially with the high levels of debt being used by the government to stimulate the economy. Doing a Roth IRA conversion now versus later could potentially be a tax-savvy decision if the Roth IRA grows at a respectable rate and if tax rates increase. Having a Roth IRA to use or offer to your beneficiaries in a high-tax environment will prove to be extremely tax beneficial."

"Where does the Roth stretch IRA fit into the estate-planning benefits?" Rich asked.

"I'm glad you brought up the Roth stretch IRA because it's actually a really neat estate-planning tool that I almost forgot to mention," John said. "Unlike the original Roth IRA owner, a nonspousal beneficiary of a Roth IRA is required to take minimum distributions over his or her life expectancy. Remember, a spousal beneficiary of a Roth IRA is not required to take a Roth IRA distribution."

"Great," Rich said.

"In the case of a nonspousal Roth IRA beneficiary," John continued, "when the beneficiary is relatively young, there is the potential for the distributions to be less than the annual earnings of the Roth IRA, so the Roth IRA grows while the distributions are being taken. Of course, the beneficiary can take more than the minimum, even the entire Roth IRA, at any time tax-free. In other words, using a self-directed Roth stretch IRA will allow an individual to transfer tax-free assets to children or other beneficiaries and allow those individuals to benefit from tax-free income while the Roth IRA continues to grow tax-free. The Roth stretch IRA strategy generally works best when the beneficiary is young so that Roth IRA distributions can be taken over a longer period of time, allowing the Roth IRA to continue to grow tax-free."

"I really like the Roth IRA concept a lot," Rich said. "How do you decide between the traditional IRA and Roth IRA?"

"Unfortunately there is no right or wrong answer when it comes to deciding whether you should make contributions to a self-directed IRA or self-directed Roth IRA. The decision generally depends on a variety of factors, which are generally fact- and circumstance-based:

- If you expect your retirement tax rate to be equal or higher than it is today, a self-directed Roth IRA should yield the greatest benefit.
- If you expect your retirement tax rate to be much lower than it is today, you may want to choose making contributions to a self-directed traditional IRA.

- If you expect your investment to generate strong returns, then a self-directed Roth IRA could be an option.
- The younger one is, the more attractive a self-directed Roth IRA is because your Roth IRA will have more time to grow without paying any tax."

Roth IRA Proposed Legislation

"I've read that President Obama has proposed certain new rules with respect to IRAs and specifically Roth IRAs," Rich said. "What about that?"

"There've been some proposals floated by President Obama over the last few years concerning limiting the value of IRAs, even eliminating the pretax IRA, as well as eradicating the backdoor Roth IRA strategy. Most of these proposals were in the president's budgets in 2014, 2015, and 2016 and have not gone anywhere. The president has floated a number of proposals limiting the ability for one to accumulate retirement funds, especially after-tax Roth IRA funds. There are a few IRA proposals the president has floated over the last few years since 2014:

- Required minimum distributions, or RMDs, from Roth IRAs once savers turn 70½—similar to the distributions that people must make from traditional IRAs and other retirement accounts.
- Individuals with less than $100,000 in their combined retirement accounts would no longer have to take required minimum distributions.
- Ending the stretch IRA. That proposal would require nonspouse beneficiaries of deceased IRA owners and retirement plan participants to take inherited distributions over no more than five years instead of being allowed to stretch out the distributions over their lifetimes.
- Limit the size of IRA accounts to $3.4 million.
- Require the original Roth IRA owner to take distributions after 70½.
- Create a 28 percent maximum tax benefit for contributions to retirement accounts.

"Just to be crystal clear," John continued, "none of these proposals are law and none of them apply today. The president and his team stated that one of the reasons behind the IRA proposals is to simplify tax law when it comes to retirement accounts. I am not sold on this answer. I think the real impetus behind the president's numerous proposals to curtail the growth of retirement accounts is to limit the ability of the wealthy to generate and maintain wealth in a tax-friendly manner, which seems to go against some of his social policies. Again, this is just my opinion, but I can't see why if people are able to save and can save a lot of money for their retirement, why that is a negative thing."

"What is the myRA I have heard so much about lately?" Rich asked.

"The myRA is a pilot program and a new type of savings account for Americans who don't have access to an employer-sponsored retirement savings plan. Workers who sign up will be able to have a portion of their paycheck directly deposited into their myRA automatically every payday. But unlike private Roth IRAs, myRAs will be invested solely in government bonds and will be backed by the US government—meaning you can never lose your original investment. Plus, there will be no fees to eat into your annual returns."

"What do you think of it?" Rich asked.

"The myRA is a nice idea to help people who don't have access to a retirement plan at work save money for their retirement," John said. "I am never against retirement savings. The investments will be safe and secure because the funds will be invested in Treasury securities, which means they will be backed by the full faith and credit of the United States. myRAs feature government-backed principal protection, so the account balance will never decrease in value and will earn the same interest rate that is available to federal employees for their retirement savings."

"Is there any downside?" Rich asked.

"The downside is that the myRA requires your funds to be invested in Treasury securities and will earn the same rate as the Thrift Savings Plan's Government Securities Investment Fund that's offered to federal workers. That fund earned less than 2 percent in 2013, although it earned around

5 percent before the financial crisis. Not a great return when you look at what your funds can generate by simply buying an S&P mutual fund. In addition, myRA accounts cannot exceed a maximum balance of $15,000. At that point (or when an account has been open for thirty years), it must be rolled over into a private-sector Roth IRA, where the money can continue to grow tax-free."

"So it's a nice idea but…" Rich said.

"Exactly," John said. "The *but* is that an individual can generally do a lot better just by making a contribution to a pretax or Roth IRA, which is available to any individual with earned income, and in the IRA you are not limited to Treasury securities and can better diversify your retirement portfolio. Also, you would not be capped at $15,000, which is not very significant in terms of retirement savings anyway."

"I really like the Roth IRA and will strongly consider converting my self-directed IRA to a Roth IRA either this year or next," Rich said.

"Okay," John said. "I think that could be a wise move, especially because you are relatively young and you do have the capacity to pay the tax on the conversion. One thing to consider when doing a Roth conversion is that you are paying the tax up front, so if your investment does not work out (remember Enron), you have just paid tax for money you will never see, which is a double whammy. All in all, the Roth IRA is a really great solution for accumulating tax-free wealth while at the same time building a strong estate-planning platform for your family."

"That sounds great," Rich said.

IX

Helpful Tips for Making Investments with a Self-Directed IRA

"So," John began, "now that we've discussed which types of investments can be made with a self-directed IRA and which investments can't be made with a self-directed IRA as covered by the prohibited transaction rules under IRC 408 & 4975, I want to highlight some great tips that helped my clients use a self-directed IRA to make a variety of alternative-asset investments, such as real estate."

"Great. I'm looking forward to this," Rich said.

"First," John said, "what is it that you can and can't do? A self-directed IRA LLC offers you the ability to use your retirement funds to make almost any type of investment on your own without requiring the consent of any custodian or third party. As a gentle reminder, the IRS and Department of Labor only describe the types of investments that are prohibited, which are very few. Those prohibited transaction rules are based on the premise that investments involving the IRA and related parties are handled in a way that should benefit the retirement account and not the IRA owner. The rules prohibit transactions between the IRA and certain individuals known as disqualified persons. The outline for these rules can be found in IRC Section 4975. In general, the definition of a disqualified person [IRC Section 4975(e)(2)] extends to a variety of related-party scenarios but generally includes the IRA holder, any ancestors or lineal descendants of the IRA holder, and entities in which the IRA holder holds a controlling equity or management interest."

Investment Options with My Self-Directed IRA

"Can you give me some examples of the types of investments that can be made with my self-directed IRA LLC?" Rich asked.

"Sure," John said. "Let's go over the list:

- Residential or commercial real estate
- Raw land
- Foreclosure property
- Mortgages
- Mortgage pools
- Deeds
- Private loans
- Tax liens
- Private businesses
- Limited liability companies
- Limited liability partnerships
- Private placements
- Precious metals and certain coins
- Stocks, bonds, mutual funds
- Foreign currencies."

Real Estate

"The IRS permits you to use a self-directed IRA LLC to purchase real estate or raw land."

"Great," Rich said.

"And since you're the manager of the self-directed IRA LLC, making a real estate investment is as simple as writing a check from your self-directed IRA bank account. The advantage of purchasing real estate with your self-directed IRA LLC is that all gains are tax-deferred until a distribution is taken, and distributions are not required until the IRA holder turns 70½. In the case of a Roth self-directed IRA, all gains are tax-free as long as certain requirements are satisfied, and there are no distribution requirements."

"Can you give me an example?" Rich asked.

"Sure. If you purchased a piece of property with your self-directed IRA LLC for $100,000 and later sold the property for $300,000, the $200,000 of gain appreciation would generally be tax-deferred. But if you purchased the property using personal funds (nonretirement funds), the gain would be subject to federal income tax and in most cases state income tax."

"The following are a number of helpful tips that should be kept in mind when using a self-directed IRA to buy real estate."

John handed Rich a list:

Helpful Tips When Using a Self-Directed IRA to Buy Real Estate

- The deposit and purchase price for the real estate property should be paid using self-directed IRA LLC funds or funds from a nondisqualified third party.
- No personal funds or funds from a disqualified person should be used.
- All expenses, repairs, taxes incurred in connection with the self-directed IRA real estate investment should be paid using retirement funds—no personal funds should be used.
- If additional funds are required for improvements or other matters involving the real estate investments, all funds should come from the self-directed IRA or from a nondisqualified person.
- If financing is needed for a real estate transaction, only nonrecourse financing should be used. A nonrecourse loan is a loan that is not personally guaranteed and whereby the lender's only recourse is against the property and not against the borrower.

- With a self-directed IRA, the use of a nonrecourse loan would be subject to tax pursuant to IRC Section 514. The tax rate could reach 35 percent.
- No services should be performed by the IRA holder or disqualified person in connection with the real estate investment. In general, only necessary and required tasks in connection with the maintenance of the self-directed IRA structure, no active services should be performed by the IRA holder or any disqualified person with respect to the real estate transaction.
- Title of the real estate purchased should be in the name of the self-directed IRA LLC. For example, if Joe Smith established a self-directed IRA LLC and named the LLC XYZ, LLC, title to real estate purchased by Joe's self-directed IRA LLC would be as follows: XYZ LLC.
- Keep good records of income and expenses generated by the real estate investment.
- All income, gains, and losses from the self-directed IRA LLC real estate investment should be allocated to the IRA.
- Make sure you perform adequate diligence on the property you will be purchasing, especially if it is in a state you do not live in.
- Make sure you will not be engaging in any self-dealing real estate transactions, which would involve buying or selling real estate that will personally benefit you or a disqualified person.

Tax Liens and Tax Deeds

"How about tax liens or tax deeds?" Rich asked.

"The IRS permits the purchase of tax liens and tax deeds with a self-directed IRA. By using a self-directed IRA to purchase tax liens or tax deeds, your profits are tax-deferred back into your retirement account until a distribution is taken. More importantly," John said, "with a self-directed IRA, you, as manager of the self-directed IRA LLC, will have checkbook control over your retirement funds, allowing you to make purchases on the spot without custodian consent. In other words, purchasing a tax-lien or tax deed is as easy as writing a check!"

John handed Rich a list that described some helpful tips to keep in mind when using a self-directed IRA LLC to purchase tax liens or tax deeds:

Helpful Tips When Using a Self-Directed IRA to Buy Tax Liens/ Deeds

- The deposit and purchase price for the tax lien should be paid using self-directed IRA funds or funds from a nondisqualified third party.
- No personal funds or funds from a disqualified person should be used.
- A check from the self-directed IRA account should be taken to auction or used for the tax lien purchase—no personal checks or cash should be used.
- No credit card should be applied for in the name of the self-directed IRA, as that would violate the IRS prohibited transaction rules. A pure debit card is allowable.
- All income, gains, and losses from tax lien investments should be allocated to the IRA.

Loans and Notes

"As previously discussed, the IRS permits using IRA funds to make loans or purchase notes from third parties. By using a self-directed IRA to make loans or purchase notes from third parties, all interest payments received would be tax-deferred until a distribution is taken (pretax IRA). Distributions are not required until the plan participant turns 70½. In the case of a Roth self-directed IRA, all gains are tax-free."

"And for my example?" Rich said.

"If you use a self-directed IRA to loan money to a friend," John said, "all interest you receive would flow back into your self-directed IRA tax-free. But if you lent your friend money from personal funds (nonretirement funds), the interest received would be subject to federal and, in most cases, state income tax."

"Makes sense," Rich said.

John handed Rich another list that set forth a number of helpful tips to keep in mind when using a self-directed IRA LLC to make a loan or purchase a note.

Helpful Tips When Using a Self-Directed IRA to Buy Loans/Notes

- The loan or note amount should be paid using self-directed IRA funds or funds from a nondisqualified third party.
- No personal funds or funds from a disqualified person should be used in the loan transaction.
- The loan or note should not involve a disqualified person directly or indirectly.
- The loan or note should have a stated interest rate of at least prime as per the *Wall Street Journal* (3.25 percent as of January 1, 2015).
- All interest and principal associated with the loan or note should be allocated to the self-directed IRA.
- It is good practice to have the loan terms documented in a promissory note or loan agreement.
- If you will be acting as the lender, consider securing the loan with an interest or lien in an asset owned by the borrower.
- Make sure you will not be engaging in any self-dealing loan transaction, which would involve a loan or note that will personally benefit you or a disqualified person.

Private Business Investments

"You can also purchase an interest in a privately held business with a self-directed IRA," John said. "The business you purchase can be any entity other than an S corporation (i.e., limited liability company, C corporation, partnership, etc.). When investing in a private business using 401(k) funds, especially if the business will be run through a pass-through entity such as an LLC, it's important to keep in mind the disqualified person and prohibited transaction rules under IRC 4975 and the unrelated business taxable income rules under IRC 512, which would impose a hefty tax on the self-directed IRA private business investment."

John handed Rich yet another list that detailed a number of helpful tips to keep in mind when using a self-directed IRA to make private business investments.

Helpful Tips When Using a Self-Directed to Make Private Business Investments

- The deposit and purchase price for the business should be paid using self-directed IRA or funds from a nondisqualified third party.
- No personal funds or funds from a disqualified person should be used to purchase the business.
- The purchase of the stock or assets of the business should not directly or indirectly benefit the plan participant personally or any disqualified person.
- The purchase of a business operated via an LLC or partnership will potentially trigger the unrelated business taxable income rules under IRC 512 and a corresponding tax of approximately 35 percent would be applied.
- Stock of an S corporation should not be purchased with retirement funds as the S corporation rules only allow individuals to be S corporation shareholders.
- The purchase of stock of a C corporation would not trigger the application of the unrelated business taxable income rules under IRC 512.
- All income, gains, and losses from the purchased business should be allocated to the self-directed IRA.
- The IRA holder or any disqualified person should not have any ownership in the business being purchased and should not directly or indirectly personally benefit from the acquisition.

- Make sure to perform adequate diligence on the business you will be purchasing or investing in, especially if you will be buying the stock/interests and not the assets.
- Make sure you will not be engaging in any business acquisition transaction that would involve buying or selling a business that will personally benefit you or a disqualified person.

IRS-Approved Precious Metals and Coins

"And what about gold and coins?" Rich asked.

"Do you remember our previous discussion on the rules found in IRC 408 pertaining to the type of precious metals and coins that may be purchased with retirement funds?" John asked.

"Yes, I remember that my IRA can invest in one, one-half, one-quarter, or one-tenth ounce US gold coins, or one-ounce silver coins minted by the Treasury Department. It can also invest in certain platinum coins and certain gold, silver, palladium, and platinum bullion."

"That's correct," John replied "The self-directed IRA structure allows for investments into precious metals and certain coins. The advantage of using a self-directed IRA to purchase precious metals and/or coins is that their values generally keep up with or exceed inflation rates better than other investments and any appreciation or gains would be tax-deferred. In addition, IRS-approved metals (bullion) and coins must be held in the physical possession of a US bank or depository."

John slipped Rich another list to add to his collection. "I believe this will offer some very insightful tips when considering purchasing IRS-approved precious metals and coins with a self-directed IRA."

Helpful Tips when Using a Self-Directed IRA to Buy IRS-Approved Precious Metals or Coins

- Only IRS-approved metals and coins may be purchases as per IRC 408(m).

- The IRS-approved precious metals or coins being purchased by the plan should be paid for using self-directed IRA funds or funds from a nondisqualified third party.
- With respect to IRS-approved precious metals, the metals should not be held in the personal possession of any individual.
- With respect to the IRS-approved precious metals, the metals must be held in the physical possession of a US depository or at a US bank.
- An affidavit signed by the manager of the IRA LLC confirming that the IRS-approved precious metals or coins are being purchased and being held in the sole interest of the self-directed IRA and not for any personal benefit is good practice.
- A detailed inventory of the purchased metals and/or coins would be a good idea.
- Copies of all contracts or invoices showing the purchase of the metals or coins would be helpful.
- Pictures of the purchased precious metals and or coins would be helpful proof to show that the assets being held are what was purchased and that there has been no personal benefit derived from the transaction.
- All income, gains, and losses from the purchased precious metals or coins should be allocated to the self-directed IRA.
- IRS-approved precious metals should not be held at a bank outside the United States.
- Perform adequate diligence on the dealer with which you will be transacting for the purchase of metals or coins.

Foreign Currencies

"And there's nothing against foreign currencies, correct?" Rich asked.

"Correct," John said. "The IRS does not prevent the use of IRA funds to purchase foreign currencies. In fact, the self-directed IRA plan structure permits the purchase of foreign currencies. Many believe that foreign currency investments offer liquidity advantages to the stock market as well as significant investment opportunities."

"Is there any limit to which currencies?"

"Not really," John said. "By using a self-directed IRA to purchase foreign currencies, all foreign currency gains generated are tax-deferred until a distribution is taken (pretax IRA distributions are not required until the plan participant turns 70½). In the case of a Roth self-directed IRA, all gains are tax-free."

John provided Rich with a short list that detailed some helpful tips when using a self-directed IRA to purchase foreign currency.

Helpful Tips When Using a Self-Directed IRA to Buy Foreign Currency

- Make sure you have a solid background in trading currencies—they are highly volatile and significantly risky
- If you will be investing with a third party, perform adequate diligence on the individual and make sure the individual has the knowledge to trade foreign currencies and all his/her securities licenses are in good standing.
- Beware of leverage—it is allowable but it would trigger the application of the unrelated business taxable income rules under IRC 512 and thereby a corresponding tax.
- No personal guarantee of any leverage or loan obligation is permitted.
- All income, gains, and losses from the foreign currency transactions should be allocated to the self-directed IRA.

Stocks, Bonds, Mutual Funds, CDs

"And good old-fashioned equities and CDs?" Rich asked.

"You bet," John said. "In addition to nontraditional investments such as real estate, a self-directed IRA may purchase stocks, bonds, mutual funds, and CDs. The advantage of using a self-directed IRA is that you are not limited to just making these types of investments. With a self-directed IRA with checkbook control you can open a stock trading account with any financial institution as well as purchase real estate or tax liens or lend money to a third party. Your investment opportunities are endless! When purchasing stocks or securities with a self-directed IRA, all income and gains, including dividends, would flow back to the plan without tax. With a Roth self-directed IRA LLC, all gains are tax-free. But if you purchased stocks with personal funds, all income and gains would be subject to short-term or long-term capital gains tax.

John handed Rich another list that offered some helpful tips when using a self-directed IRA to purchase traditional equities and the like.

Helpful Tips for Making Stock-Related Investments with a Self-Directed IRA

- If you will be investing with a third party, perform adequate diligence on the individual and make sure the individual has the knowledge to trade stocks or securities and all his/her securities licenses are in good standing.
- Beware of promoters who are promising high returns and who do not work at reputable financial institutions—there is a high likelihood of fraud.
- Beware of leverage—it is allowable but it would trigger the application of the unrelated business taxable income rules under IRC 512 and thereby a corresponding tax.
- No personal guarantee of any leverage or loan obligation is permitted.
- Open up a brokerage account in the name of the self-directed IRA—not a personal account (in the case of a self-directed IRA LLC, the account should be in the name of the LLC).
- All income, gains, and losses from the stock investments should be allocated to the self-directed IRA.

Beware of the Prohibited Transaction Rules

"What about those prohibited transactions?" Rich asked.

"Definitely," John said. "You need to make sure that you're not engaged in any self-dealing when buying or selling real estate or violating any of the prohibited transaction rules in connection with any self-directed IRA investment. In other words, if the purchase or sale personally benefits you or a disqualified person in any way, directly or indirectly, it would likely be a prohibited transaction. Similarly, no active services should be performed by you or any disqualified person in connection with the real estate investment. So, you can't use a disqualified person as your real estate agent, tax accountant, adviser, property manager, and so on. Remember, the IRC does not describe what a self-directed IRA can invest in, only what it cannot invest in. IRC Sections 408 & 4975 prohibit disqualified persons from engaging in certain types of transactions. The purpose of these rules is to encourage the use of IRAs for the accumulation of retirement savings and to prohibit those in control of IRAs from taking advantage of the tax benefits for their personal account."

Beware of the Unrelated Business Income Tax

"Is there anything else I need to watch out for?" Rich asked.

"A couple things," John said. "In general, when it comes to using a self-directed IRA to make investments, those investments are exempt from federal income tax. This is because an IRA is exempt from tax pursuant to IRC Section 408, and IRC Section 512 exempts most forms of investment income generated by an IRA from taxation. Some examples of exempt types of income include interest from loans, dividends, annuities, royalties, most rentals from real estate, and gains/losses from the sale of real estate or other capital assets. In almost all cases, the UBTI tax will not apply to your self-directed IRA investments since most IRA investments generally generate income exempt from the UBTI tax."

"What kind of income could subject a self-directed IRA to UBTI?" Rich asked.

"Income generated from the following sources," John said.

- Income from the operations of an active trade or business—i.e., a restaurant, gas station, store, etc.
- Business income generated via a pass-through entity, such as an LLC or partnership
- Using a nonrecourse loan to purchase a real estate asset
- Using margin on a stock purchase

"Margin, huh?" Rich said.

John nodded. "You do need to be careful about investments that involve margins, a nonrecourse loan, or an investment in any active trade or business made through a pass-through entity, such as an LLC, or with any active business or an investment fund that will use leverage or invest in active businesses operated as pass-through entities."

"What about buying public stock, such as Apple or IBM, or investing in a business run by a nondisqualified person that operates as a C corporation?" Rich asked. "I want to avoid UBTI at all costs."

"That sort of investment will not trigger the UBTI tax," John said. "But you're right to want to avoid it. Triggering the UBTI tax could be the difference between the investment making economic sense or not. Being required to pay close to 35 percent tax on investment income that you expected to be tax-deferred or tax-free really changes things for most people in terms of whether the investment makes sense or not."

Beware of Fraud

"Is there anything to worry about in terms of the safety of the investments?" Rich asked.

"As with any investment, you always have to beware of fraud," John said. "While self-directed IRAs and 401(k) plans can be a safe way to invest retirement funds, investors should be mindful of potential fraudulent schemes when using a self-directed retirement structure."

"Any examples?" Rich said.

"Recently the Securities and Exchange Commission (SEC) issued an investor alert to warn investors of the potential risks of fraud associated with investing through self-directed individual retirement accounts [self-directed IRAs and solo 401(k) plans]."

John handed Rich a copy of the SEC Investor Alert (see Exhibit K). The SEC notes that there has been an increase in reports or complaints of fraudulent investment schemes that utilized a self-directed IRA or solo 401(k) plan as a key feature."

"So what do you watch out for?" Rich asked.

"You always need to undertake your own evaluation of the merits of any proposal, and you should check with regulators about the background and history of an investment and its promoters before making a decision when considering a self-directed retirement structure. You should understand that the custodians of a self-directed retirement account may have limited duties to investors, and that the custodians and trustees for these accounts will generally not evaluate the quality or legitimacy of an investment and its promoters. As with every investment, investors also need to undertake their own evaluation of the merits of a proposal, and should check with regulators about the background and history of an investment and its promoters before making a decision."

"So how would fraud occur?" Rich asked.

"Fraud occurs when a person or business intentionally deceives another with promises of goods, services, or financial benefits that do not exist, were never intended to be provided, or were misrepresented. Typically, victims give money but never receive what they paid for."

"Who are the typical victims of fraud?" Rich asked.

"Virtually anyone can fall prey to fraudulent crimes. Con artists do not pass over anyone due to such factors as a person's age, finances, educational level, gender, race, culture, ability, or geographic location. In fact, fraud perpetrators often target certain groups based on these factors."

"Who commits fraud crimes?" Rich asked.

"According to the US government, fraud criminals, like their victims, vary educationally, socially, geographically, and financially. Most con artists make a career of their criminal activities. Some even join professional organizations to legitimize their schemes and project a respectable front."

"What are some common types of fraud?" Rich asked.

"The weapon of choice for fraud criminals is not a gun or a knife. Rather, it's most often a telephone, letter, glossy publication, or brochure offering free vacations, merchandise, investment opportunities, or services. Not all frauds involve the direct selling of goods to consumers. Some frauds target institutions or businesses."

Examples:

- Telemarketing fraud (telephone solicitation for phony goods or services)
- Mail fraud
- Health care and insurance fraud
- Pension and trust fund fraud
- Credit card and check fraud (including fraud by impersonation resulting from theft of mail or credit cards)
- Identity theft
- Fraud related to securities, commodities, and other investments
- Bank fraud
- Embezzlement
- Pyramid or Ponzi schemes
- Advance fee schemes
- Internet fraud

John handed Rich a list of some helpful information and links to a number of organizations that can help a retirement investor better protect his or her retirement assets from fraud.

- SEC: The SEC provides information on different products, asset allocations, and risk. http://www.sec.gov/investor/seniors.shtml

- FINRA: FINRA provides an online service for investors to check the backgrounds of brokers called Broker Check. http://www.finra. org/Investors/ToolsCalculators/BrokerCheck/
- FINRA's website also has tools and resources to protect senior investors and help them make informed investment decisions, including "Investor Alerts" that provide timely information on steering clear of investment scams and problems. See http://www.finra.org/Investors/ProtectYourself/InvestorAlerts/index.htm.
- The North American Securities Administrators Association (NASAA) also has helpful information available for specific states. This organization is very proactive in providing resources for senior investors. http://www.nasaa.org/investor-education/
- The Federal Trade Commission (FTC) works for the consumer to prevent fraudulent, deceptive, and unfair business practices in the marketplace and to provide information to help consumers spot, stop, and avoid them. They also enter Internet, telemarketing, identity theft, and other fraud-related complaints into Consumer Sentinel, a secure online database available to hundreds of civil and criminal law enforcement agencies in the US and abroad. The FTC website is http://www.ftc.gov or call 877-FTC-HELP.
- The Better Business Bureau (BBB) www.BBB.org is also an excellent resource for researching businesses that have been reported for fraudulent or deceptive practices.
- The American Association of Retired Persons (AARP) has provided resources and funding for many research projects in various states in order to uncover scams targeted at senior citizens. They also have numerous free publications to help seniors become more astute investors. Go to http://www.aarp.org.

John then gave Rich another list that covered some helpful tips that will help avoid fraudulent self-directed IRA investments and avoid being financially cheated.

- Shred financial documents and paperwork with personal information before you discard them.
- Protect your social security number. Give it out only if absolutely necessary or ask to use another identifier.
- Don't give out personal information over the phone, mail, or Internet unless you know who you are dealing with.
- Don't give out passwords for any of your accounts to anyone.
- Don't give out your credit card numbers to any strangers.
- If you believe the contact is legitimate, go to the company's website by typing in the site address directly or using a page you have previously bookmarked, instead of a link provided in an email.
- Be aware of being kept on the phone for a long time.
- Be wary of promises of quick profits, offers to share "inside" information, and pressure to invest before you have an opportunity to investigate.
- Words like *guarantee, high return, limited offer,* or *as safe as a CD* are red flags.
- Watch out for offshore scams and investment opportunities in other countries.
- Watch out if a company is not registered with the SEC or the secretary of State where it is located.
- Be cautious if a financial adviser cannot be found through FINRA.
- Ask the online promoter whether—and how much—they are being paid to sell the product.
- Make sure you understand the investment before you invest your money.
- Take your time to make decisions.
- Be sure to talk over all financial decisions with a trusted family member, friend, or financial adviser.
- Report any frauds and any potential investment frauds affecting Americans to local, state, or federal regulators.
- Never make a check out to a financial adviser.

- Never allow statements or confirmations to be sent directly to your financial adviser without receiving copies.
- Be wary of pressure to trade the account in a manner that is inconsistent with your investment goals and the risk you want or can afford to take.

"In general, the best prevention technique is to identify and research the persons, products, and companies offering their services," John said. "The more education and understanding of the product features, especially investment products, the higher the level of scrutiny you can apply. In the event of any suspicious calls, emails, or personal solicitations, you should report them to the proper authorities."

"Got it," Rich said.

"Always take the time you need to understand and evaluate a potential investment. Make sure you understand the investment you will be making and thoroughly understand how the promoter will be able to generate the returns being promised. Also, make sure the promoter of the investment has the necessary qualifications or licenses, if applicable, to offer the investment. Be cautious if a sponsor or adviser uses the affiliation as the reason to make the investment, rather than relying on the underlying merits of the investment or trust in the salesperson."

"Sounds good," Rich said.

Keeping Your Self-Directed IRA LLC in Good Standing

"You also need to make sure you meet your LLC tax return filing requirements," John said.

"How do I do that?" Rich asked.

"If your self-directed IRA LLC is owned by one IRA, the LLC is treated as a disregarded entity for federal income tax purposes. So no federal income tax return is required to be filed. But, if two or more IRAs own your LLC, the LLC is treated as a partnership for tax purposes and a federal partnership tax return (IRS Form 1065) and state return must be filed.

You should consult a tax professional for more information to determine whether your self-directed IRA LLC may have any federal or state income tax filing requirements."

"What about annual LLC fees?" Rich asked.

"Some states require annual reports and impose an annual fee for every LLC that was formed in the state," John said. "The state should notify you of this, however, the link below will provide a summary of the LLC annual fees per state. You should consult a tax professional for more information on what annual fees, if any, may apply to your self-directed IRA LLC."

John handed Rich the same chart he had handed him some weeks earlier, which detailed the LLC formation fees in all fifty states and the District of Columbia (see Exhibit D).

Valuing Your Self-Directed IRA

"Finally," John said, "you need to report the valuation of your IRA LLC each year. Your IRA custodian will send you a notice at the end of each year requesting that you provide a valuation of your IRA LLC. The valuation will then be submitted by the IRA custodian to the IRS on Form 5498, which every custodian by law is required to complete. You should consult a tax professional for assistance."

"Will do," Rich said. "That's helpful."

"All in all," John said, "using a self-directed IRA LLC is quite easy and stress-free. However, there are a number of items that you should be careful about when making an investment with a self-directed IRA. Working with a self-directed IRA facilitation firm or consulting with a tax professional is highly advisable."

"I'll make sure to do that," Rich said.

X

Moving Money out of Your Self-Directed IRA

"So, we've spent a lot of time discussing the ins and outs of the self-directed IRA and checkbook control self-directed IRA solution," John said, "including, the process and rules for establish and funding the self-directed IRA, the types and categories of permitted and prohibited investments."

"It's been very helpful," Rich said.

"Let's now look at how you can take funds out of your self-directed IRA by way of distribution as well as how you would go about rolling funds out of the structure to a new custodian."

"That sounds good," Rich said. "I plan on keeping my checkbook control self-directed IRA LLC structure for several years because I don't expect to have any exit strategy with respect to my real estate investment for a number of years. But I am curious how I can get money out of the structure if I need to, or if I want to simply move funds to another IRA custodian."

"We spent some time earlier," John said, "discussing some of the distribution rules for pretax traditional IRAs and Roth IRAs, but let's briefly review them."

Taking a Distribution from a Traditional IRA

"An IRA owner may take distributions from his or her IRA at any time," John said. "The determination of whether the distribution is taxed depends on the type of IRA (i.e., traditional or Roth), the age of the IRA owner, and in the case of a Roth IRA, the duration of time the account has been established. The IRA owner is required to include traditional IRA distributions in his or her taxable gross income. The IRA owner who receives a distribution will report the distribution on his or her individual federal income tax return (Form 1040) and pay tax on the distribution based on the individual's federal income tax rate."

"What kind of IRA-related transactions are not treated as distributions subject to tax?" Rich asked.

"Those would be:

- Rollovers
- Transfers
- Recharacterizations
- Revoked IRA within seven-day period
- The portion of a distribution relating to nondeductible traditional IRA contributions

Exemption from the Early Distribution 10 Percent Tax

"In general," John said, "traditional IRAs are designed to encourage retirement saving and at the same time discourage people from taking money away from their retirement savings before reaching the age of 59½. The age 59½ was selected by Congress because it was believed to be the age when one began transitioning from active employment to retirement. Remember that early distributions are subject to an additional tax. The IRS assesses a 10 percent penalty on the taxable portion of early distributions. However, the 10 percent early distribution penalty does not apply in the following situations:

Death of the IRA Owner

An IRA distribution to beneficiaries is not subject to the 10 percent early distribution penalty. In other words, upon the death of the

IRA owner, the distribution of the owner's IRA to his or her beneficiaries is not subject to the 10 percent penalty.

Disability

Distributions received by a disabled IRA owner are not subject to the 10 percent early distribution penalty. Prior to making the disability distribution, the financial organization may require written evidence from the disabled IRA owner to verify disability. The IRA owner can demonstrate this by using IRS Form 1040, Schedule R, Credit for the Elderly or Disabled.

Rollovers and Conversions

Amounts rolled over to an IRA or properly converted to an IRA are not subject to the 10 percent early distribution penalty.

First-Time Homebuyer Expenses

Distributions taken for qualified first-time homebuyer expenses are not subject to the 10 percent early distribution penalty. There is a $10,000 lifetime limit with this exemption.

Return of Nondeductible Contributions

The 10 percent early distribution penalty would not apply to the portion of a distribution that represents a return of nondeductible contributions or after-tax assets received through a rollover.

Substantially Equal Periodic Payment

The 10 percent early distribution penalty shall not apply to distributions that are part of a series of substantially equal periodic payments made at least annually over the IRA owner's life expectancy or joint life expectancy of the IRA owner and his or her beneficiary. The rules that apply to this option can be found in IRC 72(t) and are quite complex.

Health Insurance

An IRA owner who received federal or state unemployment compensation for twelve consecutive weeks may take IRA distributions to pay for health insurance. These distributions are not subject to the 10 percent early distribution penalty. The IRA owner must take a distribution in the year he received his unemployment or in the year that follows. This exemption does not apply to distributions taken more than sixty days after the IRA owner regains employment.

Medical Expenses

Distributions used for reimbursed medical expenses that exceed 7.5 percent of the IRA owner's adjusted gross income are not subject to the 10 percent early distribution penalty.

Higher Education Expenses

IRA distributions used for qualified education expenses of the IRA owner, his or her spouse, spouse's child, or grandchild are not subject to the 10 percent early distribution penalty.

IRS Levy

Distributions taken because of IRS tax levies imposed on the IRA owner are not subject to the 10 percent early distribution penalty.

Qualified Reservist Distributions

Qualified reservists (including National Guard personnel) called to active duty after September 11, 2001, for a period of at least 180 days or for an indefinite amount of time are permitted to take penalty-free distributions from their IRA. This applies to distributions taken between the date of the order or call to duty and the end of the active duty period. **Note:** The distribution taken will still be subject to federal income tax.

Taking a Distribution from a Self-Directed Roth IRA

"As we discussed earlier, in the case of a Roth IRA, distributions from a Roth IRA that are *not* qualified may be subject to income tax and an additional 10 percent early distribution penalty. A qualified distribution is a distribution from a Roth IRA that meets both of the following two categories of requirements:

1. It occurs at least five years after the Roth IRA was established and the owner funded his or her first Roth IRA.
2. It is distributed under one of the following circumstances:
    *   The Roth IRA holder is at least age 59½ when the distribution occurs.
    *   The Roth IRA holder becomes disabled before the distribution.
    *   The beneficiary of the Roth IRA holder receives the assets after his or her death.

"It's also important to remember that the IRS uses special rules when determining the source of the Roth IRA assets being distributed and the potential tax implications, including funds converted to a Roth IRA," John continued. "Based on the IRS ordering rules, Roth IRA assets are distributed in the following order, keeping in mind that once assets from one source run out, the assets from the next source are distributed:

1. Regular Roth IRA participant contributions
2. Taxable conversion and rollover amounts
3. Nontaxable conversion and rollover amounts
4. Earnings on all Roth IRA assets

"In determining what portion of the distribution is considered to come from contributions as opposed to earnings, you must follow the ordering rules outlined above. For example, Jim made a $5,000 contribution to his Roth IRA in 2010. In 2011, at age 45, Jim's Roth IRA was worth $6,000 and he needed all $6,000 to pay a personal expense. Based on the Roth IRA ordering rules, Jim would be able to take his $5,000 Roth contribution back without tax or penalty but would be required to pay tax and a 10 percent early distribution penalty on the $1,000 of income. This is in contrast to a Roth 401(k) plan that follows a pro rata basis formula for determining the taxation of Roth 401(k) distributions, which is less taxpayer-friendly than the Roth IRA distribution ordering rules discussed above. Also, it is important to remember that the Roth IRA distribution ordering rules apply to all your IRAs in the aggregate.

Taking Early Distributions from Funds Converted to a Roth IRA

"The penalty rules regarding taking early distributions from Roth IRA conversion funds add a twist. The early withdrawal penalty applies to a distribution of conversion money from Roth IRA assets if the plan participant is under the age of 59½ in a few situations," John said.

1. The distribution is made within the five-tax-year period starting with the year that the conversion was distributed from a pretax IRA; and
2. Only to the extent that the distribution is attributable to amounts that were includable in gross income as a result of the conversion.

"In general, when thinking about taking early distribution from funds converted to a Roth IRA, you must realize that there could be a tax implication because of the ordering rules for determining the taxation of a nonqualified Roth distribution."

"Do you have an example?" Rich asked.

"For example, in 2010, Bill converted all $60,000 in his traditional IRA to his Roth IRA. Jim's Forms 8606 from previous years show that $10,000 of the amount converted is his basis. Bill included $50,000 ($60,000 - $10,000) in his gross income. In 2014, Bill made a regular contribution of $5,000 to a Roth IRA. In early 2015, at age 61, Bill took an $8,000 distribution from his Roth IRA. The first $5,000 of the distribution is a return of Bill's regular contribution and cannot be included in his income. The next $3,000 of the distribution cannot be included in income because it was included previously."

"I remember we discussed the required minimum distribution rules in great detail," Rich said. "Can you just briefly summarize them because I know with a pretax IRA I will be required to take a certain amount of my traditional IRA as a distribution upon reaching the age of 70½ ."

"I'll try to make it as painless as possible," John laughed. "As a general theme, the IRS will not allow you to keep retirement funds in your account indefinitely. You generally have to start taking withdrawals from your pretax traditional IRA when you reach age 70½. Remember, a Roth IRA is not subject to the RMD rules until after the death of the owner and the funds are in the hands of a nonspouse. In general, you must begin withdrawing money by April 1 of the year following the year that you turn 70½. In general, your age and account value determine the amount you must withdraw."

"So 70½ is just the age when a required minimum distribution is required. Can I also withdraw more than the minimum required amount?"

"Yes. Just like any pretax IRA distribution, RMD will be included in your taxable income except for any part that was taxed before (your basis) or that can be received tax-free (such as qualified distributions from designated Roth accounts)."

"How do you calculate it?" Rich asked.

"To calculate your RMD for any year, you look at the account balance as of the end of the immediately preceding calendar year divided by a distribution period from the IRS's Uniform Lifetime Table. A separate table is used if the sole beneficiary is the owner's spouse who is ten or more years younger than the owner."

"What happens when you reach 70½?"

"The IRA custodian that holds your IRA will help guide you in terms of when the first RMD is to be made. But in general, the first RMD is due April 1 of the year following the calendar year in which you reach age 70½. For each subsequent year after your required beginning date, you must withdraw your RMD by December 31. The first year following the year you reach age 70½ you will generally have two required distribution dates: an April 1 withdrawal (for the year you turn 70½), and an additional withdrawal by December 31 (for the year following the year you turn 70½). To avoid having both of these amounts included in your income for the same year, you can make your first withdrawal by December 31 of the year you turn 70½ instead of waiting until April 1 of the following year."

"How about some examples?" Rich said.

Example 1:

Bill is seventy-two years old and the value of his IRA is $150,000 as of December 31. His RMD for 2014 would be $5,859.38 using a 25.6 withdrawal factor.

Example 2:

Joe is seventy-seven years old and the value of his IRA is $300,000 as of December 31. His RMD for 2014 would be $14,150.94 using a 21.2 withdrawal factor.

Example 3:

Gary is eighty-five years old and the value of his IRA is $50,000 as of December 31. His RMD for 2014 would be $3,378.38 using a 14.8 withdrawal factor.

"As you can see," John said, "the RMD regime was designed by the IRS to prohibit retirees from accumulating wealth without paying tax and passing on the wealth to their heirs tax-free. The IRS gave you a tax deduction for making the pretax IRA contributions and allowed you defer the tax on the income generated by the IRA investments for many years; they feel it is only fair to eventually ask you to pay tax on some of the deferred income generated. In addition, having retirees spend some of their RMD is perceived by the government to have a positive impact on the economy."

"What happens if I forget to take an RMD from my self-directed IRA?" Rich asked.

"If you don't take any distributions," John said, "or if the distributions are not large enough, you may have to pay a 50 percent excise tax on the amount not distributed as required."

"I guess not having to take RMDs is another benefit of having a Roth IRA," Rich said.

"Yes," John said. "You would not have to take RMD from your Roth IRA and neither would your spouse after your death, but if there are still Roth funds left after your spouse passes, your children would eventually have to take RMDs, but no tax would be due."

"Okay," Rich said, "if I die and leave my IRA to my spouse, how do the RMD rules work for my spouse?"

"Your spouse would have a bunch of choices," John said. "Essentially, your spouse could (i) treat an IRA as her own, (ii) base RMDs on her own current age, (iii) base RMDs on your age at death, reducing the distribution period by one each year, or (iv) withdraw the entire account balance by the end of the fifth year following the account owner's death if the account owner died before the required beginning date. In addition, if the account owner died before the required beginning date, the surviving spouse can wait until the owner would have turned 70½ to begin receiving RMDs. The most popular approach is for the spouse to simply move the IRA of the deceased spouse into the surviving spouse's name and operate the IRA that way."

"What about if I leave my IRA to a nonspouse—like my children?" Rich asked.

"Essentially the nonspouse has several options: (i) withdraw the entire account balance by the end of the fifth year following the account owner's death, if the account owner died before the required beginning date, (ii) calculate RMDs using the distribution period from the Single Life Table based on whether the owner died after RMDs began; or if the account owner died before RMDs began, the beneficiary's age at year-end following the year of the owner's death, reducing the distribution period by one for each subsequent year. I don't want to get too heavily into these rules and calculations now because I touched on a lot of them earlier and they can get pretty convoluted."

Taking Distributions from a Checkbook Control Self-Directed IRA

"With my checkbook control self-directed IRA," Rich said, "I will have all my funds at a local bank. So how do I take a distribution?"

"That's a great question and it causes confusion with a number of my clients. The way to take a distribution from your checkbook control self-directed IRA or an RMD is to first send the funds to the IRA custodian and then request a distribution from the custodian. This is very important because if you simply wrote yourself a check from the LLC account and by-passed the IRA custodian, the transaction could be treated as a prohibited transaction. Any time you want to take a distribution or do a rollover from your checkbook control self-directed IRA LLC, you will need to go through the IRA custodian. This is very important and will mean the difference between taking a distribution and engaging in a prohibited transaction."

"Can you give some examples of how this will work?"

"Sure," John said. "Let's start with the self-directed IRA custodian-controlled structure. In that case, in which the IRA custodian is in control of the self-directed IRA investment, taking a distribution is quite simple since the custodian is in full control of the account. All you need to do is complete a distribution request form and the IRA custodian will then send you the distribution funds by check or wire. Let's say, for example, that Joe has a self-directed IRA with Custodian ABC valued at $150,000. Joe directs ABC custodian to buy real estate and purchased a home valued at $95,000. Joe receives $1,000 of rent each month, which is sent by the tenant to the IRA custodian by check and the IRA custodian then deposits the funds into Joe's IRA account. If Joe wishes to take a distribution from his IRA account or needs to satisfy an RMD, he would simply complete a distribution request form from ABC Custodian and submit it to the custodian for processing. The custodian then sends a check or executes a wire transfer for the amount of the distribution and sends it to Joe. Joe is then responsible for paying tax and a 10 percent early distribution penalty, if applicable. The same procedure applies whether Joe has a pretax traditional IRA or Roth IRA. The key is that all distribution activity must go through the IRA custodian. Joe couldn't ask the tenant to send him a check personally—all distribution requests and payments must go through the IRA custodian. The same applies to rollovers or contributions. If Joe wants to roll over other IRA or 401(k) funds to the self-directed IRA with ABC custodian, the funds go from his existing custodian to ABC Custodian, and the funds are then treated as a tax-free rollover. Joe could ask for the funds to be sent to him, but that would be considered an indirect rollover and he could only do one of these every twelve months for all his IRAs. Alternatively, if the funds were coming from a 401(k) plan, there could be withholding on this amount or the funds could be rolled directly to another IRA custodian, which is called a direct rollover and can be done without limit. A direct rollover is almost always the method used to move funds between retirement accounts. Also, any IRA contributions will need to be made to the IRA custodian directly."

"What about the checkbook control self-directed IRA LLC?" Rich asked.

"Of course, with a self-directed IRA LLC, the investment is occurring at the LLC level and not the IRA custodian so there is an additional step the IRA holder must satisfy in order to take a distribution. Let's go back to the example of Joe. Joe has set up a checkbook control self-directed IRA LLC with custodian XYZ Trust Company. Joe had his tax attorney establish an LLC for him in Texas, where he purchased real estate. Joe named his LLC Texas RE 5555, LLC. Joe transferred $200,000 from his former IRA custodian to XYZ custodian, who then invested the $200,000 into Joe's LLC account in return for 100 percent interest in his LLC. Joe opened his LLC bank account with EFG Bank. Joe then purchased a piece of property in Texas for $125,000. Joe took title in the property in the name of his LLC. And he was able to collect $1,300 a month in rent. Joe set up a direct payment system so the tenant could wire the funds into Joe's LLC bank account each year and pay his rent. Joe, who is sixty years old, had some personal debts he wanted to pay off and decided to take a $20,000 distribution from his IRA. Joe was over the age of 59½ so he would just be subject to tax on the amount of the distribution and the 10 percent early distribution penalty would not apply. Also, Joe was under the age of seventy so he was under no obligation to take a required minimum distribution but still wanted to take the distribution. In order to take the distribution, Joe wrote a check made out to XYZ Trust Company, Custodian of the Joe Smith IRA. Joe wrote a check from the IRA LLC bank account, included his IRA account number on the check, and mailed the check to XYZ Trust Company, his IRA custodian. Joe then went online to XYZ custodian's website and printed the distribution request form, on which he indicated the amount of the distribution he was seeking to take and the payment information. Joe signed the form and submitted it to the custodian. Several days later Joe received a check made out to him from his IRA custodian (XYZ Trust Company) for the amount of his distribution—$20,000. There is no withholding when taking an IRA distribution. Joe was then able to use the funds for any personal purposes. Joe sent a copy of the check to his accountant so that the distribution amount would be reported on his federal income tax return (IRS Form 1040). His accountant mentioned that the IRA custodian would report the amount of the distribution on IRS Form 1009-R and he would receive a copy as well."

"Why couldn't Joe just take the money from his LLC and report it on his tax return?" Rich asked.

"Do you remember when we talked about the prohibited transaction rules under IRC 4975?" John asked.

"Yes," Rich said.

"And do you remember that IRC 4975(c)(1)(A) states that sale or exchange, or leasing, of any property between a plan and a disqualified person is a prohibited transaction?"

"Yes," Rich said.

"So, even if Joe had the right intentions and paid tax on his tax return for the distribution amount, the fact that the funds would have gone from his IRA LLC to himself personally, a disqualified person, means that he would have triggered the prohibited transaction rules under IRC 4975. Joe would be slapped with a penalty and the immediate termination of his IRA."

"That's a bad option," Rich said.

"You know it," John agreed. "It's very important to remember that anytime you want to make an IRA contribution, execute a rollover, or take a distribution, your funds go through the IRA custodian first."

Taking an RMD from Your Checkbook Control Self-Directed IRA

"Okay," Rich said, "that's seems easy enough. What about taking an RMD?"

"Essentially if Joe was over the age of 70½ and was required to take an RMD, the process would be the same," John said. "The amount of the RMD would need to be sent from the LLC to the IRA custodian. Joe would title the check the same way he did in the prior example. He would then complete the IRA custodian distribution request form and indicate the amount of the RMD. The IRA custodian would then send Joe a check for the amount of the RMD and issue a 1099-R to the IRS. Joe would then need to report the RMD amount on his federal income tax return (IRS Form 1040)."

"Would I have to figure out the RMD amount?" Rich asked.

"No," John said. "The IRA custodian who holds your self-directed IRA will notify you of the amount of the RMD you have to take based on the value of your account as of December 31 of the previous year."

"What value is used for the RMD?" Rich asked.

"Remember that with a checkbook control self-directed IRA LLC you, as manager of the LLC, have control over the LLC investments," John said. "So, the IRA custodian in reality doesn't have any control or detailed knowledge of the type of investments you will be making with your checkbook control self-directed IRA LLC. Taking this a step further, the checkbook control IRA custodian wouldn't know if you were buying real estate in Texas, Florida, or California with your LLC."

"I get it," Rich said.

"Good," John said. "As we discussed earlier, the IRA custodian will send you a letter toward the end of the year requesting a valuation of your IRA LLC. In the case of RMDs the value is obviously quite important because it will have a direct correlation to the amount of RMD you will be taking. If your LLC has cash and publicly traded securities or precious metals, attaining a fair market value for the LLC is not a problem. However, in the case of alternative assets, such as real estate, it's important that the IRA holder acquire an independent value of the real estate and provide a copy to the IRA custodian. Some custodians will then ask for supporting documentation backing up the valuation when the LLC holds alternative assets, such as real estate. The IRA custodian would then provide the value of the IRA account to the IRS on IRS Form 5498 but will also use the value to determine the RMD amount for the IRA holder."

"How do I determine the RMD amount if I have multiple IRA accounts in addition to my self-directed IRA?" Rich asked.

"Each IRA custodian is required to provide you with the RMD amount with respect to the IRA accounts held at that institution. It would be impossible for your self-directed IRA custodian to know the value of any IRAs you have at other financial institutions. So, each IRA custodian will provide you the RMD amount for the IRA held at that institution. Remember, as long as you satisfy the overall RMD amount for the year with IRA funds, it is not important which IRA account the RMD comes from."

"What happens if I don't have enough cash in my self-directed IRA LLC to make the RMD payment?" Rich asked.

"Well that is a really important question I probably should have addressed earlier," John said. "If one is buying alternative assets with their self-directed IRA LLC, such as real estate, precious metals, notes, etc., and is approaching the age of 70, the IRA holder must be conscious of the RMD rules and make sure he or she has enough cash on hand to make the RMD payment. If there is not enough cash in any IRA account to cover the RMD for the year, then the IRA holder may have to take an IRA asset, such as real estate, as an RMD even if the value of the asset is in excess of the RMD amount."

"Wait, for real estate, I can't just take a portion of the property as an RMD?" Rich asked. "Generally no, unless the asset is raw land that can be subdivided. Splitting a portion of a house where the house will be partly owned by the IRA and the IRA holder in order to satisfy an RMD could become problematic and could trigger a prohibited transaction. Even if the property title can be re-deeded, I think it is best practice to never own an asset with a mixture of IRA and personal funds from a disqualified person," John said.

"What about if I used a self-directed IRA LLC?" Rich asked.

"Well," John responded, "remember the Swanson case? The issue is that when the asset was purchased, one or more IRAs owned the LLC 100%. If a portion of the asset was then taken as a distribution to cover the RMD, the individual IRA holder, a disqualified person, along with the IRA, will now own the LLC. The Swanson case clearly states that a newly established entity with no shares cannot be a disqualified person, but only after the shares were issued would the entity become a disqualified person. Hence, an argument can be made that if an IRA LLC-owned asset was taken as a partial distribution by the individual IRA holder, the LLC could be treated as a disqualified person since a disqualified person will now own a percentage of the entity. I have heard different ideas presented by other tax practitioners, and there is certainly a need for more clarity or guidance from the

IRS, but I believe it is always good practice to never own an asset with a combination of IRA and personal funds from disqualified persons. In such a situation, I would suggest satisfying the RMD with cash from an IRA or taking the entire asset as a distribution in order to satisfy the RMD," John stated. "I know it can be painful, especially if the IRA asset is valued significantly more than the minimum RMD amount, but I believe it is the safer approach in light of the IRS prohibited transaction rules," John added. "This is why it so important for someone who is using IRA funds to make alternative asset investments and is reaching the age of 65 to starting thinking about satisfying the RMD rules. Typically, five or so years is sufficient time to start preparing ones IRA portfolio to have sufficient cash on hand to satisfy the RMD amount, especially for someone investing IRA funds in real estate. This could potentially save one from having to take an IRA owned asset, such as a house, which could be valued much higher than the minimum RMD amount, as a RMD."

"Okay," Rich said, "this makes sense. So can we talk about strategy now? What happens when I want to move my funds out of a self-directed IRA LLC and back to a traditional custodian or want to take my entire IRA as a distribution?"

"That's a very important question," John said, "because it makes a lot of sense to think not only about how you will be making investments with a self-directed IRA but also how you will recap the benefits of the investment. As we previously discussed, when you want to move funds out of your self-directed IRA LLC structure, the funds will need to go first to the IRA custodian and then you can direct the IRA custodian to either move the funds to another IRA custodian or request a distribution and the IRA custodian will send you the funds for personal use."

Taking an In-Kind Distribution from a Self-Directed IRA

"Can I distribute the assets my IRA LLC owns, such as real estate, or do I need to sell the asset?" Rich asked.

"Great question and I should have touched upon this earlier," John said. "When you take a distribution, you can distribute cash or any IRA asset, which is known as an in-kind distribution. The same would apply to rollovers to another IRA custodian. You can roll over cash or IRA assets, as long as the new IRA custodian will accept that asset category to be held in an IRA. For example, say you had your self-directed IRA account with ABC custodian and owned real estate in the self-directed IRA account. If you wanted to change custodians and move the real estate to a new IRA custodian, you would need to find an IRA custodian that will accept the real estate as an IRA asset. As we discussed, most of the traditional banks will not allow your IRA to own real estate because of the a lack of financial incentive for them, so if you want to roll over a self-directed IRA account that holds alternative assets, such as real estate, you will need to find an IRA custodian that allows an IRA to invest in real estate or the alternative asset in question."

"How would I take an in-kind distribution of real estate?" Rich asked.

"It would pretty much follow the same process as taking a cash distribution," John said, "except there are some minor differences. The first thing you would need to do is value the real estate asset you will be taking as a distribution. This is especially important if you have a pretax IRA as there would be a tax imposed on the value of the real estate being taken as a distribution, as well as potentially a 10 percent early distribution tax. Once you get a value for the real estate, you will then need to complete a distribution request form with the IRA custodian and indicate that you will be taking an in-kind distribution of the real estate. When the distribution process has been completed and submitted to the IRA custodian, you would need to retitle the real estate from the name of the LLC to you own personal name. This can be done via a title company or a real estate attorney locally. I've had several clients who wanted to keep the real estate in the LLC simply draft an amended LLC operating agreement showing that the LLC is now owned by the individual personally and having the IRA custodian acknowledge its removal as member of the LLC. Either way works; the key is to show that the ownership of the real estate has been changed from the IRA to the IRA holder personally."

"Just to be clear," Rich said, "I'll be responsible for paying tax on the fair market value of the real estate or other asset I take as a distribution if I have a pretax IRA?"

"Yes," John said, "that's 100 percent correct. The tax due on an in-kind distribution is the fair market value of the asset on the date the distribution was taken and not the price you paid for the asset. For example, if the self-directed IRA LLC purchased a home for $100,000 and ten years later the house has appreciated to $300,000, and if the IRA holder wants to take the house as a distribution but she wants to live in it, she would be deemed to have taken a $300,000 distribution because that is what the house was valued at on the date of the distribution. The same would go for stock, precious metals, or any other alternative asset. Taking cash as a distribution is simple because the distribution equals the amount of cash that was taken as a distribution. This is why obtaining an independent valuation of the in-kind asset that will be taken as a distribution is so important—because the amount of tax due will be directly based on the fair market value of the asset. It's not a surprise that the IRS will pay special attention to the value of any asset being taken as an in-kind distribution."

In-Kind Rollover of IRA-Owned Real Estate to a Checkbook Control Self-Directed IRA

"I know we talked about the rollover before," Rich said, "but how can I roll over real estate I own with a full-service IRA custodian to a checkbook control self-directed IRA LLC?"

"I'm happy you brought this up again since it fits in nicely when talking about taking in-kind distributions," John said. "Since your real estate is titled in the name of the IRA custodian, it will need to be retitled or reregistered in the name of the new IRA custodian. The deed typically must be filed by the authorized representative of the IRA custodian currently holding title to the real estate. The signature will then essentially allow the real estate to be released to the new IRA custodian. The deed will have to be rerecorded in the appropriate county showing the new IRA custodian, as the custodian for the IRA is now the new owner of the real estate."

"What about with a checkbook control self-directed IRA LLC?" Rich asked.

"You're getting good," John said. "In that case, there's one more step to the process. The deed actually has to be retitled and rerecorded a third time so that title to the real estate will ultimately be in the name of the self-directed IRA LLC. Don't worry, the IRA custodian or the tax professional you would be working with will be able to assist you in accomplishing this type of in-kind rollover."

Dissolving Your Self-Directed IRA LLC Structure

"Okay," Rich said, "I think I have a handle on how to take a distribution from my self-directed IRA and how to accomplish an in-kind rollover. But what happens with the LLC for my checkbook control self-directed IRA if I want to dissolve the structure?"

"That's an important question," John said, "and it touches on state law, which would govern the dissolution process for the LLC in the state. So let me talk in general terms. It's best practice, even in the case of a single-member LLC, in which the IRA is the sole owner of the LLC, for the manager to draft a resolution approving the dissolution of the LLC. Most tax professionals who work on drafting self-directed IRA LLC operating agreements will include a provision that the manager(s) of the LLC can elect to dissolve the LLC. In some cases, I've seen provisions that require that the IRA custodian as member of the LLC also sign the resolution to dissolve the LLC. Either way works; it's just important to confirm that the dissolution process outlined satisfies state law. To that end, having the LLC manager and IRA custodian sign the resolution as member(s) of the LLC is the safest approach since all interested parties in the LLC have thereby agreed to the dissolution."

"And then you're done?" Rich asked.

"Not quite," John said. "After that, the LLC articles of dissolution will need to be filed by the state. These documents are necessary to legally separate the IRA custodian as member from the LLC from the entity. And the articles of dissolution are to be filed with the appropriate state agency, along with any state-required paperwork. The cost is generally around $25 to file the LLC articles of dissolution. Then you have to cancel your LLC employer identification number (EIN), which is how your LLC alerts the IRS to its dissolution. Technically speaking, the IRS does not actually cancel an EIN; it refers to EIN cancellation as 'account closure.' The final step is to distribute the LLC's assets to the IRA member or members. Any remaining funds in the LLC will be distributed to the IRA custodian as member(s) of the LLC. Once the funds from the LLC have been distributed to the IRA custodian as member(s) of the LLC, you can then direct the IRA custodian to either move the funds to a new IRA custodian or request a distribution. You would then want to close your LLC bank account since the LLC has been dissolved."

"Got it," Rich said.

"Of course, if you're using a custodian-controlled self-directed IRA structure without an LLC," John added, "there would be no need to dissolve an LLC since no LLC was used. All you would need to do is direct the custodian to move the funds or IRA assets to the new IRA custodian of your choice."

"Do most self-directed IRA custodians charge you for closing your self-directed IRA account?" Rich asked.

"Yes," John said. "Most do, and they'll charge you anywhere from $50 to $250 depending on the institution and facts involved. That's probably the last step in dissolving your self-directed IRA structure."

"Okay," Rich said, "that seems pretty easy. I'll keep this in mind when I'm at the point of closing out my self-directed IRA LLC investments. I really appreciate you taking so much time to explain the self-directed IRA and specifically the checkbook control self-directed IRA LLC structure in such great detail. It's really hard to find knowledgeable tax professionals who are well versed in the self-directed IRA rules, especially as they pertain to checkbook control and the IRS prohibited transaction rules. I can't tell you how much misinformation I received before finding you and I really appreciate it."

"It was my pleasure," John said. "Using a self-directed IRA or checkbook control self-directed IRA LLC structure can offer some great retirement and investment benefits, but you must always be careful when making IRA investments to make sure the investment does not violate the IRS prohibited transaction rules. And before making an investment you need to perform due diligence on the investment to make sure it makes financial sense and doesn't involve any potential for fraud. Also, an understanding of the UBTI rules is really important because it could be the difference between making a tax-efficient investment or not."

"Yes," Rich said. "It's really clear when you lay out the advantages and potential pitfalls like that."

"I'll leave you with something I tell all my clients," John said. "The self-directed IRA can become your best friend and strongest retirement asset, but you must treat it with respect. You've got a very high level of personal control, especially when using an LLC to make investments, and you need to navigate the prohibited transaction rules carefully. Working with qualified tax professionals is always wise when using a self-directed IRA to make alternative asset investments. I hope the time we spent together has been valuable and has helped you see some of the benefits involved in using a self-directed IRA as well as some of the responsibilities that come along with it."

"Thanks a million," Rich said.

The two smiled and shook hands.

Conclusion

You Are What You Eat

As the saying goes, "You are what you eat." This is true in life and when it comes to retirement savings. Your retirement account will become whatever you put into it, both in monetary terms and in terms of your time.

The primary objective of this book is to reveal the exciting benefits that the self-directed IRA can offer you from a retirement, tax, and investment perspective. I used the characters of Rich and John to illustrate the kind of dialogue I have experienced talking with more than 15,000 retirement investors exploring the ins and outs of the self-directed IRA. Rich and John and the fictitious questions and answers they exchanged were designed to give you a sense of the types of issues and matters that you need to consider when (1) choosing the right self-directed IRA, (2) establishing a self-directed IRA, (3) contributing to a self-directed IRA, (3) making self-directed IRA investments, (4) using the self-directed Roth IRA option, and ultimately (4) taking distributions from the IRA.

Rich represented the typical self-directed IRA investor who is interested in real estate and has more than $100,000 to invest. Most of the individuals I speak to who are looking at the self-directed IRA want to make alternative asset investments, such as real estate, either as a way to diversify their retirement portfolios, to make a hedge against inflation, to seek higher returns, or to gain the ability to invest in something they know, understand, or can touch. The questions Rich posed to John are typical of the questions someone looking at the self-directed IRA would ask a tax professional. It was my hope that using this type of dialogue format would allow the book to address the self-directed IRA structure in detail while still being engaging and interesting.

Hopefully, I've helped you understand the different types of self-directed IRA options that are available to you and some of their advantages and disadvantages. Most importantly, I hope the book has been able to show you the enormous benefits of having and growing a retirement account and some of the ways you can accomplish this. Whether you have a pretax traditional IRA or after-tax Roth IRA, or convert from a pretax IRA to a Roth IRA, taking the time to focus on growing your IRA through contributions and investments will be the difference between retiring rich and working the rest of your life.

With the self-directed IRA you can accomplish all this and have the opportunity to invest in some different types of asset classes, such as real estate, that you may feel more comfortable with than stocks or mutual funds. I also hope that this gives you a stronger interest in your retirement account than you had before. I've found that when people are interested in and understand what they are investing in, they generally have a greater chance of success. Like everything in life, you get more out of whatever you put into it.

I'm not telling you that you should invest only in what you like or understand or you should take all your retirement funds and buy alternative assets. That's not the purpose of this book and that's a conversation best left for you to have with your investment adviser or financial planner.

First, I want to make sure you understand that you are allowed to buy real estate, gold, and tax liens, and make private loans or invest in private businesses with your IRA funds. It's 100 percent legal and easy to do.

Second, I want to also impress upon you that retirement investing can be fun and engaging and does not have to be as dry as reading a financial website or analyzing a company's financials.

Finally, I know many of you are probably wondering why this is the first book you've read on how much personal control and influence you can have on your retirement funds. People ask me, "How can that be?" They think that it sounds almost too good to be true.

Don't blame yourself for not knowing. You are not alone. I have talked to tens of thousands of retirement account holders and am always amazed at how few people realize you can buy real estate or invest in other nontraditional assets with retirement money. I understand how they feel. I have a law degree and a master's in taxation and have worked at some of the largest law firms in the world. While I am not the most sophisticated investor, I have a diverse tax and investment background. But I only learned about alternative investment options through research I did for a client.

Since then, I've helped a number of tax partners I used to work with—one who even went to Yale Law School—who were unaware that retirement assets can be invested outside of the traditional financial markets.

I can't stress it enough. This is what the major financial institutions want. The increasingly huge retirement investment world is a $20 trillion industry with billions of dollars in potential fees. Many Americans are cash poor but retirement rich and these financial institutions are counting on the fees from those accounts to bolster their bottom lines.

The Pros

There are many reasons for considering a self-directed IRA to make traditional as well as alternative-asset investments. This book looked closely at some of the primary reasons retirement investors want to establish a self-directed IRA, but I want to take a brief moment to summarize some of the most popular ones.

Tax Advantages:

With the self-directed IRA LLC you have all the tax advantages of traditional IRAs, as well as tax deferral and tax-free gains. All income and gains generated by your IRA investment will flow back to your IRA tax-free. By using a self-directed IRA to make investments, the IRA owner is able to defer taxes on any investment returns, thus allowing the IRA owner to benefit from tax-free growth. Instead of paying tax on the self-directed IRA returns of an investment, tax is paid only at a later date when a distribution is taken, leaving the investment to grow tax-free without interruption.

Imagine if someone explained to you at a young age that if you begin funding an individual retirement account with $3,000 or so per year at age twenty and continue on through age sixty-five, you will end up with $2.5 million at retirement (assuming you can earn the long-run annual compound growth rate in stocks, which was 9.88 percent from 1926 to 2011). That's not a bad result for investing only $3,000 a year. Or, if you want, you could turn $1400 a year of IRA contributions into over a million dollars upon retirement. In other words, saving just $4 a day can be the difference between having a million dollars tax-free when you retire. That's one less Starbucks coffee, Big Mac, Burrito, or ITunes download—and all the difference in the world.

These are not just numbers; this is the difference between retiring in style and having to work your entire life just to survive. I hope that this book has made that point clear and shown you how saving for retirement can be easy and fun and does not have to be tough or painful. The self-directed IRA can make this all possible while allowing you to invest in assets you know and understand.

Investment Options:

With the self-directed IRA LLC, you can invest in almost any type of investment, including real estate, private business entities, tax liens, precious metals and commercial paper tax-free. The IRC does not describe what a retirement account can invest in, only what it *cannot* invest in. IRC Sections 408 & 4975 prohibits Disqualified Persons from engaging in certain type of transactions, which generally involve life insurance, collectibles, and any transaction that directly or indirectly personally benefits a disqualified person (a prohibited transaction). The self-directed IRA offers you a world of investment opportunities and the ability to invest in what you know and understand.

Whether it is real estate or some other type of alternative asset—as long as it does not fit into one of the prohibited type of transaction categories—the investment can generally be made. The investment options with a self-directed IRA LLC are infinite, but it is important to remember that if your investment will involve margin, leverage, or be made in an active trade or business through a pass-through entity, such as an LLC, the unrelated business taxable income tax regime could apply.

The following are some examples of the type of popular investments that can be made with your self-directed IRA LLC:

- Residential or commercial real estate
- Raw land
- Foreclosure property
- Mortgages
- Mortgage pools
- Deeds
- Private loans
- Tax liens
- Private businesses
- Limited Liability Companies
- Limited Liability Partnerships
- Private placements
- Precious metals and certain coins
- Stocks, bonds, mutual funds
- Foreign currencies

Diversification:

With the self-directed IRA LLC, you can invest in almost any type of investment, including real estate, allowing you to diversify and better protect your retirement portfolio. If the 2008 financial crisis had any positive features it was that many Americans started asking about alternative investment options for their retirement accounts. Diversification is a strategy to help make sure all your retirement assets aren't concentrated in a certain type of investment or area.

Retirement account diversification has become a popular concept for many retirement account holders. It is believed that the financial crisis cost retirees almost 25 percent of their retirement assets and many are still trying to get back to where they were before the crisis. The sudden and steep stock market fall, coupled with the lack of faith in Wall Street and the global financial markets, caused many Americans to seek a more balanced and diversified retirement portfolio. This shift brought a sharp increase in the number of Americans looking at a self-directed IRA as the vehicle for attaining a level of account diversification. Accordingly, balance and diversification have become popular hallmarks of a strong investment retirement portfolio.

Alternative investments such as real estate have always been permitted in IRAs; it even says so right on the IRS website. But few people seemed to know about this option until the last several years. The alternative asset and self-directed retirement market were relatively small and unknown prior to 2008. There were a few small groups of early adopters in the retirement world who had heard about the nontraditional asset option and took advantage of it to buy real estate and other nontraditional assets. These groups were on the cutting edge of investment options and largely did not have an impact on the greater retirement investment community. The crossover only started after the 2008 financial crisis, when many Americans actively set out to determine whether alternative investment options were available to them rather than waiting for these options to be advertised or offered.

After the 2008 financial crisis, allocating a portion of an investment portfolio to alternative asset investments, such as real estate or precious metals, was seen as a way to help diversify a retirement investment portfolio of stocks and bonds and reduce risk. Alternative asset investments for retirement accounts were also shown to provide an income stream and hedge against inflation.

Of course, there is no certainty that a diversified investment retirement portfolio will provide greater benefits to stockholders than a portfolio that is more concentrated in any particular individual real estate investment sector or location. History still suggests that stocks are a solid investment over the long term. For example, according to historical records, the average annual return for the S&P 500 since its inception in 1928 through 2014 is approximately 10 percent. However, that number can be very misleading. Accurate calculations of average returns, taking all significant factors into account, can be challenging. Nevertheless, having your retirement account properly diversified and not wholly subjected to the ups and downs of Wall Street has become a priority since the 2008 financial crisis and is one of the factors behind the emergence of the self-directed IRA solution.

Control:

In general, a retirement investor looking to make self-directed IRA investments has the choice of using a full-service custodian to make the alternative asset investment or using a checkbook control IRA LLC to make the investment.

This book has detailed some of the advantages and disadvantages of both types of self-directed IRA solutions. The primary reason many people choose one self-directed IRA structure over another is based on the level of control and access the individual wants over his or her retirement accounts. This decision is typically investment-based and is dependent on the type of investment that individual will be making with his or her self-directed IRA. Investing in a hedge fund that has a five-year lockup period versus buying and selling real estate will have a significant impact on the type of self-directed IRA structure one chooses.

The ability to make investments quickly and to have fast and easy access to a checkbook also plays a role, especially in certain types of investments such as tax liens or tax deeds. There is no right or wrong choice; it all depends on your desire for control, which is generally tied into the investments that the self-directed IRA will make. Fees do also play a significant role in the type of self-directed IRA structure that will be used, but, again, that choice will be affected by the type of investments the IRA will be making.

For example, an investor looking to buy real estate or tax liens may be okay with paying a bit more in up-front costs for a checkbook control self-directed IRA LLC because of the level of access and control he or she would likely need to have over the investment. In contrast, an individual buying precious metals to hold may be more fee-sensitive. No matter what self-directed IRA structure you choose, you will have a greater level of investment opportunity and greater control over your retirement asset allocation than you would with a traditional IRA bank or financial institution.

Limited Liability:

The limited liability feature applies only if you use a self-directed IRA LLC to make investments. For some investors, having an LLC and gaining limited liability protection is not crucial because of the type of investments involved. Investments into hedge funds, private equity funds, precious metals, and hard money loans are just a few of the types of investments in which having limited liability protection would not be as crucial because of the relatively low level of potential creditor attack. In contrast, real estate is the main asset class in which having an LLC does make some sense from a limited liability standpoint. Remember, having limited liability protection will only protect IRA funds held outside the LLC. So if all your IRA funds will be tied up in a piece of real estate held via an LLC, a creditor could attack the assets of the LLC in the case of a liability claim but would not be able to attack the assets held outside the LLC. Someone making multiple real estate purchases with his or her IRA and who has other IRA assets, in addition to those IRA funds invested in real estate, would likely find the limited liability protection afforded by the LLC rather valuable.

Asset and Creditor Protection:

Retirement accounts have become many Americans' most valuable assets. That means it is vital that you have the ability to protect them from creditors, such as people who have won lawsuits against you. By using a self-directed IRA, the IRA holder's IRA will be protected for up to $1 million in the case of personal bankruptcy under the 2005 Bankruptcy

Act. In addition, most states will shield a self-directed IRA from creditor attack against the IRA holder outside of bankruptcy, but this is something that should be discussed with a local attorney specializing in asset protection. Using a self-directed IRA LLC, the IRA will generally be protected against a creditor attack of the IRA holder personally. This feature is especially important to individuals who have somewhat high-risk professions, such as doctors, dentists, lawyers, and real estate developers. Being able to build an asset portfolio that is tax-efficient and also generally protected from creditors inside and outside of bankruptcy is especially important for many people.

Tax-Free Wealth for Your Retirement:
I spent a chapter in this book exploring the amazing tax benefits of using a Roth IRA to make investments. The Roth IRA is truly the best legal tax shelter available, and it is accessible to everyone. Remember, a Roth IRA is an after-tax account in which no tax deduction is received on the contribution, but all income and gains associated with the Roth IRA would be tax-free, in general, as long as the Roth IRA has been open at least five years and the Roth IRA holder is at least 59½. Along with the great tax benefits of generating tax-free asset growth and income, especially in light of an expected higher tax environment in the near future, the Roth IRA can serve as a valuable estate-planning tool by allowing you to pass tax-free wealth to your heirs.

Using retirement funds to make alternative asset investments is not for everyone. That being said, buying real estate or making other alternative assets with retirement funds through a self-directed IRA is an option that more and more people are starting to consider. According to the data provider Preqin[3], the alternative assets industry's leading source of data and intelligence, the alternative assets industry added more than $600 billion in assets under management in 2015, and as of January 2015, the assets under management of alternative asset classes now stand at $6.9 trillion.

3 https://www.preqin.com/docs/reports/Preqin-Investor-Outlook-Alternative-Assets-H1-2015.pdf

Certainly the 2008 financial crisis had a large impact on many Americans looking to alternative assets as a source of diversification. These numbers are even more impressive when you consider that the alternative asset investment market is not advertised to the average American, especially when it comes to retirement accounts. When is the last time you saw a TV commercial from a major bank or financial institution proclaiming an opportunity to buy real estate or gold through your IRA? Those institutions do not allow their IRA accounts to invest in any alternative asset class for the simple reason that they don't make money when you purchase real estate or other alternative assets, but they do make money when you buy their financial products. The genie is now out of the bottle, and more and more American retirement investors are starting to learn about the self-directed IRA and some of the exciting retirement, tax, and investment benefits it presents.

I hope this book was able to show you how beneficial retirement saving can be and how easy and fun it should be when you can invest in what you know and understand. No matter what type of self-directed IRA structure you choose, the potential for asset diversification, inflation protection, asset growth, tax-free investing, asset protection, and estate-planning opportunities is too great to ignore. Yes, there are rules to follow, such as the prohibited transaction rules, and there is the potential for fraud from shady investment promoters. But if you work with a qualified self-directed IRA facilitation company, tax attorney, or CPA, having a self-directed IRA is easy, stress-free, and fun, and it can be very rewarding financially. It also can be the difference between retiring with financial freedom and having to work for the rest of your life.

Appendix

Exhibit A

 IRA Required Minimum Distribution Worksheet

Use this worksheet to figure this year's required withdraw for your traditional IRA UNLESS your spouse[1] is the sole beneficiary of your IRA and he or she is more than 10 years younger than you.

Deadline for receiving required minimum distribution:
- Year you turn age 70 ½ - by April 1 of the following year
- All subsequent years - by December 31 of that year

1. IRA balance[2] on December 31 of the previous year. $_____

2. Distribution period from the table below for your age on your birthday this year.   _____

3. Line 1 divided by number entered on line 2. This is your required minimum distribution for this year from this IRA. $_____

4. Repeat steps 1 through 3 for each of your IRAs.

Table III (Uniform Lifetime)

Age	Distribution Period	Age	Distribution Period	Age	Distribution Period	Age	Distribution Period
70	27.4	82	17.1	94	9.1	106	4.2
71	26.5	83	16.3	95	8.6	107	3.9
72	25.6	84	15.5	96	8.1	108	3.7
73	24.7	85	14.8	97	7.6	109	3.4
74	23.8	86	14.1	98	7.1	110	3.1
75	22.9	87	13.4	99	6.7	111	2.9
76	22.0	88	12.7	100	6.3	112	2.6
77	21.2	89	12.0	101	5.9	113	2.4
78	20.3	90	11.4	102	5.5	114	2.1
79	19.5	91	10.8	103	5.2	115 and over	1.9
80	18.7	92	10.2	104	4.9		
81	17.9	93	9.6	105	4.5		

Once you determine a separate required minimum distribution from each of your traditional IRAs, you can total these minimum amounts and take them from any one or more of your traditional IRAs.

For additional information, see:

- Publication 590-B, *Distributions from Individual Retirement Arrangements (IRAs)*
- Retirement Topics – Required Minimum Distributions

[1] Generally, your marital status is determined as of January 1 of each year. If your spouse is the beneficiary of your IRA on January 1, he or she remains a beneficiary only for purposes of calculating the required minimum distribution for that IRA even if you get divorced or your spouse dies during the year.

[2] You must increase your IRA balance by any outstanding rollover and recharacterized Roth IRA conversions that were not in any traditional IRA on December 31 of the previous year.

Exhibit B

Ages										
(Joint Life and Last Survivor Expectancy) (For Use by Owners Whose Spouses Are More Than 10 Years Younger and Are the Sole Beneficiaries of Their IRAs)										
	20	21	22	23	24	25	26	27	28	29
69	63.1	62.2	61.2	60.2	59.3	58.3	57.3	56.4	55.4	54.5
70	63.1	62.2	61.2	60.2	59.3	58.3	57.3	56.4	55.4	54.4
71	63.1	62.1	61.2	60.2	59.2	58.3	57.3	56.4	55.4	54.4
72	63.1	62.1	61.2	60.2	59.2	58.3	57.3	56.3	55.4	54.4
73	63.1	62.1	61.2	60.2	59.2	58.3	57.3	56.3	55.4	54.4
74	63.1	62.1	61.2	60.2	59.2	58.2	57.3	56.3	55.4	54.4
75	63.1	62.1	61.1	60.2	59.2	58.2	57.3	56.3	55.3	54.4
76	63.1	62.1	61.1	60.2	59.2	58.2	57.3	56.3	55.3	54.4
77	63.1	62.1	61.1	60.2	59.2	58.2	57.3	56.3	55.3	54.4
78	63.1	62.1	61.1	60.2	59.2	58.2	57.3	56.3	55.3	54.3
79	63.1	62.1	61.1	60.1	59.2	58.2	57.2	56.3	55.3	54.3
80	63.1	62.1	61.1	60.1	59.2	58.2	57.2	56.3	55.3	54.3
81	63.1	62.1	61.1	60.1	59.2	58.2	57.2	56.3	55.3	54.3
82	63.1	62.1	61.1	60.1	59.2	58.2	57.2	56.3	55.3	54.3
83	63.1	62.1	61.1	60.1	59.2	58.2	57.2	56.3	55.3	54.3
84	63.0	62.1	61.1	60.1	59.2	58.2	57.2	56.3	55.3	54.3
85	63.0	62.1	61.1	60.1	59.2	58.2	57.2	56.3	55.3	54.3
86	63.0	62.1	61.1	60.1	59.2	58.2	57.2	56.3	55.3	54.3
87	63.0	62.1	61.1	60.1	59.2	58.2	57.2	56.2	55.3	54.3
88	63.0	62.1	61.1	60.1	59.2	58.2	57.2	56.2	55.3	54.3
89	63.0	62.1	61.1	60.1	59.2	58.2	57.2	56.2	55.3	54.3
90	63.0	62.1	61.1	60.1	59.1	58.2	57.2	56.2	55.3	54.3

Exhibit C

(Single Life Expectancy)
(For Use by Beneficiaries)
As Indicated in IRS Publication 590-B

Age	Life Expectancy	Age	Life Expectancy
0	82.4	56	28.7
1	81.6	57	27.9
2	80.6	58	27.0
3	79.7	59	26.1
4	78.7	60	25.2
5	77.7	61	24.4
6	76.7	62	23.5
7	75.8	63	22.7
8	74.8	64	21.8
9	73.8	65	21.0
10	72.8	66	20.2
11	71.8	67	19.4
12	70.8	68	18.6
13	69.9	69	17.8
14	68.9	70	17.0
15	67.9	71	16.3
16	66.9	72	15.5
17	66.0	73	14.8
18	65.0	74	14.1
19	64.0	75	13.4
20	63.0	76	12.7
21	62.1	77	12.1
22	61.1	78	11.4
23	60.1	79	10.8
24	59.1	80	10.2
25	58.2	81	9.7
26	57.2	82	9.1
27	56.2	83	8.6
28	55.3	84	8.1
29	54.3	85	7.6
30	53.3	86	7.1
31	52.4	87	6.7
32	51.4	88	6.3
33	50.4	89	5.9
34	49.4	90	5.5
35	48.5	91	5.2
36	47.5	92	4.9
37	46.5	93	4.6
38	45.6	94	4.3
39	44.6	95	4.1
40	43.6	96	3.8
41	42.7	97	3.6
42	41.7	98	3.4
43	40.7	99	3.1
44	39.8	100	2.9
45	38.8	101	2.7
46	37.9	102	2.5
47	37.0	103	2.3
48	36.0	104	2.1
49	35.1	105	1.9
50	34.2	106	1.7
51	33.3	107	1.5
52	32.3	108	1.4
53	31.4	109	1.2
54	30.5	110	1.1
55	29.6	111 and over	1.0

Exhibit D

STATE	FILING FEES
Alabama - Tel: 334-242-1170 Press 8	$100 ($75 plus county fee) Business Privilege Tax Return $10 No Annual Report filing
Alaska - Tel: 907-465-2530	$250 (online) $25 fee for reserving an LLC name
Arizona - Tel: 602-542-6187	LLCS are formed through the Arizona Corporations Commission $85 ($50 +35 Expedited fee) Application to Reserve Limited Liability Company Name $10 Regular $45 Expedited $150 publishing fee (within 3 months of formation) Need original signature of registered agent
Arkansas - Tel: 888-233-0325	Form LL-01 $45 Online $50 Paper $150-franchise tax report must be filed by May 1st of each year.
California - Tel: 916-653-6814	$85 ($70 + $15 walk in fee) Within 90 days of your formation, you will need to send in your statement of information along with a $20 filing fee. LLCs also pay an $800 annual tax, due within 3 1/2 months of your LLC's formation and every April 15 thereafter.
Colorado - Tel: 303-894-2200	File $60 Amend $25 Amend and Restate $25 Dissolve $25
Connecticut - Tel: 860-509-6002 Department of Revenue - Tel: 860-297-5962	$120 Filing Fee $100 Expedited Service
Delaware - Tel: 302-739-3073	$140 ($90 + $50 for certified copy) If necessary the expedite fee for Delaware LLC $100 Same Day $50 24-Hour Fee
D.C. - Tel: 202-442-4411	$220
Florida - Tel: 850-245-6500	$155 ($125 +30 for certified copy)
Georgia - Tel: 404-656-2817	$25 for Name reservation $100 for filing articles online (articles immediate online if name reservation has been done first) = $125 $50 annual filing fee due within 90 days of filing – client obligation
Hawaii - Tel: 808-586-2744 Alt: 808-586-2727	$75 ($50 + $25 expedited fee)
Idaho - Tel: 208-334-2301	$120 ($100 filing fee +$20 expedited fee)
Illinois - Tel: 217-782-6961	$500 by hand (receive in 7 days) or $600 online (receive in 24hrs)
Indiana - Tel: 317-232-6576	$90 Mail $85 Online
Iowa - Tel: 515-281-5204	$50
Kansas - Tel: 785-296-4564	$160 Online $165 Paper
Kentucky - Tel: 502-564-2848	$40
Louisiana - Tel: 225-925-4704	$130 ($100 +30 expedited fee)
Maine - Tel: 207-626-8400	$225 ($175 +$50 expedited fee)

STATE	FILING FEES
Maryland - Tel: 410-767-1340	$150 ($100 +$50 expedited fee) $300 annual fee for personal property return filing fee due each year
Massachusetts - Tel: 617-727-9640	$500 $20 Expedite Fee
Michigan - Tel: 888-767-6424	$50
Minnesota - Tel: 651-296-2803	$135 Mail $155 In Person or Online
Mississippi - Tel: 601-359-1633	$50 Online only
Missouri - Tel: 573-751-4153	$50 Online $105 In Person
Montana - Tel: 406-444-3665	$70 $ 20 Expedited Fee within 24 hours
Nebraska - Tel: 402-471-4079	$100 plus $10 for a certificate and $5 a page ($125)
Nevada - Tel: 775-684-5708	$75 (plus $125 expedited fee is client wants = $200) – Need signature of registered agent IF FILE ONLINE - $75
New Hampshire - Tel: 603-271-3244	$100 $50 for certification
New Jersey - Tel: 609-292-9292	$125 Online or In Person
New Mexico - Tel: 505-827-4508	$50
New York - Tel: 518-473-2492	$200 +$25 (expedited fee) = $225 Publication requirement within 120 days of forming LLC. Onetime fee – amount varies by county. Cost can vary from $400 to $1800 for Manhattan.
North Carolina - Tel: 919-807-2225	$125 (plus $100 if client wants expedited)
North Dakota - Tel: 701-328-2900	$135
Ohio - Tel: 614-466-3910	$125 $100 Expedite
Oklahoma - Tel: 405-521-3912	$104 e-filing $100 by mail
Oregon - Tel: 503-986-2200	$100 Online
Pennsylvania - Tel: 717-787-1057	$125
Rhode Island - Tel: 401-222-3040	$150
South Carolina - Tel: 803-734-2158	$110 (need signature of registered agent)
South Dakota - Tel: 605-773-4845	$150
Tennessee - Tel: 615-741-2286 Department of Revenue – Tel: 615-253-0700	$300
Texas - Tel: 512-463-5555	$300 ($20 expedited fee if client is in a big hurry)
Utah - Tel: 801-530-4849	$70 Online $5 extra for Expedite
Vermont - Tel: 802-828-2386	$125
Virginia - Tel: 804-371-9733	$100
Washington - Tel: 360-725-0377	$200 Online $180 Mail
West Virginia - Tel: 304-558-8000	$100 Online
Wisconsin - Tel: 608-261-7577	$130 Online $170 Mail

Exhibit E

6/7/2011

ROLLOVER CHART

Roll From \ Roll To	Roth IRA	IRA (traditional)	SIMPLE IRA	SEP-IRA	457(b) (government)	Qualified Plan[1] (pre-tax)	403(b) (pre-tax)	Designated Roth Account (401(k), 403(b) or 457(b)[2])
Roth IRA	YES	NO	NO	NO	NO	NO	NO	NO
IRA (traditional)	YES[3]	YES	NO	YES	YES[4]	YES	YES	NO
SIMPLE IRA	YES,[3] after two years	YES, after two years	YES	YES, after two years	YES,[4] after two years	YES, after two years	YES, after two years	NO
SEP-IRA	YES[3]	YES	NO	YES	YES[4]	YES	YES	NO
457(b) (government)	YES[3]	YES	NO	YES	YES	YES	YES	YES,[3,5] after 12/31/10
Qualified Plan[1] (pre-tax)	YES[3]	YES	NO	YES	YES[4]	YES	YES	YES,[3,5] after 9/27/10
403(b) (pre-tax)	YES[3]	YES	NO	YES	YES[4]	YES	YES	YES,[3,5] after 9/27/10
Designated Roth Account (401(k), 403(b) or 457(b)[2])	YES	NO	NO	NO	NO	NO	NO	Yes, if a direct trustee to trustee transfer

[1]Qualified plans include, for example, profit-sharing, 401(k), money purchase, and defined benefit plans
[2]Governmental 457(b) plans, after December 31, 2010
[3]Must include in income
[4]Must have separate accounts
[5]Must be an in-plan rollover
For more information regarding retirement plans and rollovers, visit Tax Information for Retirement Plans Community.

Exhibit K

SEC
OFFICE of INVESTOR
EDUCATION and ADVOCACY

Investor Alert: Self-Directed IRAs and the Risk of Fraud

The SEC's Office of Investor Education and Advocacy (OIEA) and the North American Securities Administrators Association (NASAA) are issuing this Investor Alert to warn investors of the potential risks associated with investing through self-directed Individual Retirement Accounts (self-directed IRAs). NASAA has noted a recent increase in reports or complaints of fraudulent investment schemes that utilized a self-directed IRA as a key feature. State securities regulators have investigated numerous cases where a self-directed IRA was used in an attempt to lend credibility to a fraudulent scheme. Similarly, the SEC has brought numerous cases in which promoters of fraudulent schemes steered investors to self-directed IRAs. While self-directed IRAs can be a safe way to invest retirement funds, investors should be mindful of potential fraudulent schemes when considering a self-directed IRA. Investors should understand that the custodians and trustees of self-directed IRAs may have limited duties to investors, and that the custodians and trustees for these accounts will generally *not* evaluate the quality or legitimacy of an investment and its promoters. As with every investment, investors should undertake their own evaluation of the merits of a proposal, and should check with regulators about the background and history of an investment and its promoters before making a decision.

I. Investing through Self-Directed IRAs

An Individual Retirement Account (IRA) is a form of retirement account that provides investors with certain tax benefits for retirement savings. Some common examples of IRAs used by investors include the traditional IRA, Roth IRA, Simplified Employee Pension (SEP) IRA, and Savings Incentive Match Plan for Employees (SIMPLE) IRA. All IRA accounts are held for investors by custodians or trustees. These may include banks, trust companies, or any other entity approved by the Internal Revenue Service (IRS) to act as a trustee or custodian.

A self-directed IRA is an IRA held by a trustee or custodian that permits investment in a broader set of assets than is permitted by most IRA custodians. Most IRA custodians are banks and broker-dealers that limit the holdings in IRA accounts to firm-approved stocks, bonds, mutual funds and CDs. Custodians and trustees for self-directed IRAs, however, may allow investors to invest retirement funds in other types of assets such as real estate, promissory notes, tax lien certificates, and private placement securities. While self-directed IRAs may offer investors access to an array of private investment opportunities that are not available through other IRA providers, investments in these kinds of assets may have unique risks that investors should consider. Those risks can include a lack of disclosure and liquidity -- as well as the risk of fraud.

II. Self-Directed IRAs and the Risk of Fraud

According to a 2011 report by the Investment Company Institute, U.S. investors held approximately $4.7 trillion in IRAs. Estimates from various sources approximate that investors hold 2 percent, or $94 billion, of IRA retirement funds in self-directed IRAs. The large amount of money held in self-directed IRAs makes them attractive targets for fraud promoters. Fraud promoters also may target other types of retirement accounts by attempting to lure investors into transferring money from those accounts to new self-directed IRAs in order to participate in the fraud promoter's scheme.

In particular, fraud promoters who want to engage in Ponzi schemes or other fraudulent conduct may exploit self-directed IRAs because they permit investors to hold unregistered securities and the custodians or trustees of these accounts likely have not investigated the securities or the background of the promoter. There are a number of ways that fraud promoters may use these weaknesses and misperceptions to perpetrate a fraud on unsuspecting investors. For example:

- Misrepresentations Regarding Custodial Responsibilities – Fraud promoters can misrepresent the responsibilities of self-directed IRA custodians to deceive investors into believing that their investments are legitimate or protected against losses. Fraud promoters often explicitly state or suggest that self-directed IRA custodians investigate and validate any investment in a self-directed IRA. Self-directed IRA custodians are responsible only for holding and administering the assets in a self-directed IRA. Self-directed IRA custodians generally do not evaluate the quality or legitimacy of any investment in the self-directed IRA or its promoters. Furthermore, most custodial agreements between a self-directed IRA custodian and an investor explicitly state that the self-directed IRA custodian has no responsibility for investment performance.

- Exploitation of Tax-Deferred Account Characteristics – Self-directed IRAs are tax-deferred retirement accounts that carry a financial penalty for prematurely withdrawing money before a certain age. This financial penalty may induce self-directed IRA investors to keep funds in a fraudulent scheme longer than those investors who invest through other means. Also, the prospect of an early withdrawal penalty could encourage an investor to become passive with a lesser degree of oversight than a managed account might receive, allowing a fraud promoter to perpetrate his fraud longer.

- Lack of Information for Alternative Investments – Self-directed IRAs usually allow investors to hold alternative investments such as real estate, mortgages, tax liens, precious metals, and private placement securities. Unlike publicly-traded securities, financial and other information necessary to make a prudent investment decision may not be as readily available for these alternative investments. Even when financial information for these alternative investments is available, it may not be audited. Furthermore, self-directed IRA custodians usually do not investigate the accuracy of this financial information. This lack of available information for alternative investments makes them a popular tool for fraud promoters' schemes.

III. Ways to Avoid Fraud with Self-Directed IRAs

Verify information in self-directed IRA account statements. Alternative investments may be illiquid and difficult to value. As a result, self-directed IRA custodians often list the value of the investment as the original purchase price, the original purchase price plus returns reported by the promoter, or a price provided by the promoter. *Investors should be aware that none of these valuations necessarily reflect the price at which the investment could be sold, if at all.*

Avoid unsolicited investment offers. Investors should be very careful when they receive an unsolicited investment offer. Whether from a total stranger or from a friend, trusted co-worker, or even family member, investors should ask themselves, "Why would anyone tell me about a really great investment opportunity?" *Investors also should be especially wary of an unsolicited investment offer that promotes the use of a self-directed IRA.* As noted above, fraud promoters may attempt to lure investors into transferring money from traditional IRAs and other retirement accounts into new self-directed IRAs in order to participate in the fraud promoter's scheme.

Ask questions. Always ask if the person offering the investment is licensed and if the investment is registered, then check out the answers with an unbiased source, such as the SEC or your state securities regulator. The SEC has a short publication called "Ask Questions" that discusses many of the other questions investors should ask of anyone who wants them to make an investment. Please take a look at it before making any investment decision.

Be mindful of "guaranteed" returns. Every investment carries some degree of risk, and the level of risk typically correlates with the return an investor can expect to receive. Low risk generally means low yields, and high yields typically involve higher risk. Fraud promoters often spend a lot of time trying to convince investors that extremely high returns are "guaranteed" or "can't miss." Don't believe it. High returns represent potential rewards for investors who are willing and financially able to take big risks.

Ask a professional. For complex investment opportunities, particularly those which involve the opening or creation of a new account outside a traditional financial institution or well-recognized broker, investors should consider getting a second opinion from a licensed unbiased investment professional or an attorney.

IV. Recent Cases Involving Self-Directed IRAs

Some recent examples of SEC and state enforcement cases that involve funds from self-directed IRAs invested in fraudulent schemes include:

SEC v. United American Ventures

The SEC filed charges alleging that two companies and four individuals misrepresented and concealed numerous material facts in connection with the offer and sale of $10 million in bonds to approximately 100 individual investors in various states. In particular, the SEC alleged that the defendants promised guaranteed returns in purported investments in medical technologies and raised money by convincing investors to invest through self-directed IRAs and steering them to custodians who offered the self-directed IRAs. Approximately $3.5 million of the funds invested in the bonds came from self-directed IRAs.

SEC v. Stinson

The SEC filed charges alleging that an individual perpetrated an offering fraud and Ponzi scheme in which at least $16 million was raised from more than 140 investors. In particular, the SEC alleged that the defendant promised "safe and risk free" returns in purported investments in real estate and commercial mortgage loans. The defendant raised money by targeting, among others, investors in self-directed IRAs. Approximately $9.2 million of the funds invested in the fraudulent scheme came from self-directed IRAs.

SEC v. Durmaz

The SEC filed charges alleging that a company and its partners perpetrated a Ponzi scheme in which at least $20 million was raised from more than 120 investors. In particular, the SEC alleged that the defendants promised safe, guaranteed returns in purported investments in foreign bonds and raised money by convincing investors to invest in self-directed IRAs and steering them to custodians who offered the self-directed IRAs. $20 million of the funds invested in the fraudulent scheme came from self-directed IRAs.

State v. Smith (24C02-1102-FB-00044) and State v. Snelling (24C02-1102-FB-00046) (Indiana)

The Indiana state securities regulators pursued an action alleging that Jerry Smith and Jasen Snelling bilked investors out of more than $4.5 million in a nearly decade-long Ponzi scheme where Mr. Smith and Mr. Snelling told investors they were talented day traders and promised up to 20% returns. Mr. Smith and Mr. Snelling, through various companies, encouraged investors to roll over their traditional IRA accounts into self-directed IRAs at a trust company. Mr. Smith and Mr. Snelling would immediately take the funds from those accounts and use them for personal living expenses, but investors continued to receive statements from the trust company, as well as bills for custodial fees, even after their money was taken out of the accounts. Mr. Smith and Mr. Snelling are charged with more than fifty counts of violations of the Indiana Uniform Securities Act.

In re: Stephen Edward Gwin, et al. (Missouri)

The Missouri Securities Division issued final orders against Stephen Gwin in two separate cases where Mr. Gwin, a federal felon, and others misled senior citizens into investing in unregistered securities, and diverting investment proceeds through self-directed IRAs at trust companies into accounts that Mr. Gwin controlled. Mr. Gwin promoted his million dollar scam through free lunch investment seminars. Mr. Gwin and his co-respondents were found liable and ordered to pay various civil penalties.

Texas v. Warr Investment Group, LLC, et al. (Texas)

The Texas State Securities Board has filed a petition alleging that James Elton Warr through Warr Investment Group LLC and other entities encouraged investors to transfer their funds to a self-directed IRA that was not independent, but instead was secretly controlled by his daughter. According to the petition the Warr entities defrauded the public through their illegal and deceptive sales of securities in real estate investment programs. Mr. Warr claimed that investors would receive a guaranteed 8% annual return and that the real estate investments were a safe and lucrative alternative to more traditional investments such as certificates of deposit and stocks. Mr. Warr and his entities raised at least $970,000 from 30 investors. A Texas court granted the Texas State Securities Board request to freeze Mr. Warr's assets and appoint a receiver to take control of Warr Investment Group LLC and its related entities.

V. Recourse for Fraud Victims

If you have lost money in a fraudulent investment or scheme involving a self-directed IRA or a third-party custodian or trustee, or have information about one of these scams, you should contact:

- The SEC Complaint Center.

- Your state's securities administrator. You can find links and addresses for your state regulator by visiting the North American Securities Administrators Association's website.

You also can check the SEC's Investor Claims Funds webpage for information concerning the appointment of a receiver or claims administrator in any SEC enforcement action.

Additional Information

For additional educational information for investors, see the SEC's Office of Investor Education and Advocacy's homepage, the SEC's Investor.gov website or NASAA's investor education webpage. For additional information related to avoiding fraud, also see:

- Questions You Should Ask About Your Investments
- How to Avoid Fraud

For additional information regarding IRAs, please see the Internal Revenue Service's IRA Online Resource Guide.

The Office of Investor Education and Advocacy has provided this information as a service to investors. It is neither a legal interpretation nor a statement of SEC policy. If you have questions concerning the meaning or application of a particular law or rule, please consult with an attorney who specializes in securities law.

About the Author

Adam Bergman, Esq., a recognized expert on IRAs and 401(k)s, is a senior tax partner with the IRA Financial Group LLC, and managing partner of the Bergman Law Group LLC. Founder of the BergmanIRAReport.com and the Bergman401KReport.com, he is also the author of *Going Solo: America's Best Kept Retirement Secret For the Self-Employed;* and a frequent contributor to *Forbes*. Additionally, he has been interviewed on *CBS News*, and his retirement tax planning advice has been quoted in such publications as *Businessweek*, *CNN Money*, *Smart Money*, and *USA Today*.

Previously, Bergman worked as a tax and ERISA attorney at White & Case LLP, Dewey LeBoeuf LLP, and Thelen LLP, three of the most prominent corporate law firms in the world. He is a member of the tax division of the American Bar Association and the New York State Bar Association.

41077379R00278

Made in the USA
Middletown, DE
03 April 2019